Homer

The Odyssey

Translated by
by
Ian Johnston
Malaspina University-College
Nanaimo, BC
Canada

Front Cover Illustration
by Ian Crowe

Richer Resources Publications
Arlington, Virginia

Homer
The Odyssey

Reprint requests and requests for additional copies
of this book can be addressed to
Richer Resources Publications
1926 N. Woodrow Street
Arlington, Virginia 22207
or via our website at:
www.RicherResourcesPublications.com

ISBN 978-0-9776269-9-1
Library of Congress Control Number
2006927447

Published by Richer Resources Publications
Arlington, Virginia
Printed in the United States of America

For Colleen

Translator's Note

This text uses the traditional Latinate spellings and common English equivalents for the Greek names, e.g., Achilles, Clytaemnestra, Achaeans, Menelaus, rather than modern renditions which strive to stay more closely to the Greek: Akhilleus, Klytaimnestra, Akhaians, Menelaos, and so on, with the exception of a very few names of gods (e.g., Cronos) and a few others. And where there is a common English rendition of the name (e.g., Ajax, Troy), I have used that. A dieresis over a vowel indicates that it is pronounced by itself (e.g., Deïphobus is pronounced "Day-ee-phobus" not "Day-phobus" or "Dee-phobus").

In the line numbers of this translation, the short indented lines are normally included with the shorter lines above them, so that the two partial lines count as a single line. The line numbers are between twenty-five and thirty percent higher than the lines in the Greek text.

The numbers in the text indicate links to explanatory footnotes at the bottom of the page. These have been provided by the translator.

Table of Contents

Book One
Athena Visits Ithaca

[The invocation to the Muse; the gods discuss Odysseus and decide he should return; Athena goes to Ithaca to encourage Telemachus, speaks to him disguised as Mentes, offering advice about dealing with his mother and the suitors and suggesting he go on a trip to Pylos and Sparta; Penelope speaks to Phemius, the singer, asking him to change the song; Telemachus criticizes her; Penelope goes upstairs; Eurycleia carries the lit torches to escort Telemachus to his rooms.]

Muse, speak to me now of that resourceful man
who wandered far and wide after ravaging
the sacred citadel of Troy. He came to see
many people's cities, where he learned their customs,
while on the sea his spirit suffered many torments,
as he fought to save his life and lead his comrades home.
But though he wanted to, he could not rescue them—
they all died from their own stupidity, the fools.
They feasted on the cattle of Hyperion,
god of the sun—that's why he snatched away their chance   10
of getting home someday. So now, daughter of Zeus,
tell us his story, starting anywhere you wish.[1]

The other warriors, all those who had escaped
being utterly destroyed, were now back safely home,
facing no more dangers from battle or the sea.
But Odysseus, who longed to get back to his wife
and reach his home, was being held in a hollow cave
by that mighty nymph Calypso, noble goddess,
who wished to make Odysseus her husband.
But as the seasons came and went, the year arrived   20
in which, according to what gods had once ordained,
he was to get back to Ithaca, his home—
not that he would be free from troubles even there,
among his family. The gods pitied Odysseus,
all except Poseidon, who kept up his anger

[1]The Muses, the divine patrons of the arts, are daughters of Zeus.

against godlike Odysseus and did not relent
until he reached his native land.

             But at that moment,
Poseidon was among the Ethiopians,
a long way off, those same Ethiopians,
the most remote of people, who live divided   30
in two different groups, one where Hyperion goes down,
the other where he rises. Poseidon went there
to receive a sacrificial offering to him—
bulls and rams—and was sitting at a banquet,
enjoying himself. But other gods had gathered
in the great hall of Olympian Zeus. Among them all,
the father of gods and men was first to speak.
In his heart he was remembering royal Aegisthus,
whom Orestes, Agamemnon's famous son,
had killed.[1] With him in mind, Zeus addressed the gods: 40

      "It's disgraceful how these humans blame the gods.
They say their tribulations come from us,
when they themselves, through their own foolishness,
bring hardships which are not decreed by Fate.
Now there's Aegisthus, who took for himself
the wife of Agamemnon, Atreus' son,
and then murdered him, once the man came home.
None of that was set by Fate. Aegisthus knew
his acts would bring about his total ruin.
We'd sent Hermes earlier to speak to him.   50
The keen-eyed killer of Argus told him
not to slay the man or seduce his wife,[2]
for Orestes would avenge the son of Atreus,
once he grew up and longed for his own land.

[1] *. . . had killed:* Aegisthus had seduced Agamemnon's wife while the latter was in
Troy and, when he returned from the war, the two lovers killed Agamemnon and
took control of Argos. Orestes, who was away at the time, came back to Argos in
disguise and avenged his father. This famous story is referred to a number of times in
the *Odyssey* (the account in Book 3 is the most detailed).
[2] *. . . keen-eyed killer of Argus:* Hermes, Zeus's divine son, killed the monster Argus,
whom Hera had told to guard the goddess Io to prevent her getting into sexual
mischief with Zeus.

That's what Hermes said, but his fine words
did not persuade Aegisthus in his heart.
So he has paid for everything in full."

Athena, goddess with the gleaming eyes, answered Zeus:

"Son of Cronos and father to us all,
you who rule on high, yes indeed, Aegisthus   60
now lies dead, something he well deserved.
May any other man who does what he did
also be destroyed! But my heart is torn
for skillful Odysseus, ill-fated man,
who has had to suffer such misfortune
for so many years, a long way from friends.
He's on an island, surrounded by the sea,
the one that forms the ocean's navel stone.[1]
In the forests of that island lives a goddess,
daughter of tough-minded Atlas, who knows   70
the ocean depths and by himself holds up
those gigantic pillars which separate
earth and heaven. That's the one whose daughter
prevents the sad, unlucky man from leaving.
With soft seductive speech she keeps tempting him,
urging him to forget his Ithaca.
But Odysseus yearns to see even the smoke
rising from his native land and longs
for death. And yet, Olympian Zeus, your heart
does not respond to him. Did not Odysseus   80
offer you delightful sacrifices
on Troy's far-reaching plain beside the ships?
Why then, Zeus, are you so angry with him?"

Cloud-gatherer Zeus then answered her and said:

                              "My child,
what a speech has passed the barrier of your teeth!

---

[1] ... *navel stone*: the Greek word *omphalos* (navel stone) Homer uses here to describe
Calypso's island of Ogygia. More commonly in later works the word designates "the
world's navel stone" at Delphi.

How could I forget godlike Odysseus,
pre-eminent among all mortal men
for his intelligence and offerings
to the immortal gods, who hold wide heaven?
But Earthshaker Poseidon is a stubborn god,   90
constantly enraged about the Cyclops,
the one whose eye Odysseus destroyed,
godlike Polyphemus, the mightiest
of all the Cyclopes.[1] Thoosa bore him,
a nymph, a daughter of that Phorcys
who commands the restless sea. Poseidon,
down in those hollow caves, had sex with her.
That's the reason Earthshaker Poseidon
makes Odysseus wander from his country.
Still, he has no plans to kill him. But come,   100
let's all of us consider his return,
so he can journey back to Ithaca.
Poseidon's anger will relent. He can't
fight the immortal gods all by himself,
not with all of us opposing him."

Goddess Athena with the gleaming eyes replied to Zeus:

"Son of Cronos and father to us all,
ruling high above, if the immortal gods
now find it pleasing for the wise Odysseus
to return back home, then let's send Hermes,   110
killer of Argus, as our messenger,
over to the island of Ogygia,
so he can quickly tell that fair-haired nymph
our firm decision—that brave Odysseus
will now leave and complete his voyage home.
I'll go to Ithaca and urge his son
to be more active, put courage in his heart,
so he will call those long-haired Achaeans
to assembly, and there address the suitors,
who keep on slaughtering his flocks of sheep   120

[1] . . . *all the Cyclopes*: the Cyclopes, as we find out later in the poem, are aggressive uncivilized cannibal monsters with only one eye.

10

and shambling bent-horned cattle. I'll send him
on a trip to Sparta and sandy Pylos,
to learn about his father's voyage home—
he may hear of it somewhere—and to gain
a worthy reputation among men."[1]

Athena spoke. Then she tied those lovely sandals
on her feet, the immortal, golden sandals
which carry her as fast as stormy blasts of wind
across the ocean seas and endless tracts of land.
She took with her that weighty, powerful spear—   130
immense and sturdy, with a point of sharpened bronze—
with which she conquers ranks of human warriors
when they annoy her, daughter of a mighty father.
She raced down from the peak of Mount Olympus,
sped across to Ithaca, and then just stood there,
at Odysseus' outer gate before the palace,
on the threshold, gripping the bronze spear in her fist.
She looked like Mentes, a foreigner, the chief
who ruled the Taphians. There she met the suitors,
those arrogant men, who were enjoying themselves   140
playing checkers right outside the door, sitting down
on hides of cattle they themselves had butchered.
Some heralds and attendants were keeping busy
blending wine and water in the mixing bowls.
Some were wiping tables down with porous sponges
and setting them in place, while others passed around
huge amounts of meat. God-like Telemachus
observed Athena first, well before the others.
He was sitting with the suitors, his heart troubled,
picturing in his mind how his noble father   150
might get back, scatter the suitors from his home,
win honour for himself, and regain control
of his own household. As he thought about all this,
sitting there among the suitors, he saw Athena.
He immediately walked over to the outer gate,
for in his heart he considered it disgraceful

[1]The Suitors are the rich young aristocratic men of Ithaca and the islands who are
seeking to marry Penelope, Odysseus' wife, in the belief that Odysseus is dead.

that a stranger should remain a long time at his door.
He moved up near Athena, grasped her right hand,
and took her bronze-tipped spear. Then he spoke to her—
his words had wings:

> "Welcome to you stranger.   160
> You must enjoy our hospitality.
> Then, after you have had some food to eat,
> you can tell us what you need."

Saying this,
Telemachus led Pallas Athena into his home.
She followed. Once they'd come inside the high-roofed house,
he walked to a tall pillar carrying the spear
and set it in a finely-polished rack, which held
many other spears belonging to Odysseus.
He brought Athena in and sat her in a chair,
a beautifully crafted work. Under it   170
he rolled out a linen mat and then arranged
a foot stool for her feet. Beside her he drew up
a lovely decorated chair for him to sit in.
They were some distance from the other people,
in case the noise the suitors made disturbed the guest
and made him hate the meal because he'd had to share
the company of overbearing men. Then, too,
Telemachus wanted to discuss his absent father.
A female servant carried in a fine gold jug
and poured water out into a silver basin,   180
so they could wash their hands. Beside them she set down
a polished table. Then the worthy housekeeper
brought in the bread and set it down before them.
Next, she laid out a wide variety of food,
drawing freely on supplies she had in store.
A carver sliced up many different cuts of meat
and served them. He set out goblets made of gold,
as a herald went back and forth pouring their wine.

Then, one after another, the proud suitors came.
They sat down on reclining seats and high-backed chairs.   190

Heralds poured water out for them to wash their hands,
and women servants piled some baskets full of bread,
while young lads filled their bowls up to the brim with drink.
The suitors reached out with their hands to grab
the tasty food prepared and placed in front of them.
When each and every man had satisfied his need
for food and drink, their hearts craved something more—
dancing and song—the finest joys of dinner feasts.
A herald gave a splendid lyre to Phemius,
so he was forced to sing in front of all the suitors.   200
On the strings he plucked the prelude to a lovely song.
But then Telemachus, leaning his head over
close to Athena, so no one else could listen,
murmured to her:

                    "Dear stranger, my guest,
          if I tell you something, will I upset you?
          These men here, they spend all their time like this,
          with songs and music—it's so easy for them,
          because they gorge themselves on what belongs
          to someone else, and with impunity,
          a man whose white bones now may well be lying   210
          on the mainland somewhere, rotting in the rain,
          or in the sea, being tossed around by waves.
          If they saw him return to Ithaca,
          they'd all be praying they had swifter feet
          rather than more wealth in gold or clothes.
          But by now some evil fate has killed him,
          and for us there is no consolation,
          not even if some earth-bound mortal man
          should say that he will come. The day has passed
          when he might have reached home. But tell me,   220
          and speak candidly—Who are your people?
          Who are you? What city do you come from?
          What about your parents? What kind of ship
          did you sail here in? And the sailors,
          by what route did they bring you to Ithaca?
          Who do they say they come from? For I know
          there's no way you could reach me here on foot.

And I also need to understand one point,
so tell me the truth—this present visit,
is it your first journey here, or are you   230
a guest-friend of my father's? Many men
have come here to our home as strangers,
since he became a roaming wanderer
among all sorts of people."[1]

                          Then Athena,
goddess with the gleaming eyes, answered Telemachus:

"To you I will indeed speak openly.
I can tell you that my name is Mentes,
son of the wise Anchialus, and king
of the oar-loving Taphians. I've come,
as you surmise, with comrades on a ship,   240
sailing across the wine-dark sea to men
whose style of speech is very different,
on my way to Temese for copper,
and carrying a freight of shining iron.
My ship is berthed some distance from the city,
close to the fields, in Reithron's harbour,
below Mount Neion's woods. We can both claim
that we are guest-friends, the two of us,
just as our fathers were so long ago.
If you want, go up and ask Laertes,   250
that old warrior, who, men say, no longer comes
down to the city, but who bears his troubles
in fields far out of town. But he has with him
an old attendant woman, who prepares
his food and drink, once his legs grow weary
hobbling up and down his vineyard hills.
I've come now because some people claim
your father has apparently come home.

[1] . . . *guest-friend*: this phrase indicates a special relationship established between two
people, one of whom has been a guest welcomed in the other's house, or who have
exchanged visits to each other's houses. Telemachus is trying to establish if Mentes, whom
Athena is impersonating, has come to Ithaca with this special bond already established
between himself and Odysseus on the basis of a previous visit, or whether Mentes is, like
so many other recent visitors, a stranger coming to Ithaca for the first time.

But the gods are still preventing him
from getting back. For there's no chance
that brave Odysseus has died somewhere.
No. He's still alive but being detained
on an island, surrounded by the sea,
with wild and dangerous men restraining him,
holding him back against his will. But now,
let me tell you about a prophecy
the gods have set here in my heart,
which, I think, will happen—even though
I am no prophet and have no sure skills
in reading omens from the birds. I say   270
Odysseus will not stay away much longer
from his dear native land, not even if
he's chained in iron fetters. He'll devise
some way to get back home, for he's a man
of infinite resources. But come now,
tell me this, and speak straight and to the point.
Are you in truth Odysseus' son? You're tall,
your head and handsome eyes look just like his,
astonishingly so. We used to spend
a lot of time together, before he left   280
and sailed away to Troy, where other men,
the best of all the Argives, voyaged, too,
in their hollow ships. But since those days,
Odysseus and I have not seen each other."

Noble Telemachus then answered her and said:

"Stranger, I will speak quite frankly to you.
My mother says I am Odysseus' son.
I can't myself confirm that, for no man
has ever yet been sure about his parents.
I wish I'd been the son of some man blest   290
to reach old age among his own possessions,
for now—and I say this because you asked—
I'm the son of a man who is, they say,
of all mortal men, the most unfortunate."

Goddess Athena with the gleaming eyes answered him:

"Then at least the gods have given you
a family which, in days to come, will have
a famous name, since Penelope
has given birth to such a noble son.
But come, speak openly and tell me this—   300
What is this feast? Who are these crowds of men?
Why do you need this? Is it a wedding?
Or a drinking party? It seems clear enough
this is no meal where each man brings his share.
It strikes me that these men are acting here
in an insulting, overbearing way,
while dining in your home. Looking at them
and their disgraceful conduct, any man
who mingled with them, if he had good sense,
would lose his temper."

                    Noble Telemachus   310
then said to Athena in reply:

                              "Stranger,
since you've questioned me about the matter,
I'll tell you. Our house was once well on its way
to being rich and famous—at that time
Odysseus was alive among his people.
But now the gods with their malicious plans
have changed all that completely. They make sure
Odysseus stays where nobody can see him—
they've not done this to anyone before.
I would not show such grief if he were dead,   320
not if he'd died among his comrades
in the land of Troy, or if he'd perished
in his friends' arms, after finishing the war.
Then the Achaeans all would have put up
a tomb for him, and he'd have won great fame
in future days—so would his son, as well.
But as things stand, some spirits of the storm
have snatched him off and left no trace. He's gone

16

where people cannot see or hear him,
abandoning me to tears and sorrow.   330
But it's not him alone who makes me sad
and cry out in distress. For now the gods
have brought me other grievous troubles.
All the best young men who rule the islands,
Dulichium and wooded Zacynthus,
and Same, as well as those who lord it here
in rocky Ithaca—they are all now
wooing my mother and ravaging my house.[1]
She won't turn down a marriage she detests
but can't bring herself to make the final choice.   340
Meanwhile, these men are feasting on my home
and soon will be the death of me as well."

This made Pallas Athena angry—she said to him:

"It's bad Odysseus has wandered off
when you need him here so much! He could lay
his hands upon these shameless suitors.
I wish he'd come home now and make a stand
right at the outer gate, with helmet on,
two spears and his own shield—the sort of man
he was when I first saw him in our house,   350
drinking and enjoying himself. At that time,
he was returning from the home of Ilus,
son of Mermerus, from Ephyre.
Odysseus had gone there in his fast ship,
seeking a man-killing poison, something
he could smear on his bronze arrow points.
However, Ilus did not give him any,
for he revered the gods who live for ever.
But my father did, because he felt
a very strong affection for Odysseus.   360
How I wish Odysseus from way back then
would now return and mingle with the suitors.
They'd all come to a speedy end and find

---

[1] *Dulichium . . . Zacynthus . . . Same*: these are islands close to Ithaca, part of Odysseus'
kingdom.

their courtship painful. But all these matters
lie in the laps of gods—he may return
and take out his revenge in his own hall,
or he may not. But I'd encourage you
to think of ways to force these suitors out,
to rid your halls of them. So hear me out.
Listen now to what I'm going to tell you.   370
Tomorrow you must call Achaea's warriors
to an assembly and address them all,
appealing to the gods as witnesses.
Tell the suitors to return to their own homes.
As for your mother, if her heart is set
on getting married, then let her return
to where her father lives, for he's a man
of power with great capabilities.
He'll organize the marriage and arrange
the wedding gifts, as many as befit   380
a well-loved daughter. Now, as for yourself,
if you'll listen, I have some wise advice.
Get yourself a crew of twenty rowers
and the best boat you possess. Then leave here—
set off in search of news about your father,
who's been gone so long. Some living mortal
may tell you something, or you may hear
a voice from Zeus, which often brings men news.
Sail first to Pylos—speak to noble Nestor.
After you've been there, proceed to Sparta   390
and fair-haired Menelaus, the last one
of all bronze-clad Achaeans to get home.
If you hear reports your father is alive
and coming home, you could hang on a year
still wasting his resources. But if you hear
that he is dead and gone, then come back here,
to your dear native land, build him a tomb,
and carry out as many funeral rites
as are appropriate. Give your mother
over to a husband. When you've done that   400
and brought these matters to a close, then think,
deep in your mind and heart, how you might kill

these suitors in your home, either openly
or by some trick. You must not keep on acting
like a child—you're now too old for that.
Have you not heard how excellent Orestes
won fame among all men when he cut down
his father's murderer, sly Aegisthus,
because he'd slain his famous father?
You are fine and strong, I see, and you, too,   410
should be brave, so people born in future years
will say good things of you. I must go now,
down to my swift ship and to my comrades.
I suspect they're getting quite impatient
waiting for me. Make sure you act with care—
and think about what I've been telling you."

Prudent Telemachus then answered her:

"Stranger, you've been speaking as a friend,
thinking as a father would for his own son—
and what you've said I never will forget.   420
But come now, though you're eager to be off,
stay here a while. Once you've had a bath
and your fond heart is fully satisfied,
then go back to your ship with your spirit
full of joy, carrying a costly present,
something really beautiful, which will be
my gift to you, an heirloom of the sort
dear guest-friends give to those who are their friends."

Goddess Athena with the gleaming eyes then said to him:

"Since I'm eager to depart, don't keep me here   430
a moment longer. And whatever gift
your heart suggests you give me as a friend,
present it to me when I come back here,
and pick me something truly beautiful.
It will earn you something worthy in return."

This said, Athena with the gleaming eyes departed,

flying off like some wild sea bird. In his heart she put
courage and strength. She made him recall his father,
even more so than before. In his mind, Telemachus
pictured her, and his heart was full of wonder.   440
He thought she was a god. So he moved away.
And then the noble youth rejoined the suitors.
Celebrated Phemius was performing for them,
as they sat in silence, listening. He was singing
of the return of the Achaeans, that bitter trip
Athena made them take when they sailed home from Troy.

In her upper room, the daughter of Icarius,
wise Penelope, heard the man's inspired song.
She came down the towering staircase from her room,
but not alone—two female servants followed her.   450
Once beautiful Penelope reached the suitors,
she stayed beside the door post in the well-built room,
with a small bright veil across her face. On either side
her two attendants stood. With tears streaming down,
Penelope addressed the famous singer:

                              "Phemius,
        you know all sorts of other ways to charm
        an audience, actions of the gods and men
        which singers celebrate. As you sit here,
        sing one of those, while these men drink their wine
        in silence. Don't keep up that painful song,   460
        which always breaks the heart here in my chest,
        for, more than anyone, I am weighed down
        with ceaseless grief which I cannot forget.
        I always remember with such yearning
        my husband's face, a man whose fame has spread
        far and wide through Greece and central Argos."

Sensible Telemachus answered her and said:

        "Mother, why begrudge the faithful singer
        delighting us in any way his mind
        may prompt him to? One can't blame the singers.   470

20

It seems to me it's Zeus' fault. He hands out
to toiling men, each and every one of them,
whatever he desires. There's nothing wrong
with this man's singing of the evil fate
of the Danaans, for men praise the most
the song which they have heard most recently.
Your heart and spirit should endure his song.
For Odysseus was not the only man
at Troy who lost his chance to see the day
he would come back. Many men were killed.   480
Go up to your rooms and keep busy there
with your own work, the spindle and the loom.
Tell your servants to perform their duties.
Talking is a man's concern, every man's,
but especially mine, since in this house
I'm the one in charge."

              Astonished at his words,
Penelope went back to her own chambers,
setting in her heart the prudent words her son had said.
With her attendant women she climbed the stairs
up to her rooms and there wept for Odysseus,   490
her dear husband, until bright-eyed Athena
cast sweet sleep upon her eyelids.

              In the shadowy halls
the suitors started to create an uproar,
each man shouting out his hope to lie beside her.
Then shrewd Telemachus began his speech to them:

        "You suitors of my mother, who all have
such insolent arrogance, let us for now
enjoy our banquet, but no more shouting,
for it's grand to listen to a singer
as fine as this one—his voice is like a god's.   500
But in the morning let us all assemble,
sit down for a meeting, so I can speak
and tell you firmly to depart my home.
Make yourself some different meals which eat up

21

your own possessions, moving house to house.
But if you think it's preferable and better
for one man's livelihood to be consumed
without paying anything, I'll call upon
the immortal gods to see if Zeus
will bring about an act of retribution.   510
And if you are destroyed inside my home,
you will not be avenged."

                                    Telemachus finished.
They all bit their lips, astonished that he'd spoken out
so boldly. Then, Antinous, son of Eupeithes,
declared:

              "Telemachus, the gods themselves,
       it seems, are teaching you to be a braggart
       and give rash speeches. I do hope that Zeus,
       son of Cronos, does not make you king
       of this sea island Ithaca, even though
       it is your father's legacy to you."   520

Shrewd Telemachus then answered him and said:

       "Antinous, will you be angry with me,
       if I say something? I would be happy
       to accept that, if Zeus gave it to me.
       Are you claiming that becoming king
       is the very worst of trials for men?
       No. To be king is not something evil.
       One's family gets rich immediately,
       and one receives more honours for oneself.
       But there are other kings of the Achaeans,   530
       many of them here in sea-girt Ithaca,
       young and old, one of whom could well be king,
       since lord Odysseus is dead, but I
       will rule our home and slaves, battle spoils
       which brave Odysseus won for me."

Then Eurymachus, son of Polybus, replied:

                         22

"Telemachus, these matters surely lie
in the gods' laps—which of the Achaeans
will rule sea-girt Ithaca. But you can keep
all your possessions for yourself as king   540
in your own home. Let no man come with force
and seize your property against your will,
no, not while men still live in Ithaca.
But I would like to ask you, my good man,
about that stranger. Where does he come from?
From what country does he claim to be?
Where are his family, his paternal lands?
Does he bring news your father's coming,
or is he here pursuing his own business?
He jumped up so fast and left so quickly!   550
He did not stay to let himself get known.
And yet to look at him, he didn't seem
a worthless man."

                    Prudent Telemachus
then answered him and said:

                              "Eurymachus,
my father's journey back to Ithaca
is no doubt done for. I no longer trust
in messages, no matter what the source.
Nor do I care for any prophecy
my mother picks up from those soothsayers
she summons to these halls. That stranger   560
is a guest-friend of my father's. He says
that he's from Taphos. His name is Mentes,
son of wise Anchialus. He rules as king
over oar-loving Taphians."

                         He said this,
but in his heart Telemachus had recognized
the immortal goddess. At that point, the suitors
switched to dancing and to singing lovely songs.
They amused themselves until dark evening came.
Then each man went to his own house to sleep.

23

Telemachus moved up to where his room was built,   570
high in the splendid courtyard, with a spacious view,
his mind much preoccupied on his way to bed.
Accompanying him, quick-minded Eurycleia
held two flaming torches. She was Ops's daughter,
son of Peisenor. Some years ago Laertes
had purchased her with his own wealth—at the time,
she was in her early youth—paying twenty oxen.
In his home he honoured her the way he did
his noble wife, but not once did he have sex with her,
because he wanted to avoid annoying his wife.   580
She was now carrying two blazing torches for him.
Of all the female household slaves she was the one
who loved him most, for she had nursed him as a child.
He opened the doors of the well-constructed room,
sat on the bed, and pulled off his soft tunic,
handed it to the wise old woman, who smoothed it out,
and folded it, then hung the tunic on a peg
beside the corded bedstead. Then she left the room,
pulling the door shut by its silver handle.
She pulled the bolt across, using its leather thong.   590
Telemachus lay there all night long, wrapped up
in sheep's wool, his mind thinking of the journey
which Athena had earlier proposed to him.

Book Two
Telemachus Prepares for His Voyage

[Telemachus summons all the Achaeans to an assembly; Aegyptius speaks first; Telemachus complains about the suitors and threatens them; Antinous replies, blaming Penelope, describing how she has deceived the suitors, and issuing an ultimatum to Telemachus; Telemachus says he will never send his mother away; Zeus sends two eagles as an omen; Halitherses prophesies trouble for the suitors if they don't stop; Eurymachus replies with a threat and an ultimatum; Telemachus announces his intention of making a sea voyage; Telemachus prays to Athena, who reappears as Mentor and gives instructions for the trip; the suitors mock Telemachus; Telemachus tells Eurycleia to prepare supplies for the voyage; Athena organizes a ship and a crew for Telemachus and puts the suitors to sleep; Telemachus and the crew collect the supplies, load them onboard, and sail away from Ithaca.]

As soon as rose-fingered early Dawn appeared,
Odysseus' dear son jumped up out of bed and dressed.
He slung a sharp sword from his shoulders, then laced
his lovely sandals over his shining feet.
Then he left his room, his face resembling a god's.
At once he asked the loud-voiced heralds to summon
all the long-haired Achaeans to assembly.
They issued the call, and the Achaeans came,
gathering quickly. When the assembly had convened,
Telemachus moved straight into the meeting,   10
gripping a bronze spear. He was not by himself—
two swift-footed hunting dogs accompanied him.
Athena cast down over him a god-like poise—
all the people were astonished at his presence,
as he entered and sat down in his father's chair,
while the senior men gave way. Among those present,
heroic Aegyptius was the first to speak,
a man stooped with age, but infinitely wise.
His son, the warrior Antiphus, had sailed to Troy,
that horse-rich city, along with lord Odysseus,   20
in their hollow ships. But in his cave the wild Cyclops
had slaughtered him and made him his final meal.

Aegyptius had three other sons. One of them,
Eurynomus, was with the suitors. The other two
were always working in their father's fields. But still,
Aegyptius could not forget the son who'd died.
And now, racked with grief and mourning, he shed tears
as he addressed them:

                "Men of Ithaca,
    listen now to what I have to say.
    We have not held a general meeting   30
    or assembly since the day Odysseus
    sailed off in his hollow ships. What man
    has made us gather now? What's his reason?
    Is he a younger or a senior man?
    Has he heard some news about the army
    and will tell us details of its journey home,
    now that he has heard the news himself?
    Or is it some other public business
    he will introduce and talk about?
    He has my blessing! I pray that Zeus   40
    fulfils whatever he has in his heart
    and makes his wishes work out for the best."

Aegyptius spoke. Odysseus' dear son rejoiced
at such auspicious words. But he did not sit long,
for he was very keen to speak. So he stood up
in the middle of the meeting. In his hand,
Peisenor, a herald who provided shrewd advice,
placed the sceptre.[1] Telemachus began to speak,
talking to Aegyptius first of all:

                "Old man,
    the one who called the people to this meeting   50
    is not far off, as you will quickly learn.
    I did. For I'm a man who suffers more
    than other men. But I have no reports
    of our returning army, no details

---

[1] . . . *the sceptre*: in a traditional assembly a sceptre was passed to the man who was to speak next.

I've just heard myself to pass along to you,
nor is there other public business
I'll announce or talk about. The issue here
is my own need, for on my household
troubles have fallen in a double sense.
First, my noble father's perished, the man   60
who was once your king and my kind father.
And then there's an even greater problem,
which will quickly and completely shatter
this entire house, and my whole livelihood
will be destroyed. These suitors, the dear sons
of those men here with most nobility,
are pestering my mother against her will.
They're don't want to journey to her father,
Icarius, in his home, where he himself
could set a bride price for his daughter   70
and give her to the man he feels he likes,
the one who pleases him the most. Instead,
they hang around our house, day after day,
slaughtering oxen, fat goats, and sheep.
They keep on feasting, drinking sparkling wine
without restraint, and they consume so much.
There's no man to guard our home from ruin,
as Odysseus did before. I cannot act
the way he used to and avert disaster.
If I tried, I would be hopeless, a man   80
who had not learned what courage is. And yet,
if I had power, I would defend myself,
because we can't endure what's happening.
My home is being demolished in a way
that is not right. You men should be ashamed.
You should honour other men, your neighbours,
who live close by. And you should be afraid
of anger from the gods, in case their rage
at your bad acts turns them against you.
I beg you by Olympian Zeus and Themis,   90
who summons and disperses men's assemblies,
restrain yourselves, my friends—leave me alone
to suffer my own bitter grief, unless

Odysseus, my noble father, for spite
has hurt well-armed Achaeans, and now,
in recompense for this, you angry gods
are harming me by urging these men on.
For me it would be better if you gods
ate up my landed property and flocks.
If you gorged yourselves, then someday soon   100
there might be recompense. All the time
you were doing that, we'd walk up and down,
throughout the city, asking for our goods
to be returned, until the day every piece
was given back. But now you load my heart
with pain beyond all hope."

                              Telemachus spoke.
Then in his anger he threw the sceptre on the ground
and burst out crying. Everyone there pitied him,
so all the others men kept silent, unwilling
to give an angry answer to Telemachus.   110
Antinous was the only one to speak. He said:

"Telemachus you boaster, your spirit
is too unrestrained. How you carry on,
trying to shame us, since you so desire
the blame should rest on us. But in your case,
Achaean suitors aren't the guilty ones.
Your own dear mother is, who understands
how to use deceit. It's been three years now—
and soon it will be four—since she began
to frustrate hearts in our Achaean chests.   120
She gives hope to each of us, makes promises
to everyone, and sends out messages.
But her intent is different. In her mind
she has thought up another stratagem:
in her room she had a large loom set up,
and started weaving something very big,
with thread that was quite thin. She said to us:

     'Young men, those of you who are my suitors,

since lord Odysseus is dead, you must wait,
although you're keen for me to marry,   130
till I complete this cloak—otherwise
my weaving would be wasted and in vain.
It is a shroud for warrior Laertes,
for the day a lethal fate will strike him.
Then none of the Achaean women here
will be annoyed with me because a man
who acquired so many rich possessions
should lie without a shroud.'

                          "That's what she said.
And our proud hearts agreed. And so each day
she wove at her great loom, but every night   140
she set up torches and pulled the work apart.
Three years she fooled Achaeans with this trick.
They trusted her. But as the seasons passed,
the fourth year came. Then one of her women
who knew all the details spoke about them,
and we caught her undoing her lovely work.
Thus, we forced her to complete the cloak
against her will. The suitors now say this,
so you, deep in your heart, will understand
and all Achaeans know—send your mother back.   150
Tell her she must marry whichever man
her father tells her and who pleases her.
But if she keeps on doing this for long,
teasing Achaea's sons because in her heart
she knows that she's been given by Athena,
more than any other woman, a skill
in making lovely things, a noble heart,
and cunning of a sort we never hear about
in any fair-haired woman of Achaea,
even those who lived so long ago—   160
Tyro, Alcmene, and Mycene,
the one who wore the lovely headband—
none of them had shrewdness which could match

29

Penelope's.[1] Yet in one thing at least
her scheme did not go well. Your livelihood
and your possessions will keep being consumed
as long as in her mind she follows plans
the gods have now put in her heart. And so,
while she is gaining a great reputation,
you're sad about so much lost sustenance.   170
But we are not going back to our own lands,
or some place else, not until she marries
an Achaean man of her own choosing."

Prudent Telemachus then said in reply:

"Antinous, there's no way I will dismiss
out of this house against her will the one
who bore and nursed me. As for my father,
he's in a distant land, alive or dead.
It would be hard for me to compensate
Icarius with a suitable amount,   180
as I would have to do, if I sent her back.
If I didn't do that, then her father
would treat me badly, and some deity
would send other troubles, since my mother,
as she left this house, would call upon
the dreaded Furies. Men would blame me, too.
That's why I'll never issue such an order.
And if your heart is angry about this,
then leave my home, go have your feasts elsewhere.
Eat up your own possessions, changing homes,   190
one by one. But if you think it's better,
more in your interests, that one man's goods
should be destroyed without repayment,
then use them up. But I will call upon
the immortal gods to ask if somehow Zeus
will give me retribution. Then you'll die
here in my home and never be avenged."

[1] *Tyro, Alcmene, and Mycene:* Tyro had sex with Poseidon, producing two twin sons
Pelias and Neleus; Alcmene was the mother of Hercules (by Zeus) and Iphicles; Mycene
was a daughter of Inachus: all are well known mythic figures.

Telemachus spoke. Then from a mountain peak
far-seeing Zeus replied by sending out two eagles,
flying high up in the sky. For some time they soared   200
like gusts of wind, with their wings spread out, side by side.
But when they reached the middle of the crowded meeting,
with quick beats of their wings they wheeled around,
swooping down on everyone, destruction in their eyes.
Then with their talons they attacked each other,
clawing head and neck, and flew off on the right,
past people's homes, across the city. They were amazed
to see these birds with their own eyes. In their hearts
they were stirred to think how everything would end.
Then old warrior Halitherses, Mastor's son,   210
addressed them. He surpassed all men of his own time
in knowledge about birds and making prophecies
of what Fate had in store. Thinking of their common good,
he spoke up and said:

                                          "Listen to me, men of Ithaca.
        Hear what I say. In what I'm going to speak,
        I'm talking to the suitors most of all.
        A mighty ruin is rolling over them.
        For Odysseus will not be away for long
        from his own friends. I think even now
        he's near by, planning a disastrous fate   220
        for all the suitors. And he'll be a scourge
        to many others here in sunny Ithaca.
        Long before that we should be considering
        how to stop this. Or rather, these suitors
        should end it themselves. That would achieve
        what's best for them and do so right away.
        For I am not unskilled in prophecy—
        I understand things well. To Odysseus
        I say that everything is turning out
        just as I told him. Back when the Achaeans,   230
        with resourceful Odysseus in their ranks,
        were sailing off to Troy, I prophesied
        he'd suffer many troubles and would lose
        all his companions, before returning home

                                    31

in twenty years unknown to anyone.
Now everything I said is coming true."

Eurymachus, Polybus' son, then spoke out in reply:

"Old man, you should go home and prophesy
to your own children, so that something bad
does not happen to them later. In these things   240
I can foretell events much better than you can.
There are lots of birds flying here and there
beneath the sunshine, and not all of them
are omens of disaster. Odysseus
has perished far away, and how I wish
you had died there with him. If you had,
you wouldn't utter prophecies like these
or be encouraging Telemachus
when he's enraged, in hopes you'll get a gift,
something he might give you for your house.   250
But I tell you this—and it will happen.
You know many things an old man knows,
so if your words deceive a younger man
and incite him to get angry, first of all,
he'll be worse off, and, with these men here,
won't have the slightest power to act.
And on you, old man, we'll lay a penalty
that will pain your heart to pay—your sorrow
will be difficult to bear. But now here,
among you all, I will myself provide   260
Telemachus advice. He must command
his mother to return home to her father.
They will prepare a wedding and provide
as many lovely presents as befit
a well-loved daughter. Before that happens,
I don't think Achaea's sons will end
their unwelcome wooing, for there's no one
we're afraid of yet—not Telemachus,
for all his wordiness—nor do we care
about a prophecy which you, old man,   270
may spout. It won't come to fruition,

and people will despise you all the more.
And his possessions will be eaten up
in this shameful way. There will never be
compensation given, so long as she
keeps putting off Achaeans in this marriage.
Because she's so desirable, we wait here,
day after day, as rivals, and don't seek
different women, any one of whom
might be suitable for us to marry."   280

Shrewd Telemachus then said in reply:

                                      "Eurymachus,
all you other noble suitors, no longer
will I make requests of you or speak of it,
for gods and all Achaeans understand.
Just give me a swift ship and twenty rowers—
so I can make a journey and return
to various places, to sandy Pylos
and then to Sparta, to see if I can find
some news about my father's voyage home—
he's been gone so long—if any mortal man   290
can tell me. Or I'll hear Zeus' voice perhaps,
which commonly provides men information.
If I hear my father is still living
and returning home, I could hold out here
for one more year, although it's hard for me.
If I learn he's dead and gone, I'll come back
to my dear native land, build him a tomb,
and there perform as many funeral rites
as are appropriate. And after that,
I'll give my mother to a husband."   300

Telemachus said this, then sat down. Next Mentor,
who'd been noble Odysseus' companion,
stood up among them. When he'd sailed off in his ships,
Odysseus had made Mentor steward of his household,
charging them to follow what the old man ordered
and telling Mentor to keep all property secure.

Keeping in mind their common good, he spoke them:

"Men of Ithaca, listen now to me.
Hear what I have to say. From now on
let no sceptred king ever be considerate   310
or kind or gentle. Let him in his heart
ignore what's right, act with cruelty,
and strive for evil, for no one here,
none of those whom divine Odysseus ruled,
remembers him, yet in his role as father,
he was compassionate. Not that I object
to these proud suitors and the violent acts
which they, with their malicious minds, commit,
for they are putting their own heads at risk,
when they use force to drain Odysseus' home   320
of its resources and claim he won't come back.
But at this point it's the other people
I am angry with, you who sit in silence
and don't say anything to criticize
or make the suitors stop, even though
there are many of you and few of them."

Then Leocritus, son of Euenor, spoke in reply:

"Mentor, you mischief maker, your wits
have wandered off. What are you saying,
urging men to make us stop? It would be hard   330
to fight against those who outnumber you—
and about a feast. Even if Odysseus,
king of Ithaca, were to come in person,
eager in his heart to drive out of his halls
these noble suitors eating up his home,
his wife would not rejoice at his arrival,
although she yearned for him. For if he fought
against so many men, then he would meet
a shameful death right here. What you've just said
is quite irrelevant. So come on now,   340
you people should disperse, each one
go off to his own land. As for Telemachus,

34

well, Mentor and Halitherses, comrades
of his ancestral house from years ago,
will speed him on his way. But still, I think
he'll be sitting here a long time yet,
collecting his reports in Ithaca.
He's never going to undertake that trip."

Leocritus spoke and soon dissolved the meeting.
The men dispersed, each man to his own house.   350
The suitors went inside godlike Odysseus' home.

Telemachus walked away to the ocean shore.
There, once he'd washed his hands in gray salt water,
to Athena he made this prayer:

                                        "O hear me,
          you who yesterday came to my home
          as a god and ordered me to set out
          in a ship across the murky seas,
          to learn about my father's voyage back
          after being away so long. All this
          Achaeans are preventing, most of all,   360
          the suitors with their wicked arrogance."

As he said this prayer, Athena came up close to him,
looking and sounding just like Mentor. She spoke—
her words had wings:

                              "Telemachus,
          in future days you will not be worthless
          or a stupid man, if you have in you now
          something of your father's noble spirit.
          He's the sort of man who, in word and deed,
          saw things to their conclusion. So for you
          this trip will not be useless or without result.   370
          If you're not sprung from Penelope and him,
          then I have no hope that you'll accomplish
          what you desire to do. It's true few men
          are like their fathers. Most of them are worse.

35

Only very few of them are better.
But in future you'll not be unworthy
or a fool, and you do not completely lack
Odysseus' wisdom, so there is some hope
you will fulfill your mission. So set aside
what those foolish suitors have advised. 380
They lack all discretion, all sense of justice,
for they have no idea of death, the dark fate
closing in on them, when in a single day
they will all perish. You must not delay
that trip you wish to make. I am a friend
of your ancestral home, so much so that I
will furnish a fast ship for you and come
in person with you. But now you must go home.
Mingle with the suitors. Collect provisions,
and put everything in some containers— 390
wine in jars and barley meal, which strengthens men,
in thick leather sacks. I'll go through the town
and quickly round up a group of comrades,
all volunteers. In sea-girt Ithaca,
I'll choose from the many ships, new and old,
the best one for you, and then, when that ship
has been made ready and is fit to sail,
we'll launch it out into the wine-dark sea."

Athena, Zeus' daughter, finished speaking,
Telemachus did not stay there for long, 400
once he had heard the goddess speak. He set off
toward his home, with a heavy heart, and there
he found the arrogant suitors in the palace,
by the courtyard, skinning goats and singeing pigs.
Antinous came up laughing at Telemachus.
He grabbed his hand and spoke to him, saying:

"Telemachus,
you're such a braggart—an untamed spirit.
You should never let that heart of yours
entertain any further nasty words
or actions. I think you should eat and drink, 410

just as you did before. Achaeans here
will certainly see to it you acquire
all the things you need—some hand-picked oarsmen
and a ship, so you can quickly travel
to sacred Pylos in search of some report
about your noble father."

                         Prudent Telemachus
then answered him and said:

                              "Antinous,
it's quite impossible for me to eat
and stay quiet with your overbearing group
or to enjoy myself with my mind relaxed.   420
Is it not sufficient that in days past,
while I was still a child, you suitors
consumed so much of my fine property?
But now that I've grown up and teach myself
by listening to others and my spirit
gets stronger here inside me, I will try
to counteract the wicked fate you bring,
either by going to Pylos, or else here,
in this community. For I will set out,
and the voyage which I've talked about   430
will not be useless, even though I travel
as a passenger and not the master
of the ship or oarsmen. It seems to me
you think that will improve things for you."

Telemachus spoke. Then he casually pulled his hand
out of Antinous' grasp. Meanwhile, the suitors,
preoccupied with feasting in the house, mocked him
and kept up their abusive insults. One of them,
an over-proud young man, would speak like this:

          "It seems Telemachus really does intend   440
to murder us. He'll bring men to help him
back from sandy Pylos or from Sparta.
That's how terrible his resolution is.

Or else he wants to head off to Ephyre,
that rich land, so he can fetch from there
some lethal medicines and then throw them
in the wine bowl, to destroy us all."

And after that another proud young man would say:

"Who knows whether he might die himself,
once he sets off in his hollow ship, roaming   450
far away from friends, just like Odysseus?
If so, he'll provide still more work for us.
We'll have to split up everything he owns
and hand this house over to his mother
and the man she marries."

                              That's how the suitors talked.
But Telemachus just walked away, going down
to the high-roofed chamber which stored his father's wealth,
an extensive place. Bronze and gold lay there stacks,
with clothing packed in chests and stores of fragrant oil.
Huge jars of old sweet wine stood there—each one contained   460
drink fit for gods and not yet mixed with water—
arranged in rows along the wall, in case Odysseus,
after so many hardships, ever reached his home.
The close-fitting double doors were firmly closed,
and a female steward stayed there day and night,
protecting everything, the shrewd Eurycleia,
daughter of Ops, Peisenor's son. Telemachus
called her into the storage room, then said:

                              "Old Nurse,
pour some sweet wine into jars for me,
the best wine you've got after the stock   470
you've planned to store here for Odysseus,
that ill-fated man, born from Zeus, in case,
after evading death and fate, he shows up
from somewhere. Fill twelve jars and fit them all
with covers. Pour me out some barley grain
in well-stitched leather sacks. Make sure there are

38

twenty measures of ground-up barley meal.
But keep this knowledge to yourself. Just get
all these things assembled. In the evening,
once my mother goes upstairs into her room   480
to get some sleep, I'll come to collect them.
I'm off to sandy Pylos and to Sparta,
to see if I can get some information
about my dear father's journey home,
if there is any news I can find out."

Telemachus spoke. The dear nurse Eurycleia
let out a cry and began to weep. Then she spoke—
her words had wings:

                          "Oh my dear child,
how did this thought gain entry to your heart?
Where on this wide earth do you intend to roam,   490
with you an only son and so well loved?
In some distant land among strange people
Odysseus, a man born from Zeus, has died.
As soon as you have gone from here, the suitors
will start their wicked schemes to hurt you later—
how they can have you killed by trickery
and then parcel out among themselves
all your possessions. You must stay here
to guard what's yours. You don't need to suffer
what comes from wandering on the restless sea."   500

Shrewd Telemachus then answered her and said:

    "Be brave, dear nurse, for I have not planned this
without help from a god. But you must swear
you won't mention this to my dear mother,
until eleven or twelve days from now,
or until she misses me or learns I've gone,
so she does not mar her lovely face with tears."

Once Telemachus said this, the old woman swore
a mighty oath by all the gods she'd tell no one.

39

When she had sworn and the oath had been completed,   510
she went immediately to pour wine into jars
and fill the well-stitched leather sacks with barley meal.
Telemachus went up into the dining hall
and there rejoined the company of suitors.
Then goddess Athena with the gleaming eyes
thought of something else. Looking like Telemachus,
she went all through the city. To every man
she came up to she gave the same instructions,
telling them to meet by the fast ship that evening.
Next, she asked Noemon, fine son of Phronius,   520
for a swift ship, and he was happy to oblige.
Then the sun went down, and all the roads grew dark.
Athena dragged the fast ship down into the sea
and stocked it with supplies, all the materials
well-decked boats have stowed on board, then moved the ship
to the harbour's outer edge. There they assembled,
that group of brave companions, and the goddess
instilled fresh spirit in them all. Then Athena,
goddess with the glittering eyes, thought of one more thing.
She set off, going to divine Odysseus' home.   530
There she poured sweet drowsiness on all the suitors.
She made them wander round as they were drinking
and knocked the cups out of their hands. When sleep
fell down across their eyelids, the suitors felt an urge
not to stay sitting there for any length of time,
but to get themselves some rest down in the city.
Then bright-eyed Athena told Telemachus
to come outside, by the entrance to the spacious hall.
In her voice and form she resembled Mentor:

        "Telemachus, your well-armed companions   540
        are already sitting beside their oars,
        waiting for you to launch the expedition.
        Let's be off, so we don't delay the trip
        a moment longer."

        With these words, Pallas Athena
quickly led the way, and Telemachus followed

in her footsteps. Once they'd come down to the sea
and reached the ship, on shore they came across
their long-haired companions. Telemachus spoke to them
with strength and power:

                  "Come, my friends, let's gather
our supplies. They've already been assembled,   550
all together in the hall. My mother
knows nothing of all this, and neither do
any other women of the household.
I've mentioned this to only one of them."

After saying this, Telemachus led them away,
and the group then followed. They carried everything
to the well-decked ship and stowed it all in place,
as Odysseus' dear son instructed them to do.
Then, with Athena going on board ahead of him,
Telemachus embarked. She sat in the stern.   560
Telemachus sat right beside her, as the men
untied the stern ropes, then climbed aboard the ship
and went to seat themselves beside their oarlocks.
Bright-eyed Athena arranged a fair breeze for them,
a strong West Wind blowing across the wine-dark sea.
Telemachus then called out to his companions
to set their hands to the ship's rigging. Once they heard,
they went to work, raising the mast cut out of fir,
setting it in its hollow socket, securing it
with fore-stays, and hoisting the white sail aloft   570
with twisted ox-hide thongs. The belly of the sail
filled up with wind, and the ship sailed on its way.
As it sliced straight through the swell on its way forward,
around the bow began the great song of the waves.
When they had lashed the rigging on that fast black ship,
they set out bowls brimful of wine and poured libations
to the eternal ageless gods, and of them all
especially to Athena, Zeus' bright-eyed daughter.
Then all night long and well beyond the sunrise,
their ship continued sailing on its journey.   580

Book Three
Telemachus Visits Nestor in Pylos

[Telemachus and his crew reach Pylos and are welcomed by Nestor;
Nestor describes events at Troy and on the voyage home; Nestor gives
a detailed account of Aegisthus' plan to seduce Clytaemnestra and
murder Agamemnon; Nestor offers a sacrifice to Poseidon, then invites
Athena and Telemachus to stay the night with him; Athena declines
but Telemachus goes with Nestor; Nestor and his sons offer a sacrifice
to Athena; Polycaste gives Telemachus a bath; Nestor orders a chariot
for Telemachus; Telemachus and Peisistratus leave Pylos, spend the
night in Pherae, then continue their journey.]

When the sun had left the splendid sea and risen up
into an all-bronze heaven, giving light to gods
and mortal men and grain to farmers' fields,
the ship and crew reached Pylos, a well-built city
ruled by Nestor. There by the sea the city folk
were preparing black bulls as holy offerings
to Poseidon, dark-haired Shaker of the Earth.[1]
There were nine groups, each with five hundred people
and nine offerings of bulls ready to sacrifice.
As they were tasting samples of the innards   10
and cooking thigh parts for the gods, the ship and crew
were heading straight for shore. They hauled in and furled
the sails on their trim ship, moored it, and disembarked.
With Athena showing him the way, Telemachus
stepped from the ship. The bright-eyed goddess spoke to him:

"Telemachus, no need to feel embarrassed,
not in the least, for this is why you've sailed
across the sea, to get information
about your father—where he is buried
and what fate has befallen him. Come now,   20
go directly to horse-taming Nestor.
Let's find out what advice his heart contains.

---

[1] *. . . shaker of the earth*: Poseidon was god of the sea and of earthquakes (hence, two
common epithets applied to him: "encircler of the earth" and "shaker of the earth" or
"earthshaker").

You yourself must beg him to report the truth.
He will not lie, for he is truly wise."

Prudent Telemachus then answered her and said:

"Mentor, how shall I go up there and greet him?[1]
I've had no practice with such formal speech.
And then, when a young man seeks to question
an older one, that could bring him shame."

Athena, goddess with the gleaming eyes, then said: 30

"Telemachus, your heart will think of something,
and power from heaven will provide the rest.
For I don't think that you were born and raised
without being favoured by the gods."

                                        She spoke.
Pallas Athena then quickly led them off.
Telemachus followed in the goddess' footsteps.
They reached the group of Pylians gathered there,
where Nestor sat among his sons. Around them
his companions were preparing for the feast,
cooking meat and setting other pieces onto spits.   40
When they saw the strangers, they came thronging round,
clasping their hands and inviting them to sit.
Nestor's son Peisistratus approached them first,
took Athena and Telemachus both by the hand,
asked them to sit down on soft cushions and eat
beside his brother Thrasymedes and his father
on the beach. He gave them portions of the innards,
and then into a cup of gold he poured some wine.
He made a toast to Pallas Athena, daughter
of aegis-bearing Zeus, then said to her:[2]   50

"Stranger, you must now pray to lord Poseidon,

[1] *Mentor*. as in Book 2, Athena has the form and voice of Mentor.
[2] *. . . aegis-bearing*. The aegis is a shield borne by Zeus (or by a god to whom he lends
it), symbolic of the storm cloud. Its powers make men afraid and run off in a panic.

43

for the feast which you have chanced upon
is in his honour. When you have offered
your libation and have prayed, as is right,
hand your comrade the cup of honey wine,
so he can pour out his libation, too,
for he looks like someone who offers prayers
to the immortals. All men need the gods.
Since he's a younger man of my own age,
I'll start by giving you this golden cup."   60

Saying this, he set the cup of sweet wine in her hand.
Athena rejoiced at such a wise and righteous man,
because he'd offered the gold cup to her first.
At once she made a solemn prayer to lord Poseidon:

"Hear me, Poseidon, you who enfold the earth—
do not hold back from bringing to fulfillment
those events we pray for. And to begin with,
give Nestor and his sons a glorious name,
and then grant all other men of Pylos
a pleasing recompense in answer to   70
these lovely offerings. And in addition,
grant that Telemachus and I get back,
once we've accomplished all those things
for which we came here in our swift black ship."

That's the prayer Athena uttered then, while she herself
was taking care that everything would work out well.
She gave Telemachus the fine two-handled cup.
Odysseus' brave son then made a prayer like hers.
Once they'd finished roasting the upper cuts of meat
and pulled them off the spits, they served out portions   80
and had a sumptuous feast. When every one of them
had taken food and drink to his own heart's content,
Nestor, the Geranian horseman, began to speak:[1]

"It seems to me that it's a good time now

---

[1] *Geranian horseman*: Nestor is frequently called the "Geranian horseman,"
presumably because as a young lad he was raised in Gerania, away from his family in
Pylos.

44

to ask our guests to tell us who they are,
now they've enjoyed our food. And so, strangers,
who are you? What country did you sail from,
when you set your course across the water?
Are you on business? Or are you roaming
on the seas at random, like those pirates   90
who sail around, risking their own lives,
posing a threat to men from other lands?"

Then shrewd Telemachus spoke up in reply,
and boldly, too, because Athena herself had put
courage in his heart, so he might talk about
his absent father and acquire for himself
a noble reputation:

                         "Nestor, son of Neleus,
great glory of Achaeans, you asked us
where we come from, so I'll tell you.
We're from Ithaca below Mount Neion.   100
My business, which I'll speak about, is private,
not a public matter. I am pursuing
wide-spread rumours of the brave Odysseus,
my father, who, they say, fought at your side
and utterly destroyed the Trojans' city.
We have heard reports about the others,
all those who went to war against the Trojans—
where each met his bitter fate—but Zeus,
son of Cronos, has made Odysseus' death
something unknown, for none of us can say   110
with any confidence where he was killed,
whether he was overwhelmed by enemies
on land or killed at sea by waves stirred up
by Amphitrite.[1] That's why I've come
to sit now in your home, for there's a chance
you could tell me something of his death,
which you may have seen with your own eyes.
Or perhaps you've heard about his wanderings

---

[1] . . . *Amphitrite*: Amphitrite, a sea goddess, is wife to Poseidon. The reference
may be to the Atlantic Ocean.

from someone else. For his mother bore him
to go through trouble more than other men.   120
Do not pity me or, from compassion,
just offer me words of consolation,
but tell me truly how you chanced to see him.
If my father, brave Odysseus, in word or deed,
ever promised you something and kept his word,
way over there among the Trojans,
where Achaeans suffered such distress,
I ask you now—remember what he did,
and give me the truth."

                    Responding to Telemachus,
Geranian horseman Nestor said:

                        "My friend,   130
you make me call to mind the suffering
and boundless courage of Achaea's sons
in all they went through over there, the things
we had to endure while on board the ships,
as we roamed across the misty waters,
in search of loot, with Achilles in the lead,
and all the fights around great Priam's city,[1]
where so many of our finest men were killed.
That's where warlike Ajax and Achilles lie,
and Patroclus, too, a man whose counsel   140
was like the gods'. My own dear son fell there,
Antilochus, as strong as he was noble,
outstanding for his speed and fighting skill.
And we endured countless other hardships
apart from these. Who could possibly describe
every detail of the men who perished?
If you were to spend five or six years here
questioning me about the brave Achaeans
and the troubles they went through, you'd grow tired
and sail back home well before I'd finished.   150
Nine years we spent scheming to bring them down
with every sort of trick, but Cronos' son

[1] . . . *Priam's city*: Priam was king of Troy during the Trojan War.

made all our plans so hard to carry out.
Over there no one ever tried to claim
he could match Odysseus' shrewd advice.
In devising every kind of devious scheme
he was easily the best, your father,
if indeed you are his son. Looking at you,
I am astonished, for you really speak
the way he did. No one would ever think   160
a younger man could talk so much like him.
All that time back then, never once did I
and lord Odysseus, in council or assembly,
disagree. We spoke with a single heart
and gave the Argives wise and useful views
about how those events would best turn out.
But when Priam's towering city was destroyed
and our ships set off, the Achaean fleet
was scattered by some god. And even so,
Zeus planned in his heart to give Achaeans   170
a sorrowful return. They had not been wise
or righteous, so many met a nasty fate,
thanks to the mortal anger of Athena,
bright-eyed goddess with a mighty father.
She incited the two sons of Atreus
to quarrel with each other. The two men
had quickly called Achaeans to assembly,
not in the usual way, but at sunset.
Achaea's sons arrived all flushed with wine.
Both kings delivered speeches. They explained   180
why they had called the meeting. Menelaus
told Achaeans to plan on going home
on the broad back of the sea. What he said
did not please Agamemnon in the least,
because he wished to keep the army there,
so they could all offer sacrifices
to appease Athena's dreadful anger.
The fool! He didn't know there was no chance
that she was going to hear what he would say.
For the minds of gods, who live forever,   190
are not altered quickly. So these two men

stood there, trading hard words with each other.
The armed Achaeans jumped up on their feet,
making an amazing noise. Two different plans
were popular among them, and that night
no one slept, as both sides kept arguing,
each one with harsh opinions of the other,
for Zeus was bringing us a wretched fate.
In the morning, some of us dragged our ships
down to the sparkling sea, put goods on board—   200
our women, too, who wore their girdles low.
But half the soldiers stayed, remaining there
with Agamemnon, son of Atreus,
shepherd of his army. So half of us
embarked and rowed away. Our ships moved fast—
some god had made the yawning sea grow calm.
We came to Tenedos and sacrificed
to all the gods, still keen to get back home.[1]
But even then Zeus had not decided
to let us all return—a stubborn god!   210
He stirred up a second nasty quarrel.
So some men turned their curving ships around
and sailed back, among them lord Odysseus,
that wise and cunning man, with his soldiers.
Once again he favoured Agamemnon,
son of Atreus. Then I fled away
with the remaining ships, which followed me.
I knew a god was planning something bad.
And Diomedes, warrior son of Tydeus,
urged his comrades on to act as we did.   220
Fair-haired Menelaus and his ships
sailed later. They caught up with us at Lesbos.
We'd been arguing about the major stretch—
should we sail to the north of rugged Chios
towards the island of Psyria, keeping
Chios on our left, or take the southern route,
below Chios and past stormy Mimas.
So we asked a god to give us a sign.
He did and ordered us to carve our way

[1] . . . *Tenedos*: an island near Troy.

48

across the great sea straight to Euboea—   230
that way we would escape from trouble
as quickly as we could.[1] A blustery wind
began to blow, and so our ships moved fast
across the fish-filled seas. That very night
we landed at Geraestus, where we offered
many bulls' thighs to Poseidon, our thanks
for crossing the great sea. On the fourth day,
the crews of Diomedes, son of Tydeus,
tamer of horses, berthed their well-built ships
in Argos, but I sailed on to Pylos.[2]   240
Once a god sent that wind to blow us home,
it never once let up. And so, my lad,
I made it back. But of the Achaeans—
the ones who died and those who got back home—
I didn't learn a thing. I just don't know.
But what I have found out, as I've sat here,
in my own home, you'll hear. You have that right.
I'll not conceal it from you. People say
great spear-fighting Myrmidons reached home safely,
led by the glorious son of brave Achilles,   250
as did the noble son of Poias, too,
Philoctetes. And Idomeneus
took all his comrades back to Crete, the ones
who'd made it through the war. Not one of them
was lost at sea. As for Agamemnon,
although you live a long way off, you've heard
of his return—how he came home and then
how Aegisthus planned his cruel slaughter.
He later paid a terrible reckoning.
That's why it's good for any murdered man   260
to leave a worthy son. For Orestes

[1] . . . *as quickly as we could*. The choice of routes back home offers a number of options, particularly if the fleet wishes to move from island to island (a slow but safer course). The god advises a straight rush across open water ("the great sea") to Euboea, a large island just off the mainland of Attica, a faster but potentially more dangerous course.

[2] . . . *Argos*. Diomedes is king of Argos, a town in the Peloponnese. It is not the same as the Argos ruled by Agamemnon, which is in the south-east Peloponnese (and sometimes called Achaean Argos, a city often identified as Mycenae, although these two are also at times identified as two neighbouring places).

got his revenge against his father's killer,
sly Aegisthus, who'd killed Agamemnon,
that splendid man. And you, my friend, I see
that you're a strong, fine-looking man,
but you must act with courage, so those born
in future years will say good things of you."

Shrewd Telemachus then said in reply:

                                    "Nestor,
son of Neleus, great glory of Achaeans,
yes, indeed, that son got his revenge.   270
Achaeans all will celebrate his fame
and sing of it to men in years to come.
If gods would only give me strength like that,
so I could pay these haughty suitors back—
they bring me such distress. In all their pride
they keep on plotting wretched things for me.
But happiness like that the gods deny me,
me and my father. But now, in spite of that,
I must keep going."

                        Geranian horseman Nestor
then said to Telemachus:

                                    "My friend,   280
since you mentioned this and made me think of it,
they say that many suitors in your home,
seeking to become your mother's husband,
keep devising wicked schemes against you,
over your objections. So tell me this—
are you being oppressed with your consent?
Or in response to what some god has said,
have people turned against you? Who knows
whether Odysseus will return some day
to pay them back for all their violence,   290
either alone or with a combined force
of all Achaeans? Ah, how I wish
Athena with her bright eyes were willing

50

to cherish you the way she cared back then
for fine Odysseus in the land of Troy,
where we Achaeans had to undergo
such grievous times. For I have never seen
the gods display their love so openly
as Pallas Athena did supporting him.
If she was keen to love you in that way   300
and to take you to her heart, those suitors
would soon forget about the marriage."

Shrewd Telemachus then answered Nestor, saying:

"Old man, I don't think what you've described
will ever happen. What you have said
is too much to expect. I am surprised
you mention it. I entertain no hopes
that it could happen to me, even if
the gods themselves were willing."

                                Then Athena,
bright-eyed goddess, answered him:

                                    "Telemachus,   310
what a speech just passed the barrier of your teeth!
A god could easily bring someone home
from a long way off, if he wanted to.
But I'd prefer to go through many hardships
and then see the day when I got back
and reached my home, than to complete my trip
only to be butchered by my own hearth,
the way that Agamemnon was cut down,
tricked by his own wife and by Aegisthus.
But the gods cannot protect a man from death—   320
which comes to all—even ones they love,
once the destroying fate of a harsh doom
has seized him."

                        Shrewd Telemachus
then said in answer to Athena:

51

                                                    "Mentor,
although we're sad, let's not discuss this further.
For him there'll be no more returning home.
No. For by this time the immortal gods
have planned some dismal fate for him. I'd like
to change the subject and ask Nestor something.
He's a righteous and intelligent man,   330
more so than others. He's been king, they say,
over three human generations. To me,
as I look at him, he seems immortal.
O Nestor, son of Neleus, tell me the truth.
How did wide-ruling Agamemnon,
son of Atreus, meet his death? And where
was Menelaus? As for Aegisthus,
that deceitful man, what did he devise
to kill a man much finer than himself?
Was Menelaus not in Achaean Argos,   340
but wandering around some foreign land?
Was that what made Aegisthus brave enough
to carry out the killing?"

              Geranian horseman Nestor
then answered Telemachus and said:

                                          "My boy,
I'll tell you all this and speak frankly, too.
You yourself obviously understand
what would have taken place if Menelaus,
Atreus' fair-haired son, had come home
from Troy and found Aegisthus living there,
in his own house. He would have killed the man.   350
No one would have heaped up a tomb for him—
he'd have been eaten by the dogs and birds,
as he lay on the plain outside the city.
And not one of the Achaean women
would have lamented him, the one who planned
the monstrous act. We were over there in Troy,
fighting hard in battle after battle,
while he was having a good time, tucked away

in horse-breeding Argos, seeking to seduce
the wife of Agamemnon with his talk.   360
Lady Clytaemnestra at first turned down
such a repulsive crime, for she possessed
a noble heart. Besides, she had with her
a singer whom the son of Atreus
had firmly charged to watch out for his wife,
when he'd set out for Troy. But when fate
sent from the gods caught her and she succumbed,
Aegisthus took that singer far away,
to a deserted island, and left him there,
a trophy for the birds to prey upon.   370
And when he wished to take her to his home,
she agreed to go. Then Aegisthus burned
many thigh cuts on the holy altars
sacred to the gods and offered up
all sorts of treasure, woven goods and gold,
for he had managed a tremendous act,
something his heart had never dreamed of.
Well, once we'd left Troy, we sailed together,
Menelaus and myself. At the time,
our relationship was very friendly.   380
But when we came to holy Sunium,
the Athenian headland, Phoebus Apollo
with his gentle shafts struck down and killed
Menelaus' helmsman, Phrontis,
Onetor's son, as he gripped the steering oar
on the swift-moving ship.[1] He was a man
pre-eminent among the tribes of men
in piloting a ship through stormy winds.
Now, though Menelaus was still very keen
to keep going on his trip, he stayed there,   390
to bury his companion and provide
the funeral rites. But when he re-launched
his hollow ships upon the wine-dark sea
and quickly reached the steep crag of Malea,

---

[1] . . . swift-moving ship. The line about the "gentle" shafts of Apollo refers to some
fatal but non-violent illness (like a fever), for which Apollo was considered
responsible.

then far-seeing Zeus carried out a scheme
to make his voyage dreadful. He sent down
blasting winds and immense waves, like mountains.
Splitting Menelaus' fleet in two,
Zeus pushed some to Crete, where Cyndians live
beside banks of the river Iardanus.   400
There's a steep cliff there, a rock facing the sea
right in the misty surf, on Gortyn's borders,
where the South-West Wind smashes mighty waves
against the promontory on the left,
by Phaestus. A small rock in that spot holds back
the mighty waves. Some of his ships came there.
After making desperate efforts, the men
escaped destruction, but on that rock
the ships were smashed to pieces by the waves.
The wind then drove five other dark-nosed ships   410
over the waves and carried them to Egypt,
where Menelaus and his ships then sailed
among some folk who spoke a foreign language,
gathering plentiful supplies and gold,
while at home Aegisthus planned the murder.
After he had killed the son of Atreus,
he ruled gold-rich Mycenae seven years.
Under his kingship people were oppressed.
But in the eighth year brave Orestes came
back from Athens—bad news for Aegisthus.   420
Orestes slew his father's murderer,
sly Aegisthus, because he had cut down
his famous father. Once he'd killed the man,
he held a funeral feast for all the Argives,
in remembrance of his hateful mother
and cowardly Aegisthus. That same day,
Menelaus, so good at battle shouts,
arrived, bringing large amounts of treasure,
as much freight as his ships could carry.
So now, my friend, you must not wander off   430
and stay away from home too long, leaving
your possessions there, with such arrogant men
in your own house, in case they take over

all your wealth or eat it up. That would make
your voyage here quite useless. I'd urge you—
and this I strongly recommend—to go
to Menelaus. For he's just come home
from foreign places very recently,
when no one in his heart had any hope
he might be returning from those people.   440
For stormy winds had driven him off course
at first, into a sea so large that birds
take a year or more to fly back from there.
That's how huge and terrifying it is.
But you and your companions should leave now
in your ship. If you'd like to go by land,
there are chariots and horses here for you.
My sons will help, as well, and be your guides
to fair-haired Menelaus, where he lives
in noble Sparta.[1] Make sure you ask him   450
to speak to you and to be quite candid.
He will not lie, for he is far too wise."

As Nestor finished, the sun was going down,
with darkness coming on. So Athena,
the bright-eyed goddess, said to them:

                              "Old man,
what you've just said is true and relevant.
But now you should slice out the victims' tongues
and mix the wine, so we can make libations
to lord Poseidon and to other gods,
and then think of rest. It's that time of day.   460
For now the light has slid below the darkness,
and it's not right for us to linger here
at a banquet for the gods. We must get back."

Zeus' daughter spoke, and they heard what she had said.
Heralds poured out water for them to wash their hands,

---

[1] . . . *noble Sparta*: Nestor offers Telemachus a choice here, but it is difficult to imagine
how Telemachus could sail directly to Sparta, which is far inland in the
mid-Peloponnese.

and young boys filled up wine bowls to the brim with drink,
served everyone, pouring wine out in the cups,
the first drops for libations. They threw the bulls' tongues
on the fire and, standing up, poured out their offerings.
That tribute made, they drank wine to their heart's content.   470
Then both Athena and godlike Telemachus
wished to get back to their hollow ship. But Nestor,
wanting them to stay, appealed to them and said:

> "Zeus and other eternal gods forbid
> that you should leave my home for your fast ship
> as if you were departing from a man
> who has no clothes or wealth, some pauper,
> whose home has no rich store of cloaks or blankets
> to give him and his guests a gentle sleep.
> No. My house has coverlets and lovely rugs.   480
> Surely the dear son of brave Odysseus
> will not lie down to sleep on a ship's deck,
> not while I'm alive and still have children
> left in my own halls to welcome strangers,
> whoever visits me in my own home."

Athena, bright-eyed goddess, then answered Nestor:

> "No doubt what you have said, old friend, is wise,
> and Telemachus should follow your advice.
> It would be far better if he did. But now,
> when he goes back with you to get some sleep   490
> in your own home, I'll go to our black ship,
> to rally the morale of our companions
> and tell them everything. Among our group
> I'm the only one who can make the claim
> that I'm an older man. The rest are young,
> all the same age as brave Telemachus.
> They follow us because they are our friends.
> I'll lie down on the black hollow ship tonight
> and in the morning go to the Caucones,
> where there's an old debt they still owe me,   500
> not a small amount. Since Telemachus

56

has visited your home, give him horses,
the strongest and the fastest ones you have,
and send him off in a chariot with your son."

Gleaming-eyed Athena said these words and left,
taking on the form of a sea eagle. Amazement
gripped all the Achaeans. And the old man, too,
was astonished as his eyes took in the sight.
He grabbed Telemachus' hand and said to him:

> "My friend, I don't think you'll turn out to be   510
> a bad or feeble man, if gods follow you
> to be your guide, when you're so very young.
> Of all those who live on Mount Olympus,
> that is none other than Zeus' daughter,
> the glorious Tritogeneia,[1] the god
> who held your splendid father in such honour
> among the Argives. But now, dear goddess,
> be gracious and give me a noble fame,
> me, my children, and the wife I cherish.
> And in return I'll sacrifice to you   520
> a broad-faced heifer, still unbroken,
> which no man yet has put beneath the yoke.
> I'll offer her to you with gold-wrapped horns."

Nestor spoke this prayer, and Pallas Athena heard him.
Then Geranian horseman Nestor led them away,
with his sons and sons-in-law, to his lovely home.
Once they reached the splendid palace of the king,
they sat down in rows on high-backed chairs and couches.
When they'd all come in, the old man mixed for them
a bowl of sweet wine ten years old, which his steward   530
opened after loosening the lid. The old man
had some of it mixed in a bowl, and then poured out
libations, as he prayed in earnest to Athena,
daughter of aegis-bearing Zeus. Others did the same.
Then they drank wine to their heart's content and left,

---

[1] *Tritogeneia*: the word means "Trito-born" (thrice born?) and is an epithet often given to Athena. Its precise significance is not known.

each to his own home, to get some sleep. Nestor,
the Geranian horseman, told Telemachus,
god-like Odysseus' dear son, to sleep right there,
on a corded bed in the echoing corridor,
with spear-fighter Peisistratus, leader of men,   540
there with him in the palace. Of all his sons
he was the only one as yet unmarried.
Nestor himself slept in an inner chamber
inside the high-roofed house, with his noble wife,
who had prepared the bed, lying down beside him.

As soon as rose-fingered early Dawn appeared,
Geranian horseman Nestor got up out of bed,
went outside, and sat down before his high white doors
on polished stones, which glistened, as if rubbed with oil.
Neleus in earlier times used to sit on them,   550
a man whose wise advice was equal to the gods.
But Fate had overtaken him by now. He'd gone
to Hades, so now Geranian horseman Nestor,
protector of Achaeans, sat on those stones,
a sceptre in his hand. His sons came from their rooms
and gathered round him in a throng—Echephron,
Stratius, Perseus, Aretus, and godlike Thrasymedes.
Then the sixth son joined them, warrior Peisistratus.
They brought in godlike Telemachus, asking him
to sit among them. Geranian horseman Nestor   560
then began to speak to them:

                    "My dear children,
          you must act on my desires, and quickly,
          so I can propitiate Athena,
          before the other gods. She came to me
          in manifest form, at Poseidon's feast.
          So come—one of you must fetch a heifer
          out there in the plain. And just to guarantee
          the beast gets here as quickly as it can,
          have the cattle herder drive it to me.
          Then someone must set off for the black ship   570
          of brave Telemachus and bring back

all his companions, leaving only two.
And tell the goldsmith Laerces to come,
so he can wrap the heifer's horns with gold.
All the rest of you stay here together.
Inform the inside household servants
to prepare a fine banquet in the house,
with chairs and logs set all around. Make sure
they bring fresh water."

                  Once Nestor finished speaking,
the men all set to work. The heifer from the plain   580
was driven in, and brave Telemachus' comrades
arrived from their fine ship. The goldsmith came, as well,
gripping the bronze tools he needed for his trade,
an anvil, hammer, and well-crafted tongs, the things
he used to work the gold. And Athena also came,
ready to receive the sacrifice. Then Nestor,
the old chariot fighter, produced the gold. The smith
worked it into a rich design and wrapped it
around the heifer's horns, so that the goddess,
when she saw the offering, would rejoice. Stratius   590
and noble Echephron led in the heifer by the horns,
as Aretus entered from an inner room,
bringing water in a basin etched with flowers
for them to wash their hands. In his other hand
he brought in a basket filled with barley grains.
Steadfast Thrasymedes stood holding a sharp axe
to cut down the heifer. And Perseus held a bowl
to catch the victim's blood. Then old man Nestor,
the chariot fighter, began the ritual washing
and sprinkled barley grains, intoning many prayers   600
to Athena. Then, as the initial offering,
from the beast's head he cut off a single hair
and threw it on the fire. When they'd made their prayers
and scattered barley grains, then Thrasymedes,
Nestor's daring son, approached the animal
and struck it. The axe sliced through sinews on its neck,
and the spirit of the beast ebbed out. The women—
Nestor's daughters, his sons' wives, his cherished wife,

59

Eurydice, eldest daughter of Clymenus—
raised the sacred cry, as the men then lifted up   610
the animal's head above the much-travelled earth.
Peisistratus, leader of men, slit its throat,
and its black blood flowed. The spirit left its bones.
They carved the body quickly, cutting thigh bones out,
all in proper order, and then covered them
in a double fold of fat and set raw meat on top.
Next, the old man burned the pieces on split wood
and poured gleaming wine on them. Beside Nestor
stood young men holding five-pronged forks. Once the thighs
had been completely burned and they'd sampled innards,   620
they cut up the remaining meat, placed it on spits,
and held the pointed skewers on the fire.

Then lovely Polycaste, youngest daughter
of Nestor, son of Neleus, bathed Telemachus.
When the bath was finished, she rubbed him with rich oil
and gave him a tunic and fine cloak to wear.
Coming from his bath, he looked just like a god.
He went and sat by Nestor, the people's shepherd.

When they had cooked the upper cuts of meat
and pulled them off the spits, they sat and ate.   630
The servers were distinguished men, who poured the wine
in goblets made of gold. Once they had all eaten
their fill of food and drink, Geranian horseman Nestor
was the first to speak. He said:

                              "Come now, my sons,
                    hitch up some fine-maned horses to a chariot,
                    so Telemachus can start his journey."

Nestor spoke. They heard and carried out his orders,
eagerly and quickly harnessing swift horses
onto the chariot. In it a servant woman
stored bread and wine and special delicacies,   640
assortments that those kings Zeus cherishes
eat with delight. Then Telemachus climbed up

inside the splendid chariot, and Nestor's son
Peisistratus, leader of men, stepped up
beside him in the chariot, grabbed the reins,
and then cracked the whip. The pair of horses
raced willingly across the plain, leaving
the steep citadel of Pylos. All day long
they rattled the yoke and harness on their necks.

Then the sun set, and darkness covered all the roads.   650
They reached the home of Diocles in Pherae.
He was Ortilochus' son, whose father
was Alpheus, and there they spent the night.
Diocles offered them the hospitality
he owed to strangers who stayed there as his guests.

As soon as rose-fingered early Dawn appeared,
they hitched their horses, climbed in the splendid chariot,
and set off from the echoing portico and gate.
With a touch of the whip, the horses raced along,
eager to run. The two men reached plains full of wheat,   660
in a hurry to complete their journey, so quickly
did their pair of horses pull them onward.
The sun then set, and all the roads grew dark.

Book Four
Telemachus Visits Menelaus in Sparta

[Telemachus and Peisistratus arrive at Menelaus' home in Sparta; Menelaus
welcomes them, talks of Agamemnon and Odysseus; Helen questions
Menelaus about the guests, drugs the wine, tells the story of Odysseus visiting
Troy disguised as a beggar; Menelaus talks about the Trojan Horse;
Telemachus' asks Menelaus' advice; Menelaus gives a long account of his
travels in Egypt, especially his adventures with the Old Man of the Sea, the
death of the lesser Ajax, and the death of Agamemnon; Menelaus invites
Telemachus to stay, but Telemachus declines; the Suitors hatch a plan to kill
Telemachus; Penelope hears of their plans and is anxious; Athena sends her
a phantom to reassure her; some of the suitors sail off to ambush Telemachus.]

When Telemachus and Peisistratus reached
the Spartan plain and its surrounding hills,
they went straight to splendid Menelaus' palace.[1]
They found him inside his house, at a marriage feast
he was providing for his many relatives,
in honour of his noble son and daughter.
He was sending her away to Neoptolemus,
son of man-destroying Achilles—back in Troy
he had first promised he would offer her to him.
He'd pledged his word, and now the gods were making sure   10
the marriage would take place. He was seeing her off
with chariots and horses for her journey
to the famous city of the Myrmidons,
whom her husband ruled. For his son, Menelaus
was bringing Alector's daughter home to Sparta.
That son, mighty Megapenthes, born to a slave,
was his favorite, for the gods had granted Helen
no more children after she had given birth
to the lovely girl Hermione, as beautiful
as golden Aphrodite. So they were feasting   20
in the massive palace with its high-pitched roof—
neighbours and relatives of glorious Menelaus,

---

[1]Sparta is the name of the central city in the district of Lacedaemon or Lacedaemonia.
The two names are sometimes used interchangeably.

all enjoying themselves. Among them was a singer,
accompanying his godlike song by playing the lyre.
As he began to sing, two tumblers ran and jumped
here and there, through the middle of the crowd.

As the two visitors, heroic Telemachus
and Nestor's noble son, stood at the palace gates
with their two horses, lord Eteoneus came out,
a diligent attendant to splendid Menelaus.   30
When he noticed them, he went back inside the house,
to tell the shepherd of his people what he'd seen.
Standing close to Menelaus, he spoke to him—
his words had wings:

                         "Menelaus, raised by gods,
          there are two strangers here, two men who look
          as if they are descended from great Zeus.
          So tell me if we should, on their behalf,
          take their fast horses out of harness,
          or send them off to find some other host
          who'll welcome them as friends."

                         These words he uttered   40
really irritated fair-haired Menelaus,
so he replied as follows:

                         "Before today,
          Eteoneus, son of Boethous,
          you haven't been a fool. But now you talk
          just like a silly child. For both of us
          often feasted on the hospitality
          of other men before we got back here,
          hoping that Zeus would give us some relief
          from later suffering. So unhitch those horses
          the strangers brought, and bring the men inside,   50
          so they may dine."

                         Menelaus finished.
Then Eteoneus left, rushing from the hall

and calling out to other diligent attendants
to follow him. They took the sweating horses
from the harness and hitched them in the stables,
scattering wheat for them, mixed with white barley grains,
leaned the chariot against the luminescent wall,
and led the men into the godlike building.
Telemachus and Peisistratus were amazed
by what they noticed in the regal palace—   60
for the high-roofed home of splendid Menelaus,
a man raised by Zeus, shimmered in the light,
as if illuminated by the sun or moon.
When their eyes had gazed on it with great delight,
they went in well-polished bathing tubs to wash.
After women servants had given them a bath,
rubbed them down with oil, and helped them put on
thick cloaks and tunics, they sat down on chairs
right by Menelaus, son of Atreus. A serving woman
carried in a lovely pitcher made of gold   70
containing water for them to rinse their hands.
She poured it out into a silver basin,
so they could wash. Then beside them she pulled up
a polished table. A valued female servant
brought in bread and set it down before them,
and added many tasty delicacies as well,
taking freely from the food she had in store.
A carver lifted platters with all sorts of meat
and served them, then set down in front of the two men
goblets made of gold. Fair-haired Menelaus   80
welcomed both of them and said:

                                        "Help yourselves.
        Enjoy our food. And once you've had your meal,
        we'll ask you who you are. For in you two
        your parents' breeding has not been destroyed—
        since you are from a royal human stock,
        from god-nurtured kings who wield a sceptre.
        Worthless men could not father sons like you."

Menelaus spoke. Then with his own hands he picked up

the roasted meat and set it down in front of them,
the fat back-cut of beef they'd placed in front of him,   90
a mark of honour. So the two men helped themselves,
eating the fine meal prepared and set before them.
When they'd had their heart's content of food and drink,
Telemachus leaned his head close to Nestor's son,
so no one else could hear, and spoke to him:

> "Son of Nestor, who brings my heart such joy,
> look at how, throughout this echoing hall,
> there's so much sparkling bronze and gold,
> electrum, silver, ivory—to me
> it's the interior of Zeus' home   100
> on Mount Olympus, so much untold wealth—
> I'm amazed just looking at it."[1]

As he said this,
fair-haired Menelaus heard his words and spoke
to both of them—his words had wings:

> "Dear lads,
> no mortal man can really rival Zeus,
> since his possessions and his palaces
> endure forever. But among human beings,
> someone else might challenge me or not
> about our wealth. I carried riches back
> inside my ships, after we'd endured so much   110
> while we were wandering. We made it home—
> it took us more than seven years. We'd roamed
> to Cyprus, Egypt, and Phoenicia.
> We even reached the Ethiopians,
> Sidonians, and Erembi—Lydia, too,
> where lambs are born with horns and ewes give birth
> three times in one full year. No master there,
> nor any shepherd, ever lacks sweet milk
> or cheese or meat, and through the entire year
> their flocks are ready to produce their milk.   120
> While I was wandering around these lands,

[1]Electrum is a naturally occurring alloy of gold and silver with other trace mineral elements.

gathering all sorts of goods, another man
slaughtered my own brother unexpectedly,
in secret, thanks to the duplicity
of his murderous wife. So you can understand
there is no joy for me in being king
of these possessions. You may have heard this
from your fathers, whoever they may be.
I suffered many troubles and allowed
a really well-established home, endowed   130
with many noble riches, to collapse.
I wish I could live with one third my wealth
here in my home, if those men could be safe,
the ones who died in the wide land of Troy,
far from horse-breeding Argos. And yet,
although I often sit here in my house
feeling sorry and in mourning for them all,
sometimes groaning to relieve my spirit
and sometimes calling for a end to moaning,
for one can quickly get too much of sorrow,   140
still, for all my grieving, I do not lament
all those men as much as I do one man,
who, when I think of him, makes me despise
both sleep and food, for of all Achaeans
no one toiled as hard as did Odysseus,
who took so much upon himself. For him,
it seems, there would be no end of trouble,
and I cannot forget to grieve for him.
He's been away so long. And we don't know
if he's alive or dead. Old man Laertes,   150
I would think, is in mourning for him,
and so is sensible Penelope,
and Telemachus, as well, whom he left
a new-born child at home."

                                  Menelaus spoke.
His words stirred up a desire in Telemachus
to lament his father. So from his eyelids
he shed a tear onto the ground, as he heard
what Menelaus said about Odysseus.

With both his hands he pulled up the purple cloak
to hide his eyes. Noticing this, Menelaus   160
debated in his mind and heart: Should he allow
Telemachus to speak about his father,
or should he first question him and sound him out
on each and every detail? As he thought of this
in his mind and heart, Helen came into the room,
emerging from her fragrant high-roofed chamber.
She looked like golden-arrowed goddess Artemis.
Adreste came with her. She set in place for her
a finely crafted chair. Alcippe carried in
a soft wool rug. Phylo brought a silver basket,   170
which Helen had been given by Alcandre,
wife to Polybus, who lived in Thebes in Egypt,
where the most massive hordes of rich possessions
lie in people's homes. He'd given Menelaus
a pair of tripods and two silver bathing tubs,
as well as ten gold talents. In addition,
his wife presented Helen with some lovely gifts—
a golden spinning staff and silver basket,
with wheels below and rims of plated gold.
The servant woman Phylo brought this basket in   180
and placed it by her side, filled with fine-spun yarn.
On it lay the spinning rod full of purple wool.
Helen sat down on the chair, a stool beneath her feet.
At once she started speaking to her husband,
asking detailed questions.

           "Do we know,
my divinely cherished Menelaus,
who these men who've come into our home
claim to be? Shall I speak up and pretend,
or shall I tell the truth? My heart tells me
I must be frank. I can't say I've ever seen   190
someone who looks so much like someone else,
whether man or woman. When I see it,
I'm amazed—this man looks just like the son
of brave Odysseus—I mean Telemachus,
whom he left at home a new-born child,

when, because I'd acted so disgracefully,
you Achaeans all marched off to Troy,
your hearts intent on brutal war."

Fair-haired Menelaus then said in reply:

"This likeness you've just noticed, my dear wife,   200
I've observed, as well. His feet are similar,
as are his hands, the glances from his eyes,
his head, and his hair on top. And just now,
as I was remembering Odysseus,
discussing all the troubles he'd endured
because of me, he let a bitter tear
fall from his eyes and raised the purple cloak
across his eyelids."

                          Then Peisistratus, Nestor's son,
spoke out and said:

                          "Menelaus, son of Atreus,
Zeus-fostered leader of your people,   210
this man here is indeed, as you have said,
Odysseus' son. But he's a prudent man—
in his heart he's too ashamed to come
on his first visit here and put on a show
with some assertive speech in front of you,
whose voice we listen to with great delight,
as if it were a god's. I've been sent here
by Geranian horseman Nestor as his guide.
He wants to see you and get your advice,
in word or deed. For with his father gone,   220
a child has many troubles in his home,
and there is no one there to help him.
That's what's happened with Telemachus.
His father's vanished, and there's no one else
to protect his house from ruin."

                          Fair-haired Menelaus
then answered Peisistratus, saying:

68

"Well now,
this is strange indeed—to my home has come
the offspring of a man I cherish, someone
who, on my behalf, endured much hardship.
If he'd returned, I thought I'd welcome him   230
above all other Argives, should far-seeing Zeus
on Mount Olympus let the two of us
make it home by sea in our swift ships.
I would have given him an Argive city
and built a home for him, where he could live,
bringing him from Ithaca with all his wealth,
his son, and his own people. I'd have emptied
some neighbouring city in the region,
whose people all acknowledge me as king—
then we could live here and be together,   240
and nothing would have separated us.
We could have often entertained each other,
getting joy from one another's company,
until Death's black cloud came to embrace us.
But god himself must have been envious,
to make that unlucky man the only one
who didn't get back home."

Menelaus finished.
What he'd just said made them all feel like weeping.
Argive Helen, daughter of Zeus, began to cry,
as did Telemachus and Menelaus, too,   250
son of Atreus. Nestor's son could not keep the tears
out of his eyes. In his heart he was remembering
valiant Antilochus, killed by Dawn's courageous son.[1]
With him in mind, Peisistratus spoke—his words had wings:

"Son of Atreus, old warrior Nestor
used to say, when we conversed together
and your name was mentioned in our home,
that, as far as sound thinking was concerned,
you were pre-eminent among all men.

---

[1]*Antilochus . . . son*: Antilochus, Peisistratus' brother, was killed at Troy by Memnon, son of Dawn. He was buried with Achilles and Patroclus at Troy.

So, if it seems somehow appropriate,   260
you should listen to me now. I don't enjoy
weeping at dinner time, and early Dawn
will soon be here. I don't think it shameful
to cry for any mortal man who's died
and met his fate. In fact, this ritual
is the only ceremony we give
for these unhappy men—we cut our hair
and let the tears run down our cheeks. I have
a brother who was killed, not the worst man
among the Argives. Perhaps you knew him.   270
I never met him, never even saw him,
but they say Antilochus surpassed all men
in running fast and fighting well."

                          Fair-haired Menelaus
then answered Peisistratus, saying:

                         "My friend,
you have truly mentioned everything
a right-thinking man might say or do,
even someone older than yourself.
The kind of father you were born from
enables you to speak so sensibly.
To recognize someone's inheritance   280
is easy, when the son of Cronos spins
good fortune's threads at marriage and at birth,
the way he now has done for Nestor,
granting him for all his days continually
to reach a ripe old age in his own home,
with sons who are, in turn, intelligent
and great spear fighters, too. But we must stop
and let that earlier weeping cease. Let's have
water poured upon our hands, then once again
turn our minds to dinner. In the morning   290
there'll be stories for Telemachus and I
to tell each other to our heart's content."

He finished speaking. Then one of his attendants,

diligent Asphalion, poured water on their hands,
and they reached for the rich food spread out before them.

Then Helen, Zeus' daughter, thought of something else.
She quickly dropped into the wine they were enjoying
a drug which eased men's pains and irritations,
making them forget their troubles. A drink of this,
once mixed in with wine, would guarantee no man   300
would let a tear fall on his cheek for one whole day,
not even if his mother and his father died,
or if, in his own presence, men armed with swords
hacked down his brother or his son, as he looked on.
Zeus' daughter had effective healing potions,
like that drug, which she'd obtained from Polydamna,
wife of Thon, who came from Egypt, where the fields,
so rich in grain, produce the greatest crop of drugs,
many of which, once mixed, are beneficial,
and many poisonous. Every person there   310
is a physician whose knowledge of these things
surpasses that of every other human group,
for through their ancestry they stem from Paeeon.[1]
When Helen had stirred in the drug and told them
to serve out the wine, she rejoined the conversation
and spoke up once again:

                    "Menelaus, son of Atreus,
      whom gods cherish, and you sons of noble men—
      since both good and bad are given by Zeus,
      sometimes to one man and, at other times,
      to someone else, for he is capable   320
      of all things, you should now sit in the hall
      and dine. After that, enjoy your stories.
      I'll tell you one I think is suitable.
      I will not speak of, nor could I recite,
      everything about steadfast Odysseus,
      all the hardships he went through. But there's that time
      when you Achaeans were in such distress
      and that strong man endured and did so much—

---

[1] *Paeeon* is the god of healing who knows all the remedies available for human ills.

right in homeland of those Trojans, too!
With savage blows he beat up his own body,   330
threw a ragged garment on his shoulders,
so he looked like a slave, and then sneaked in,
along the broad streets of that hostile city.
He hid his own identity, pretending
he was someone else, a beggar—something
he'd never been among Achaean ships—
and then went in the Trojans' city. None of them
suspected anything. I was the only one
who recognized him, in spite of his disguise.
I questioned him, but his skill in deception   340
made him evasive. Still, when I had bathed him,
rubbed him with oil, and was helping him get dressed—
once I'd sworn a mighty oath not to reveal
among the Trojans that he was Odysseus
until he'd reached the swift ships and the huts—
he told me all about Achaean plans.
Then his long sword slaughtered many Trojans,
and he returned, bringing the Achaeans,
lots of information. Other Trojan women
began to cry aloud, but I was glad.   350
My heart by then had changed—it now desired
to go back. I was sorry for that blindness
Aphrodite brought, when she'd led me there,
far from my own land, abandoning my child,
my bridal room, and my own husband, too,
who lacked nothing in good looks or wisdom."

In reply to Helen, fair-haired Menelaus said:

"Yes, indeed, dear wife, everything you've said
is true. Before now, I've come to understand
the minds and plans of many warriors.   360
I've roamed through many lands. But my eyes
have never seen a man to match Odysseus.
How I loved his steadfast heart! What about
the things that forceful man endured and did
in the wooden horse? Achaea's finest men—

72

all of us—were sitting in it, carrying
a lethal fate to Trojans. Then you came there,
perhaps instructed by some god who wished
to give great glory to the Trojans.
And, where you walked, noble Deïphobus   370
followed, too. Three times you circled round,
feeling that hollow trap. Your voice called out,
naming the best warriors among Danaans,
and you made it sound just like the voice
of each man's Argive wife. Now, I was there,
sitting with lord Odysseus in the middle,
and with Tydeus' son.[1] We heard you call.
Two of us—Diomedes and myself—
were eager to get up and charge outside
or else to answer back from where we were,   380
inside the horse. But Odysseus stopped us—
we were really keen, but he held us in check.
Then all the other sons of the Achaeans
kept their mouths shut, except for Anticlus,
the only one still keen to cry aloud
and answer you. But Odysseus clapped his hand
firmly over Anticlus' mouth and held him,
thus rescuing all Achaeans. He kept
his grip on Anticlus until Athena
led you away."

            Then prudent Telemachus replied: 390

"Menelaus, son of Atreus, cherished by Zeus,
leader of your people, that incident
is more painful still—it could not save him
from a bitter death, not even if the heart
inside him had been made of iron.
But come, send us to bed, so sweet Sleep
can bring us joy once we lie down to rest."

---

[1] *Deïphobus*: a son of Priam, king of Troy, was an important Trojan warrior during the war.
Tydeus' son is Diomedes, a major Achaean warrior-king, whose return home Nestor has
talked about earlier (in Book 3).

Once Telemachus spoke, Helen told her slaves
to set up mattresses within the corridor
and spread out lovely purple blankets over them,   400
with rugs on top, and over these some woolen cloaks.
The women left the hall with torches in their hands
and arranged the beds. A herald led the guests away.
And so they slept there in the palace vestibule,
prince Telemachus and Nestor's noble son.
The son of Atreus slept in an inner room,
inside the high-roofed home, with long-robed Helen,
goddess among women, lying there beside him.

As soon as rose-fingered early Dawn appeared,
Menelaus, skilled at war shouts, got out of bed   410
and put his clothes on, slinging a sharp sword
around his shoulders. He laced up lovely sandals
over his sleek feet. Then, looking like some god,
he left his room. He sat beside Telemachus
and then addressed him, saying:

                              "Prince Telemachus,
          what do you need that's brought you all this way
          on the sea's broad back to lovely Sparta?
          Is it a public or a private matter?
          Tell me about it, and be frank."

                              Shrewd Telemachus
then said in reply:

                              "Menelaus, son of Atreus,   420
          cherished by Zeus and leader of your people,
          I've come to see if you could give me news
          about my father. My home's being eaten up,
          my rich estates destroyed. My house is full
          of enemies who keep on butchering
          flocks of sheep and shambling bent-horned cattle.
          They are suitors for my mother—their pride
          makes them supremely arrogant. That's why
          I've now come to your knee, to see if you

74

perhaps can tell me of his mournful death—   430
in case your own eyes witnessed it somewhere,
or else you've found out from some other man
the story of his wandering. For his mother
delivered him into a life of sorrow,
more so than other men. And do not speak
from pity, or give me words of consolation,
but tell me truly how you chanced to see him.
I'm begging you, if ever in word or deed
my father, brave Odysseus, over there,
on Trojan soil, where you Achaean men   440
endured so much, made you a promise
and then kept his word, speak to me now,
and give me the truth."

                Fair-haired Menelaus,
very annoyed by what he'd heard, replied:

                  "It's disgraceful
how such wretched cowards want to lie
in that brave warrior's bed, as if a deer
had lulled her new-born suckling fawns to sleep
in a mighty lion's den and then gone roaming
through mountain fields and grassy valleys
in search of forage—then the lion comes   450
back to his lair and brings to both of them
a shameful death. That just how Odysseus
will bring those suitors their disgraceful doom.
O Father Zeus, Athena, and Apollo,
how I wish Odysseus would come back
and meet the suitors with the strength he had
when he stood up in well-built Lesbos once
in a wrestling match with Philomeleides.
With his great power, he threw him down,
and all Achaean men rejoiced. Those suitors   460
would quickly find their bitter courtship
ends in a swift death. But these things you ask,
what you've begged me about, I'll not digress
to speak of other things, nor will I lie.

75

No. What the Old Man of the Sea told me—
and did so truthfully—I'll not hide from you.
I won't conceal a single word.

                              "In Egypt,
though I was eager to get home, the gods
prevented me—I had not offered them
a full and proper sacrifice, and gods   470
always demand obedience to their orders.
Now, just in front of Egypt there's an island,
right in the crashing sea—it's called Pharos—
as far off shore as a hollow ship can sail
in one whole day, when a fine stiff breeze
blows up behind her. There's a harbour there
with excellent moorage, and from that spot
men launch well-balanced ships into the sea,
once they have taken on supplies of water.
For twenty days the gods detained me there.   480
Not once was there a favourable wind,
the sort of offshore breeze which makes men's ships
race out across the broad back of the sea.
Then my provisions would have all been spent,
together with the spirit in my crew,
if a goddess had not felt pity for me
and rescued us—the goddess Eidothea,
daughter of the Old Man of the Sea,
great Proteus. For I had moved her heart,
more so than other men. When she met me,   490
I was by myself, for I'd wandered off,
away from my companions, who'd gone out,
as they always did, to scour the island,
fishing with bent hooks, their stomachs cramped
from hunger. She came up close to me and said:

      'Stranger, are you a slow-witted idiot,
      or are you happy just to let things go
      and find delight in your own suffering?
      You've been stranded so long on this island,
      unable to discover any sign of help,   500

                              76

while your companions' spirits waste away.'

"That's what she said. So then I answered her:

'Whoever you may be among the gods,
I'll tell you I have not been pent up here
with my consent. Something must have happened
to make me act against immortal gods,
who occupy wide heaven. But tell me this—
for gods know all things—which immortal one
keeps my feet shackled here and blocks my way?
Tell me how I find my way back home,   510
how I sail across the fish-filled seas.'

"I finished speaking. The lovely goddess
immediately gave me her answer:

'All right, stranger, I'll be truthful with you.
The Old Man of the Sea comes here from Egypt,
I mean infallible, eternal Proteus,
a god who knows the depths of every sea,
Poseidon's servant and, so people say,
my father, too, the one who sired me.
Now, if somehow you could set an ambush   520
and catch hold of him, he'd show you your way.
He'd chart the course for your return and map
how you could sail across the fish-filled seas.
And, Zeus-fostered man, if you were willing,
he'd tell you all the good and evil things
which have been taking place in your own house
while you've been traveling away from home
on such a long and arduous journey.'

"When she'd told me this, I replied and said:

'Could you yourself produce a strategy   530
to ambush this divine old man, in case
he sees me first and, knowing all my plans,
escapes me. It's difficult for mortal men

77

to overcome a god.'

  "Once I'd said this,
the lovely goddess answered right away:

'Stranger, I'll be frank—tell you the truth
in everything. When the sun has made its way
up into the middle of the heavens,
that infallible Old Man of the Sea
emerges from the brine, where he's concealed   540
by dark waves stirred up by the West Wind's breath.
Once he gets here, he lies down to rest
in these hollow caves, and around him sleeps
a herd of seals—they are the offspring
of the lovely daughter of the sea and swim up
out of the gray water. Their breath gives off
the sharp salt smell of the deep sea. At daybreak,
I'll take you there and organize an ambush.
You must carefully select three comrades,
the best men in those well-decked ships of yours.   550
Now I'll describe for you all the sly tricks
that old man has. First, he'll inspect the seals.
He'll count them, numbering them off by fives.
Once he's looked them over, he'll lie down
in their midst, like a shepherd with his sheep.
As soon as you see him stretched out to sleep,
then you must use all your strength and courage
to hold him there for all his desperate moves,
as he struggles to escape. For he'll attempt
to change himself into all sorts of shapes   560
of everything that crawls over the earth,
or into water or a sacred flame.
You must not flinch—keep up your grip on him—
make it even tighter. And finally,
when he begins to speak and questions you
in the same shape you saw him go to sleep,
then, warrior king, you can relax your grip
and let the old man go. Ask him which god
is angry at you and how you'll get back,

"Saying this, she plunged into the crashing sea.
I went to where my ships were on the beach—
my dark heart thinking, as I walked, of many things.
Once I'd reached the ships along the shore,
we prepared and ate our evening meal.
When immortal night arrived, we lay down
beside the breaking surf. Then, as the streaks
of rose-fingered early Dawn appeared,
I walked along the shores of that wide sea,
praying in earnest to the gods. Then I took   580
three comrades, the ones I trusted most
in any enterprise. That sea goddess,
who'd plunged into the bosom of the sea,
brought up four seal skins from the ocean depths,
each one freshly skinned, then set up the plot
against her father. She scooped out in the sand
some pits to hide in, and then waited there.
Once we'd come up really close beside her,
she made us lie down in a row and threw
a seal skin over each of us. That ambush   590
would have been too horrible to bear,
for the atrocious stench of sea-born seals
was dreadful. Who would let himself lie down
with creatures from the sea? But Eidothea
personally helped us out by thinking up
a useful remedy—she got ambrosia,
sweet-smelling oil of the immortal gods,
and put it under each man's nose. That killed
the foul stink coming from those animals.
With patient hearts we waited there all morning.   600
Crowds of seals emerged and then lay down
in rows along the seashore. At noon,
the old man came up out of the water,
discovered the plump seals, looked at each one,
and made his count, beginning first with us,
whom he included with the animals.
His heart did not suspect there was a trick.

Then he lay down. We charged up with a shout
and grabbed him in our arms. But the old man
did not forget his skillful tricks. At first, 610
he turned himself into a hairy lion,
and then into a serpent and a leopard,
then a huge wild boar. He changed himself
to flowing water and a towering tree.
We didn't flinch but kept our grip on him.
Our hearts were resolute. When the old man,
for all his devious skills, got tired out,
he spoke up, asking me some questions:

'Son of Atreus, which god helped your plan
and forged a scheme so you could lie in wait 620
and ambush me against my will? And why?
What do you need?'

"When he'd said this to me,
I answered him and said:

'You know that, old man,
so why mislead me with such questioning?
I've been stranded too long on this island
and can't discover any sign of help.
The heart is growing faint inside me.
So tell me, for you gods know everything,
which one of the immortals chains my feet
and blocks my way. And speak to me as well 630
about my journey back, how I may sail
across the fish-filled seas.'

"When I'd said that,
he answered me at once:

'Before you left,
you should have offered a fine sacrifice
to Zeus and other gods, so you could sail
across the wine-dark sea and then arrive
in your own land as fast as possible.

Your fate decrees you will not see your friends
or reach your homeland or your well-built house,
until you've gone back once more to Egypt,   640
to the waters of that Zeus-fed river,
and made holy sacrifices to the gods,
the immortal ones who hold wide heaven.
The gods will then give you that journey home
which you so yearn for.'

         "As the old man spoke,
my fond heart broke apart inside me,
because he'd told me I must go once more
across the misty seas, on that long trip
to Egypt, a painful journey. But still,
I answered him and spoke these words:

                    'Old man,   650
I will carry out what you have told me.
But come now, tell me—and speak truthfully—
did Achaeans in those ships get safely back,
all those men Nestor and myself left there
when we set out from Troy? Did any die
a bitter death on board, or in the arms
of those who loved them, after they'd tied up
the loose threads of the war?'

             "That's what I asked,
and he gave me his answer right away:

'Son of Atreus, why question me on this?   660
You don't need to know or to read my mind.
For once you've learned the details of all this,
you'll not hold back your tears for very long.
Many of those warriors were destroyed,
and many men survived. Among Achaeans,
armed in bronze, only two leading warriors
were killed on their way home. As for the fights,
you were there yourself. There is one leader
held back by the sea somewhere, but still alive.

81

Ajax perished among his long-oared ships[1]— 670
at Gyrae Poseidon first propelled his boat
against huge rocks, then saved him from the sea.
Although Athena hated him, he'd have been saved,
if he'd not grown insanely foolish—
he stated he had managed to escape
the sea's huge depths, in spite of all the gods.
Poseidon heard him make this boastful claim.
Immediately those mighty hands of his
picked up his trident and then brought it down
on that rock at Gyrae, splitting it apart. 680
One piece stayed in place—the other one
sheared off and fell into the sea, the part
where Ajax sat when his mind first became
so utterly deluded. He fell down
into the endless surging waves and died
by swallowing salt water. But your brother
escaped that fate—he and his hollow ships
survived, for queen Hera rescued him.
And then, when he was just about to reach
the steep height at Malea, storm winds caught him. 690
As he groaned in distress, they carried him
across the fish-filled seas to the remotest part
of where Thyestes used to live, now the home
of Thyestes' son Aegisthus.[2] But then,
once the gods had changed the wind's direction,
it seemed that he could make it safely back.
So he got home. And he was full of joy
to set foot on his native land once more.
He embraced the earth and kissed it—shedding
numerous warm tears—he was so delighted 700
at the sight. But a watchman spied him out,
someone Aegisthus had placed as lookout,

---

[1] *Ajax*. This is a reference to Oïlean Ajax, king of Locris (or the "Lesser" Ajax), not to Ajax, king of Salamis, the greatest Achaean warrior after Achilles, who had died and was buried at Troy (as Nestor has pointed out in Book 3).

[2] Thyestes was the brother of Atreus, father of Agamemnon and Menelaus. Atreus had killed Thyestes' small sons and fed them to him at dinner. Aegisthus, the remaining son, took his revenge on Agamemnon, in collaboration with Agamemnon's wife.

to promote his plot, promising the man,
as his reward, two gold talents. He'd been there,
on watch, for one whole year, just in case
Agamemnon should succeed in getting back
without being noticed and remind them all
of his ferocious power. The watchman went
straight to the palace to report the news
to the shepherd of the people. So then,   710
Aegisthus came up with a treacherous plan.
He picked out twenty men, the best there were
in the whole state, and set up an ambush.
Then, in another section of the house,
he had a feast made ready and went off
with chariot and horses to escort
Agamemnon, shepherd of his people,
all the while intending to destroy him.
Aegisthus then accompanied him home—
he suspected nothing of the murder—   720
and then, after the feast, he butchered him,
just as one might slay an ox in its own stall.
Of those companions of the son of Atreus
who followed him, not one was left alive.
Nor were any of Aegisthus' comrades—
they were all slaughtered in the palace.'

"The old man finished speaking. My fond heart
was shattered, and, as I sat in the sand,
I wept—my spirit had no wish to live
or gaze upon the light of day. But then,   730
when I'd had my fill of rolling in the sand
and weeping, the Old Man of the Sea
spoke frankly to me, saying,

               'Son of Atreus,
you must not spend so much time like this,
in constant weeping. That's no help to us.
You must strive, as quickly as you can,
to get back to your native land. It may be
you'll find Aegisthus is still living there,

or else Orestes has preceded you
and killed the man. If so, then there's a chance   740
you'll get back for Aegisthus' funeral feast.'

"The old man finished speaking. In my chest
my heart and spirit, for all my grieving,
felt strong once again. So I answered him—
my words had wings:

                    'Now I understand
what's happened to these men. But tell me
about the third one—whether he still lives,
held back by the wide sea, or has been killed.
I wish to hear that, for all my sorrow.'

"I spoke, and he at once replied, saying,   750

'You mean Laertes' son, from Ithaca.
I saw him on an island. He was weeping
in the palace of the nymph Calypso,
who keeps him there by force. He has no way
of getting back to his own land—he lacks
companions and ships equipped with oars,
to carry him across the sea's broad back.
As for you, Zeus-fostered Menelaus,
it's not ordained that you will meet your fate
and die in horse-rich Argos. No. The gods   760
will send you off to the Elysian fields,
and to the outer limits of the earth—
the place where fair-haired Rhadamanthus lives
and life for human beings is really easy—
there's no snow or heavy storms or even rain,
and Oceanus sends a steady breeze,
as West Wind blows to keep men cool and fresh.
Helen is your wife—that's why they'll do this,
because they see you as the man who married
Zeus daughter.' [1]

---

[1] *Elysian Fields . . . Rhadamanthus.* These lines suggest that Menelaus will not die, like the
other warriors, but live on in a paradise of the Elysian Fields. This special treatment for

"With these words, 770
the old man plunged back in the surging sea.
I went to my ships and godlike ship mates.
As I walked, my heart was darkly troubled,
but once I'd reached my ships beside the sea
and we'd prepared a meal, immortal night
came down, and we slept there on the shore."

"As soon as rose-fingered early Dawn appeared,
we dragged our boats into the sacred sea,
then fitted masts and sails on our trim ships.
The men climbed in, went to their rowing seats, 780
and, sitting well in order, raised their oars
and struck the gray salt sea. So I sailed back
to Egypt's heaven-fed river once again,
and there I offered a full sacrifice.
Once I'd appeased the anger of those gods
who live forever, I made a funeral mound
for Agamemnon, to make sure his fame
would never die, and when I'd finished that,
I set off on my journey home. The gods
gave me fair winds and brought me with all speed 790
back to the native land I love.

                    "But come now,
you must stay with me in my palace here
ten or eleven days, and after that
I'll send you off with honour. I'll give you
lovely gifts—a finely polished chariot
and three horses, too, and, as well as these,
a gorgeous cup, so you can pour libations
to eternal gods and remember me
for all your days to come."

                    Shrewd Telemachus
then said to Menelaus in reply:

Menelaus is very unusual. He receives it because he's a son-in-law of Zeus (since Helen
is Zeus' daughter). *Rhadamanthus* is a son of Zeus and Europa, so famous for his wise
judgment that Zeus made him one of a trio of judges in the underworld.

85

"Son of Atreus,   800
you must not hold me up for very long.
To tell the truth, I'd like to stay right here,
sitting in your palace an entire year,
and I'd not miss my parents or my home,
for I get such astonishing delight
from what you say and from your stories.
But my companions are already restless
back in sacred Pylos, and time has passed
while you've detained me here. As for gifts,
give me whatever you wish, just let it be   810
something you treasure. But I'll not take
those horses back with me to Ithaca—
I'll leave them here to bring you pleasure.
For you are king of an extensive plain
in which huge quantities of lotus grow,
with sedge, broad-eared white barley, wheat, and rye.
But there are no wide plains in Ithaca,
no meadows. It has grazing land for goats,
something I prefer to lush horse pasture.
No island sloping down into the sea   820
has meadows fit for raising horses,
and that's especially true of Ithaca."

Then the great war-shouter Menelaus smiled,
patted Telemachus with his hand, and said:

       "My lad, the way you've spoken out proclaims
       your noble blood. So I'll exchange those gifts.
       That I can do. Of all the things stored up
       here in my home, I'll give you the finest,
       the most expensive one. I'll offer you
       a beautifully crafted mixing bowl.   830
       It's all silver, with rims of hammered gold.
       Hephaestus made it. Warrior Phaedimus,
       the Sidonians' king, presented it to me
       when I went there and his home sheltered me.
       Now I'd like to give that mixing bowl to you."

So these men kept conversing with each other.

Meanwhile, back in Telemachus' Ithaca,
the banqueters had reached the royal palace,
driving sheep there and carrying strong wine.
Their well-dressed wives were sending bread for them.   840
As these men were in the hall preparing dinner,
the suitors were outside Odysseus' palace,
enjoying themselves by throwing spears and discus
on level ground in front—with all the arrogance
they usually displayed. Their two leaders,
Antinous and handsome Eurymachus,
were sitting there—by far the best of all the suitors.
Then Noemon, Phronius' son, came up
to question Antinous. He said:

                        "Antinous,
        in our hearts do we truly know or not   850
        when Telemachus will journey back
        from sandy Pylos? He went away
        taking a ship of mine which I now need
        to make the trip across to spacious Elis,
        where I have twelve mares and sturdy mules
        still sucking on the teat, not yet broken.
        I want to fetch and break in one of them."

He finished. In their hearts the suitors were amazed.
They had no idea Telemachus had gone
to Pylos, land of Neleus, and still believed   860
he was somewhere with the flocks on his estates
or with the swineherd. So in answer to Noemon,
Antinous, son of Eupeithes, spoke up:

                        "Tell me the truth—
        when did he leave? What young men went with him?
        Did he take citizens of Ithaca,
        or were those men his slaves and servants?
        That's something he could do. And tell me this—
        I want the truth, so I know what happened—

87

did he take that black ship against your will,
by force, or did you volunteer to give it up,   870
because he begged you to?"

                    Noemon, son of Phronius,
then answered Antinous:

                    "I agreed to give it to him.
Would anyone have acted otherwise,
when a man like him, with a grief-stricken heart,
makes a request? It would be difficult
to deny him what he asked. The young men—
the ones who went with him—are excellent,
except for us, the best this land affords.
As they embarked, I observed their leader,
Mentor, or some god who looks just like him.   880
I'm surprised at that—at dawn yesterday
I saw lord Mentor, though by that time
he'd already gone on board for Pylos."

Once he finished speaking, Noemon went away,
back to his father's house. But those two suitors,
Antinous and Eurymachus, had angry hearts.
They quickly got the suitors to give up their games
and had them sit down all together in a group.
Antinous, Eupeithes' son, then spoke to them.
He was annoyed, his black heart filled with rage,   890
his flashing eyes a fiery blaze:

                    "Here's trouble.
In his overbearing way Telemachus,
with this voyage of his, has now achieved
significant success. And we believed
he'd never see it through. Against our will,
this mere youngster has simply gone away,
launching a ship and choosing our best men,
the finest in the land. He'll soon begin
creating problems for us. I hope Zeus
will sap his strength before he comes of age   900

and reaches full maturity. Come now,
give me a swift ship and twenty comrades,
so I can watch for him and set an ambush,
as he navigates his passage through the strait
dividing Ithaca from rugged Samos,
and bring this trip searching for his father
to a dismal end."

              When Antinous had finished,
all of them agreed, and they instructed him
to carry out what he'd proposed. Then they got up
and went back inside the palace of Odysseus.   910

Now, Penelope was not ignorant for long
of what those suitors were scheming in their hearts.
For the herald Medon told her. He'd been listening
outside the hall, as they were making plans inside,
weaving their plot. He proceeded through the house
to tell Penelope the news. As he came out
just across the threshold, Penelope called him:

      "Herald, why have these noble suitors
sent you out here? Are you supposed to tell
the female household slaves of lord Odysseus   920
to stop their work and then make them a feast?
After this whole courtship, I hope they never
get together somewhere else. And today,
may they make the banquet in this house
their latest and their last, all those of you
who by gathering here consume so much,
the wealth of wise Telemachus. It seems,
when you were children all that time ago,
you didn't pay attention to your fathers,
as they talked about the kind of man   930
Odysseus was among their generation—
in Ithaca he never did or said
a hurtful thing to anyone, unlike
the usual habits of our godlike kings,
who hate one man and love another one.

89

He never did the slightest injury
to any man. But your heart and wicked acts
are plain to see—you show no gratitude
for kindness shown to you in earlier days."

Then Medon, an intelligent man, said to her: 940

       "My queen, I wish that what you've just described
were the worst of it. But now these suitors
are planning something much more dangerous
and troubling—I hope the son of Cronos
never permits them to succeed. They mean
to kill Telemachus with their sharp swords,
as he comes home. He's sailed off to Pylos
and then to sacred Sparta, seeking news
about his father."

                As Medon spoke, Penelope
felt her heart and knees give way where she was standing.   950
For some time she couldn't speak a word to him—
both her eyes were full of tears, and she'd lost her voice.
But finally she spoke to him and said:

                          "Herald,
why did my son leave? There was no need
for him to go on board swift-moving ships,
men's salt-water horses, to sail across
enormous seas. Did he do it to make sure
he'd never leave a name among all men?"

Wise Medon then answered Penelope and said:

       "I don't know if some god was urging him   960
or if his own heart prompted him to sail
for Pylos, to learn about his father—
whether he was coming home again
or had met his fate."

                    After saying this,

Medon went away, down through Odysseus' home.
A cloud of heart-destroying grief fell on Penelope.
She lacked the strength to sit down on a chair—
and there were many in the room. She collapsed,
crouching on the threshold of that splendid room,
moaning in distress. Around her, all her servants   970
cried out, too, all those inside the house, young and old.
Still weeping with that group, Penelope spoke out:

"Friends, listen. For Zeus has given me
    more sorrows than any other woman
    born and raised with me. Some time ago
    I lost my noble husband—a man
    who had a lion's heart and qualities
    which made him stand out among Danaans
    in all sorts of ways, a courageous man,
    whose famous name is well known far and wide   980
    throughout all Greece and middle Argos.
    And now, without a word, storm winds sweep
    my son, whom I so love, away from home,
    and I don't even hear about his journey.
    You are too cruel. In your minds, not one of you
    thought to rouse me from my bed, though you knew,
    deep in your hearts, the moment he embarked
    in his black hollow ship. If I had known
    he was going to undertake this journey,
    he would have stayed here. He really would,   990
    for all his eagerness to make the trip.
    Or else I would have perished in these rooms
    before he left me. But now one of you
    must quickly summon old man Dolius,
    my servant, whom my father gave to me
    before I ever came to Ithaca,
    the one who tends my orchard full of trees,
    so he may go as quickly as he can,
    to sit beside Laertes and tell him
    all these things. Perhaps Laertes then   1000
    in his mind can somehow weave a plan,
    then go and weep his case before those men

91

intent on wiping out his family,
the race of heavenly Odysseus."

The good nurse Eurycleia answered Penelope:

"Dear lady, you may kill me with a sword
or keep me in the house, but I'll not hide
a word from you. For I knew all this.
I gave him everything he asked for,
bread and sweet wine, too. He made me swear   1010
a mighty oath I would not tell you,
not until he'd been away eleven days
or you yourself should miss him and find out
he'd left—in case you harmed your lovely skin
with weeping. But you should have a bath,
put clean clothing on your body, then go—
take your servants to your room upstairs
and make your prayers there to Athena,
daughter of great Zeus who bears the aegis.
She may rescue him from death. Don't bother   1020
that old man with still more troubles.
I don't think the family of Arcesius
is so completely hated by the gods,
that one of them cannot still somehow
protect this high-roofed home and its estates,
so rich and far away."

                Eurycleia spoke.
What she said eased the sorrow in Penelope,
whose eyes stopped weeping. She left to bathe herself,
put fresh clothing on her body, and went away,
taking her female servants to her room upstairs.   1030
She placed some grains of barley in a basket
and then prayed to Athena:

              "O untiring child
of aegis-bearing Zeus, hear my prayer.
If resourceful Odysseus in his home
ever burned a sacrifice to you—

plump cattle thighs or sheep—recall that now,
I pray. Save my dear son and guard him well
from those suitors and their murderous pride."

With these words, Penelope raised a sacred cry,
and the goddess heard her prayer.

But the suitors   1040
were still carousing in those shadowy halls.
One overbearing youth would say something like this:

"Ah ha, our queen with many suitors
is really getting ready for the marriage,
knowing nothing of the preparations
for the killing of her son."

That's the sort of thing
any one of them would say, in his ignorance
of how things finally would end. Then Antinous
addressed them all and said:

"Noble lords,
you must not speak out so intemperately—   1050
no more talk like that. Someone may report it,
especially to those inside the house.
Come now, let's get up quietly and work
to carry out that plan which all our hearts
responded to with such delight."

After saying this, Antinous picked out his men,
twenty of the best. They went down to the shore
and dragged a swift black ship into deep water.
They set the mast in place, carried sails on board,
and fitted oars into their leather rowing loops,   1060
all in due order, then spread the white sail out.
Their proud attendants brought up weapons for them.
They moored the ship quite near the shore, then disembarked
and ate a meal there, waiting until evening fell.

Wise Penelope lay there in her upstairs room,
taking no food—she wouldn't eat or drink—
worrying if her fine son could avoid being killed,
or if those arrogant suitors would slaughter him.
Just as a lion grows tense, overcome with fear,
when encircled by a crowd of crafty hunters,   1070
that's how her mind was working then, as sweet sleep
came over her. Then she lay back and got some rest,
and all her limbs relaxed.

                                        But then Athena,
goddess with the glittering eyes, thought of something else.
She made a phantom shape, exactly like a woman,
Iphthime, daughter of the brave Icarius
and wife to Eumelus, who lived in Pherae.
Athena sent this shape to lord Odysseus' home,
while Penelope was in distress and grieving,
to tell her she should end her tears and sorrow.   1080
The phantom passed through the thong which held the bolt
and went into Penelope's room. Standing there
above her head, it spoke to her, saying:

                              "Penelope,
        is your heart anxious as you lie asleep?
        It shouldn't be. The gods who live at ease
        will not bring you distress and suffering—
        your son will still get home. For he's someone
        who's never been offensive to the gods."

Wise Penelope remained in her sweet sleep
beside the gate of dreams. But she replied and said: 1090

        "Sister, why have you come here?[1] Up to now
        you haven't visited—your home's so far away.
        You tell me to end my cries and suffering,
        all the pains which grieve my mind and heart.
        But I've already lost my noble husband,
        that lion-hearted man, whose qualities

[1] *Sister.* Iphthime, the identity of the phantom image, is Penelope's sister.

made him pre-eminent among Danaans
in all sorts of ways—a courageous warrior,
whose fame is widely known throughout wide Greece
and middle Argos. And now the son I love   1100
has set off in a hollow ship—poor child—
with no idea of how men struggle on
or conduct themselves in meetings. That's why
I grieve for him much more than for my husband.
He makes me tremble—I am so afraid
he'll run into troubles with those people
in the land he's visiting or out at sea.
Many enemies are now devising schemes
to hurt him, in their eagerness to kill him
before he gets back to his native land."   1110

The dim phantom then answered Penelope:

"Be brave. And do not let your mind and heart
succumb to fear too much. He has with him
the sort of guide whom other men have prayed
to stand beside them, and she has power—
yes, Pallas Athena. While you've been grieving,
she's taken pity on you. She's the one
who sent me here to tell you this."

                              Wise Penelope
then spoke out in reply:

                         "If you're indeed a god
and have listened to that goddess when she speaks,   1120
then tell me news of that ill-fated man.
I'm begging you. Is Odysseus still alive
and looking at the sunlight, or is he dead,
already down in Hades' home?"

The faint image then answered Penelope and said:

"No, no. I cannot talk of him in any detail
and tell you whether he's alive or dead.

It's a bad thing to chatter like the wind."

Once it said this, the phantom slipped away,
through the door bolt out into a breath of wind.   1130
The daughter of Icarius woke from her sleep,
her heart encouraged that so clear a dream
had raced towards her in the dead of night.

The suitors then embarked and sailed away
on their trip across the water, minds fully bent
on slaughtering Telemachus. Out at sea,
half way between Ithaca and rugged Samos,
there's the rocky island Asteris. It's small,
but ships can moor there in a place with openings
in both directions. The Achaeans waited there   1140
and set up their ambush for Telemachus.

Book Five
Odysseus Leaves Calypso's Island
and Reaches Phaeacia

[The assembled gods decide to send Hermes to tell Calypso to let
Odysseus go; Calypso welcomes Hermes on her island, hears Zeus's orders
and complains; Calypso tells Odysseus he can go and helps him build a
raft; Odysseus sets sail from Calypso's island and gets within sight of
Phaeacia; Poseidon sends a storm which destroys the raft; Odysseus gets
help from the sea goddess Leucothea (once Ino), who gives him a
protective veil; Odysseus has trouble finding a place to come ashore, finds
a river mouth, climbs ashore, and falls asleep in the woods near the river.]

As Dawn stirred from her bed beside lord Tithonus,
bringing light to eternal gods and mortal men,
the gods were sitting in assembly, among them
high-thundering Zeus, whose power is supreme.
Athena was reminding them of all the stories
of Odysseus's troubles—she was concerned for him
as he passed his days in nymph Calypso's home.

> "Father Zeus and you other blessed gods
> who live forever, let no sceptred king
> be prudent, kind, or gentle from now on,   10
> or think about his fate. Let him instead
> always be cruel and treat men viciously,
> since no one now has any memory
> of lord Odysseus, who ruled his people
> and was a gentle father. Now he lies
> suffering extreme distress on that island
> where nymph Calypso lives. She keeps him there
> by force, and he's unable to sail off
> and get back to his native land—he lacks
> a ship with oars and has no companions   20
> to send him out across the sea's broad back.
> And now some men are setting out to kill
> the son he loves, as he sails home. The boy
> has gone to gather news about his father,

off to sacred Pylos and holy Sparta."

Cloud-gatherer Zeus then answered her and said:

"My child,
what a speech has slipped the barrier of your teeth!
Did you not organize this plan yourself,
so that Odysseus, once he made it home,
could take out his revenge against those men?   30
As for Telemachus, you should use your skill
to get him to his native land unharmed—
that's well within your power. The suitors
will sail back in their ship without success."

Zeus spoke and then instructed Hermes, his dear son:

"Hermes, since in every other matter
you are our herald, tell the fair-haired nymph
my firm decision—the brave Odysseus
is to get back home. He'll get no guidance
from the gods or mortal men, but sail off   40
on a raft of wood well lashed together.
He'll suffer hardships, but in twenty days
he reach the fertile land of Scheria,
the territory of the Phaeacians,
people closely connected to the gods.
They will honour him with all their hearts,
as if he were divine, then send him off,
back in a ship to his dear native land.
They'll give him many gifts of bronze and gold
and clothing, too, a greater hoard of goods   50
than Odysseus could have ever won at Troy,
even if he'd got back safe and sound
with his share of the loot they passed around.
That's how Fate decrees he'll see his friends
and reach his high-roofed house and native land."

Zeus finished speaking. The killer of Argus,
his messenger, obeyed. At once he laced up

on his feet those lovely golden ageless sandals
which carry him as fast as stormy blasts of wind
across the ocean seas and boundless tracts of land.   60
He took the wand with which he puts to sleep
or wakes the eyes of any man he chooses.
With this in hand, the mighty killer of Argus
flew off—speeding high above Pieria,
then leaping from the upper sky down to the sea.
Across the waves he raced, just like a cormorant,
which hunts for fish down in the perilous gulfs
of the restless sea, soaking his thick plumage
in the brine—that how Hermes rode the crowded waves.
But when he reached the distant island, he rose up,   70
out of the violet sea, and moved on shore,
until he reached the massive cave, where Calypso,
the fair-haired nymph, had her home. He found her there,
a huge fire blazing in her hearth—from far away
the smell of split cedar and burning sandal wood
spread across the island. With her lovely voice
Calypso sang inside the cave, as she moved
back and forth before her loom—she was weaving
with a golden shuttle. All around her cave
trees were in bloom, alder and sweet-smelling cypress,   80
and poplar, too, with long-winged birds nesting there—
owls, hawks, and chattering sea crows, who spend their time
out on the water. A garden vine, fully ripe
and rich with grapes, trailed through the hollow cave.
From four fountains, close to each other in a row,
clear water flowed in various directions,
and all around soft meadows spread out in full bloom
with violets and parsley. Even a god,
who lives forever, coming there, would be amazed
to see it, and his heart would fill with pleasure.   90
The killer of Argus, god's messenger, stood there,
marveling at the sight. But once his spirit
had contemplated all these things with wonder,
he went inside the spacious cave. And Calypso,
that lovely goddess, when she saw him face to face,
was not ignorant of who he was, for the gods

are not unknown to one another, even though
the home of some immortal might be far away.
But Hermes did not find Odysseus in the cave—
that great-hearted man sat crying on the shore,   100
just as before, breaking his heart with tears and groans,
full of sorrow, as he looked out on the restless sea
and wept. Calypso invited Hermes to sit down
on a bright shining chair. Then the lovely goddess
questioned him:

>"Hermes, my honoured and welcome guest,
why have you come here with your golden wand?
You haven't been a visitor before.
Tell me what's on your mind. My heart desires
to carry out what you request, if I can,
and if it's something fated to be done.   110
But bear with me now, so I can show you
the hospitality I give my guests."

After this speech, Calypso set out a table
laden with ambrosia, then mixed red nectar.
And so the messenger god, killer of Argus,
ate and drank. When his meal was over and the food
had comforted his heart, Hermes gave his answer,
speaking to Calypso with these words:

>"You're a goddess,
and you're asking me, a god, why I've come.
Since you've questioned me, I'll tell you the truth.   120
Zeus told me to come here against my will.
For who would volunteer to race across
that huge expanse of sea—so immense
it cannot be described? There's no city there
of mortal men who offer sacrifices
or choice gifts to the gods. But there's no way
that any other god can override
or shun the will of aegis-bearing Zeus.
He says that you have here with you a man
more unfortunate than all the other ones   130

who fought nine years round Priam's city,
which in the tenth year they destroyed and left
to get back home. But on that voyage back
they sinned against Athena, and she sent
tall waves and dangerous winds against them.
All his other noble comrades perished,
but winds and waves still carried him ahead
and brought him here. Now Zeus is ordering you
to send him off as soon as possible.
For it is not ordained that he will die   140
far from his friends. Instead his fate decrees
he'll see his family and still make it home
to his high-roofed house and native land."

Hermes finished. Calypso, the lovely goddess,
trembled as she spoke to him—her words had wings:

"The gods are harsh and far too jealous—
more so than others. They are unhappy
if goddesses make mortal men their partners
and take them to bed for sex. That's how it was
when rose-fingered Dawn wanted Orion—   150
you gods that live at ease were jealous of her,
until golden-throned sacred Artemis
came to Ortygia and murdered him
with her gentle arrows.[1] In the same way,
when fair-haired Demeter was overcome
with passion and had sex with Iasion
in a thrice-ploughed fallow field, soon enough
Zeus heard of it and annihilated him
by throwing down his dazzling lightning bolt.
Now once again you gods are envious,   160
because a mortal man lives here with me.
I saved him when he was all by himself,
riding his ship's keel—his swift ship smashed
by a blow from Zeus' flaming lightning,
while in the middle of the wine-dark sea,

[1] *Orion*: Orion was a mythical hunter, son of Poseidon. By some accounts he was
mistakenly killed by Artemis in an archery contest with Apollo.

where all his other brave companions died.
Wind and waves brought him here. This is a man
I cherished and looked after, and I said
I'd make him ageless and immortal
for all days to come. But since there's no way   170
another god can override the plans
of aegis-bearing Zeus or cancel them,
let him be off across the restless seas,
if Zeus has so commanded and decreed.
But I'll have no part of escorting him
away from here—I have no ships with oars
nor any crew to take him on his way
across the broad back of the sea. But still,
I can make sincere suggestions to him
and keep nothing hidden, so he can reach   180
his native land and get back safe and sound."

Then the killer of Argus, Zeus' messenger,
said to Calypso:

                              "Yes, send him away.
        Think of Zeus's rage. He may get angry
        and make things hard for you in days to come."

The killer of Argus, the gods' great messenger,
said these words and left. The regal nymph Calypso,
once she'd heard Zeus's message, went off to find
great-hearted Odysseus. She found him by the shore,
sitting down, with his eyes always full of tears,   190
because his sweet life was passing while he mourned
for his return. The nymph no longer gave him joy.
At night he slept beside her in the hollow cave,
as he was forced to do—not of his own free will,
though she was keen enough. But in the daylight hours
he'd sit down on the rocks along the beach, his heart
straining with tears and groans and sorrow. He'd look out,
through his tears, over the restless sea. Moving up,
close to him, the lovely goddess spoke:

                                              "Poor man,
spend no more time in sorrow on this island   200
or waste your life away. My heart agrees—
the time has come for me to send you off.
So come now, cut long timbers with an axe,
and make a raft, a large one. Build a deck
high up on it, so it can carry you
across the misty sea. I'll provision it
with as much food and water and red wine
as you will need to satisfy your wants.
I'll give you clothes and send a favouring wind
blowing from your stern, so you may reach   210
your own native land unharmed, if the gods
are willing, the ones who hold wide heaven,
whose will and force are mightier than my own."

Calypso finished. Lord Odysseus trembled,
then spoke to her—his words had wings:

                                   "Goddess,
in all this you're planning something different.
You're not sending me back home, when you tell me
to get across that huge gulf of the sea
and in a raft—a harsh and dangerous trip.
Not even swift well-balanced ships get through   220
when they enjoy fair winds from Zeus. Besides,
without your consent I'd never board a raft,
not unless you, goddess, would undertake
to swear a mighty oath on my behalf,
you'll not come up with other devious plans
to injure me."

                          Odysseus finished speaking.
Calypso, the lovely goddess, smiled, caressed him,
and then replied by saying:

                         "You're a cunning man,
with no lack of wit—to consider
giving such a speech. But let the earth   230

stand witness, and wide heaven above,
and the flowing waters of the river Styx—
the mightiest and most terrible oath
the blessed gods can make—I will not plan
any other injury against you. No.
I'll think of things and give advice, as if
I was scheming for my own advantage,
if ever I should be in such distress.
For my mind is just, and inside my chest
there is no iron heart—it feels pity,   240
just like your own."

       The beautiful goddess
finished speaking, then quickly led him from the place.
He followed in her footsteps. Man and goddess
reached the hollow cave. He sat down in the chair
Hermes had just risen from, and the nymph set down
all kinds of food to eat and drink, the sort of things
mortal human beings consume.[1] Then she took a seat
facing god-like Odysseus, and her servants
placed ambrosia and nectar right beside her.
So the two of them reached out to take the fine food   250
spread out before them. When they'd had their fill
of food and drink, beautiful divine Calypso
was the first to speak:

       "Nobly born son of Laertes,
resourceful Odysseus, so you now wish
to get back to your own dear native land
without delay? In spite of everything
I wish you well. If your heart recognized
how much distress Fate has in store for you
before you reach your homeland, you'd stay here
and keep this home with me. You'd never die,   260
even though you yearned to see your wife,
the one you always long for every day.

---

[1] . . . *mortal human beings consume:* The diet of the gods is different from what human beings eat. Calypso serves Hermes ambrosia and nectar and has those herself, but Odysseus, as a human being, has to have different things to eat and drink.

I can boast that I'm no worse than her
in how I look or bear myself—it's not right
for mortal women to complete with gods
in form and beauty."

Resourceful Odysseus
then answered her and said:

"Mighty goddess,
do not be angry with me over this.
I myself know very well Penelope,
although intelligent, is not your match   270
to look at, not in stature or in beauty.
But she's a human being and you're a god.
You'll never die or age. But still I wish,
each and every day to get back home,
to see the day when I return. And so,
even if out there on the wine-dark sea
some god breaks me apart, I will go on—
the heart here in my chest is quite prepared
to bear affliction. I've already had
so many troubles, and I've worked so hard   280
through waves and warfare. Let what's yet to come
be added in with those."

Odysseus finished.
Then the sun went down, and it grew dark. The two of them
went inside the inner chamber of the hollow cave
and lay down beside each other to make love.

As soon as rose-fingered early Dawn appeared,
Odysseus quickly put on a cloak and tunic,
and the nymph dressed in a long white shining robe,
a lovely lightly woven dress. Around her waist
she fixed a gorgeous golden belt and placed a veil   290
high on her head. Then she organized her plans
so brave Odysseus could leave. She handed him
a massive axe, well suited to his grip, and made
of two-edged bronze. It had a finely crafted shaft

of handsome olive wood. Next she provided him
a polished adze. Then she led him on a path
down to the edges of the island, where tall trees grew,
alder, poplar, and pine that reached the upper sky,
well-seasoned, dried-out wood, which could keep him afloat.
Once she'd pointed out to him where the large trees grew,   300
Calypso, the lovely goddess, went back home.
Odysseus then began to cut the timber. His work
proceeded quickly. He cut down twenty trees,
used his bronze axe to trim and deftly smooth them,
then lined them up. The fair goddess Calypso
then brought him augers, so he bored each timber,
fastened them to one another, and tightened them
with pins and binding. Odysseus made the raft
as wide as the broad floor of a cargo ship
traced out by someone very skilled in carpentry.   310
Then he worked to add the deck, attaching it
onto the close-set timbers, then finished it
with extended gunwales. Next he set up a mast
with a yard arm fastened to it and then made
a steering oar to guide the raft. From stem to stern
he wove a fence of willow reeds reinforced
with wood to guard him from the waves. Calypso,
the beautiful goddess, brought him woven cloth
to make a sail—which he did very skillfully.
On it he tied bracing ropes, sheets, and halyards.   320
Then he levered the raft down to the shining sea.

By the fourth day he had completed all this work.
So on the fifth beautiful Calypso bathed him,
dressed him in sweet-smelling clothes, and sent him
from the island. The goddess stowed on board the raft
a sack full of dark wine and another large one,
full of water, and a bag of food, in which she put
many tasty things for him to eat. She sent him
a warm and gentle wind, and lord Odysseus
was happy as he set his sails to catch the breeze.   330
He sat beside the steering oar and used his skill
to steer the raft. Sleep did not fall upon his eyelids

as he watched the constellations—the Pleiades,
the late-setting Bootes, and the Great Bear,
which men call the Wain, always turning in one place,
keeping watch over Orion—the only star
that never takes a bath in Ocean.[1] Calypso,
the lovely goddess, had told him to keep this star
on his left as he moved across the sea. He sailed
for ten days on the water, then for seven more,   340
and on the eighteenth day some shadowy hills appeared,
where the land of the Phaeacians, like a shield
riding on the misty sea, lay very close to him.

But at that moment, the mighty Earthshaker,
returning from the Ethiopians, saw him
from the distant mountains of the Solymi.
Poseidon watched Odysseus sailing on the sea,
and his spirit grew enraged. He shook his head
and spoke to his own heart:

                            "Something's wrong!
The gods must have changed what they were planning   350
for Odysseus, while I've been far away
among the Ethiopians. For now,
he's hard by the land of the Phaeacians,
where he'll escape the great extremes of sorrow
which have come over him—so Fate ordains.
But still, even now I think I'll push him
so he gets his fill of troubles."

                           Poseidon spoke.
Then he drove the clouds together, seized his trident,
and shook up the sea. He brought on stormy blasts
from every kind of wind, concealing land and sea   360
with clouds, so darkness fell from heaven. East Wind
clashed with South Wind, while West Wind, raging in a storm,

---

[1] . . . *in Ocean*: the Great Bear or Wain (in modern times often called the Plough) turns
more or less around the same spot in the night sky and at the latitudes of the eastern
Mediterranean never disappears below the horizon (i.e., never seems to vanish into the
sea or bathe in the Ocean). The Bootes (Herdsman) is the constellation Arcturus.

smashed into North Wind, born in the upper sky,
as it pushed a massive wave. Odysseus's knees gave way,
his spirit fell, and in great distress he spoke aloud,
addressing his great heart:

"I've got such a wretched fate!
How is all this going to end up for me?
I'm afraid everything the goddess said
was true, when she claimed that out at sea,
before I got back to my native land,   370
I'd have my fill of troubles. And now
all that is taking place—just look how Zeus
has covered the wide sky with clouds, stirred up
the sea with stormy blasts from different winds
swooping down on me. My sheer destruction
is now beyond all doubt. O those Danaans,
three and four times blessed, who died back then
in spacious Troy, while doing a favour
for the sons of Atreus![1] How I wish
I'd died as well and met my Fate that day   380
when companies of Trojans hurled at me
their bronze-tipped spears, in the fighting there
around the corpse of Peleus's dead son.[2]
Then I'd have had my funeral rites,
and Achaeans would've made me famous.
But now I'm fated to be overwhelmed
and die a pitiful death."

As he said this,
a massive wave charged at him with tremendous force,
swirled round the raft, then from high above crashed down.
Odysseus let go his grip on the steering oar   390
and fell out, a long way from the raft. The fierce gusts
of howling winds snapped the mast off in the middle.

---

[1] *. . . sons of Atreus.* These are, of course, Menelaus and Agamemnon, for whose sake
many Achaean kings joined the expedition to Troy, because of a promise they had made
to Menelaus to help him recover his wife, Helen.

[2] *Peleus's dead son.* This is a reference to Achilles and to a famous incident in the Trojan
war when the Achaean leaders fought to protect the body of Achilles.

The sail and yard arm dropped down into the sea,
some distance off. For many moments he was held
under the water—he found it difficult
to rise above the power of that mighty wave,
because the clothes he'd got from beautiful Calypso
dragged him down. But finally he reached the surface,
spitting tart salt water from his mouth, as it streamed down
from off his head. But even so, though badly shaken,   400
he did not forget about the raft. Through the waves
he swam, grabbed hold, and crouched down in the middle,
trying to escape destructive Fate. The huge wave
carried him along its course this way and that.
Just as in autumn North Wind sweeps the thistle down
along the plain, and the tufts bunch up together,
that how the winds then drove his raft to and fro
across the sea. Sometimes South Wind would toss it
over to North Wind to carry. At other times,
East Wind would let West Wind lead on the chase.   410

Then Ino with the lovely ankles noticed him—
Cadmus' daughter, once a mortal being with human speech,
but now, deep in the sea, she was Leucothea
and had her share of recognition from the gods.[1]
She felt pity for Odysseus as he suffered
in his wandering. She rose up from the water,
like a sea gull on the wing, perched on the raft,
and spoke to him, saying:

                              "You poor wretch,
            why do you put Earthshaker Poseidon
            in such a furious temper, so that he   420
            keeps making all this trouble for you?
            No matter what he wants, he won't kill you.
            It seems to me you've got a clever mind,
            so do just what I say. Take off these clothes,
            and leave the raft. Drift with the winds.
            But paddle with your hands, and try to reach

[1]*Ino . . . Leucothea*: Ino was the mortal daughter of Cadmus and Harmonia (king and
queen of Thebes). After her death Zeus changed Ino into a goddess of the sea, Leucothea.

the land of the Phaeacians, where Fate says
you will be rescued. Here, take this veil—
it's from the gods—and tie it round your chest.
Then there's no fear you'll suffer anything   430
or die. But when your hand can grab the shore,
then take it off and throw it far from land
into the wine-dark sea. Then turn away."

The goddess spoke and handed him the veil. Then she left,
diving like a sea bird down in the heaving sea.
A dark wave swallowed her. Then lord Odysseus,
who had endured so much, considered what to do.
In his distress he addressed his own brave heart:

      "I'm in trouble. I hope none of the gods
      is weaving dangers for me once again   440
      with this advice of hers to leave the raft.
      Well, I won't follow what she says—not yet.
      For I can see with my own eyes how far off
      that land is where she said I would be saved.
      So what I'll do is what seems best to me—
      as long as these planks hold firm in place,
      I'll stay here and bear whatever troubles come,
      but once the waves have smashed my raft apart,
      I'll swim for it. There is no better way."

As his mind and heart were thinking about this,   450
Earthshaker Poseidon set in motion
a monstrous, menacing, and terrifying wave,
arching high above his head, and drove it at him.
Just as a storm wind scatters dry straw in a heap,
blowing pieces here and there in all directions—
that's how that wave split the long planks on the raft.
But straddling a board, as if riding a horse,
Odysseus stripped away the clothing he'd received
from fair Calypso. He wound the veil across his chest,
and then, with arms outstretched, fell face first in the sea,   460
trying to swim. The mighty Shaker of the Earth
saw him, shook his head, then spoke to his own heart:

"So now, after suffering so much anguish,
keep wandering on the sea until you meet
a people raised by Zeus. Still, I don't think
you'll be laughing at the troubles still in store."

With these words Poseidon lashed his fine-maned horses
and left for Aegae where he has his splendid home.
Then Athena, Zeus's daughter, thought up something new.
She blocked the paths of every wind but one   470
and ordered all of them to stop and check their force,
then roused the swift North Wind and broke the waves in front,
so divinely born Odysseus might yet meet
the people of Phaeacia, who love the oar,
avoiding death and Fates. So for two days and nights
he floated on the ocean waves, his heart filled
with many thoughts of death. But when fair-haired Dawn
gave rise at last to the third day, the wind died down,
the sea grew calm and still. He was lifted up
by a large swell, and as he quickly looked ahead,   480
Odysseus saw the land close by. Just as children
rejoice to see life in a father who lies sick,
in savage pain through a long wasting illness,
with a cruel god afflicting him, and then,
to their delight, the gods release him from disease,
that's how Odysseus rejoiced when he could see
the land and forests. He swam on ahead, eager
to set foot on the shore. But when he'd come in close,
as far as man's voice carries when he shouts,
he heard the crashing of the sea against the rocks—   490
huge waves with a dreadful roar smashing on dry land
and foaming spray concealing everything—
there were no harbours fit for ships to ride or coves,
but jutting headlands, rocks, and cliffs—at that point
Odysseus felt his knees and spirit give way,
and in despair he spoke to his great heart:

                    "What's this?
Zeus has given me a glimpse of land,
just when I'd lost hope, and I've made my way

cutting across this gulf, but I can't find
a place where I can leave this cold gray sea.   500
There's an outer rim of jagged boulders
where waves come crashing with a roar on them.
The rock face rises sheer, the water there
is deep, so there's no way to gain a foothold
and escape destruction. If I try to land,
a huge wave may pick me up and smash me
on those protruding rocks, and my attempt
would be quite useless. But if I keep swimming
and hope I'll find a sloping beach somewhere
or havens from the sea, then I'm afraid   510
the stormy winds will grab me once again
and carry me, for all my heavy groaning,
across the fish-filled seas, or else some god
may set some monstrous creature of the sea
against me—illustrious Amphitrite
raises many beasts like that. I know well
how great Earthshaker has been angry at me."

As he debated in his mind and heart like this,
a huge wave carried him toward the rocky shore.
His skin would have been stripped and all his bones smashed up,   520
but the goddess with the gleaming eyes, Athena,
put a thought inside his mind. As he surged ahead,
he grabbed a rock with both his hands and held on,
groaning, until that giant wave had passed him by.
So he escaped. But as the wave flowed back once more,
it charged, struck, and flung him out to sea. Just as
an octopus is dragged out of its den with pebbles
clinging to its suckers, that's how his skin was scraped
from his strong hands against the rocks, as that great wave
engulfed him. And then unfortunate Odysseus   530
would have perished, something not ordained by fate,
if bright-eyed Athena had not given him advice.
Moving from the surf where it pounded on the shore,
he swam out to sea, but kept looking at the land,
hoping to come across a sloping beach somewhere
or a haven from the sea. He kept swimming on

and reached the mouth of a fair-flowing river,
which seemed to him the finest place to go onshore.
There were no rocks, and it was sheltered from the wind.
Odysseus recognized the river as it flowed   540
and prayed to him deep in his heart:

> "Hear me, my lord,
> whoever you may be. I've come to you,
> the answer to my many prayers, fleeing
> Poseidon's punishment from the deep sea.
> A man who visits as a wanderer
> commands respect, even with deathless gods—
> just as I've now reached your stream and knees,
> after suffering so much. So pity me,
> my lord—I claim to be your suppliant."

Odysseus spoke. At once the god held back his flow,   550
checked the waves, calmed the water up ahead of him,
and brought him safely to the river mouth. Both knees bent,
he let his strong hands fall—the sea had crushed his spirit.
All his skin was swollen, and sea water flowed in streams
up in his mouth and nose. He lay there breathless,
without a word, hardly moving—quite overcome
with terrible exhaustion. But when he revived
and spirit moved back in his heart, he untied
the veil the goddess gave him and let the river
take it as it flowed out to the sea. A great wave   560
carried it downstream, and then without delay
Ino's friendly hands retrieved it. But Odysseus
turned from the river, sank down in the rushes,
and kissed life-giving earth. Then in his anxiety,
he spoke to his great heart:

> "What now? What's next for me?
> How will I end up? If I stay right here
> all through the wretched night, with my eye on
> the river bed, I fear the bitter frost
> and freshly fallen dew will both combine
> to overcome me when, weak as I am,   570

my spirit's breath grows faint—the river wind
blows cold in early morning. But if I climb
uphill into shady woods and lie down
in some thick bushes and so rid myself
of cold and weariness, sweet sleep may come
and overpower me, and then, I fear,
I may become some wild beast's prey, its prize."

As he thought it through, the best thing seemed to be
to move up to the woods. Close by the water
he found a place with a wide view. So he crept   580
underneath two bushes growing from one stem—
one was an olive tree, the other a wild thorn.
Wet winds would not be strong enough to ever blow
through both of these, nor could the bright sun's rays shine in,
and rain would never penetrate—they grew so thick,
all intertwined with one another. Under these
Odysseus crawled and immediately gathered up
with his fine hands a spacious bed—fallen leaves
were all around, enough to cover two or three
in winter time, however bad the weather.   590
When resourceful lord Odysseus noticed that,
he was happy and lay down in the middle,
heaping fallen leaves on top of him. Just as
someone on a distant farm without a neighbour
hides a torch underneath black embers, and thus saves
a spark of fire, so he won't need to kindle it
from somewhere else, that's how Odysseus spread the leaves
to cover him. Athena then poured sleep onto his eyes,
covering his eyelids, so he could find relief,
a quick respite from his exhausting troubles.   600

Book Six
Odysseus and Nausicaa

[Athena visits Nausicaa while she is sleeping in the palace and tells her to take the washing to the river; Nausicaa asks her father, Alcinous, to provide a wagon and mules; Nausicaa and her attendants go the river, wash the clothes, and wake up Odysseus; Odysseus emerges naked and talks to Nausicaa; she agrees to help him; Odysseus bathes, dresses, and eats; they set off for the city and reach the outskirts; Odysseus prays to Athena.]

While much-enduring lord Odysseus slept there,
overcome with weariness and sleep, Athena
went to the land of the Phaeacians, to their city.
Many years ago these people used to live
in wide Hypereia, close to the Cyclopes,
proud arrogant men and much more powerful,
who kept on robbing them. So god-like Nausithous
had taken them away and led them off to settle
in Scheria, far from any men who have to work
to earn their daily bread. He'd had them build a wall   10
around the city, put up homes, raise temples
to the gods, and portion out the land for farming.
But some time past his fate had struck him and he'd gone
down to the house of Hades. Now Alcinous was king,
a man to whom the gods had granted wisdom.
Athena, bright-eyed goddess, went to this man's home,
to arrange a journey home for brave Odysseus.
She moved into a wonderfully furnished room
where a young girl slept, one like immortal goddesses
in form and loveliness. She was Nausicaa,   20
daughter of great-hearted Alcinous. Close by her,
beside each door post, her two attendants slept,
girls whose beauty had been given by the Graces.[1]
The shining doors were closed. Like a gust of wind,
Athena slipped over to the young girl's bed,
stood there above her head, and then spoke to her.

[1] *Graces:* the Graces are the goddesses of charm and graceful temperament. There are three of them: Aglaia, Euphrosyne, and Thalia.

Her appearance changed to look like Dymas' daughter—
he was a man famous for the ships he owned.
His daughter was the same age as Nausicaa,
whose heart was well disposed to her. In that form,   30
bright-eyed Athena spoke out and said:

          "Nausicaa,
how did your mother bear a girl so careless?
Your splendid clothes are lying here uncared for.
And your wedding day is not so far away,
when you must dress up in expensive robes
and give them to your wedding escort, too.
You know it's things like these that help to make
a noble reputation among men
and please your honoured mother and father.
Come, at day break let's wash out the clothing.   40
I'll go as well to help you, so with all speed
you can prepare yourself—it won't be long
before you, too, are a married woman.
You've already got men from this country
asking for your hand in marriage, the finest
in all Phaeacia, from whom you yourself
derive your lineage. So come on now,
ask your noble father to provide you,
this morning early, a wagon and some mules,
so you can carry the bright coverlets,   50
the robes and sashes. That would be better
than going on foot, because the washing tubs
stand some distance from the town."

       With these words,
bright-eyed Athena went back to Olympus,
where, men say, gods' home endures forever,
undisturbed by winds and never drenched with rain
or covered by the snow—instead high overhead
the air is always bright. Blessed gods are happy there
each and every day. The bright-eyed goddess went there,
once she'd finished speaking to Nausicaa.
                                                                       60

As soon as Dawn on her splendid throne arrived
and woke fair-robed Nausicaa, she was curious
about her dream. So she went through the house
to tell her dear father and her mother. She found them
in the house—her mother sitting by the hearth
with her servant women, spinning purple yarn.
She came across her father as he was going out
to meet some well-known kings in an assembly—
he'd been summoned by Phaeacian noblemen.
Nausicaa went to stand close by her father   70
and then spoke to him:

                              "Dear father, can you prepare
             a high wagon with sturdy wheels for me,
             so I can carry my fine clothing out
             and wash it in the river? It's lying here
             all dirty. And it's appropriate for you
             to wear fresh garments on your person
             when you're with our leading men in council.
             You have five dear sons living in your home—
             two are married, but three are now young men
             still unattached, and they always require   80
             fresh-washed clothing when they go out dancing.
             All these things I have to think about."

Nausicaa said these words because she felt ashamed
to remind her father of her own happy thoughts
of getting married. But he understood all that
and answered, saying:

                              "I have no objection,
             my child, to providing mules for you,
             or any other things. Go on your way.
             Slaves will get a four-wheeled wagon ready
             with a high box framed on top."

                              Once he'd said this,   90
he called out to his slaves, and they did what he ordered.
They prepared a smooth-running wagon made for mules,

led up the animals, and then yoked them to it.
Nausicaa brought her fine clothing from her room.
She placed it in the polished wagon bed. Her mother
loaded on a box full of all sorts of tasty food.
She put in delicacies, as well, and poured some wine
into a goat skin. The girl climbed on the wagon.
Her mother also gave her some smooth olive oil
in a golden flask, so she and her attendants   100
could use it when they'd bathed. Then Nausicaa
took the bright reins and whip and lashed the mules ahead.
With a clatter of hooves, the mules moved quickly off,
carrying the clothing and the girl, not by herself,
for her attendants went with her as well.

When they reached the stream of the fair-flowing river,
where the washing tubs were always standing ready,
full of fresh water flowing up from underneath
and spilling over, enough to clean one's clothing,
even garments really soiled, they took the mules   110
out of their wagon harnesses, then drove them
along the banks beside the swirling river,
to let them graze on clover sweet as honey.
The girls picked up the clothing from the wagon,
carried it in their arms down to the murky water,
and trampled it inside the washing trenches,
each one trying to work more quickly than the others.
Once they'd washed the clothes and cleaned off all the stains,
they laid the items out in rows along the sea shore,
right where the waves which beat upon the coast   120
had washed the pebbles clean. Once they had bathed themselves
and rubbed their bodies well with oil, they ate a meal
beside the river mouth, waiting for the clothes to dry
in the sun's warm rays. When they'd enjoyed their food,
the girl and her attendants threw their head scarves off
to play catch with a ball, and white-armed Nausicaa
led them in song. Just as when archer Artemis
moves across the mountains, along the lofty ridges
of Erymanthus or Taygetus, full of joy,
as she pursues wild boars and swiftly running deer,   130

118

with nymphs attending on her, daughters of Zeus,
who bears the aegis, taking pleasure in the hunt,
and Leto's heart rejoices, while Artemis
holds her head and eyebrows high above them all,
so recognizing her is easy, though all of them
are beautiful—that's how that unmarried girl
stood out then from her attendants.

                       But when the girl
was going to harness up the mules and start to fold
the splendid clothes to make the journey homeward,
Athena, bright-eyed goddess, thought of something else,   140
so that Odysseus might wake up and then could see
the lovely girl, who would conduct him to the city
of Phaeacian men. So when the princess threw the ball
at one of those attendants with her, she missed the girl
and tossed it in the deep and swirling river.
They gave a piercing cry which woke up lord Odysseus.
So he sat up, thinking in his heart and mind:

        "Here's trouble! In this country I have reached,
        what are the people like? Are they violent
        and wild, without a sense of justice?   150
        Or are they kind to strangers? In their minds
        do they fear the gods? A young woman's shout
        rang out around me—nymphs who live along
        steep mountain peaks and by the river springs
        and grassy meadows. Could I somehow be
        near men with human speech? Come on then,
        I'm going to try to find out for myself."

With these words, lord Odysseus crept out from the thicket.
With his strong hands, he broke off from thick bushes
a leafy branch to hold across his body and conceal   160
his sexual organs. He emerged, moving just like
a mountain lion which relies on its own strength—
though hammered by the rain and wind, it creeps ahead,
its two eyes burning, coming in among the herd
of sheep or cattle, or stalking a wild deer—

his belly tells him to move in against the flocks,
even within a well-built farm. That how Odysseus
was coming out to meet those fair-haired girls,
although he was stark naked. He was in great distress,
but, caked with brine, he was a fearful sight to them,   170
and they ran off in fear and crouched down here and there
among the jutting dunes of sand. The only one
to stand her ground was Alcinous' daughter.
For Athena had put courage in her heart
and taken from her arms and legs all sense of fear.
So she stood there facing up to him. Odysseus
wondered whether he should grasp the lovely girl
around her knees and plead his case or keep his distance,
remaining where he was, and with gentle words
entreat her to inform him where the city was   180
and provide him clothing. As he thought about it,
it seem to him a better plan to stand apart
and appeal to her with words of reassurance,
in case her heart grew angry when he clasped her knee.
So he quickly used his cunning and spoke to her
with soothing language:

                       "O divine queen,
I come here as a suppliant to you.
Are you a goddess or a mortal being?
If you're one of the gods who hold wide heaven,
then I think you most resemble Artemis,   190
daughter of great Zeus, in your loveliness,
your stature, and your shape. If you're human,
one of those mortals living on the earth,
your father and noble mother are thrice-blest,
and thrice-blest your brothers, too. In their hearts
they must glow with pleasure for you always,
when they see a child like you moving up
into the dance. But the happiest heart,
more so than all the rest, belongs to him
who with his wedding gifts will lead you home.   200
These eyes of mine have never gazed upon
anyone like you—either man or woman.

As I observe you, I'm gripped with wonder.
In Delos once I saw something like this—
a youthful palm-tree shoot growing up
beside Apollo's altar. I'd gone there,
with many others in my company,
on the trip where Fate had planned for me
so many troubles. But when I saw that,
my heart looked on a long time quite astonished—   210
I'd never noticed such a lovely tree
springing from the earth. And, lady, that's how
I am amazed at you, lost in wonder,
and am very much afraid to clasp your knee.
But great distress has overtaken me.
Yesterday, my twentieth day afloat,
I escaped the wine-dark sea. Before that,
waves and swift-driving storm winds carried me
from Ogygia island. And now a god
has tossed me on shore here, so that somehow   220
I'll suffer trouble in this place as well.
For I don't think my problems will end now.
Before that day, there are still many more
the gods will bring about. But, divine queen,
have pity. You're the first one I've approached,
after going through so much grief. I don't know
any other people, none of those who hold
the city and its land. Show me the town.
Give me some rag to throw around myself,
perhaps some wrapping you had for the clothes   230
when you came here. As for you, may gods grant
all your heart desires—may they give you
a husband, home, and mutual harmony,
a noble gift—for there is nothing better
or a stronger bond than when man and wife
live in a home sharing each other's thoughts.
That brings such pain upon their enemies
and such delight to those who wish them well.
They know that themselves, more so than anyone."

White-armed Nausicaa then answered him and said: 240

"Stranger, you don't seem to be a wicked man,
or foolish. Olympian Zeus himself
gives happiness to bad and worthy men,
each one receiving just what Zeus desires.
So he has given you your share, I think.
Nonetheless you still must bear your lot.
But now you've reached our land and city,
you'll not lack clothes or any other thing
we owe a hard-pressed suppliant we meet.
I'll show the town to you, and I'll tell you   250
what our country's called—the Phaeacians
own this city and this land. As for me,
I am the daughter of brave Alcinous—
Phaeacian power and strength depend on him."

Nausicaa finished speaking. Then she called out
to her fair-haired attendants:

                              "Stand up, you girls,
Have you run off because you've seen a man?
Surely you don't think he is an enemy?
For there's no man now alive or yet to be
who'll reach this land of the Phaeacians   260
bringing war, because gods truly love us,
and we live far off in the surging sea,
the most remote of people. Other men
never interact with us. No. So this man
is some poor wanderer who's just come here.
We must look after him, for every stranger,
every beggar, comes from Zeus, and any gift,
even something small, is to be cherished.
So, my girls, give this stranger food and drink.
Then bathe him in the river, in a place   270
where there's some shelter from the wind."

Nausicaa finished. They stood up and called out
to one another. Then they took Odysseus aside,
to a sheltered spot, following what Nausicaa,
daughter of great-hearted Alcinous, had ordered.

They set out clothing for him, a cloak and tunic,
and gave him the gold flask full of smooth olive oil.
They told him to bathe there in the flowing river,
but lord Odysseus said to the attendants:

> "Would you young ladies move some distance off,   280
> so I can wash salt water off my shoulders
> by myself and then rub on the olive oil.
> It's a long time since oil was on my skin.
> I won't wash myself in front of you,
> for I'm ashamed to stand stark naked
> in the presence of such fair-haired girls."

Once he'd said this, the two attendants moved away
and told Nausicaa. Then lord Odysseus
washed his body in the river, rinsing off the salt
covering his broad shoulders and his back,   290
and wiping the encrusted brine out of his hair.
When he'd washed himself all over and rubbed on oil,
he put on clothes the unmarried girl had given him.
Then Athena, Zeus's daughter, made him appear
taller and stronger, and on his head she curled
his hair—it flowed up like a flowering hyacinth.
Just as a skillful workman sets a layer of gold
on top of silver, a craftsman who's been taught
all sorts of arts by Athena and Hephaestus,
and what he creates is truly beautiful,   300
that's how the goddess graced his head and shoulders.
Then Odysseus went to sit some distance off,
beside the shore, glowing with charm and beauty.
Nausicaa gazed at him in admiration,
then spoke to her fair-haired attendants, saying:

> "Listen to me, my white-armed followers—
> I have something to say. This man here
> has not come among god-like Phaeacians
> against the will of those immortals
> who possess Olympus. Previously I thought   310
> he was crude and rough, but now he seems

like the gods who occupy wide heaven.
Would a man like that could be my husband,
living here and happy to remain. But come,
my girls, give the stranger food and drink."

When Nausicaa had spoken, they heard her words
and quickly did what they'd been told. They set out
food and drink before resourceful lord Odysseus.
He ate and drank voraciously—many days had passed
since he'd last tasted food. Then white-armed Nausicaa   320
thought of something else. She folded up the clothes,
put them in the handsome wagon, harnessed up
the strong-hooved mules, and climbed up by herself.
She called out to Odysseus, then spoke to him:

> "Get up now, stranger, and go to the city.
> I'll take you to my wise father's house,
> where, I tell you, you will get to meet
> all the finest of Phaeacians. You seem
> to me to have good sense, so act as follows—
> while we are moving through the countryside   330
> past men's farms, walk fast with my attendants
> behind the mules and wagon. I'll lead the way.
> Then we'll come up to the city. A high wall
> runs round it, and there are lovely harbours
> on both sides—each has a narrow entrance,
> with curving boats drawn up along the road,
> since each man has a place for his own ship.
> The assembly ground stands there as well,
> around the splendid temple to Poseidon,
> built with huge stones set deep within the earth.   340
> Here the people tend to their black ships,
> busy with the gear—fixing ropes and sails
> and shaping tapered oars. The Phaeacians
> have no use for bow or quiver, but for masts,
> boat oars, and well-trimmed ships, in which with joy
> they cross the gray salt sea. Their talk is crude,
> and that I would avoid, in case someone
> insults me later on—among the people

there are really insolent men, and thus
one of the nastier types might well say,   350
if he bumped into us: 'Who's the man
who's following Nausicaa? A stranger—
he's tall and handsome! Where did she find him?
No doubt he'll be her husband. She's brought here
some shipwrecked vagrant, a man whose people
live far away, for no one dwells near us,
or he's some god come down from heaven,
answering those prayers she's always making.
She'll have him as her husband all her days.
It's better that way, even if she went   360
and found herself someone to marry
from another place—she has no respect
for those Phaeacians, her own countrymen,
the many noble men who'd marry her.'
That's what they would say, and their remarks
would injure me. But I would do the same
to some other girl who acted just like that,
who, while her father and her mother lived,
against their wishes hung around with men
before the day she married one in public.   370
So, stranger, pay attention to what I say,
and with all speed you can get my father
to arrange an escort for your journey home.
You'll come across a fine grove to Athena—
it's near the road, a clump of poplar trees.
There's a fountain, with meadows all around.
My father has a fertile vineyard there
and some land, too, within shouting distance
of the town. Sit down there, and wait a while,
until we move into the city and reach   380
my father's house. When you think we've had time
to reach my home, then go in the city
of the Phaeacians and inquire about
my father's house, great-hearted Alcinous.
It's easy to pick out—an infant child
could lead you to it. For Phaeacians homes
are built in a style utterly unlike

125

the palace of heroic Alcinous.
Once inside the house and in the courtyard,
move through the great hall quickly till you reach   390
my mother seated at the hearth, in the firelight,
against a pillar, spinning purple yarn—
a marvelous sight. Servants sit behind her.
My father's chair is there by the same pillar,
where, like a god, he sits and sips his wine.
Move past him. Then with your arms embrace
my mother's knees, if you desire to see
the joyful day of your return come soon,
even though your home is far away.
If her heart and mind are well-disposed to you,   400
then there's hope you'll see your friends and reach
your well-built house and your own native land."

Saying this, Nausicaa cracked the shining whip
and struck the mules. They quickly left the flowing river,
moving briskly forward at a rapid pace.
Using her judgment with the whip, she drove on
so Odysseus and her servants could keep up on foot.
Just at sunset, they reached the celebrated grove,
sacred to Athena. Lord Odysseus sat down there
and made a quick prayer to great Zeus' daughter: 410

"Hear me, child of aegis-bearing Zeus,
unwearied goddess, listen to me now,
for you did not respond to me back then,
when I was being beaten down at sea
and the great Earthshaker destroyed my raft.
Grant that I come to the Phaeacians
as a friend, someone worthy of their pity."

So he prayed. And Pallas Athena heard him.
But she did not reveal herself to him directly—
she feared her father's brother, who was still furious,   420
and would rage against godlike Odysseus
until he reached his native land at last.

Book Seven
Odysseus at the Court of Alcinous in Phaeacia

[Nausicaa reaches the palace; Odysseus sets out for the city and meets Athena on the way, disguised as a young girl; she leads him to the palace; Odysseus admires Alcinous' palace and the nearby orchard; Odysseus enters the palace and makes a plea to Arete, the queen; the Phaeacians offer Odysseus a meal; after the meal Odysseus converses with Arete and Alcinous, telling them of his voyage from Ortygia and his meeting with Nausicaa; Alcinous offers to help Odysseus get home; servants prepare a bed for him, and he goes to sleep out in the portico.]

So lord Odysseus, who had endured so much, prayed there,
while two strong mules took the girl into the city.
Once she reached her father's splendid palace,
she halted at the outer gates, while her brothers,
godlike men, crowded round her. They unhitched the mules,
then brought the clothes inside. The girl went to her room.
There her old chamber maid lit a fire for her—
Eurymedusa, an old woman from Apeire.
Curved ships had carried her from there some years ago,
when she'd been chosen as a prize for Alcinous,   10
because he was the king of all Phaeacians
and people listened to him as if he were a god.
She'd raised white-armed Nausicaa in the palace.
Now she lit the fire and set food out in the room.

Then Odysseus got up and set off for the city.
Athena took good care to veil him in thick mist,
so no bold Phaeacian who ran into him
would cast verbal taunts and ask him who he was.
As he was about to enter the fine city,
bright-eyed Athena met him—she was disguised   20
as a young girl carrying a pitcher. When she stopped
in front of him, noble Odysseus said to her:

"My child, could you direct me to the home

of the man called Alcinous. He's the king
of people here, and I'm a foreigner,
coming from a distant country far away.
I've suffered a great deal, and I don't know
any of the men who own this city
or the farmland."

                              Bright-eyed Athena
then said in reply:

                                    "Honoured stranger,   30
in that case I'll show you the very house
you've just questioned me about. It's near by,
close to my good father's home. But go quietly,
and I will lead the way. You must not look
at people or ask anyone a question.
The people here are not fond of strangers—
they don't extend a friendly welcome
to those from other lands, but put their trust
in their swift ships to carry them across
vast gulfs of the sea, something Poseidon   40
has permitted them, for their ships move fast,
as swift as birds in flight or as a thought."

That said, Pallas Athena led off rapidly—
he followed closely in the goddess' footsteps.
The Phaeacians, so celebrated for their ships,
did not see him as he moved across the city
in their midst. Athena, fair-haired fearful goddess,
would not permit that. Her heart cared about him,
so she cast around him an amazing mist.
Odysseus was astonished by the harbours   50
and well-tended ships, by the meeting places,
where those heroes gathered, by the lofty walls,
topped with palisades—it was a marvelous sight.
When they reached the splendid palace of the king,
bright-eyed Athena was the first to speak:

                                    "Honoured stranger,

here is the house you asked me to point out.
You'll find Zeus-fostered kings in there feasting.
But go inside, and do not be afraid.
In a man, boldness is always better
at getting good results, even in the case   60
where he's a stranger from another land.
Inside the palace, you'll first greet the queen.
Her name is Arete, born of the same line
as Alcinous, the king. Originally,
Nausithous was born to the Earthshaker,
Poseidon, and to Periboea,
loveliest of women, youngest daughter
to great-hearted Eurymedon, once king
of the rebellious Giants. But he destroyed
his reckless people and was killed himself.   70
Poseidon then had sex with Periboea,
who bore him a son, courageous Nausithous,
who ruled Phaeacians and who had two sons,
Rhexenor and Alcinous. Rhexenor,
a married man but with no sons, was killed
by Apollo's silver bow in his own home.
He left an only daughter, Arete.
Alcinous made her his wife and honoured her
beyond all other women on this earth,
all the wives who now control their homes   80
under the direction of their husbands.
That's how much she's honoured from the heart
by her dear children, by Alcinous himself,
and by the people, too, who look on her
as if she were a goddess, when they greet her
as she walks through town. She does not lack
a fine intelligence, and thus for women
to whom she's well disposed she can resolve
disputes they go through with their husbands.
So if you win her favour, there's a hope   90
you'll see your friends and make that journey back
to your own high-roofed home and native land."

Bright-eyed Athena finished. Then she went away,

across the restless sea, leaving lovely Scheria.
She came to Marathon and the wide streets of Athens
and entered the well-built palace of Erectheus.

Odysseus moved towards Alcinous's splendid home.
He stood there, his heart thinking over many things
before he came up to the threshold made of bronze.
Above the high-vaulted home of brave Alcinous   100
there was a radiance, as if from sun or moon.
Bronze walls extended out beyond the threshold
in various directions to the inner rooms.
They had a blue enamel cornice. Golden doors
blocked the way into the well-constructed palace.
The bronze threshold had silver doorposts set inside
and a silver lintel. The handles were of gold.
On both sides of the door stood gold and silver dogs,
immortal creatures who would never age,
created by Hephaestus's matchless artistry,   110
to guard the palace of great-hearted Alcinous.[1]
On either side within, seats were set against the wall,
from the doorway right through to the inner room,
with soft rugs covering them, elegantly woven
women's handiwork. On these, Phaeacian leaders
would sit to eat and drink from their abundant stores.
Gold statues of young men stood on sturdy pedestals,
holding torches in their hands to give light at night
for people feasting in the hall. And Alcinous
had fifty women servants in the palace: 120
some at the millstone ground up yellow grain,
some wove fabric, or sitting down, twisted yarn,
hands fluttering like leaves on a tall poplar tree,
while olive oil dripped down.[2] Just as Phaeacian men
have more skill than anyone at sailing a fast ship
across the sea, so their women have great skill
at working on the loom—for Athena gave them,

---

[1] *Hephaestus*: one of the Olympian gods, the divine son of Zeus and Hera, is the craftsman-creator god of the forge.

[2] *. . . dripped down*: olive oil was and in some places still is an important ingredient in some weaving processes, working as a mild bleaching agent and strengthening the fibres.

above all others, a knowledge of fine handiwork
and keen intelligence. Beyond the courtyard,
but near the door, stands an enormous orchard,   130
four land measures, with a hedge on either side.
Huge and richly laden trees grow there—pomegranates,
pears, and apple trees with shining fruit, sweet figs,
and fertile olive trees. And in this orchard
no fruit gets destroyed or dies in winter time
or during summer. It lasts all year long. West Wind,
as he blows in, always brings some fruits to life
and ripens others—pear growing above pear,
apple upon apple, grapes in cluster after cluster,
and fig after fig. And inside that orchard,   140
Alcinous has a fertile vineyard planted, too.
In part of it, a sunny patch of level ground,
grapes are drying in the sun. In another place
men are gathering up and treading other grapes.
In front the unripe grapes are shedding blossoms,
while others change into a purple colour.
Beside the final row of vines there are trim beds
with every kind of plant growing all year round.
There are two springs inside—one sends its water
through all the garden, and on the opposite side   150
the other runs below the threshold of the yard,
where people of the town collect their water,
towards the high-roofed palace. These glorious things
were gifts from the gods to the home of Alcinous.

Lord Odysseus, who had endured so much, stood there
and gazed around. When his heart had marveled at it all,
he moved fast across the threshold into the house.
There he found Phaeacian counselors and leaders
making libations to honour keen-eyed Hermes,
killer of Argus. They poured him a final tribute   160
whenever they intended to retire to bed.
Long-suffering lord Odysseus, still enclosed in mist,
the thick covering poured around him by Athena,
went through the hall until he came to Arete
and Alcinous, the king. With his arms Odysseus

embraced the knees of Arete, and at that moment
the miraculous mist dissolved away from him.
The people in the palace were all silent,
as they gazed upon the man, struck with wonder
at the sight. Odysseus then made this entreaty: 170

       "Arete, daughter of godlike Rhexenor,
       I've come to you and to your husband here,
       to your knees, in supplication to you—
       a man who's experienced so much distress—
       and to those feasting here. May gods grant them
       happiness in life, and may they each pass on
       riches in their homes to all their children,
       and noble honours given by the people.
       Please rouse yourself to help me return home,
       to get back quickly to my native land.   180
       I've been suffering trouble for a long time
       so far away from friends."

                         Odysseus finished.
Then he sat down by the fire, right on the ashes
inside the hearth. All the people there were silent.
No one said a word. Then, finally, an old man,
lord Echeneus, a Phaeacian elder statesman,
a skilful speaker full of ancient wisdom,
with their common good in mind, spoke up and said:

       "Alcinous, it's not at all appropriate
       or to our credit that this stranger's sitting   190
       at our hearth, in the ashes on the ground.
       The people here are holding themselves back,
       waiting for your word. Come, tell the stranger
       to get up. Then invite the man to sit
       on a silver-studded chair. Tell the heralds
       to mix wine, so we may make an offering
       to thunder-loving Zeus, who accompanies
       all pious suppliants. And tell the steward
       to provide this stranger with a dinner
       from what she has in store."

When he heard these words,
brave and kingly Alcinous stretched out his hand,
reached for Odysseus, that wise and crafty man,
raised him from the hearth, and invited him to sit
in a shining chair, after he had asked his son,
handsome Laodamas, the son he loved the most,
who sat beside him, to stand up and offer it.
An attendant carried in a fine gold pitcher,
then poured some water out into a silver basin,
so he could wash his hands. A polished table
was set up beside him, and the housekeeper,   210
a well-respected female servant, brought in food,
set it in front of him, with many tasty treats
offered freely from her store. And so Odysseus,
that long-suffering noble man, could eat and drink.
Then noble Alcinous spoke to his herald:

> "Pontonous, prepare wine in the mixing bowl,
> then serve it to all people in the hall,
> so we may pour libations out to Zeus,
> who loves lightning, for he accompanies
> all pious suppliants."

Once Alcinous said this,   220
Pontonous prepared the honeyed wine, and then poured
the first drops for libation into every cup.
When they'd made their offering and drunk their fill of wine,
Alcinous then addressed the gathering and said:

> "You Phaeacians counselors and leaders,
> pay attention to me so I can say
> what the heart here in my chest commands.
> Now that you have all finished eating,
> return back to your homes and get some rest.
> In the morning we'll summon an assembly   230
> with more elders, entertain this stranger
> here in our home; and also sacrifice
> choice offerings to the gods. Then after that,
> we'll think about how we can send him off,

so that this stranger, with us escorting him
and without further pain or effort, may reach
his native land, no matter how far distant.
Meanwhile he'll not suffer harm or trouble,
not before he sets foot on his own land.
After that he'll undergo all those things   240
Destiny and the dreaded spinning Fates
spun in the thread for him when he was born,
when his mother gave him birth.[1] However,
if he's a deathless one come down from heaven,
then gods are planning something different.
Up to now, they've always shown themselves to us
in their true form, when we offer up to them
a splendid sacrifice. They dine with us,
sitting in the very chairs we also use.
If someone traveling all by himself   250
meets them, they don't hide their true identity,
because we are close relatives of theirs,
like Cyclopes and the wild tribes of Giants."[2]

Resourceful Odysseus then answered Alcinous:

"Alcinous, you should not concern yourself
about what you've just said—for I'm not like
the immortal gods who hold wide heaven,
not in my form or shape. I'm like mortal men.
If, among human beings, you know of some
who bear a really heavy weight of trouble,   260
I might compare myself with them for grief.
Indeed, I could recount a longer story—

---

[1] *dreadful spinning Fates*: the three Fates, who are sisters, are called Atropos, Lachesis, and
Clotho. At a person's birth they allot his or her share of pain and suffering and good.
According to some accounts, Clotho sets the wool around the spindle, Lachesis spins the
yarn, and Atropos cuts the thread when death comes. The Olympian gods cannot or will
not alter the decisions of the Fates.

[2] *Cyclopes . . . Giants*: the Cyclopes are divinely born creatures of ambiguous origin, who
supported Zeus in his struggle against his father Cronos; they are famous for having only
one eye in their foreheads and for being gigantic, aggressive, and uncivilized. The Giants
are divine, often monstrous, creatures created from the castration of Uranus, the first
ruling god. They fought against Zeus and were imprisoned deep in Tartarus.

all those hardships I have had to suffer
from the gods. But let me eat my dinner,
though I'm in great distress. For there's nothing
more shameless than a wretched stomach,
which commands a man to think about its needs,
even if he's really sad or troubles
weigh down his heart, just the way my spirit
is now full of sorrow, yet my belly   270
is always telling me to eat and drink,
forgetting everything I've had to bear,
and ordering me to stuff myself with food.
But when dawn appears, you should stir yourselves
so you can set me in my misery
back on my native soil, for all I've suffered.
If I can see my goods again, my slaves,
my large and high-roofed home, then let life end.”

Once Odysseus finished, they all approved his words,
and, because he'd spoken well and to the point,   280
they ordered that their guest should be sent on his way.
Then, after they had poured libations and had drunk
to their heart's content, each of them returned back home
to get some rest. In the hall, lord Odysseus was left
sitting by Arete and godlike Alcinous.
Servants cleared away the remnants of the feast.
White-armed Arete spoke first, for when she saw
his cloak and tunic, she recognized his lovely clothes
as ones made by her servant women and herself.
So she spoke to him—her words had wings:

                                        “Stranger,   290
    first of all, I'll ask you this: Who are you?
    What people do you come from? And those clothes—
    who gave them to you? Did you not tell us
    you came here wandering across the sea?”

Resourceful Odysseus then answered her and said:

    “O queen, it would be hard to tell the story

of my miseries from start to finish—
heavenly gods have given me so many.
But in answer to what you have asked me
I can tell you this. There is an island   300
called Ogygia far off in the sea.
A cunning, fearful goddess lives there,
fair-haired Calypso, Atlas's daughter.
None of the gods associates with her,
nor any mortal men. But one of the gods
led me in my misfortune to her hearth.
I was alone, for Zeus had struck my ship
with his bright lightning bolt and shattered it,
right in the middle of the wine-dark sea.
All my other fine companions perished there,   310
but I clung to the keel of my curved ship
and drifted for nine days. The tenth black night,
gods brought me to Ogygia, the island
where that fair-haired, fearful goddess lives—
I mean Calypso. She received me kindly,
loved, and fed me. She promised she'd make me
ageless and immortal for eternity.
But she never won the heart here in my chest.
I stayed there seven years, the entire time,
always soaking the immortal clothing   320
Calypso gave me with my constant tears.
But, as the circling years kept moving past me,
the eighth year came. Then she commanded me,
with her encouragement, to sail back home—
either because she'd got some news from Zeus,
or else her mind had changed. She sent me off
on a well-lashed raft, and she provided
many things—food and sweet wine. She dressed me
in immortal clothing, and sent a wind,
a warm and gentle breeze. Seventeen days   330
I sailed across the sea. On the eighteenth
the shadowy mountains of your country
came in sight, and my fond heart was happy.
But I had no luck—I still had to learn
great torments, which the Shaker of the Earth,

Poseidon, sent at me. He stirred up winds
against me, blocked my route, and shook the sea
in an amazing way. The surging waves
did not allow the raft to carry me,
for all my heavy groaning, since that storm   340
smashed my raft to pieces. But I swam on,
cutting across the gulf, until wind and wave
carried me ahead and left me on your shore.
If I'd tried to land there, the pounding surf
would've tossed me up onshore, throwing me
against huge rocks in a perilous place.
So I moved back again, kept on swimming,
until I reached a river, which I thought
the best place I could land—it was free of rocks,
and there was shelter from the wind, as well.   350
I staggered out and fell down on the beach,
gasping for breath. Immortal night arrived.
So I climbed up from that heaven-fed river,
gathered leaves around me in the bushes,
and fell asleep. Some god poured over me
an endless sleep, so there among the leaves,
my fond exhausted heart slept through the night,
past daybreak and noon—not until the sun
was in decline did that sweet sleep release me.
Then I observed your daughter's servants   360
playing on the shore, and she was with them,
looking like a goddess. I entreated her,
and she revealed no lack of noble sense,
the sort you would not hope to come across
in one so young at a first encounter—
young people always act so thoughtlessly.
She gave me lots of food and gleaming wine,
bathed me in the river, and gave me clothes.
Though I'm in pain, I've told the truth in this."

Alcinous then answered him and said:

                                       "Stranger,   370
my child was truly negligent this time.

She did not bring you with her servants
here to our home, although it was to her
that you first made your plea."

                              Resourceful Odysseus
then said in answer to the king:

                                        "My lord,
in this you must not criticize your daughter,
I beg you, for she is quite innocent.
She did indeed tell me to follow her
with her attendants, but I was unwilling,
afraid and shamed in case, when you saw us,   380
you would be angry, for on this earth
groups of men are quick to grow enraged."

Alcinous then said in answer to Odysseus:

                                        "Stranger,
the heart here in my chest is not like that.
It does not get incensed without a reason.
It's better in all things to show restraint.
By Father Zeus, Athena, and Apollo,
I wish, given the kind of man you are,
with a mind that thinks so like my own,
you'd marry my child and become my son,   390
and then stay here. I'd give you a home
and wealth, as well, if you chose to remain.
But no Phaeacian will detain you here,
against your will. No. May that never be
the will of Father Zeus. I'll arrange a time,
so you can know for certain when you're leaving—
let it be tomorrow. While you lie asleep,
they'll carry you across the tranquil sea,
until you reach your native land and home,
or whatever place you wish, even though   400
it may take them far past Euboea.
Some of our people who saw that island
when they carried fair-haired Rhadamanthus

to visit Tityus, the son of Gaea,
say it is the most remote of places.[1]
They went there and, without any effort,
made the journey home in the same day.
So you, too, will discover for yourself
I have the finest ships and young men, too,
who toss salt water with their oar blades." 410

Alcinous finished. Long-suffering lord Odysseus
was pleased and spoke out in prayer, saying:

                                        "Father Zeus,
may Alcinous complete all he has said.
Then on this grain-giving earth his fame
will never be extinguished, and I
will reach my native land."

                        As they conversed like this,
white-armed Arete commanded her attendants
to set a bed outside, under the portico,
placing fine purple blankets on the top,
with coverlets spread over them, and then, 420
over those some woolly cloaks to keep him warm.
The servants left the chamber, torches in their hands.
Once they had worked fast to arrange the well-made bed,
they came to call Odysseus, saying:

                                        "Stranger,
        come now and rest. Your bed is ready."

When they said this, he welcomed thoughts of going to sleep.

---

[1] *Euboea . . . Rhadamanthus . . . Tityus . . . Gaea:* Euboea is a large island off the coast of
Attica, near Athens. The fact that the Phaeacians think of it as very remote suggests that
they are located far off to the south or west, perhaps off the west coast of Greece.
Rhadamanthus is a divine son of Zeus and Europa, so famous for his wise judgment that
the gods made him part of an underworld trio (along with Aeacus and Minos) who
judged the dead. Tityus, sometimes called a son of Zeus, is famous for his attempted rape
of Leto, as a result of which he was killed by Leto's children, Apollo and Artemis, and is
eternally punished in the underworld (as we see later in the poem). Gaea (or Gaia) is the
Earth, the child of Chaos.

So long-suffering lord Odysseus lay down there,
on the corded bed, beneath the echoing portico.
But Alcinous rested in an inner chamber
in the high-roofed house—his lady wife lay there, as well,   430
stretched out beside him, sharing their marriage bed.

Book Eight
Odysseus is Entertained in Phaeacia

[Odysseus attends the Phaeacian assembly; Alcinous outlines a proposal to assist Odysseus; young men prepare a boat for Odysseus; Demodocus sings of an old quarrel between Odysseus and Achilles, which makes Odysseus weep at the banquet; the young men put on a display of athletics and invite Odysseus to join in, but he declines; Euryalus insults Odysseus; Odysseus responds, and Athena encourages him; Alcinous arranges a display of Phaeacian dancing; Demodocus sings of how Hephaestus caught Ares and Aphrodite in an adulterous affair; Alcinous proposes they all give gifts to Odysseus; Euryalus apologizes; Arete gives Odysseus a gift; Nausicaa and Odysseus exchange farewells; Demodocus sings the story of the wooden horse at Troy; Odysseus weeps; Alcinous asks him to reveal his identity.]

As soon as rose-fingered early Dawn appeared,
royal and mighty Alcinous rose from his bed,
and divinely born Odysseus, sacker of cities,
got up, too. Alcinous, a powerful king, led them
to the place Phaeacians organized assemblies,
ground laid out for them beside the ships. They moved there
and sat down on polished stones arranged in rows.
Pallas Athena roamed throughout the city,
looking like one of wise Alcinous' heralds
and planning brave Odysseus' journey home.   10
To every noble she approached she spoke these words:

> "Come now, Phaeacian counselor and leader,
> come to the assembly to inform yourself
> about the stranger who has just arrived
> at the palace of our wise Alcinous.
> He's been wandering on the sea, but in form
> he looks like one of the immortals."

With such words she roused the heart and spirit in each man,
and so the seats in the assembly filled up quickly,
as people gathered there. Many of those present   20
were astonished when they saw Laertes' clever son—

Athena had poured an amazing poise on him,
across his shoulders and his head and made him look
taller and more powerful, so the Phaeacians
would welcome him, and he would win from them
respect and awe—and prevail in competition,
the many rival contests where Phaeacians
would be testing lord Odysseus. When the men
had all assembled for the meeting there,
Alcinous spoke to them and said:

                                   "Listen to me,   30
you Phaeacian counselors and leaders.
I'll tell you what the heart in my chest says.
This stranger here, a man I do not know,
a wanderer, has traveled to my house,
from people in the east or from the west.
He's asking to be sent away back home
and has requested confirmation from us.
So let us act as we have done before
and assist him with his journey. No man
arriving at my palace stays there long   40
grieving because he can't return back home.
Let's drag a black ship down into the sea
for her first voyage. Then from the citizens
choose fifty-two young men who in the past
have shown they are the best. Once they've all lashed
the oars firmly in place, they'll come ashore,
go to my house, and quickly make a meal.
I will provide enough for everyone.
That's what I'm ordering for our young men.
But all you other sceptre-bearing kings   50
should come to my fine home, so in those halls
we can make the stranger welcome. No man
should deny me this. And then summon there
the godlike minstrel Demodocus, the man
who has received from god the gift of song
above all others. He can entertain us
with any song his heart prompts him to sing."

Alcinous spoke and led them off. The sceptred kings
came after him, while a herald went to find
the godlike singer. Fifty-two hand-picked young men   60
went off, as Alcinous had ordered, to the shore
beside the restless sea. Once they'd reached the boat,
they dragged the black ship into deeper water,
set the mast and sails in place inside the vessel,
lashed the rowing oars onto their leather pivots,
then hoisted the white sail. Next, they moored the ship
well out to sea and then returned to the great home
of their wise king. Halls, corridors, and courtyards
were full of people gathering—a massive crowd,
young and old. On their behalf Alcinous slaughtered   70
eight white-tusked boars, two shambling oxen, and twelve sheep.
These carcasses they skinned and dressed and then prepared
a splendid banquet. Meanwhile the herald was returning
with the loyal singer, a man the Muse so loved
above all others. She'd given him both bad and good,
for she'd destroyed his eyes, but had bestowed on him
the gift of pleasing song. The herald, Pontonous,
then brought up a silver-studded chair for him.
He set its back against a lofty pillar in their midst,
hung the clear-toned lyre on a peg above his head,   80
then showed him how to reach it with his hands.
The herald placed a lovely table at his side,
with food in a basket and a cup of wine to drink,
when his heart felt the urge. Then all those present
reached for the splendid dinner set in front of them.
Once they'd enjoyed their heart's fill of food and drink,
the minstrel was inspired by the Muse to sing
a song about the glorious deeds of warriors,
that tale, whose fame had climbed to spacious heaven,
about Odysseus and Achilles, son of Peleus,   90
when, at a lavish feast in honour of the gods,
they'd fought each other in ferocious argument.[1]
Still, in his heart Agamemnon, king of men,

---

[1] *Odysseus . . . Achilles.* These lines refer to an argument between Odysseus and Achilles
about the best tactics to use against the Trojans. That Demodocus sings about the Trojan
War reinforces the claim that this image of the blind harper is a self-portrait of Homer,

had been glad to see the finest of Achaeans
quarreling, for that's what he'd been told would happen,
when he'd crossed the stone threshold in sacred Pytho
to consult Phoebus Apollo in his oracle
and the god had answered him with this reply—
that from this point on, disasters would begin
for Trojans and Danaans, as great Zeus willed.   100
This was the song the celebrated minstrel sang.
Odysseus's strong hands took his long purple cloak,
pulled it above his head, and hid his handsome face.
He felt ashamed to let Phaeacians look at him
with tears streaming from his eyes. So every time
the godlike minstrel stopped the song, Odysseus
would wipe away the tears, take his two-handled cup,
and pour out a libation to the gods. But then,
when Demodocus started up again, urged to sing
by Phaeacian noblemen enjoying his song,   110
Odysseus would hide his head once more and groan.
He concealed the tears he shed from all those present,
except Alcinous, the only one who noticed,
since he sat beside him and heard his heavy sighs.
So Alcinous quickly spoke to the Phaeacians,
men who love the sea:

                                   "Listen to me,
           you counselors and leaders of Phaeacians.
           Now we have refreshed our spirits. We've shared
           this food, and music has accompanied
           our splendid banquet. So let's go outside   130
           and test ourselves in all sorts of contests,
           then this stranger, once he gets back home,
           can tell his friends how much we excel
           all other men at wrestling and boxing,
           at jumping and at running."

                          Once he'd said this,
Alcinous led them out, and they followed him.
The herald hung the clear-toned lyre on the peg,
took Demodocus by the hand, and led him out,

taking him along the very path the other men,
Phaeacia's best, had walked along to watch the games.   130
So they made their way to the assembly ground.
A large crowd in their thousands followed them.
Many fine young men came forward to compete—
Acroneus, Ocyalus, and Elatreus,
then Nauteus, Prymneus, and Anchialus,
Eretmeus, too, along with Ponteus,
Proreus, Thoön, and Anabesineus,
with Amphialus, son of Polyneus,
son of Tecton. Euryalus came up, as well,
a match for man-destroying Ares, god of war,   140
son of Naubolus. His handsome looks and shape
made him, after Laodamas, who had no equal,
the finest of Phaeacians. Three sons of Alcinous
stepped out, as well—Halius, Laodomas,
and godlike Clytoneus. In the first contest
these men competed in the foot race on a course
laid out for them with markers. They all sprinted off,
moving quickly. A cloud of dust rose from the ground.
Clytoneus was by far the finest runner,
so he raced ahead and got back to the crowd,   150
leaving the others well behind, about as far
as the furrow laid down by a team of mules
in ploughing fallow land.[1] Then the competitors
tested their skill in the painful sport of wrestling,
and of all the noble princes Euryalus
proved himself the best. Next, in the leaping contest
Amphialus came out victorious, and then,
Elatreus triumphed in the discus throw,
as did Laodamas, fine son of Alcinous,
in the boxing match. Once they'd enjoyed these contests,   160
Laodamas, son of Alcinous, spoke to them:

     "Come, my friends, why don't we ask the stranger
     whether there's some contest he knows all about

---

[1] *mules . . . fallow land:* This rather obscure measurement, Butcher and Lang suggest,
seems to have something to do with the length of a furrow which a pair of mules could
plow before having to rest.

and understands. From the way his body looks
he's no weakling—not in his thighs and calves,
his thick neck and those two strong upper arms—
lots of power there, no lack of youthful strength.
He's just exhausted by his many troubles.
The sea is bad at breaking a man down,
no matter what his strength. From what I know,   170
there's nothing worse."

                                    Then Euryalus
answered him and said:

                                     "Laodamas,
what you've just said is really sensible.
So now go on your own and challenge him.
And say it so that all of us can hear."

When Alcinous's fine son heard these words, he moved
so he was standing in the middle of the crowd,
and spoke out to Odysseus:

                                "Honoured stranger,
come and test yourself in competition,
if there's some sport in which you have great skill   180
It seems to me you know how to compete,
since there's no greater glory for a man
than what he wins with his own hands and feet.
So come, make the attempt. All that sorrow—
cast it from your heart. Your journey homeward
will no longer be postponed. Your ship is launched,
your comrades are all ready to set off."

Then shrewd Odysseus answered him and said:

                                  "Laodamas,
why do you provoke me with this challenge?
My heart's preoccupied with troubles now,   190
not with competition. Up to this point,
I've suffered and struggled through so much,

and now I sit with you in this assembly
yearning to get home, pleading my case
before your king and all the people."

Euryalus then replied by taunting Odysseus
right to his face:

"No, no, stranger. I don't see you
as someone with much skill in competition—
not a real man, the sort one often meets—
more like a sailor trading back and forth   200
in a ship with many oars, a captain
in charge of merchant sailors, whose concern
is for his freight—he keeps a greedy eye
on the cargo and his profit. You don't seem
to be an athlete."

With a scowl, Odysseus,
that resourceful man, then answered Euryalus:

"Stranger, what you've said is not so wise,
like a man whose foolishness is blinding him.
How true it is the gods do not present
their lovely gifts to all men equally,   210
not beauty, shape, or skill in speaking out.
One man's appearance may not be attractive,
but a god will crown his words with beauty,
so men rejoice to look on him—he speaks
with confidence and yet sweet modesty,
and thus stands out among those in assembly.
And when he moves throughout the city,
they look at him as if he were a god.
And yet another man can be so beautiful,
he looks like an immortal, but his words   220
are empty of all grace. That's how you are.
Your appearance is particularly handsome—
a god could hardly make that any finer—
but your mind is empty. Your rude speech
has stirred the spirit in my chest. For I

am not unskilled in competition,
not the way you chat about. No. In fact,
when I relied upon my youth and strength,
I think I ranked among the very best.
Now I'm hurt and suffering, I'm holding back,   230
because I've gone through so much misery
in dealing with men's wars and painful waves.
But still, though I have undergone so much,
I'll test myself in these contests of yours.
For what you've said is gnawing at my heart—
that speech of yours provokes me."

Odysseus finished and then, still wrapped up in his cloak,
picked up a hefty discus, bigger than the others,
much heavier than the ones used by Phaeacians
when they competed with each other. With a whirl,   240
he sent it flying from his powerful hand.
The stone made a humming sound as it flew along,
and the long-oared Phaeacians, men who love their ships,
ducked down near the ground, below that flying stone.
It sailed beyond the marks of all the other men,
speeding lightly from his hand, and Athena,
in the likeness of a man, noted where it fell.
Then she called out to him and said:

                                                            "Stranger,
a blind man could find your mark by groping.
It's far out in front, not with the others.   250
So at least in this throwing competition
you can be confident. No Phaeacian
will get this far or throw it further."

Athena spoke, and resourceful lord Odysseus
was happy, glad to see someone supporting him
in the competition. So, with a more cheerful voice
he said to the Phaeacians:

                        "Equal that, you youngsters.
I'll quickly send another after it,

148

which will go as far, I think, even further.
As for other contests, let any man 260
whose heart and spirit urge him, come up here,
and test himself. You've made me so worked up.
In boxing, wrestling, or running—I don't care.
Any one at all from you Phaeacians,
all except Laodamas, for he's my host.
And what man fights against another man
who shows him hospitality? Anyone
who challenges the host who welcomes him
in a foreign land is a worthless fool,
for he is canceling his own good fortune. 270
But from the others I'll not back away,
nor will I take them lightly. No. I wish
to see their skill and test them man to man.
In all the competitions men engage in,
I am no weakling. I well understand
how to use a polished bow with skill.
I was the first to shoot an arrow off
and, in a multitude of enemies,
to kill a man, even as companions
standing close by me were still taking aim. 280
In that Trojan land, when Achaeans shot,
the only one who beat me with the bow
was Philoctetes.[1] But of all the rest
I claim I'm far the best—of mortal men,
I mean, ones now on earth who feed on bread.
For I won't seek to make myself a match
for men of earlier times—for Hercules,
or Eurytus of Oechalia, warriors
who competed with the gods in archery.
That's why great Eurytus was killed so young 290
and did not reach old age in his own home.
Apollo, in his anger, slaughtered him,
because Eurytus had challenged him

---

[1] *Philoctetes*: a famous Achaean warrior king, was left for years alone on the island of Lemnos
by the allied forces as they moved toward Troy, because a wound in his foot (from a snake
bite) produced an insupportable smell. His bow was essential for the capture of Troy, and
so Odysseus and Neoptolemus, the son of Achilles, returned to Lemnos to bring it back.

in a contest with their bows. With my spear,
I throw further than any other man
can shoot an arrow. But in the foot race
I'm afraid that one of the Phaeacians
may outrun me, for in those many waves
I was badly beaten down—on board ship
I did not have a large supply of food,   300
and so my legs are weak."

                              Odysseus finished.
All the people there were silent. No one spoke.
Then Alcinous responded to Odysseus:

        "Stranger, since you have not been ungracious
        in your speech to us and wish to demonstrate
        the merit you possess, in your anger
        that this man came up and taunted you
        in these games of ours, mocking your excellence
        in a way no one would ever do,
        if in his heart he fully understood   310
        how to speak correctly, come, hear me now,
        so you can tell this to some other hero,
        when you're back in your own home and feasting
        with your wife and children there beside you,
        remembering our qualities, the skills
        Zeus gave us when our ancestors were here,
        which still endure. We have no special gift
        in boxing fights or wrestling, but we run fast.
        We're the finest sailors, love feasts, the lyre,
        dancing, new clothes, warm baths, and going to bed.   320
        So come, all those of you among Phaeacians
        who dance the best, perform for us, and then
        our guest, when he gets back, can tell his friends
        just how much we surpass all other men
        in seamanship, speed on foot, dance, and song.
        Let a man go and get that sweet-toned lyre
        for Demodocus—it's somewhere in the hall."

Godlike Alcinous finished. The herald got up

to fetch the hollow lyre from the royal palace.
Nine officials chosen from among the people,   330
men who organized each detail of their meetings,
stood up, smoothed off a dancing space, and then marked out
a fair and spacious circle. The herald came up,
carrying the clear-toned lyre for Demodocus,
who then moved to the centre. Around the singer
stood boys in the first bloom of youth, skilled dancers,
whose feet then struck the consecrated dancing ground.
In his heart, Odysseus was amazed. He marveled
at the speed with which they moved their dancing feet.

The minstrel struck the opening chords to his sweet song—   340
how Ares loved the fair-crowned Aphrodite,
how in Hephaestus' house they first had sex
in secret, and how Ares gave her many gifts,
while he disgraced the bed of lord Hephaestus.[1]
But sun god Helios observed them making love
and came at once to tell Hephaestus. Once he'd heard
the unwelcome news, Hephaestus went into his forge,
pondering some nasty scheme deep in his heart.
He set up his massive anvil on its block,
then forged a net no one could break or loosen,   350
so they'd have to stay immobile where they were.
When, in his rage, he'd made that snare for Ares,
he went into the room which housed his marriage bed,
anchored the netting all around the bed posts,
and then hung loops of it from roof beams high above,
fine as spiders' webs, impossible to see,
even for a blessed god—that's how skillfully
he made that net. Once he'd organized the snare
around the bed, he announced a trip to Lemnos,
that well-built citadel, his favourite place by far   360

[1] *Hephaestus.* Aphrodite, the goddess of sexual love and beauty, is the wife of Hephaestus, the
divine master craftsman, the crippled god of the forge (hence, he is often called the lame god).
This famous story of the sexual affair between Ares, god of war, and Aphrodite has inspired
some famous art works. It also provides the most famous example of "Homeric laughter,"
boisterously loud continuous group laughter at the plight of someone else, the reaction of the
Olympian gods at the end of the song. This story has also prompted a good deal of negative
criticism, even in ancient times, about the lack of morality among the Olympian deities.

of all the lands on earth. Ares of the Golden Reins,
who maintained a constant watch, saw Hephaestus,
the celebrated master artisan, leaving home,
and went running over to Hephaestus' house,
eager to have sex with fair-crowned Aphrodite.
She'd just left the presence of her father Zeus,
mighty son of Cronos, and was sitting down.
Ares charged inside the house, clutched her hand, then spoke,
saying these words to her:

> "Come, my love,
> let's get into bed—make love together.   370
> Hephaestus is not home. No doubt he's gone
> to visit Lemnos and the Sintians,
> those men who speak like such barbarians."[1]

Ares spoke. To Aphrodite having sex with him
seemed quite delightful. So they went off to bed
and lay down there together. But then the crafty net
made by Hephaestus' ingenuity fell round them,
so they couldn't move their limbs or lift their bodies.
After a while, they realized they could not get out.
Then the famous crippled god came back to them—   380
he'd turned round before he'd reached the land of Lemnos.
Helios had stayed on watch and gave him a report.
With a grieving heart, Hephaestus went up to his home,
stood at the front door, where a cruel anger gripped him.
He made a dreadful cry, calling out to all the gods:

> "Father Zeus, all you other sacred gods
> who live forever, come here, so you can see
> something disgusting and ridiculous—
> Aphrodite, Zeus's daughter, scorns me
> and lusts after Ares, the destroyer,   390
> because he's beautiful, with healthy limbs,
> while I was born deformed. I'm not to blame.
> My parents are! I wish they'd never borne me!

[1] *Sintians:* a Thracian, non-Greek-speaking people living on Lemnos who had helped
Hephaestus when Zeus threw him out of heaven

See how these two have gone to my own bed
and are lying there, having sex together,
while I look on in pain. But I don't think
they want to stay lying down like this for long,
no matter how much they may be in love.
They'll both soon lose the urge to stay in bed.
But this binding snare will confine them here,   400
until her father gives back all those presents,
courting gifts I gave him for that shameless bitch—
a lovely daughter but a sex-crazed wife."[1]

Hephaestus finished. Gods gathered at the bronze-floored house.
Earthshaker Poseidon came, and Hermes, too,
the god of luck. And archer lord Apollo came.
But female goddesses were all far too ashamed
and stayed at home. So the gods, givers of good things,
stood in the doorway, looking at the artful work
of ingenious Hephaestus. They began to laugh—   410
an irrepressible laughter then pealed out
among the blessed gods. Glancing at his neighbour,
one of them would say:

                    "Bad deeds don't pay.
The slow one overtakes the swift—just as
Hephaestus, though slow, has now caught Ares,
although of all the gods who hold Olympus
he's the fastest one there is. Yes, he's lame,
but he's a crafty one. So Ares now
must pay a fine for his adultery."

That's how the gods then talked to one another.   420
But lord Apollo, son of Zeus, questioned Hermes:

        "Hermes, son of Zeus, you messenger
        and giver of good things, how would you like
        to lie in bed by golden Aphrodite,

---

[1] *wife.* Aphrodite, Ares, and Hephaestus are all children of Zeus. Aphrodite's mother was, in some accounts, the goddess Dione; in other accounts she emerged from the foam of the sea. The mother of Ares and Hephaestus is Hera, Zeus' wife and sister.

even though a strong net tied you down?"

The messenger god, killer of Argus, then said
in his reply:

> "Far-shooting lord Apollo,
> I wish there were three times as many nets,
> impossible to break, and all you gods
> were looking on, if I could like down there,   430
> alongside golden Aphrodite."

> At Hermes' words,
laughter arose from the immortal deities.
But Poseidon did not laugh. He kept requesting
Hephaestus, the celebrated master artisan,
to set Ares free. When he talked to him,
his words had wings:

> "Set him loose.
> I promise he will pay you everything,
> as you are asking, all he truly owes,
> in the presence of immortal gods."

The famous lame god then replied:

> "Poseidon,   440
> Shaker of the Earth, do not ask me this.
> It's a nasty thing to accept a pledge
> made for a nasty rogue. What if Ares
> escapes his chains, avoids the debt, and leaves—
> how then among all these immortal gods
> do I hold you in chains?"

> Earthshaker Poseidon
then answered him and said:

> "Hephaestus,
> if indeed Ares does not discharge his debt
> and runs away, I'll pay you in person."

Then the celebrated crippled god replied:

> "It would be inappropriate for me
> to refuse to take your word."

After saying this,
powerful Hephaestus then untied the netting.
Once they'd been released from their strong chains, both gods
jumped up immediately—Ares went off to Thrace,
and laughter-loving Aphrodite left for Paphos,
in Cyprus, where she has her sanctuary, her sacred altar.
There the Graces bathed and then anointed her
with heavenly oil, the sort that gleams upon the gods,
who live forever. Next, they took some gorgeous clothes   460
and dressed her—the sight was marvelous to see.

That was the song the famous minstrel sang.
As he listened, Odysseus felt joy in his heart—
long-oared Phaeacians, famous sailors, felt it, too.
Alcinous then asked Laodamas and Halius
to dance alone. No man could match their dancing skill.
The two men picked up a lovely purple ball,
which clever Polybus had made for them.
Then, leaning back, one of them would throw it high,
towards the shadowy clouds, and then the other,   470
before his feet touched ground, would catch it easily.
Once they'd shown their skill in tossing it straight up,
they threw it back and forth, as they kept dancing
on the life-sustaining earth, while more young men
stood at the edge of the arena, beating time.
The dancing rhythms made a powerful sound.
Then lord Odysseus spoke:

> "Mighty Alcinous,
> most renowned among all men, you claimed
> your dancers were the best, and now, indeed,
> what you said is true. When I gaze at them,   480
> I'm lost in wonder."

At Odysseus' words,
powerful king Alcinous felt a great delight,
and spoke at once to his Phaeacians, master sailors.

> "Leaders and counselors of the Phaeacians,
> listen—this stranger seems to me a man
> with an uncommon wisdom. So come now,
> let's give him gifts of friendship, as is right.
> Twelve distinguished kings are rulers here
> and govern in this land, and I myself
> am the thirteenth king. Let each of you   490
> bring a fresh cloak and tunic, newly washed,
> and a talent of pure gold. All of this
> we should put together very quickly,
> so this stranger has his gifts in hand
> and goes to dinner with a joyful heart.
> Euryalus must apologize in person
> to the stranger, verbally and with a gift,
> for what he said is not acceptable."

Alcinous spoke. All those present agreed with him
and said it should be done. Then every one of them   500
sent an attendant out to bring back presents.
And Euryalus addressed the king and said:

> "Lord Alcinous, most renowned among all men,
> to this stranger I will indeed apologize,
> as you instruct me. And I'll give him
> a sword completely made of bronze,
> with a silver hilt, and scabbard, too,
> of fresh-carved ivory which fits around it,
> a gift worth a great deal, and just for him."

With these words he set into Odysseus' hands   510
the silver-studded sword and then addressed him—
his words had wings:

> "Greetings, honoured stranger.
> If any harsh word has been spoken here,

let storm winds snatch it, carry it away.
As for you, may gods grant you see your wife
and reach your native land. You've suffered much,
for such a long time distant from your friends."

Then Odysseus, that resourceful man, replied and said:

"And you, my friend, best wishes to you, too.
May gods give you joyful prosperity.   520
And may you never miss this sword
which you are giving me. These words of yours
have made amends to me."

                                        Odysseus spoke
and slung the silver-studded sword around his shoulders.
As the sun went down, the splendid presents were brought in,
carried to Alcinous' home by worthy heralds.
The sons of noble Alcinous took the lovely gifts
and set them down before their honoured mother.
With powerful king Alcinous leading them,
they came in and sat down on their upraised thrones.   530
Mighty Alcinous then said to Arete:

"My lady, have a precious trunk brought here,
the best there is. You yourself should place in it
a tunic and a freshly laundered cloak.
Then heat a cauldron for him on the fire,
warm up some water, so he can bathe,
and, after he's seen safely stowed away
all the splendid gifts Phaeacian noblemen
have brought in here, he can enjoy the feast,
while listening to the minstrel's singing.   540
And I will give him this fine cup of mine—
it's made of gold—for all his days to come
he will remember me, as he pours libations
in his halls to Zeus and other gods."

Alcinous finished. Arete then told her servants
to set a large cauldron full of water on the fire

as quickly as they could. They placed it on the fire,
poured water in it, and added wood below.
So flames then licked the belly of the cauldron,
heating up the water. Meanwhile for her guest   550
Arete had brought out from her inner rooms
a splendid chest, which she filled with precious gifts,
the clothing and the gold brought by Phaeacians.
She herself added a cloak and lovely tunic.
Then she addressed Odysseus—her words had wings:

> "You must attend to the lid yourself,
> and secure it quickly with a knot,
> so no one robs you on your journey,
> perhaps when you are lost in a sweet sleep
> sometime later, as your black ship sails on."   560

Long-suffering lord Odysseus heard what she advised.
He quickly shut the lid and bound it with a knot,
a tricky one which he'd picked up from queenly Circe.
Then the housekeeper invited him to step
into the bathing tub. His heart was filled with joy
to see hot water—he'd not had such welcome care
since the day he'd left fair-haired Calypso's home.
Till then he'd been treated always like a god.
The servant women washed him, rubbed him down with oil,
and dressed him in a handsome cloak and tunic.   570
He left his bath and went to drink wine with the men.
Nausicaa, whose beauty was a gift from god,
standing by the doorway of that well-built hall,
looked at Odysseus and was filled with wonder.
She spoke winged words to him:

> "Farewell, stranger.
> When you are back in your own land,
> I hope you will remember me sometimes,
> since you owe your life to me."

                              Then Odysseus,
that resourceful man, replied to her and said:

"Nausicaa, daughter of great Alcinous,   580
may Hera's loud-thundering husband, Zeus,
grant that I see the day of my return
when I get home. There I will pray to you
all my days, as to a god. For you, girl,
you gave me my life."

                    Odysseus finished speaking.
Then he sat down on a chair beside king Alcinous.
They were already serving food and mixing wine.
A herald approached leading the faithful singer,
Demodocus, whom the people held in honour,
and sat him in the middle of the banquet,   590
leaning his chair against a lofty pillar.
Then shrewd Odysseus, as he was slicing meat
from the large amount remaining, took pieces
from the back cut of a white-tusked boar, lots of fat
on either side, and called out to the herald:

        "Herald, take this portion of our food
        to Demodocus, so that he can eat.
        Though in grief, I'll give him a warm welcome,
        for from all people living on the earth
        singers win honour and respect. The Muse   600
        has taught them song and loves their tribe."

At Odysseus' words, the herald took the serving
and handed it to noble Demodocus,
who accepted it with a delighted heart.
Their hands reached out to take the tasty food
prepared and set out there before them. And then,
when they'd had their heart's fill of food and drink,
quick-witted Odysseus said to Demodocus:

        "Demodocus, to you I give high praise,
        more so than to all other mortal men,   610
        whether it was that child of Zeus, the Muse,
        who taught you, or Apollo. For you sing
        so well and with such true expressiveness

about the destiny of the Achaeans,
everything they did and suffered, the work
they had to do—as if you yourself were there
or heard the story from a man who was.
Come, change the subject now, and sing about
the building of that wooden horse, the one
Epeius made with guidance from Athena.   620
Lord Odysseus then, with his trickery,
had it taken to the citadel, filled with men,
those who ransacked Troy. If, at my request,
you will recite the details of this story,
I'll tell all men how, of his own free will,
god gives poetic power to your song."

Odysseus spoke. And the minstrel, inspired by god,
began to sing to them, taking up the story
at the point where Argives, having burned their huts
and gone on board their well-oared ships, were sailing off,   630
while those warriors led by glorious Odysseus
were at Troy's meeting ground, hidden in the horse.[1]
Trojans had dragged the horse all by themselves
inside their citadel. It stood there, while Trojans
sat and talked around it, confused what they should do.
There were three different options people favoured—
to split the hollow wood apart with pitiless bronze,
or drag it to the heights and throw it from the rocks,
or let it stay there as a great offering to the gods,
something to assuage their anger. And that, indeed,   640
is what they finally did, for it was their fate
to be wiped out once they had within their city walls
a gigantic wooden horse in which lay hidden
all the finest Argives, bringing into Troy
death and destruction. Then Demodocus sang
how Achaea's sons left their hollow hiding place,

---

[1] *. . . in the horse*. This is the earliest surviving account of the famous story of the wooden
horse. The deception practiced on the Trojans began with the Achaean army pretending
it had abandoned the war. Hence, the army burned its camp, got on board ship, and sailed
away, apparently for home, but, in reality, hiding behind a nearby island. They left the
horse behind them.

poured from the horse, and then destroyed the city.
He sang about the various ways those warriors
laid waste that lofty city and how Odysseus,
like Ares, god of war, and godlike Menelaus   650
went to the home of Deïphobus, where, he said,
Odysseus battled in the most horrendous fight,
from which he then emerged at last victorious,
thanks to assistance from Athena's mighty heart.

That was the tale the celebrated minstrel sang.
Odysseus was moved to weep—below his eyes
his face grew wet with tears. Just as a woman cries,
as she prostrates herself on her dear husband
who's just been killed in front of his own city
and his people, trying to save his children   660
and the citizens from the day they meet their doom—
as he dies, she sees him gasping his last breath,
embraces him, and screams out her laments,
while at her back her enemies keep beating her,
with spears across her spine and shoulders,
then lead her off, cheeks ravaged by her grief,
into a life of bondage, pain, and sorrow—
that's how Odysseus let tears of pity fall
from his eyes then. But he concealed those tears
from all of them except Alcinous, who,   670
as he sat there beside him, was the only one
who noticed and could hear his heavy sighs.
He spoke out at once to his Phaeacians,
lovers of the sea.

                    "Listen to me,
        you Phaeacians counselors and leaders.
        Let Demodocus cease from playing now
        his clear-toned lyre, for the song he sings
        does not please all his listeners alike.
        Since our godlike minstrel was first moved to sing,
        as we were dining, our guest has been in pain—   680
        his mournful sighs have never stopped. His heart,
        I think, must surely overflow with grief.

Then let our singer end his song, so all of us,
both hosts and guest, can enjoy our feasting.
Things will be much better. We've done all this—
the farewell dinner and the friendship gifts,
offered up with love—in honour of our guest.
To any man with some intelligence,
a stranger coming as a suppliant
brings the same delight a brother does.   690
And you, our guest, should no longer hide
behind those cunning thoughts of yours and skirt
the things I ask you. It's better to be frank.
Tell me your name, what they call you at home—
your mother and your father and the others,
those in the town and in the countryside.
There's no one in the world, mean or noble,
who goes without a name once he's been born.
Parents give one to each of us at birth.
Tell me your country and your people,   700
your city, too, so ships can take you there,
using what they know to chart their passage.
Phaeacians have no pilots, no steering oar,
like other boats, for their ships on their own
can read men's hearts and thoughts—they know
all men's cities, their rich estates, as well,
and quickly skim across wide tracts of sea,
concealed in mist and clouds, without a fear
of shipwrecks or disaster. Still, my father,
Nausithous, once told me this story—   710
he used to say we made Poseidon angry
because we carried everyone in safety.
He claimed that one day, as a well-built ship
with a Phaeacian crew was sailing back
from such a trip, over the misty sea,
Poseidon would destroy it and then place
a massive ring of mountains round our city.
That's what the old man said. It's up to god
to make that happen or leave it undone,
whatever he finds pleasing to his heart.   720
So come, tell me this, and speak the truth—

Where have you traveled in your wanderings?
What men's countries have you visited?
Tell me of people and their well-built towns,
whether they are cruel, unjust, and savage,
or welcome strangers and fear god in their hearts.
Tell us why you weep, your heart full of pain,
to hear the fate of Argives and Danaans,
and of Troy. Gods made these things happen.
They spun out that destructive thread for men,   730
to weave a song for those as yet unborn.
Was someone in your family killed at Troy—
a good and loyal man, a son-in-law,
your wife's father, one of those we truly love
after our flesh and blood? A companion?
A fine and worthy man dear to your heart?
For a companion who's a heart's true friend
is every bit as dear as one's own brother."

Book Nine
Ismarus, the Lotus Eaters, and the Cyclops

*[Odysseus identifies himself and his origins to the Phaeacians; recounts his
first adventures after leaving Troy: the attack on the Cicones, the storm
sent from Zeus, the arrival in the land of the Lotus-eaters; the arrival in the
land of the Cyclops; the slaughter of his men; he and his men burn out
Polyphemus' eye and escape from the cave; Odysseus and his men sail on.]*

Resourceful Odysseus then replied to Alcinous:

"Lord Alcinous, most renowned of men,
it is indeed a truly splendid thing
to listen to a singer such as this,
whose voice is like a god's. For I say
there's nothing gives one more delight
than when joy grips entire groups of men
who sit in proper order in a hall
feasting and listening to a singer,
with tables standing there beside them   10
laden with bread and meat, as the steward
draws wine out of the mixing bowl, moves round,
and fills the cups. To my mind this seems
the finest thing there is. But your heart
wants to ask about my grievous sorrows,
so I can weep and groan more than before.
What shall I tell you first? Where do I stop?
For the heavenly gods have given me
so much distress. Well, I will make a start
by telling you my name. Once you know that,   20
if I escape the painful day of death,
then later I can welcome you as guests,
though I live in a palace far away.
I am Odysseus, son of Laertes,
well known to all for my deceptive skills—
my fame extends all the way to heaven.
I live in Ithaca, a land of sunshine.
From far away one sees a mountain there,

thick with whispering trees, Mount Neriton,
and many islands lying around it   30
close together—Dulichium, Same,
forested Zacynthus. Ithaca itself,
low in the sea furthest from the mainland,
lies to the west—while those other islands
are a separate group, closer to the Dawn
and rising Sun. It's a rugged island,
but nurtures fine young men. And in my view,
nothing one can see is ever sweeter
than a glimpse of one's own native land.
When Calypso, that lovely goddess, tried   40
to keep me with her in her hollow caves,
longing for me to be her husband,
or when, in the same way, the cunning witch
Aeaean Circe held me in her home
filled with keen desire I'd marry her,
they never won the heart here in my chest.
That's how true it is there's nothing sweeter
than a man's own country and his parents,
even if he's living in a wealthy home,
but in a foreign land away from those   50
who gave him life. But come, I'll tell you
of the miserable journey back which Zeus
arranged for me when I returned from Troy.[1]

"I was carried by the wind from Troy
to Ismarus, land of the Cicones.
I destroyed the city there, killed the men,
seized their wives, and captured lots of treasure,
which we divided up. I took great pains
to see that all men got an equal share.
Then I gave orders we should leave on foot—   60
and with all speed. But the men were fools.
They didn't listen. They drank too much wine
and on the shoreline slaughtered many sheep,

<hr>

[1] *Troy.* For a chart of the various adventures of Odysseus on his way home, consult the
map at the end of this book (on p. 496). His first adventure, at Ismarus with the Cicones,
seems to have been on the mainland north of Troy.

as well as shambling cows with twisted horns.
Meanwhile the Cicones set off and gathered up
their neighbours, tribesmen living further inland.
There are more of them, and they're braver men,
skilled at fighting enemies from chariots
and also, should the need arise, on foot.
They reached us in the morning, thick as leaves 70
or flowers growing in season. Then Zeus
brought us disaster—he made that our fate,
so we would suffer many casualties.
They set their ranks and fought by our swift ships.
We threw our bronze-tipped spears at one another.
While the morning lasted and that sacred day
gained strength, we held our ground and beat them back,
for all their greater numbers. But as the sun
moved to the hour when oxen are unyoked,
the Cicones broke through, overpowering 80
Achaeans. Of my well-armed companions,
six from every ship were killed. The rest of us
made our escape, avoiding Death and Fate.

"We sailed away from there, hearts full of grief
at losing loyal companions, though happy
we had eluded death ourselves. But still,
I would not let our curved ships leave the place
until we'd made the ritual call three times
for our poor comrades slaughtered on that plain,
killed by the Cicones. Cloud-gatherer Zeus 90
then stirred North Wind to rage against our ships—
a violent storm concealing land and sea,
as darkness swept from heaven down on us.
The ships were driven off course, our sails
ripped to shreds by the power of that wind.
We lowered the masts into the holds and then,
fearing for our lives, quickly rowed the ships
toward the land. For two whole days and nights
we lay there, hearts consumed with sorrow
and exhaustion. But when fair-haired Dawn 100
gave birth to the third day, we raised the masts,

hoisted white sails, and took our place on board.
Wind and helmsman held us on our course,
and I'd have reached my native land unharmed,
but North Wind, sea currents, and the waves
pushed me off course, as I was doubling back
around Malea, driving me past Cythera.[1]

"Nine days fierce winds drove me away from there,
across the fish-filled seas, and on the tenth
we landed where the Lotus-eaters live,   110
people who feed upon its flowering fruit.
We went ashore and carried water back.
Then my companions quickly had a meal
by our swift ships. We had our food and drink,
and then I sent some of my comrades out
to learn about the men who ate the food
the land grew there. I chose two of my men
and with them sent a third as messenger.
They left at once and met the Lotus-eaters,
who had no thought of killing my companions,   120
but gave them lotus plants to eat, whose fruit,
sweet as honey, made any man who sampled it
lose his desire to ever journey home
or bring back word to us—they wished to stay,
to remain among the Lotus-eaters,
feeding on the plant, eager to forget
about their homeward voyage. I forced them,
eyes full of tears, into our hollow ships,
dragged them underneath the rowing benches,
and tied them up. Then I issued orders   130
for my other trusty comrades to embark
and sail away with speed in our fast ships,
in case another man might eat a lotus
and lose all thoughts about his journey back.
They raced on board, went to their places,
and, sitting in good order in their rows,

[1] *Malea . . . Cythera*: Malea is a cape on the southeast coast of the Peloponnese, one of the
most southerly points in mainland Greece; Cythera is an island off the south coast of the
Peloponnese.

167

struck the gray sea with their oar blades.

"We sailed away from there with heavy hearts
and reached the country of the Cyclopes,
a crude and lawless people.[1] They don't grow   140
any plants by hand or plough the earth,
but put their trust in the immortal gods,
and though they never sow or work the land,
every kind of crop springs up for them—
wheat and barley and rich grape-bearing vines,
and Zeus provides the rain to make them grow.
They live without a council or assembly
or any rule of law, in hollow caves
among the mountain tops. Each one of them
makes laws for his own wives and children,   150
and they shun all dealings with each other.

"Now, near the country of the Cyclopes,
outside the harbour, there's a fertile island,
covered in trees, some distance from the shore,
but not too far away. Wild goats live there
in countless numbers. They have no need
to stay away from any human trails.
Hunters never venture there, not even those
who endure great hardships in the forest,
as they roam across the mountain peaks.   160
That island has no flocks or plough land—
through all its days it's never once been sown
or tilled or known the work of human beings.
The only life it feeds is bleating goats.
The Cyclopes don't have boats with scarlet prows

---

[1] *... and lawlelss people.* The Cyclopes (singular Cyclops) are hairy monsters, rather than
people, with only one eye in the middle of their foreheads. They originated from the
primal gods, Ouranus and Gaea, and had been imprisoned in Tartarus. But they helped
Zeus in his fight against his father, Cronos, and Zeus freed them. Odysseus, one assumes,
either doesn't know about the Cyclopes before this adventure or is not aware he is about
to meet one, since he assumes he's moving into a place where the laws of hospitality
apply. Most geographical interpretations place the incident with the Cyclops in Sicily.
We learn later that the Cyclops Odysseus meets has a name (Polyphemus) and is, along
with his neighbours, a son of Poseidon.

or men with skills to build them well-decked ships,
which would enable them to carry out
all sorts of things—like traveling to the towns
of other people, the way men cross the sea
to visit one another in their ships—   170
or men who might have turned their island
into a well-constructed settlement.
The island is not poor. All things grow there
in season. It has soft, well-watered meadows
by the shore of the gray sea, where grape vines
could flourish all the time, and level farm land,
where they could always reap fine harvests,
year after year—the sub-soil is so rich.
It has a harbour, too, with good anchorage,
no need for any mooring cable there,   180
or setting anchor stones, or tying up
with cables on the stern. One can beach a ship
and wait until a fair wind starts to blow
and sailors' hearts tell them to go on board.
At the harbour head there is a water spring—
a bright stream flows out underneath a cave.
Around it poplars grow. We sailed in there.
Some god led us in through the murky night—
we couldn't see a thing, and all our ships
were swallowed up in fog. Clouds hid the moon,   190
so there was no light coming from the sky.
Our eyes could not catch any glimpse of land
or of the long waves rolling in onshore,
until our well-decked ships had reached the beach.
We hauled up our ships, took down all the sails,
went up along the shore, and fell asleep,
remaining there until the light of Dawn.

"When rose-fingered early Dawn appeared,
we moved across the island quite amazed.
Some nymphs, daughters of aegis-bearing Zeus,   200
flushed out mountain goats, food for us to eat.
We quickly brought our curved bows from the ships
and our long spears, as well. Then, splitting up,

we fanned out in three different groups to hunt.
The god soon gave us our heart's fill of game—
I had twelve ships with me, and each of them
received nine goats by lot. I was the only one
to be allotted ten. So all day long
until the sunset, we sat there and ate,
feasting on that rich supply of meat,   210
with sweet wine, too—we'd not yet used up
the red wine in our ships and had some left.
We'd taken many jars for everyone
the day we'd seized the sacred citadel
of the Cicones. Then we looked across
toward the country of the Cyclopes,
which was nearby. We observed their smoke,
heard their talk and sounds of sheep and goats.
Then the sun went down, and darkness fell.
So we lay down to sleep on the sea shore.   220

"As soon as rose-fingered early Dawn appeared,
I called a meeting and spoke to all the men:

    'My loyal comrades, stay here where you are.
    I'll take my ship and my own company
    and try to find out who those people are,
    whether they are rough and violent,
    with no sense of law, or kind to strangers,
    with hearts that fear the gods.'

                    "I said these words,
then went down to my ship and told my crew
to loose the cables lashed onto the stern   230
and come onboard. They embarked with speed,
and, seated at the oarlocks in their rows,
struck the gray sea with their oars. And then,
when we'd made the short trip round the island,
on the coast there, right beside the sea,
we saw a high cave, overhung with laurel.
There were many flocks, sheep as well as goats,
penned in there at night. All around the cave

there was a high front courtyard made of stones
set deep into the ground—with tall pine trees   240
and towering oaks. At night a giant slept there,
one that grazed his flocks all by himself,
somewhere far off. He avoided others
and lived alone, away from all the rest,
a law unto himself, a monster, made
to be a thing of wonder, not like man
who lives by eating bread, no, more like
a lofty wooded mountain crag, standing there
to view in isolation from the rest.

"I told the rest of my trustworthy crew   250
to stay there by the ship and guard it,
while I selected twelve of my best men
and went off to explore. I took with me
a goatskin full of dark sweet wine. Maron,
Euanthes' son, one of Apollo's priests,
the god who kept guard over Ismarus,
gave it me because, to show respect,
we had protected him, his wife, and child.
He lived in a grove of trees, a piece of ground
sacred to Apollo. He gave me splendid gifts—   270
seven finely crafted golden talents,
a pure silver mixing bowl, and wine as well,
a total of twelve jars poured out unmixed,
drink fit for gods. None of his servants,
men or women in his household, knew
about this wine. He was the only one,
other than his wife and one house steward.
Each time they drank that honey-sweet red wine,
he'd fill one cup with it and pour that out
in twenty cups of water, and the smell   280
arising from the mixing bowl was sweet,
astonishingly so—to tell the truth,
no one's heart could then refuse to drink it.
I took some of this wine in a large goatskin,
a pouch of food, as well. My soldier's heart
was warning me a man might soon attack,

someone invested with enormous power,
a savage with no sense of law and justice.

"We soon reached his cave but didn't find him.
He was pasturing his rich flocks in the fields.   290
We went inside the cave and looked around.
It was astonishing—crates full of cheese,
pens crammed with livestock—lambs and kids
sorted into separate groups, with yearlings,
older lambs, and newborns each in different pens.
All the sturdy buckets, pails, and milking bowls
were awash with whey. At first, my comrades
urged me to grab some cheeses and return,
then drive the lambs and kids out of their pens
back to our swift ship and cross the water.   300
But I did not agree, though if I had,
things would've been much better. I was keen
to see the man in person and find out
if he would show me hospitality.
When he did show up, as it turned out,
he proved no joy to my companions.

"We lit a fire and offered sacrifice.
Then we helped ourselves to cheese and ate it.
We stayed inside the cave and waited there,
until he led his flocks back home. He came,   310
bearing an enormous pile of dried-out wood
to cook his dinner. He hurled his load
inside the cave with a huge crash. In our fear,
we moved back to the far end of the cave,
into the deepest corner. He then drove
his fat flock right inside the spacious cavern,
just the ones he milked. Rams and billy goats
he left outside, in the open courtyard.
Then he raised up high a massive boulder
and fixed it in position as a door.   320
It was huge—twenty-two four-wheeled wagons,
good ones, too, could not have shifted it
along the ground—that's how immense it was,

the rock he planted right in his doorway.
He sat down with his bleating goats and ewes
and milked them all, each in turn, setting
beside each one its young. Next, he curdled
half the white milk and set aside the whey
in wicker baskets, then put the other half
in bowls for him to drink up with his dinner.   330
Once he'd finished working at these tasks,
he lit a fire. Then he spied us and said:

         'Strangers,
 who are you? What sea route brought you here?
Are you trading men, or wandering the sea
at random, like pirates sailing anywhere,
risking their lives to injure other men.'

"As he spoke, our hearts collapsed, terrified
by his deep voice and monstrous size. But still,
I answered him by saying:

         'We are Achaeans
 coming back from Troy and blown off course   340
by various winds across vast tracts of sea.
Attempting to get home, we had to take
a different route and chart another course,
a scheme, I think, which gave Zeus pleasure.
We boast that we are Agamemnon's men,
son of Atreus, now the best-known man
beneath wide heaven—the city he wiped out
was such a great one, and he killed so many.
As for us, we're visitors here and come
as suppliants to your knee, in hope that you   350
will make us welcome or provide some gift,
the proper thing one does for strangers.
So, good sir, respect the gods. We're here
as suppliants to you, and Zeus protects
all suppliants and strangers—as god of guests,
he cares for all respected visitors.'

"I finished speaking. He answered me at once—
his heart was pitiless:

       'What fools you are, you strangers,
    or else you come from somewhere far away—
    telling me to fear the gods and shun their rage.   360
    The Cyclopes care nothing about Zeus,
    who bears the aegis, or the blessed gods.
    We are much more powerful than them.
    I wouldn't spare you or your comrades
    to escape the wrath of Zeus, not unless
    my own heart prompted me to do it.
    But now, tell me this—when you landed here,
    where did you moor your ship, a spot close by
    or further off? I'd like to know that.'

"He said this to throw me off, but his deceit   370
could never fool me. I was too clever.
So I gave him a cunning answer:

    'Earthshaker Poseidon broke my ship apart—
    driving it against the border of your island,
    on the rocks there. He brought us close to land,
    hard by the headland, then winds pushed us
    inshore from the sea. But we escaped—
    me and these men here. We weren't destroyed.'

"That's what I said. But his ruthless heart
gave me no reply. Instead, he jumped up,   380
seized two of my companions in his fist,
and smashed them on the ground like puppy dogs.
Their brains oozed out and soaked the ground below.
He tore their limbs apart to make a meal,
and chewed them up just like a mountain lion—
innards, flesh, and marrow—leaving nothing.
We raised our hands to Zeus and cried aloud,
to witness the horrific things he did,
our hearts unable to do anything.
Once Cyclops had stuffed his massive stomach   390

with human flesh and washed it down with milk,
he lay down in the cave, stretched out there
among his flocks. Then, in my courageous heart
I formed a plan to move up close beside him,
draw the sharp sword I carried on my thigh,
and run my hand along his chest, to find
exactly where his midriff held his liver,
then stick him there. But I had second thoughts.
We, too, would have been utterly destroyed,
there in the cave—we didn't have the strength   400
with our own hands to roll from the high door
the massive rock he'd set there. So we groaned,
and stayed there waiting for bright Dawn.

"As soon as rose-fingered early Dawn appeared,
he lit a fire and milked his flock, one by one,
with a new-born placed beside each mother.
When this work was over, he once again
snatched two of my men and gorged himself.
After his meal, he easily rolled back
the huge rock door, drove his rich flock outside,   410
and set the stone in place, as one might put
a cap back on a quiver. Then Cyclops,
whistling loudly, drove his fat flocks away
towards the mountain. He left me there,
plotting a nasty scheme deep in my heart,
some way of gaining my revenge against him,
if Athena would grant me that glory.
My heart came up with what appeared to me
the best thing I could do. An enormous club
belonging to Cyclops was lying there   420
beside a stall, a section of green olive wood
he'd cut to carry with him once it dried.
To human eyes it seemed just like the mast
on a black merchant ship with twenty oars,
a broad-beamed vessel which can move across
the mighty ocean—that's how long and wide
that huge club looked. Moving over to it,
I chopped off a piece, six feet in length,

gave it to my companions, telling them
to smooth the wood. They straightened it, while I,   430
standing at one end, chipped and tapered it
to a sharp point. Then I picked up the stake
and set it in the blazing fire to harden.
That done, I placed it carefully to one side,
concealing it beneath some of the dung
which lay throughout the cave in massive piles.
Then I told my comrades to draw lots
to see which men would risk their lives with me—
when sweet sleep came upon the Cyclops,
we'd lift that stake and twist it in his eye.   440
The crew drew lots and picked the very men
I would have chosen for myself, four of them,
with me included as fifth man in the group.
In the evening he came back, leading on
his fine-skinned animals and bringing them
inside the spacious cave, every sheep and goat
in his rich flock—not leaving even one
out in the open courtyard. Perhaps he had
a sense of something wrong, or else a god
had given him an order. He picked up   450
and put his huge rock door in place, then sat
to milk each ewe and bleating goat,
one by one, setting beside each mother
one of her young. When this task was over,
he quickly seized two men and wolfed them down.
Then I moved up and stood at Cyclops' side,
holding in my hands a bowl of ivy wood
full of my dark wine. I said:

                    'Cyclops,
     take this wine and drink it, now you've had
     your meal of human flesh, so you may know   460
     the kind of wine we had on board our ship,
     a gift of drink I was carrying for you,
     in hope you'd pity me and send me off
     on my journey home. But your savagery
     is something I can't bear. You cruel man,

176

how will any of the countless other men
ever visit you in future? How you act
is so against all human law.'

                                   "I spoke.
He grabbed the cup and gulped down the sweet wine.
Once he'd swallowed, he felt such great delight,   470
he asked me for some more, a second taste.

     'Be kind and give me some of that again.
     And now, without delay tell me your name,
     so, as my guest, I can offer you a gift,
     something you'll like. Among the Cyclopes,
     grain-bearing earth grows clusters of rich grapes,
     which Zeus' rain increases, but this drink—
     it's a stream of nectar and ambrosia.'

"He spoke. So I handed him more fiery wine.
Three times I poured some out and gave it to him,   480
and, like a fool, he swilled it down. So then,
once the wine had addled Cyclops' wits,
I spoke these reassuring words to him:

     'Cyclops, you asked about my famous name.
     I'll tell you. Then you can offer me a gift,
     as your guest. My name is Nobody.
     My father and mother, all my other friends—
     they call me Nobody.'

                         "That's what I said.
His pitiless heart replied:

                              'Well, Nobody,
     I'll eat all your companions before you   490
     and have you at the end—my gift to you,
     since you're my guest.'

                              "As he said this,
he collapsed and toppled over on his back,

                         177

lying with his thick neck twisted to one side.
All-conquering sleep then overpowered him.
In his drunken state he kept on vomiting,
his gullet drooling wine and human flesh.
So then I pushed the stake deep in the ashes,
to make it hot, and spoke to all my men,
urging them on, so no one, in his fear,   500
would hesitate. When that stake of olive wood,
though green, was glowing hot, its sharp point
ready to catch fire, I walked across to it
and with my comrades standing round me
pulled it from the fire. And then some god
breathed powerful courage into all of us.
They lifted up that stake of olive wood
and jammed its sharpened end down in his eye,
while I, placing my weight at the upper end,
twisted it around—just as a shipwright   510
bores a timber with a drill, while those below
make it rotate by pulling on a strap
at either end, so the drill keeps moving—
that's how we held the red-hot pointed stake
and twisted it inside the socket of his eye.
Blood poured out through the heat—around his eye,
lids and brows were singed, as his eyeball burned—
its roots were crackling in fire. When a blacksmith
plunges a great axe or adze in frigid water
with a loud hissing sound, to temper it   520
and make the iron strong—that's how his eye
sizzled around the stake of olive wood.
His horrific screams echoed through the rock.
We drew back, terrified. He yanked the stake
out of his eye—it was all smeared with blood—
hurled it away from him, and waved his arms.
He started yelling out to near-by Cyclopes,
who lived in caves up on the windy heights,
his neighbours. They heard him shouting out
and came crowding round from all directions.   530
Standing at the cave mouth, they questioned him,
asking what was wrong:

'Polyphemus,
what's so bad with you that you keep shouting
through the immortal night and wake us up?
Is some mortal human driving off your flocks
or killing you by treachery or force?'

"From the cave mighty Polyphemus roared:

'Nobody is killing me, my friends,
by treachery, not using any force.'

"They answered him—their words had wings:

'Well, then,   540
if nobody is hurting you and you're alone,
it must be sickness given by great Zeus,
one you can't escape. So say your prayers
to our father, lord Poseidon.'

"With these words,
they went away, and my heart was laughing—
my cunning name had pulled off such a trick.
But Cyclops groaned, writhing in agony.
Groping with his hands he picked up the stone,
removed it from the door, and sat down there,
in the opening. He stretched out his arms,   550
attempting to catch anyone who tried
to get out with the sheep. In his heart,
he took me for a fool. But I was thinking
the best thing I could do would be to find
if somehow my crewmen and myself
could escape being killed. I wove many schemes,
all sorts of tricks, the way a man will do
when his own life's at stake—and we were faced
with a murderous peril right beside us.
To my heart the best plan was as follows: 560
In Cyclops' flocks the rams were really fat—
fine, large creatures, with thick fleecy coats
of deep black wool. I picked three at a time

and, keeping quiet, tied them up together,
with twisted willow shoots, part of the mat
on which the lawless monster Polyphemus
used to sleep. The middle ram carried a man.
The two on either side were for protection.
So for every man there were three sheep.
I, too, had my own ram, the finest one   570
in the whole flock by far. I grabbed its back
then swung myself under its fleecy gut,
and lay there, face upwards, with my fingers
clutching its amazing fleece. My heart was firm.
We waited there like that until bright Dawn.

"As soon as rose-fingered early Dawn appeared,
males in the flock trotted off to pasture,
while the females, who had not been milked
and thus whose udders were about to burst,
bleated in their pens. Their master, in great pain,   580
ran his hands across the backs of all his sheep
as they moved past him, but was such a fool,
he didn't notice how my men were tied
underneath their bellies. Of that flock
my ram was the last to move out through the door,
weighed down by its thick fleece and my sly thoughts.
Mighty Polyphemus, as he stroked its back,
spoke to the animal:

                       'My lovely ram,
why are you the last one in the flock
to come out of the cave? Not once before   590
have you ever lagged behind the sheep.
No. You've always been well out in front,
striding off to graze on tender shoots of grass
and be the first to reach the river's stream.
You're the one who longs to get back home,
once evening comes, before the others.
But now you're last of all. You must be sad,
grieving for your master's eye, now blinded
by that evil fellow with his hateful crew.

180

That Nobody destroyed my wits with wine.   600
But, I tell you, he's not yet escaped being killed.
If only you could feel and speak like me—
you'd tell me where he's hiding from my rage.
I'd smash his brains out on the ground in here,
sprinkle them in every corner of this cave,
and then my heart would ease the agonies
this worthless Nobody has brought on me.'

"With these words, he pushed the ram away from him,
out through the door. After the ram had moved
a short distance from the cave and courtyard,   610
first I got out from underneath its gut
and then untied by comrades. We rushed away,
driving off those rich, fat, long-legged sheep,
often turning round to look behind us,
until we reached our ship—a welcome sight
to fellow crewmen—we'd escaped being killed,
although they groaned and wept for those who'd died.
But I would not allow them to lament—
with a scowl I told everyone to stop.
I ordered them to quickly fling on board   620
the many fine-fleeced sheep and then set sail
across the salty sea. They climbed aboard
at once, took their places on the rowing bench,
and, sitting in good order in their rows,
struck the gray sea with their oars. But then,
when I was as far from land as a man's voice
can carry when he shouts. I yelled out
and mocked the Cyclops:

                                    'Cyclops,
    it seems he was no weakling, after all,
    the man whose comrades you so wished to eat,   630
    using brute force in that hollow cave of yours.
    Your evil acts were bound to catch you out,
    you wretch—you didn't even hesitate
    to gorge yourself on guests in your own home.
    Now Zeus and other gods have paid you back.'

"That's what I said. It made his heart more angry.
He snapped off a huge chunk of mountain rock
and hurled it. The stone landed up ahead of us,
just by our ship's dark prow. As the stone sank,
the sea surged under it, waves pushed us back   640
towards the land,[1] and, like a tidal flood,
drove us on shore. I grabbed a long boat hook
and pushed us off, encouraging the crew,
and, with a nod of my head, ordering them
to ply their oars and save us from disaster.
They put their backs into it then and rowed.
But when we'd got some distance out to sea,
about twice as far, I started shouting,
calling the Cyclops, although around me
my comrades cautioned me from every side,   650
trying to calm me down:

                                        'That's reckless.
Why are you trying to irritate that savage?
He just threw a boulder in the sea
and pushed us back on shore. We really thought
he'd killed us there. If he'd heard us speak
or uttering a sound, he'd have hurled down
another jagged rock, and crushed our skulls,
the timbers on this ship, as well. He's strong,
powerful enough to throw this far.'

                                "That's what they said.
But my warrior spirit didn't listen.   660
So, anger in my heart, I yelled again:

'Cyclops, if any mortal human being
asks about the injury that blinded you,
tell them Odysseus destroyed your eye,

---

[1] *ship's dark prow . . . towards the land*: As in many other translations, line 483 in the
Greek (which mentions how the rock just missed the steering oar) has been omitted, on
the ground that if the projectile falls in front of the ship, it is nowhere close to the
steering oar in the stern. The omitted line occurs a few lines later with the description
of the second rock thrown.

182

a sacker of cities, Laertes' son,
a man from Ithaca.'

"When I said this,
he groaned and spoke out in reply:

'Alas!
Now an ancient prophecy about me
has truly been fulfilled! Telemus,
fine, tall son of Eurymus, a seer   670
who surpassed all men in prophecy,
reached old age among the Cyclopes
as a soothsayer. He said all these things
would come to pass someday—I'd lose my sight
at the hand of someone called Odysseus.
But I always expected he'd be large,
a noble man, with enormous power.
But now a puny, good-for-nothing weakling,
after overpowering me with wine,
has destroyed my eye. Come here, Odysseus,   680
so I can give you your gift as my guest,
and urge the famous Shaker of the Earth
to escort you home—I am his son,
and he boasts he's my father. If he wishes,
he himself will cure me. No other blessed god,
nor any mortal man, can do that.'

"He finished speaking. I answered him and said:

'I wish I were as certain I could end your life,
rob you of your living spirit, and send you
off to Hades' home, as I am confident   690
not even the great Shaker of the Earth
will fix your eye.'

"After I'd said this,
he stretched out his hands to starry heaven
and offered this prayer to lord Poseidon:

'Hear me, Poseidon, Enfolder of the Earth,
dark-haired god, if I truly am your son
and if you claim to be my father,
grant that Odysseus, sacker of cities,
a man from Ithaca, Laertes' son,
never gets back home. If it's his destiny   700
to see his friends and reach his native land
and well-built house, may he get back late
and in distress, after all his comrades
have been killed, and in someone else's ship.
And may he find troubles in his house.'

"That's what he prayed. The dark-haired god heard him.
Then Cyclops once again picked up a rock,
a much larger stone, swung it round, and threw it,
using all his unimaginable force.
It landed right behind the dark-prowed ship   710
and almost hit the steering oar. Its fall
convulsed the sea, and waves then pushed us on,
carrying our ship up to the further shore.

"We reached the island where our well-decked ships
were grouped together. Our comrades sat around them,
in great sorrow, always watching for us.
We rowed in, drove our ship up on the sand,
then climbed out through the surf. From the ship's hold
we unloaded Cyclops' flock and shared it out.
I took great care to see that all men there   720
received an equal part. But when the flock
was being divided up, my well-armed comrades
awarded me the ram, my special gift,
one just for me. I sacrificed that ram,
there on the shore, to Zeus, Cronos' son,
lord of the dark cloud, ruler of all,
offering him burnt pieces of the thigh.
But he did not care for my sacrifice.
Instead he started planning to destroy
all my well-decked ships and loyal comrades.   730

"So then, all day long until the sunset,
we sat feasting on the huge supply of meat
and sweet wine, too. When the sun went down
and darkness came, we lay down to rest
and slept there on the shore beside the sea.
As soon as rose-fingered early Dawn appeared,
I roused my shipmates and ordered them aboard
to untie cables fastened to the sterns.
They got in at once, moved to the rowing bench,
and sitting in good order in their rows,   740
they struck the gray sea with their oar blades.
So we sailed away from there, sad at heart,
happy to have avoided being destroyed,
although some dear companions had been killed."

Book Ten
Aeolus, the Laestrygonians, and Circe

[Odysseus continues his narrative: he and his ships reach Aeolia, home of Aeolus, god of the winds; Aeolus welcomes them and gives Odysseus a bag with all the winds tied up inside it; Odysseus sails from Aeolia, but his men open the bag, bringing on a storm which drives them back to Aeolia; Aeolus refuses Odysseus' request for further help and orders him off the island; Odysseus and his men reach the land of the Laestrygonians, who attack them and destroy all the ships except Odysseus' vessel; that one ship sails to the island of Aeaea, land of Circe; Odysseus kills a stag for a meal; half the men go to Circe's house and are changed into pigs; Eurylochus brings the news to Odysseus; Odysseus meets Hermes, who gives him an antidote to Circe's spells; Circe tries to bewitch Odysseus and fails; they go to bed together; Circe changes the men back to human beings; they stay there one year, and then sail on, heading for Hades' home.]

"Next we reached Aeolia, a floating island,
where Aeolus lived, son of Hippotas,
whom immortal gods hold dear.[1] Around it,
runs an impenetrable wall of bronze,
and cliffs rise up in a sheer face of rock.
His twelve children live there in the palace,
six daughters as well as six full-grown sons.
He gave the daughters to the sons in marriage,
and they are always at a banquet feasting,
beside their dear father and good mother,   10
with an infinite supply of tasty food
set out before them. The smells of cooking
fill the house all day. The courtyard echoes
to the sounds of celebration. At night,
they go to sleep beside their faithful wives,
on coverlets and beds well strung with cord.

"We reached the splendid palace in the city,
and for one whole month he entertained me,
always asking questions about everything—

---

[1] *Aeolia:* This next stop on Odysseus' journey is a small island to the north of Sicily.

Troy, Argive ships, how Achaeans made it home—
and I told him all from start to finish.
When, for my part, I asked to take my leave
and told him he should send me on my way,
he denied me nothing and helped me go.
He gave me a bag made out of ox-hide,
flayed from a creature nine years old,
and tied up in it all the winds that blow
from every quarter, for Cronos' son
has made Aeolus keeper of the winds,
and he could calm or rouse them, as he wished. 30
With a shining silver cord he lashed that bag
inside my hollow ship, so as to stop
even the smallest breath from getting out.
He also got a West Wind breeze to blow
to carry ships and men on their way home.
But that's not how things happened to turn out—
we ruined everything with our own folly.

"For nine whole days and nights we held our course,
and on the tenth we glimpsed our native land.
We came in so close we could see the men 40
who tend the beacon fires. But then sweet Sleep
came over me—I was too worn out.
All that time my hands had gripped the sail rope—
I'd not let go of it or passed it on
to any shipmate, so that we'd get home
more quickly. But as I slept, my comrades
started talking to each other, claiming
I was taking gold and silver back with me,
gifts of Aeolus, brave son of Hippotas.
Glancing at the man who sat beside him, 50
one of them would say something like this:

'It's not fair. Everyone adores this man
and honours him, no matter where he goes,
to any city, any land. From Troy
he's taking a huge stash of glorious loot—
but those of us who've been on the same trip

187

are coming home with empty hands. And now,
Aelous, because he's a friend of his,
has freely given him these presents.
Come on, let's see how much gold and silver   60
he has in his bag.'

                    "As they talked like this,
my companions' greedy thoughts prevailed.
They untied the bag. All the winds rushed out—
storms winds seized them, swept them out to sea,
in tears, away from their own native land.
At that point I woke up. Deep in my heart
I was of two minds—I could jump overboard
and drown at sea or just keep going in silence,
remain among the living. I stayed there
and suffered on. Covering up my head,   70
I lay down on the deck, while our ships,
loaded with my whimpering companions,
were driven by those wicked blasts of wind
all the way back to Aeolus' island.

"We went ashore there and brought back water.
My crew had a quick meal beside the ships.
After we'd had something to eat and drink,
I set off for Aeolus' splendid palace,
taking with me one comrade and a herald.
I found him feasting with his wife and children.   80
So we went into the house and sat down
on the threshold, right beside the door posts.
In their hearts they were amazed. They asked me

        'Odysseus, how is it you've come back here?
        What cruel god has been attacking you?
        We took great care to send you on your way
        so you'd get home, back to your native land
        or any other place, just as you wished.'

"That's what they asked. With a heavy heart,
I answered them:

'My foolish comrades,
aided by malicious Sleep, have injured me.
But, my friends, you can repair all this—
that's in your power.'

                    "I said these words
to reassure them. But they stayed silent.
Then their father gave me this reply:

'Of all living men, you are the worst—
so you must leave this island with all speed.
It would violate all sense of what is right
if I assisted or escorted on his way
a man the blessed gods must hate. So leave.   100
You're here because deathless gods despise you.'

"Once he'd said this, he sent me from his house,
for all my heavy groans. Then, sick at heart,
we sailed on further, my crewmen's spirits
worn down by the weary work of rowing.
Because we'd been such fools, there was no breeze
to help us on our way. We went on like this
for six whole days and nights. On the seventh
we came to Telepylus, great citadel
of Lamus, king of Laestrygonians,   110
where the herdsman driving in his flock
salutes the herdsman moving his beasts out.[1]
There a man who had no need of sleep
could earn two wages—one for tending cattle,
one for grazing sheep. Day and night-time trails
lie close together. We came up there,
into a lovely harbour, with a sheer cliff
around it on both sides. Jutting headlands
facing one another extended out

---

[1] . . . *out early*: The land of the Laestrygonians seems to be north of Sicily, possibly
Corsica. The rather odd lines following have attracted some commentary. It's not clear
why the sheep have to come in at night, just as the cattle are going out to graze. The
detail about the trails seems to suggest that one man could get the double wage because
the roads he would have to use are conveniently near each other.

beyond the harbour mouth, a narrow entrance.   120
All my shipmates brought their curved ships up
and moored them inside the hollow harbour
in a tightly clustered group—in that spot
there were never any waves, large or small.
Everything was calm and bright around them.
But I moored my black ship all by itself
outside the harbour, right against the land,
tying it to the rock. I clambered up the cliff
and stood there, on a rugged outcrop,
looking round. I could see no evidence   130
of human work or ploughing, only smoke
arising from the land. I sent some comrades out
to learn what the inhabitants were like,
the men who ate the food this land produced.
I chose two men, with a third as herald.
They left the ships and came to a smooth road,
which wagons used to haul wood to the town
from high mountain slopes. Outside the city
they met a young girl collecting water,
the noble daughter of Antiphates,   140
a Laestrygonian. She'd come down there
to the fine flowing spring Artacia,
where the townsfolk went to draw their water.
The men walked up and spoke to her. They asked
who ruled the people here and who they were.
She quickly pointed out her father's lofty home.
They reached the splendid house and found his wife,
a gigantic woman, like a mountain peak.
They were appalled. She called her husband,
strong Antiphates, out of a meeting,   150
and he arranged a dreadful death for them—
he seized one of my shipmates and prepared
to make a meal of him. The other two
jumped up, ran off, and came back to the ships.
Antiphates then raised a hue and cry
throughout the city. Once they heard his call,
the powerful Laestrygonians poured out,
thronging in countless numbers from all sides—

not like men at all, but Giants. From the cliffs
they hurled rocks down on us, the largest stones   160
a man can lift. The clamour rising from the ships
was dreadful—men were being destroyed,
ships were smashing into one another,
with those monsters spearing men like fish,
and taking them to eat a gruesome meal.
While they were slaughtering the sailors there,
trapped in the deep harbour, I grabbed my sword,
pulled it from my thigh, and cut the cables
on my dark-prowed ship, yelling to my crew,
ordering them to put their oars to work,   170
so we could get away from this disaster.
They all churned the water with their oar-blades,
terrified of being killed. We were relieved,
as my ship left the beetling cliffs behind,
moving out to sea. But all the other ships,
moored together in the harbour, were destroyed.

"We sailed on from there with heavy hearts,
grieving for dear shipmates we had lost,
though glad we had avoided death ourselves,
until we reached the island of Aeaea,   180
where fair-haired Circe lived, fearful goddess
with a human voice—sister by blood
to bloody minded Aeetes, both children
of sun god Helios, who gives men light.[1]
Perse, child of Oceanus, was their mother.
Here, in silence, we brought our ship to land,
inside a harbour with fine anchorage.
Some god was guiding us. Then we disembarked
and laid up in that spot two days and nights,
our hearts consumed with weariness and pain.   190

"When fair-haired Dawn gave birth to the third day,

---

[1] *Aeaea*: the precise location of this island is a matter of scholarly argument. In this
passage, it would seem to lie close to the land of the Laestrygonians, probably somewhere
to the west or north of Corsica. Later in the *Odyssey* references to the island seem to
place it in a more easterly location.

with my sharp sword and spear I quickly climbed
above the ships up to a vantage point,
to see if I could notice signs of men
or hear their voices. From the rocky lookout
where I stood, I could see smoke rising
from the spacious grounds of Circe's home
through dense brush and trees. Seeing the smoke,
my mind and heart considered going down
to look around. But as I thought about it,   200
the best initial action seemed to be
to get back to our swift ship by the shore,
let my comrades eat, then send them out
to reconnoiter. On my way back there,
in a lonely place close to our curved ship,
some god pitied me and sent across my path
a huge stag with massive antlers, on its way
from pastures in the woods towards the river
for a drink—the sun's heat forced it down.
As it came out, I struck it in the spine,   210
the middle of its back. My bronze-tipped spear
sliced right through—with a groan the stag collapsed
down in the dust, and its spirit left the beast.
Planting my foot, I pulled my bronze spear
out of the wound and left it lying there,
on the ground. I picked up some willow shoots
and wove a rope about six feet in length,
by plaiting them together back and forth,
until they were well twisted. After that,
I tied the huge creature's feet together,   220
and, carrying it across my back, returned
to my black ship. I had to support myself
by leaning on my spear—there was no way
I could just sling a beast as large as that
and hold it on my shoulder with one hand.[1]
I tossed the stag down right before our ship

[1] . . . one hand: The image here suggests (according to Merry, Riddell, and Monro) that
Odysseus stuck his head between the bound legs and body of the deer and carried it like
a packsack, with both his hands on the spear, because the beast was too heavy to carry
in the usual way with one hand.

and cheered up my crew with words of comfort,
standing by each man in turn:

                            'My friends,
    we're not going down to Hades' house just yet,
    Although we're grieving, not until the day   230
    our fate confronts us. So come on now,
    while there's food and drink in our swift ship,
    let's think of eating, so we don't waste away
    and die of hunger.'

                  "That's what I said. My words
soon won them over. Uncovering their heads,
they were amazed at the stag lying there,
such a huge beast beside the restless sea.
Once they'd had their fill of looking at it,
they washed their hands and made a splendid meal.
So all day long until the sun went down   240
we sat feasting on that huge supply of meat
and on sweet wine. When the sun had set
and darkness came, we lay down on the shore.

"As soon as rose-fingered early Dawn appeared,
I called a meeting and addressed them all:

    'Shipmates, though you're all feeling our distress,
    listen now to what I have to tell you.
    My friends, how far east or west we are
    we just don't know, or how far away
    from where the Sun, who brings men light,   250
    goes down underneath the earth or rises.
    But let's quickly put our heads together
    to see if we have any options left.[1]
    I don't think we do. I climbed a rocky crag,
    and from that vantage point spied out the land.

---

[1]Odysseus literally says "we don't know where the darkness is or the dawn or where the sun sets or rises," a claim that seems to mean he's so lost he doesn't know East from West any more. That seems extremely unlikely, especially since the sun has apparently been shining earlier in the story. The general sense is clear enough—they're not sure where they are.

It's an island with deep water round it,
low-lying and flat. I saw with my own eyes
smoke rising in the middle of the island,
through dense brush and trees.'

                  "That's what I said.
But their spirits fell, as they remembered   260
what Laestrygonian Antiphates had done
and the violence of great Polyphemus,
that man-eating Cyclops. They wept aloud,
shedding frequent tears. But their laments
were not much help to us. So I split up
my well-armed comrades in two separate groups,
each with its own leader. I commanded one,
and godlike Eurylochus led the other.
We shook our tokens in a bronze helmet.
When brave Eurylochus' lot fell out,   270
he set off with twenty-two companions,
all in tears, leaving us behind to grieve.
In a forest clearing they found Circe's house—
built of polished stone, with views in all directions.
There were mountain wolves and lions round it,
all bewitched by Circe's wicked potions.
But these beasts made no attack against my men.
No. They stood on their hind legs and fawned,
wagging their long tails. Just as dogs will beg
around their master when he comes from dinner—   280
since he's keeps bringing scraps to please their hearts—
that's how the wolves and sharp-clawed lions there
kept fawning round those men, who were afraid
just looking at those fearful animals.
They stood in fair-haired Circe's gateway
and heard her sweet voice singing in the house,
as she went back and forth before her loom,
weaving a huge, immortal tapestry,
the sort of work which goddesses create,
finely woven, luminous, and beautiful.   290
Then Polites, one of the men's leaders,
the man I trusted most and cherished

more than any of my comrades, spoke:

'My friends, someone's in there moving to and fro,
before a giant tapestry, and singing
so sweetly the floor echoes to her song—
perhaps a goddess, or maybe a woman—
come, let's call out to her right now.'

"He spoke,
and they all started shouting, calling her.
She came out at once, opened the bright doors,   300
and asked them in. In their foolishness,
they all accompanied her. Eurylochus
was the only one who stayed outside—
he thought it could be something of a trick.
She led the others in and sat them down
on stools and chairs, then made them a drink
of cheese and barley meal and yellow honey
stirred into Pramnian wine. But with the food
she mixed a vicious drug, so they would lose
all memories of home. When they'd drunk down   310
the drink she gave them, she took her wand,
struck each man, then penned them in her pigsties.
They had bristles, heads, and voices just like pigs—
their bodies looked like swine—but their minds
were as before, unchanged. In their pens they wept.
In front of them Circe threw down feed,
acorns, beech nuts, cornel fruit, the stuff
pigs eat when they are wallowing in mud.
Eurylochus came back immediately
to our swift black ship, bringing a report   320
of his comrades' bitter fate. But though he tried,
he couldn't say a single word, his heart
felt too much pain. His eyes were full of tears,
his mind transfixed with sorrow. When all of us,
astonished, questioned him, he spoke out,
telling us of his companions' fate:

'Lord Odysseus, we went through the woods,

195

as you had ordered and, in a clearing there,
found a splendid house built of polished stone,
with a view in all directions. Inside,   330
someone was singing in a loud clear voice,
in front of an enormous piece of weaving,
moving back and forth—some god or woman.
They all shouted, calling her. She came out,
opened up her shining doors without delay,
and asked them in. In their foolishness,
they all accompanied her inside. But I,
thinking it might be a trick, remained behind.
Then the whole bunch disappeared, all of them.
No one came out again. And I sat there   340
a long time, watching for them.'

                       "He spoke.
I slung my large bronze silver-studded sword
across my shoulder, grabbed my bow, and told him
to take me back there on the selfsame trail.
He gripped me with both hands, clasped my knees,
moaned, and spoke to me—his words had wings:

'Child raised by Zeus, don't take me there
against my will. Leave me here. I know
you won't be coming back again yourself
or bringing back the rest of your companions.   350
No. Let's get out of here and quickly, too,
with these men here. We may still escape
this day's disasters.'

                    "That's what he said.
But I gave him this answer:

                    'Eurylochus,
you can stay right here, in this very spot,
eating and drinking by our black hollow ship.
But I will go. I don't have any choice.'

"With these words, I went up from the ship and shore.

But while I was moving through the sacred groves
on my way to Circe's home, a goddess   360
skilled in many magic potions, I met
Hermes of the Golden Wand. I was going
toward the house. He looked like a young man
when the first growth of hair is on his lip,
the age when youthful charm is at its height.
He gripped my hand, spoke to me, and said:

'Where are you off to now, you poor man,
going through these hills all by yourself
and knowing nothing of the country here?
Your comrades, over there in Circe's house,   370
are penned up like swine in narrow stalls.
Are you intending now to set them free?
I don't think you'll make it back yourself—
you'll stay there with the rest of them. But come,
I'll keep you free from harm and save you.
Here, take a remedial potion with you,
go in Circe's house. It's a protection
and will clear your head of any dangers
this day brings. Now I'll describe for you
each and every one of Circe's fatal ploys.   380
She'll mix a drink for you and with the food
include a drug. But she won't have power
to cast a spell on you. This fine potion,
which I'll provide you, won't allow it.
I'll tell you now in detail. When Circe
strikes you with her elongated wand,
then draw that sharp sword on your thigh and charge,
just as if you meant to slaughter her.
She'll be afraid. And then she'll order you
to sleep with her. At that point don't refuse   390
to share a goddess' bed, if you want her
to free your crew and entertain you.
But tell her she must swear a solemn oath,
on all the blessed gods, not to make plans
to harm you with some other injury,
so when she's got you with your clothes off,

she won't change you to an unmanned weakling.'

"After saying this, the Killer of Argus
pulled a herb out of the ground, gave it to me,
and explained its features. Its roots were black,   400
the flower milk-white. Moly the gods call it.
It's hard for mortal men to pull it out,
but gods have power to do anything.
Then Hermes left, through the wooded island,
bound for high Olympus. I continued on
to Circe's home. As I kept going, my heart
was turning over many gloomy thoughts.
Once I'd made it over to the gateway
of fair-haired Circe's house, I just stood there
and called out. The goddess heard my voice.   410
She came out at once, opened her bright doors,
and asked me in. So I went in with her,
heart full of misgivings. She led me in
and sat me on a silver-studded chair,
a lovely object, beautifully made,
with a stool underneath to rest my feet.
She mixed her potion in a golden cup
for me to drink. In it she placed the drug,
her heart still bent on mischief. She gave it me,
and, when I'd drunk it, without being bewitched,   420
she struck me with her wand and said these words:

'Off now to your sty, and lie in there
with the rest of your companions.'

"She spoke. But I pulled out the sharp sword on my thigh
and charged at Circe, as if I meant to kill her.
She gave a piercing scream, ducked, ran up,
and clasped my knees. Through her tears she spoke—
her words had wings:

'What sort of man are you?
Where are you from? Where is your city?
Your parents? I'm amazed you drank this drug   430

198

And were not bewitched. No other man
who's swallowed it has been able to resist,
once it's passed the barrier of his teeth.
In that chest of yours your mind holds out
against my spell. You must be Odysseus,
that resourceful man. The Killer of Argus,
Hermes of the Golden Wand, always told me
Odysseus in his swift black ship would come
on his way back from Troy. Come, put that sword
back in its sheath, and let the two of us   440
go up into my bed. When we've made love,
then we can trust each other.'

        "Once she said this,
I answered her and said:

                    'O Circe,
how can you ask me to be kind to you?
In your own home you've changed my crew to pigs
and keep me here. You're plotting mischief now,
inviting me to go up to your room,
into your bed, so when I have no clothes,
you can do me harm, destroy my manhood.
But I won't agree to climb into your bed,   450
unless, goddess, you'll agree to swear
a solemn oath that you'll make no more plans
to injure me with some new mischief.'

"When I'd said this, she made the oath at once,
as I had asked, that she'd not harm me.
Once she'd sworn and finished with the oath,
I went up with Circe to her splendid bed.

"Meanwhile four women serving in her home
were busy in the hall, children of springs,
groves, and sacred rivers flowing to the sea.   460
One of them threw lovely purple coverlets
across the chairs and spread linen underneath.
Another pulled silver tables over to each chair

and then placed silver baskets on them.
The third one mixed deliciously sweet wine
inside a silver bowl, then served it out
in cups of gold. The fourth brought water in,
lit a large fire under a huge cauldron,
and warmed the water up until it boiled
inside the shining bronze. She sat me in a tub,   470
then, diluting water from that cauldron
so it was right for me, gave me a bath,
pouring water on my head and shoulders,
until the weariness that sapped my spirit
had left my limbs. After bathing me,
she rubbed me with rich oil, then dressed me
in a fine cloak and tunic and led me
to a handsome chair embossed with silver,
finely crafted, with a footstool underneath.
A servant brought in a lovely golden jug,   480
poured water out into a silver basin,
so I could wash, and set a polished table
at my side. Then the worthy steward
brought in bread and set it there before me,
placing with it large quantities of food,
given freely from her stores. She bid me eat.
But in my heart I had no appetite.
So I sat there, thinking of other things,
my spirit sensing something ominous.
When Circe noticed me just sitting there,   490
not reaching for the food, weighed down with grief,
she came up close and spoke winged words to me:

> 'Odysseus, why are you sitting here like this,
> like someone who can't speak, eating out your heart,
> never touching food or drink? Do you think
> this is another trick? You don't need to fear—
> I've already made a solemn promise
> I won't injure you.'

                "When she said this,
I answered her and said:

'O Circe,   500
What man with any self-respect would start
to eat and drink before he had released
his shipmates and could see them face to face?
If you are being sincere in asking me
to eat and drink, then set my comrades free,
so my own eyes can see my trusty crew.'

"When I'd said this, Circe went through the hall,
her wand clutched in her hand, and opened up
the pig-sty doors. She drove the herd out.
They looked like full-grown pigs, nine years old,
standing in front of her. She went through them,   510
smearing on each one another potion.
Those bristles brought on by that nasty drug
which they'd received from Circe earlier
fell from their limbs, and they were men again,
more youthful and much taller than before,
more handsome to the eye. Now they knew me.
Each man grabbed my hand, and all of them
were overcome with passionate weeping,
so the house around them echoed strangely.
Circe herself was moved to pity then—   520
standing close to me, the lovely goddess said:

'Son of Laertes, resourceful Odysseus,
born from Zeus, go now to the sea shore,
back to your swift ship, drag it up on land,
and stash your goods and all equipment
in the caves. Then come back here in person,
and bring your loyal companions with you.'

"Her words persuaded my proud heart. I left,
going back to our swift ship beside the sea.
I found my trusty comrades at the ship   530
lamenting miserably, shedding many tears.
Just as on a farm calves frisk around the herd
when cows, having had their fill of grazing,
return back to the yard—they skip ahead,

201

and pens no longer hold them, as they run,
mooing in a crowd around their mothers,
that's how my shipmates, once they saw me,
thronged around, weeping—in their hearts it felt
as if they they'd got back to their native land,
the rugged town of Ithaca itself,   540
where they were born and bred. In their distress
they spoke winged words to me:

      'You're back,
 you favourite of Zeus. We glad of that,
 as if we had returned to Ithaca,
 our native land. But come, tell us
 how the rest of our comrades came to grief.'

"They spoke. I replied and calmed them down:

 'First of all, let's drag the ship onshore,
 stow all our goods and tackle in the caves.
 Then you can rouse yourselves and come with me, 550
 see your comrades in Circe's sacred home,
 eating and drinking. They have lots of both.'

"The words I spoke quickly brought them round.
Of all my shipmates there, Eurylochus
was the only one to hesitate. He spoke—
his words to them had wings:

      'You wretched creatures,
 where are you going? Are you so in love
 with these disasters you'll go back there,
 to Circe's house, where she'll transform you all
 to pigs or wolves or lions, so we'll be forced 560
 to protect her great house for her? It's like
 what the Cyclops did, when our companions
 went inside his cave with this reckless man,
 Odysseus—thanks to his foolhardiness
 those men were killed.'

                         "Eurylochus finished.
Then my heart considered drawing the long sword
hanging on my sturdy thigh and striking him,
slicing off his head and knocking it to earth,
even though he was a relative of mine,
closely linked by marriage.[1] But my crewmen,   570
one by one, relaxed me with their soothing words:

    'Child of Zeus, if you give the order,
    we'll leave him behind. He can stay here,
    beside the ship, and stand guard over it,
    while you lead us to Circe's sacred home.'

"This said, they moved up from the ships and shore.
And Eurylochus was not left behind
at the hollow ship. He came along as well,
afraid I might reprimand him harshly.

"Meanwhile, Circe had been acting kindly   580
to the rest of my companions in her home.
She'd given them baths, rubbed them with rich oil,
and dressed them in warm cloaks and tunics.
We found them all quite cheerful, eating
in the hall. When my men saw each other
and recognized their shipmates face to face,
their crying and moaning echoed through the house.
The lovely goddess came to me and said:

    'Resourceful Odysseus, Laertes' son
    and Zeus' child, you should no longer rouse   590
    an outburst of such grief. I know myself
    every pain you've suffered on the fish-filled seas,
    every wrong that hostile men have done on land.
    But come now, eat my food, and drink my wine,
    until you've got back that spirit in your chest
    you had when you first left your native land
    of rugged Ithaca. You're exhausted now—
    you have no spirit—you're always brooding

[1] ... *linked by marriage.* According to some stories Eurylochus was married to Odysseus' sister.

on your painful wanderings. There's no joy
inside your hearts—you've been through so much.' 600

"Our proud hearts were persuaded by her words.
We stayed there, day by day, for one whole year,
feasting on sweet wine and large supplies of meat.
But as the months and seasons came and went,
long spring days returned. A year had passed.
My trusty comrades summoned me and said:

'You god-driven man, now the time has come
to think about your native land once more,
if you are fated to be saved and reach
your high-roofed home and your own country.' 610

"My proud heart was persuaded by their words.
So all day long until the sun went down,
we sat there, feasting on huge amounts of meat
and on sweet wine. Once the sun had set
and darkness came, they lay down to sleep
in the shadowy hall. I went to Circe,
in her splendid bed, and clasped her knees.
The goddess listened to me as I begged,
speaking these winged words to her:

'Circe, grant me the promise which you made 620
to send me home. My spirit's keen to leave,
as are the hearts in my companions, too,
who, as they grieve around me, drain my heart,
whenever you are not among us.'

"I spoke. The lovely goddess answered me at once.

'Resourceful Odysseus, Laertes' son
and Zeus' child, if it's against your will,
you should not now remain here in my house.
But first you must complete another journey—
to the home of Hades and dread Persephone. 630
Consult the shade of that Theban prophet,

204

blind Teiresias. His mind is unimpaired.
Even though he's dead, Persephone
has granted him the power to understand—
the others flit about, mere shadows.'

"As Circe finished, my spirit was breaking.
I sat weeping on her bed, for my heart
no longer wished to live or glimpse the daylight.
But when I'd had enough of shedding tears
and rolling in distress, I answered her: 640

'Circe, who'll be the guide on such a journey?
No one ever sailed a black ship down to Hades.'

"The lovely goddess gave me a quick answer:

'Resourceful Odysseus, Laertes' son
and Zeus' child, don't concern yourself
about a pilot for your ship. Raise the mast,
spread your white sail, and just take your seat.
Then the breath of North Wind Boreas
will take you on your way. But once your ship
crosses flowing Oceanus,[1] drag it ashore   650
at Persephone's groves, on the level beach
where tall poplars grow, willows shed their fruit,
right beside deep swirling Oceanus.
Then you must go to Hades' murky home.
There Periphlegethon and Cocytus,
a stream which branches off the river Styx,
flow into Acheron. There's a boulder
where these two foaming rivers meet. Go there,
heroic man, and follow my instructions—
move close and dig a hole there two feet square.[2]   660
Pour libations to the dead around it,

[1] . . . *flowing Oceanus*. Oceanus or Ocean is a river which in Homeric geography
surrounds the lands and the sea—it is, as it were, the outer rim of the world
(which is flat). It is not the same as the sea, although one can reach it by sailing
across the sea.

[2] . . . *two feet square*. The Greek reads "as great as the length of a *pugon* [the
distance from the elbow to the first finger joints] here and there," about two feet.

first with milk and honey, next sweet wine,
and then a third with water. And shake out
white barley meal. Then pray there in earnest
to many powerless heads of those who've died,
with a vow that, when you reach Ithaca,
at home, you'll sacrifice a barren heifer,
the best you have, and will cram the altar
with fine gifts, and that you'll make an offering
to Teiresias, a black ram just for him,   670
the finest creature in your flocks. And then,
when you've offered prayers of supplication
to celebrated nations of the dead,
you must sacrifice a ram and a black ewe,
twisting their heads down toward Erebus,
while you turn to face the flowing rivers,
looking backwards.[1] At that point many spirits
will emerge—they're the shadows of the dead.
Then call your crew. Tell them to flay and burn
the sheep lying there, killed by pitiless bronze.   680
Pray to the gods, to powerful Hades
and dread Persephone. Then from your thigh,
you must yourself draw that sharp sword out,
and, sitting there, prevent the powerless heads
of those who've died from coming near the blood,
until you've listened to Teiresias.
That prophet, the leader of his people,
will soon come to you. He'll tell you your course,
the distance you must go on your return,
and how to sail across the fish-filled seas.'   690

"Circe finished. Dawn soon came on her golden throne.
The nymph then dressed me in a cloak and tunic
and clothed her body in a long white robe,
a lovely, finely woven garment, and tied
a splendid golden belt around her waist.
On her head she placed a veil. Then I went

---

[1] ... *looking backwards*: Erebus is the deepest pit of Hades. Odysseus is, one assumes, not
to watch while the gods of the underworld sample the blood of the sacrificial animals in
the pit.

through her house, rousing my companions,
going up to each man and reassuring him:

'No more sleeping now, no sweet slumbering.
Let's go. Queen Circe's told me what to do.'   700

"That what I said. And their proud hearts agreed.
But I could not lead my men off safely,
not even from that place. Of all of them
the youngest was Elpenor, in battle
not all that brave or clever. He'd lain down
in Circe's sacred home some distance off,
away from his companions. Heavy with wine,
he'd climbed onto the roof, seeking cooler air.
When he heard the noise and the commotion
made by his shipmates as they moved around,   710
he jumped up on the spot, but then forgot
to use the long ladder to come down again.
He fell headfirst from the roof, snapped his neck,
and broke his spine. His spirit went to Hades.
As my men came out, I spoke to them and said:

'No doubt you now believe you're going home,
back to your dear native land. But Circe
has stated we must take a different route,
to Hades' home and dread Persephone,
to meet the shade of Teiresias from Thebes.'   720

"That's what I said, and it broke their spirits.
Sitting down right where they were, they wept,
they tore their hair. But their laments were useless.
We moved down to our swift ship by the shore,
shedding many tears of grief. Meanwhile Circe
went out and tied a ram and a black ewe
by our black ship. She'd slipped past us with ease,
for who can see a god going back and forth,
if she has no desire to be observed?"

207

Book Eleven
Odysseus Meets the Shades of the Dead

[Odysseus continues his narrative: Odysseus and his men sail to Oceanus, land there, and make a sacrifice; the shades of the dead come up out of the hole; Elpenor's shade appears first and asks for burial; then Odysseus' mother appears; Odysseus has a conversation with Teiresias, who prophesies his future and his death; Odysseus talks with his mother, who gives him news of his family; a series of female shades appears: Tyro, Antiope, Alcmene, Megara, Jocasta, Chloris, Leda, Iphimedea, Phaedra, Procis, Ariadne, Maera, Clymene, and Eriphyle; Odysseus interrupts his narrative to discuss his leaving Phaeacia with Alcinous; Odysseus resumes his story and tells of his encounters with Agamemnon, Achilles, and Ajax; Odysseus describes Minos and Orion and the punishments of Tityus, Tantalus, and Sisyphus; the final shade to appear and speak to Odysseus is the image of Hercules; Odysseus and his men return to the ship and sail away from Oceanus.]

"When we reached our boat down on the beach,
we dragged it out into the glittering sea,
set up the mast and sail in our black ship,
led on the sheep, and then embarked ourselves,
still full of sorrow, shedding many tears.
But that fearful goddess with a human voice,
fair-haired Circe, sent us a welcome breeze,
blowing from behind our dark-prowed ship—
it filled the sail, an excellent companion.
Once we'd checked the gear all through the ship,   10
we just sat—wind and helmsman held the course.
All day long, the sail stayed full, and we sped on
across the sea, until the sun went down
and all sea routes grew dark. Our ship then reached
the boundaries of deep-flowing Oceanus,
where Cimmerians have their lands and city,
a region always wrapped in mist and cloud.
Bright Helios never gazes down on them,
not when he rises into starry heaven,
or when he turns again from heaven to earth.   20

Fearful Night envelops wretched mortals.
We sailed in there, dragged our ship on land,
and walked along the stream of Oceanus,
until we reached the place Circe described.

"Perimedes and Eurylochus held the sheep,
our sacrificial victims, while I unsheathed
the sharp sword on my thigh and dug a hole,
two feet each way. I poured out libations
to all the dead—first with milk and honey,
then sweet wine, and then a third with water.   30
Around the pit I sprinkled barley meal.
Then to the powerless heads of the departed
I offered many prayers, with promises
I'd sacrifice, once I returned to Ithaca,
a barren heifer in my home, the best I had,
and load the altar with fine gifts, as well.
To Teiresias in a separate sacrifice
I'd offer up a ram, for him alone,
the finest in my flocks. With prayers and vows
I called upon the families of the dead.   40
Next I held the sheep above the hole
and slit their throats. Dark blood flowed down.

"Then out of Erebus came swarming up
shades of the dead—brides, young unmarried men,
old ones worn out with toil, young tender girls,
with hearts still new to sorrow, and many men
wounded by bronze spears, who'd died in war,
still in their blood-stained armour. Crowds of them
came thronging in from all sides of the pit,
with amazing cries. Pale fear took hold of me.   50
Then I called my comrades, ordering them
to flay and burn the sheep still lying there,
slain by cruel bronze, and pray to the gods,
to mighty Hades and dread Persephone.
And then I drew the sharp sword on my thigh
and sat there, stopping the powerless heads
of all the dead from getting near the blood,

until I'd asked Teiresias my questions.

"The first shade to appear out of the pit
was my companion Elpenor, whose corpse   60
had not been buried in the broad-tracked earth.
We'd left his body back in Circe's house,
without lament or burial—at the time
another need was driving us away.
When I saw him, I wept. My heart felt pity.
So I spoke to him—my words had wings:

    'Elpenor, how did you come to this place,
    this gloomy darkness? You got here on foot
    faster than I did, sailing my black ship.'

"I spoke. He groaned and gave me his reply: 70

    'Resourceful Odysseus, Laertes' son,
    And child of Zeus, some fatal deity
    has brought me down—that and too much wine.
    In Circe's house, after I'd been sleeping,
    I didn't think of using the long ladder
    to get back again. So I fell head first
    down from the roof. My neck was broken,
    shattering the spine. My shade departed,
    going down to Hades' house. I beg you now,
    in the name of those we left behind,   80
    the ones who are not with us, of your wife,
    your father, who reared you as a child,
    and Telemachus, whom you left at home,
    your only son. I know that your fine ship,
    once you leave here and sail from Hades' home,
    will once more reach the island of Aeaea,
    where, my lord, I ask you to remember me.
    When you sail from there, don't leave me behind,
    unburied, unlamented. Don't turn away,
    or I may bring gods' anger down on you.   90
    Burn me with all the armour I possess.
    Raise a mound for me by the gray sea shore,

memorial to an unfortunate man,
for those in times to come. Do this for me.
And on the tomb there fix the oar I used
while I lived and rowed with my companions.'

"He finished. I answered him and said:

'Unhappy man, I'll do this, complete it all.'

"So we two sat in gloomy conversation,
I, on one side, holding out my sword   100
above the blood, and, on the other side,
the shade of my companion speaking out.

"Then appeared the ghost of my dead mother,
Anticleia, brave Autolycus' daughter.
I'd left her still alive when I set off
for sacred Troy. Once I caught sight of her,
I wept, and I felt pity in my heart.
But still, in spite of all my sorrow,
I could not let her get too near the blood,
until I'd asked Teiresias my questions.   110

"Then came the shade of Teiresias from Thebes,
holding a golden staff. He knew who I was
and started speaking:

                        'Resourceful Odysseus,
Laertes' son and Zeus' child, what now,
you unlucky man? Why leave the sunlight,
come to this joyless place, and see the dead?
Move from the pit and pull away your sword,
so I may drink the blood and speak the truth.'

"Teiresias finished talking. I drew back
and thrust my silver-studded sword inside its sheath.   120
When the blameless prophet had drunk dark blood,
he said these words to me:

'Glorious Odysseus,
you ask about your honey-sweet return.
But a god will make your journey bitter.
I don't think you can evade Poseidon,
whose heart is angry at you, full of rage
because you blinded his dear son. But still,
though you'll suffer badly, you may get home,
if you will curb your spirit and your comrades.
As soon as you've escaped the dark blue sea   130
and reached the island of Thrinacia
in your sturdy ship, you'll find grazing there
the cattle and rich flocks of Helios,
who hears and watches over everything.
If you leave them unharmed and keep your mind
on your return, you may reach Ithaca,
though you'll have trouble. But if you touch them,
then I foresee destruction for your crew,
for you, and for your ship. And even if
you yourself escape, you'll get home again   140
in distress and late, in someone else's ship,
after losing every one of your companions.
There'll be trouble in your home—arrogant men
eating up your livelihood and wooing
your godlike wife by giving courtship gifts.
But when you come, you'll surely take revenge
for all their violence. Once you have killed
the suitors in your house with your sharp sword,
by cunning or in public, then take up
a well-made oar and go, until you reach   150
a people who know nothing of the sea,
who don't put salt on any food they eat,
and have no knowledge of ships painted red
or well-made oars that serve those ships as wings.
I'll tell you a sure sign you won't forget—
when someone else runs into you and says
you've got a shovel used for winnowing
on your broad shoulders, then fix that fine oar
in the ground there, and make rich sacrifice
to lord Poseidon with a ram, a bull,   160

212

and a boar that breeds with sows. Then leave.[1]
Go home, and there make sacred offerings
to the immortal gods, who hold wide heaven,
to all of them in order. Your death will come
far from the sea, such a gentle passing,
when you are bowed down with a ripe old age,
and your people prospering around you.[2]
In all these things I'm telling you the truth.'

"He finished speaking. Then I replied and said:

'Teiresias, no doubt the gods themselves   170
have spun the threads of this. But come, tell me—
and speak the truth—I can see there the shade
of my dead mother, sitting near the blood,
in silence. She does not dare confront
the face of her own son or speak to him.
Tell me, my lord, how she may understand
just who I am.'

                    "When I'd finished speaking,
Teiresias quickly gave me his reply:

'I'll tell you so your mind will comprehend.
It's easy. Whichever shadow of the dead   180
you let approach the blood will speak to you
and tell the truth, but those you keep away
will once again withdraw.'

                    "After saying this,
the shade of lord Teiresias returned

---

[1] *Then leave.* These remarks seem to suggest that Odysseus must finally propitiate
Poseidon by going somewhere far inland, where people have never heard of that god and,
in effect, make him known with the oar planted in the ground and a sacrifice. The
winnowing shovel is a device for separating grain from chaff.

[2] *. . . prospering around you.* This prophecy of the death of Odysseus has prompted much
comment, especially the phrase "far from the sea," which some interpreters wish to
emend to "from the sea" (i.e., someone will arrive by boat and bring about Odysseus'
death). It's difficult to reconcile the idea of Odysseus being far from the sea with the
mention of his people (i.e., those in Ithaca) living well all around him, unless, as some
legends have it, he leaves Ithaca and becomes a ruler somewhere else.

to Hades' home, having made his prophecy.
But I stayed there undaunted, till my mother
came and drank dark blood. Then she knew me.
Full of sorrow, she spoke out—her words had wings:

    'My son, how have you come while still alive
    down to this sad darkness? For living men   190
    it's difficult to come and see these things—
    huge rivers, fearful waters, stand between us,
    first and foremost Oceanus, which no man
    can cross on foot. He needs a sturdy ship.
    Have you only now come here from Troy,
    after a long time wandering with your ship
    and your companions? Have you not reached
    Ithaca, nor seen your wife in your own home?'

"Once she'd finished, I answered her:

                        'Mother,
    I had to come down here to Hades' home,   200
    meet the shade of Teiresias of Thebes,
    and hear his prophecy. I have not yet
    come near Achaea's shores or disembarked
    in our own land. I've been wandering around
    in constant misery, ever since I left
    with noble Agamemnon, bound for Troy,
    that city celebrated for its horses,
    to fight against the Trojans. But come now,
    tell me—and make sure you speak the truth—
    What grievous form of death destroyed you?   210
    A lingering disease, or did archer Artemis
    attack and kill you with her gentle arrows?
    And tell me of my father and my son,
    whom I left behind. Do they still possess
    my kingship, or has another man already
    taken it, because they now are saying
    I won't be coming back? Tell me of the wife
    I married. What are her thoughts and plans?
    Is she still there with her son, keeping watch

on everything? Or has she been married   220
to the finest of Achaeans?'

             "When I'd said this,
my honoured mother answered me at once:

    'You can be sure she's waiting in your home,
her heart still faithful. But her nights and days
all end in sorrow, with her shedding tears.
As for your noble kingship rights, no one else
has taken them as yet. Telemachus
controls the land unchallenged and can feast
in banquets with his equals, or at least
those which a man who renders judgment   230
should by rights attend. They all invite him.[1]
As for your father, he stays on his farm
and never travels down into the city.
He has no bed or bedding—no cloaks
or shining coverlets. In wintertime,
he sleeps inside the house beside his slaves,
close to the fire in the dirt, and wears
disgraceful clothes. During the summer months
and in fruitful autumn, he makes his bed
from fallen leaves scattered on the ground   240
here and there along his vineyard slopes.
There he lies in sorrow, nursing in his heart
enormous grief, longing you'll come back.
A harsh old age has overtaken him.
That's how I met my fate and died, as well.
I was not attacked and killed in my own home
by gentle arrows of the keen-eyed archer,
nor did I die of some disease which takes
the spirit from our limbs, as we waste away
in pain. No. It was my longing for you,   250
glorious Odysseus, for your loving care,

---

[1] *. . . all invite him:* The point here is that Telemachus, although young, is still being accorded royal honours in the social life of the palace, as if he is representing the king. Anticleia is not necessarily stating he's actually performing the work of a king. Telemachus' exact age is not known, but he must be in his mid to late teens, since he was a young child when Odysseus left for Troy about thirteen years previously.

that robbed me of my life, so honey sweet.'

"She finished. I considered how in my heart
I wished to hold the shade of my dead mother.
Three times my spirit prompted me to grasp her,
and I jumped ahead. But each time she slipped
out of my arms, like a shadow or a dream.
The pain inside my heart grew even sharper.
Then I spoke to her—my words had wings:

    'Mother, why do you not wait for me?   260
    I'd like to hold you, so that even here,
    in Hades' home, we might throw loving arms
    around each other and then have our fill
    of icy lamentation. Or are you
    just a phantom royal Persephone has sent
    to make me groan and grieve still more?'

"I spoke. My honoured mother quickly said:

    'My child, of all men most unfortunate,
    no, Persephone, daughter of Zeus,
    is not deceiving you. Once mortals die,   270
    this is what's set for them. Their sinews
    no longer hold the flesh and bone together.
    The mighty power of blazing fire
    destroys them, once our spirit flies from us,
    from our white bones. And then it slips away,
    and, like a dream, flutters to and fro.
    But hurry to the light as quickly as you can.
    Remember all these things, so later on
    you can describe the details to your wife.'

"As we talked together, some women came,   280
all wives and daughters of the noblest men,
sent out by queen Persephone. They flocked
by the black blood, throngs of them. I wondered
how I could get to question each of them.
To my heart the best idea seemed to be

to draw the sharp sword by my sturdy thigh
and stop them drinking dark blood all at once.
So they came forward one by one in turn,
and each of them described her lineage,
and I could question every one of them.   290

"There I saw high-born Tyro first of all,
daughter, she said, of noble Samoneus,
and wife of Cretheus, son of Aeolus.
She'd loved the river god Enipeus,
most beautiful by far of all the streams
that flow on earth. She used to stroll along
beside the lovely waters of Enipeus.
But the Encircler and Shaker of the Earth,
taking on the form of Enipeus.
lay with her in the foaming river mouth.   300
A high dark wave rose arching over them,
like a mountain, keeping them concealed,
the mortal woman and the god. Poseidon
removed the virgin's belt and made her sleep.
After he'd finished having sex with her,
the god then held her by the hand and said:

    'Woman, be happy about making love.
    Before the year goes by, you'll be giving birth
    to marvelous children, for a god's embrace
    does not lack power. Take good care of them,   310
    and raise them well. But now you must go home.
    Hold your tongue, and don't tell anyone.
    Know that I am Earthshaker Poseidon.'

"That said, he plunged into the surging sea.
Tyro conceived and then gave birth to sons,
Pelias and Neleus, and they became
two stalwart followers of mighty Zeus.
Pelias lived in spacious Iolcus,
where he owned many flocks, and Neleus
made his home in sandy Pylos. Tyro,   320
queen among women, bore other children

217

to Cretheus—Aeson, Pheres, and Amythaon—
who loved to go to battle in a chariot.

"Then I saw Antiope, daughter of Asopus.
She boasted she'd made love with Zeus himself,
and borne two sons, Zethus and Amphion,
who first established seven-gated Thebes,
constructing walls around it—for all their strength,
they lacked the power to live in spacious Thebes,
unless the place was fortified. After her,   330
I saw Alcmene, Amphitryon's wife,
who had sex with powerful Zeus and bore
that great fighter, lion-hearted Hercules.
And I saw Megara, proud Creon's daughter,
who married that son of Amphitryon,
a man whose fighting spirit never flagged.

"The next I saw was Oedipus' mother,
fair Jocasta, who, against her knowledge,
undertook a monstrous act—she married
her own son. Once he'd killed his father,   340
he made her his wife. And then the gods
showed everyone the truth. But Oedipus,
thanks to the fatal counsels of the gods,
for all his painful suffering, remained king
in lovely Thebes, ruling the Cadmeans.
But she descended down to Hades' home,
the mighty gaoler. She tied a fatal noose
to a roof-beam high above her head and died,
overwhelmed with grief. But she left behind
enormous agonies for Oedipus,   350
all that a mother's Furies can inflict.[1]

"Next I saw lovely Chloris, whom Neleus
married because she was so beautiful,
after he'd given countless courtship gifts.
She was the youngest child of Amphion,

---

[1] . . . *Furies can inflict*: The Furies are the goddesses of blood revenge within the
family.

son of Iasus, once the mighty king
of Minyan Orchomenus. As queen in Pylos,
she bore her husband splendid children—
Nestor, Chromius, noble Periclymenus,
and lovely Pero, a mortal wonder,   360
so much so that all the neighbouring men
sought her hand in marriage. But Neleus
wouldn't give her to anyone except the man
who drove great Iphicles' cattle herd
from Phylace—broad-faced beasts with spiral horns,
and hard to manage. A trusty prophet
was the only one who promised he would try,
but a painful fate determined by the gods
ensnared him—those savage cattle herders
imprisoned him in cruel bondage.[1]   370
But as the days and months went by, bringing
a change in seasons, the new year rolled in,
and mighty Iphicles had him released—
after he'd told them all his prophecies,
and Zeus' will then came to be fulfilled.

"Then I saw Leda, wife of Tyndareus.
She bore Tyndareus two stout-hearted sons,
horse-taming Castor and Polydeuces,
the illustrious boxer. Life-giving earth
has buried them, although they live on still.[2]   380
Even in the world below Zeus honours them.
On every other day they are alive
and then, on alternating days, are dead.
And they have won respect reserved for gods.

"After Leda, I saw Iphimedea,
wife of Aloeus. Poseidon, she said,

<hr>

[1] . . . *trusty prophet.* Later commentators have suggested that this "trusty prophet" may
have been Melampus, who was captured stealing cattle and spent a year in prison. But
he could communicate with animals and heard the worms in the roof of his prison
talking about how the timbers were about to collapse. Melampus passed this information
onto his captor (in this story Iphicles), who was so impressed he released him.

[2] . . . *illustrious boxer.* Leda is also the mother of Helen of Troy and of Clytaemnestra, two
twins with different fathers (Helen's father was Zeus).

had made love to her, and she'd had two sons,
godlike Otus and famed Ephialtes.
Though neither one of them lived very long,
grain-giving Earth had raised them up to be 390
the tallest and handsomest men by far,
after glorious Orion. They stood,
at nine years old, twenty-two feet wide
and fifty-four feet high. But they threatened
to bring the battle din of furious war
against the immortals on Olympus.
They wished to pile mount Ossa on Olympus,
then stack Pelion with its trembling forests
on top of Ossa.[1] Then they could storm heaven.
And if they'd reached their full-grown height as men, 400
they might well have succeeded. But Zeus' son,
the one whom Leto bore, killed both of them,
before the hair below their temples grew
and hid their chins beneath a full-fledged beard.[2]

"I saw Phaedra, Procis, and fair Ariadne,
daughter of Minos, whose mind loved slaughter.
Theseus brought her once away from Crete
to the hill in sacred Athens. But he got
no joy of her. Before he did, Artemis
on sea-girt Dia killed Ariadne, 410
because of something Dionysus said.[3]

"And I saw Maera and Clymene,
and hateful Eriphyle, too, who sold
her dear husband's life for precious gold.
I cannot mention all the woman I saw,
every wife and daughter of those heroes—

[1] ... on top of Ossa: Ossa and Pelion are mountains in Thessaly. This attempt to scale the heights of heaven is part of the famous stories of the war between the giants and the Olympian deities.

[2] ... full-fledged beard: The son referred to is Apollo, child of Zeus and Leto.

[3] ... Dionysus said: In the best-known version of this famous story, Theseus sails off from Crete with Ariadne, who has helped him escape from her father's labyrinth, but then deserts her on an island (Dia or Naxos). She later marries Dionysus. It is not clear here just what Dionysus may have told Artemis to make her want to kill Ariadne.

immortal night would end before I finished.
It's time to sleep, in my swift ship or here.
How I am escorted from this place
is now up to you and to the gods."   420

Odysseus paused. All Phaeacians sat in silence,
saying not a word, spellbound in the shadowy hall.
The first to speak was white-armed Arete, who said:

> "Phaeacians, how does this man seem to you
> for beauty, stature, and within himself,
> a fair, well-balanced mind? He is my guest,
> though each of you shares in this honour, too.
> So don't be quick to send him on his way,
> and don't hold back your gifts to one in need.
> Thanks to favours from the gods, you have   430
> many fine possessions stored away at home."

Then old warrior Echeneus addressed them all—
one of the Phaeacian elders there among them:

> "Friends, what our wise queen has just said to us,
> as we'd expect, is not wide of the mark.
> You must attend to her. But the last word
> and the decision rest with Alcinous."

Once Echeneus finished, Alcinous spoke out:

> "The queen indeed will have the final word,
> as surely as I live and am the king   440
> of the Phaeacians, men who love the oar.
> But though our guest is longing to return,
> let him try to stay until tomorrow.
> By then I'll have completed all our gifts.
> His leaving here is everyone's concern,
> especially mine, since I control this land."

Resourceful Odysseus then replied to him and said:

221

"Lord Alcinous, of all men most renowned,
if you asked me to stay for one whole year,
to organize my escort and give splendid gifts,   450
then I would still agree. It's far better
to get back to one's own dear native land
with more wealth in hand. I'll win more respect,
more love from anyone who looks at me,
whenever I return to Ithaca."

Alcinous then answered him and said:

                              "Odysseus,
when we look at you, we do not perceive
that you're in any way a lying fraud,
like many men the black earth nourishes
and scatters everywhere, who make up lies   460
from things no man has seen. You speak so well,
and you have such a noble heart inside.
You've told your story with a minstrel's skill,
the painful agonies of all the Argives
and your own, as well. Come then, tell me this—
and speak the truth—did you see any comrades,
those godlike men who went with you to Troy
and met their fate there? This night before us
will be lengthy, astonishingly so.
It's not yet time to sleep here in the halls,   470
so tell me of these marvelous events.
I could stay here until bright Dawn arrives,
if you'd agree to tell me in this room
the tale of your misfortunes."

                        Resourceful Odysseus
then answered him and said:

                              "Lord Alcinous,
most renowned among all men, there's a time
for many stories and a time for sleep.
If you are eager to hear even more,
I will not hesitate to speak to you

of other things more pitiful than these.   480
I mean the troubles of those friends of mine
who perished later, who managed to escape
the Trojans frightening battle cries, but died
when they returned, thanks to the deviousness
of a malicious woman.

                "Once sacred Persephone
dispersed those female shadows here and there,
then the grieving shade of Agamemnon,
son of Atreus, appeared. Around him
other shades had gathered, all those who died
and met their fate alongside Agamemnon   490
in Aegisthus' house. He knew me at once.
When he'd drunk some blood, he wept aloud,
shedding many tears, stretching out his hands,
keen to reach me. But he no longer had
any inner power or strength, not like
the force his supple limbs possessed before.
I looked at him and wept. Pity filled my heart.
Then I spoke to him—my words had wings:

    'Lord Agamemnon, son of Atreus,
    king of men, what fatal net of grievous death   500
    destroyed you? Did Poseidon stir the winds
    into a furious storm and strike your ships?
    Or were you killed by enemies on land,
    while you were cutting out their cattle
    or rich flocks of sheep? Or were you fighting
    to seize their city and their women?'

"I paused, and he at once gave me his answer:

    'Resourceful Odysseus, Laertes' son,
    and Zeus' child, Poseidon didn't kill me
    in my ships by rousing savage winds   510
    into a vicious storm. Nor was I killed
    by enemies on land. No. Aegisthus
    brought on my fatal end. He murdered me,

and he was helped by my accursed wife,
after he'd invited me into his home
and prepared a feast for me, like an ox
one butchers in its stall. And so I died
the most pitiful of deaths. Around me
they kept killing the rest of my companions,
like white-tusked pigs at some wedding feast,   520
communal meal, or fine drinking party
in a powerful and rich man's home.
You've encountered dying men before,
many of them, those slain in single combat
or the thick of war. But if you'd seen that,
your heart would've felt great pity. There we were,
lying in the hall among the mixing bowls
and tables crammed with food, the entire floor
awash with blood. The saddest thing I heard
was Cassandra, Priam's daughter, screaming.   530
That traitor Clytaemnestra slaughtered her
right there beside me. Though I was dying,
I raised my arms to strike her with my sword,
but that dog-faced bitch turned her back on me.
Though I was on my way to Hades,
she made no attempt to use her fingers
to close my eyelids or to shut my mouth.[1]
The truth is, there's nothing more disgusting,
more disgraceful, than a woman whose heart
is set on deeds like this—the way she planned   540
the shameless act, to arrange the murder
of the man she'd married. I really thought
I'd be warmly welcomed when I reached home
by my children and my slaves. That woman,
more than anyone, has covered herself
and women born in years to come with shame,
even the ones whose deeds are virtuous.'

"Agamemnon finished. I answered him at once:

---

[1] . . . *shut my mouth*: These actions were made out of respect for the dead on their way to the underworld. The refusal to carry them out shows the greatest disrespect.

'That's horrible. Surely wide-thundering Zeus
for many years has shown a dreadful hate   550
towards the family of Atreus,
thanks to the conniving of some woman.
Many died for Helen's sake, and then
Clytaemnestra organized a trap for you,
while you were somewhere far away.'

                    "I spoke,
and he immediately replied, saying:

'That's why you should never treat them kindly,
not even your own wife. Never tell her
all the things you've determined in your mind.
Tell her some, but keep the rest well hidden.   560
But in your case, Odysseus, death won't come
at your wife's hand, for wise Penelope,
Icarius' daughter, is a virtuous woman,
with an understanding heart. When we left
to go to war, she'd not been married long.
She had a young lad at her breast, a child,
who now, I think, sits down among the men,
happy his dear father will notice him
when he comes back home. Then he'll welcome him
in an appropriate way. But my wife   570
didn't let my eyes feast on my own son.
Before I could do that, she slaughtered me,
her husband. But I'll tell you something else—
keep this firmly in your mind. Bring your ship
back to your dear native land in secret,
without public display. For there's no trust
in women any more. But come, tell me—
and speak the truth—whether you chanced to hear
where my son's living now. He may well be
in Orchomenus or in sandy Pylos,   580
or perhaps in Sparta with Menelaus.
For noble Orestes has not yet died
up there on the earth.'

                              "Once Agamemnon paused,
          I gave him my answer right away:

              'Son of Atreus, why ask me that question?
              I don't know whether he's alive or dead.
              And there's no point in prattling like the wind.'

          "So we two stood there in sad conversation,
          full of sorrow and shedding many tears.
          Then Achilles' shade came up, son of Peleus,   590
          with those of splendid Antilochus
          and Patroclus, too, as well as Ajax,
          who in his looks and body was the best
          of all Danaans, after Achilles,
          who had no equal. Then the shadow
          of the swift-footed son of Aeacus[1]
          knew who I was, and with a cry of grief,
          he spoke to me—his words had wings:

              'Resourceful Odysseus, Laertes' son
              and Zeus' child, what a bold man you are!   600
              What exploit will your heart ever dream up
              to top this one? How can you dare to come
              down into Hades' home, the dwelling place
              for the mindless dead, shades of worn-out men?'

          "Achilles spoke. I answered him at once:

              'Achilles, son of Peleus, mightiest
              by far of the Achaeans, I came here
              because I had to see Teiresias.
              He might tell me a plan for my return
              to rugged Ithaca. I've not yet come near   610
              Achaean land. I've still not disembarked
              in my own country. I'm in constant trouble.
              But as for you, Achilles, there's no man
              in earlier days who was more blest than you,

---

[1] . . . *swift-footed son of Aeacus*: This is a reference to Achilles. Aeacus was a son of
Zeus and father of Peleus, hence Achilles' grandfather.

226

and none will come in future. Before now,
while you were still alive, we Argives
honoured you as we did the gods. And now,
since you've come here, you rule with power
among those who have died. So Achilles,
you have no cause to grieve because you're dead.'   620

"I paused, and he immediately replied:

'Don't try to comfort me about my death,
glorious Odysseus. I'd rather live
working as a wage-labourer for hire
by some other man, one who had no land
and not much in the way of livelihood,
than lord it over all the wasted dead.
But come, tell me of my noble son—
whether he went off to war or not.
Did he became a leader? Talk to me   630
about great Peleus, if there's something
you have heard. Is he still held in honour
among the many Myrmidons? Do men
disparage him in Greece and Phthia
because old age now grips his hands and feet?
I am not there, living in the sunlight,
to help him with the power I once had
in spacious Troy, when I killed their best men
and kept the Argives safe. But if I came
back to my father's house with strength like that,   640
though only for the briefest moment,
those who act with disrespect against him,
denying him honour, would soon come to fear
my force, these overpowering hands of mine.'

"Achilles spoke. I answered him at once:

'To tell the truth, I've heard nothing at all
of worthy Peleus. As for your son,
dear Neoptolemus, I can tell you
the entire truth, just as you requested.

227

I myself brought him in my fine ship   650
from Scyros, to join well-armed Achaeans.
And when we discussed our strategies
around the Trojans' city, I tell you,
he was always first to state his own ideas,
and when he talked, he never missed the mark.
The only ones superior to him
were godlike Nestor and myself. And then,
on the Trojan plain when we Achaeans fought,
he never stayed back in the crowds of men
with ranks of soldiers. No. He ran ahead,   660
far out in front. No man's strength matched his.
In fearful battles he killed many men.
I can't give you the names of all of them,
those he slew while fighting for the Argives.
But his sword cut down the son of Telephus,
brave Eurypylus. What a man he was!
Many of his comrades, the Ceteians,
were also slaughtered there around him
because a certain woman wanted gifts.[1]
He was the finest looking man I saw   670
after noble Memnon. And then, when we,
the noblest Argives, were climbing in
the wooden horse crafted by Epeius,
with me in overall command, telling men
to open up or close our well-built trap,
many other Danaan counselors
and leaders, too, were brushing tears aside,
and each man's legs were trembling—even then
my eyes never saw his fair skin grow pale
or watched him wipe his cheeks to clear off tears.   680
He begged me many times to let him loose,
to leave the horse, and he kept reaching for
his sword hilt and his spear of heavy bronze.
That's how keen he was to kill the Trojans.
Once we'd ravaged Priam's lofty city,
he took his share of loot and a fine prize,

---

[1] . . . *certain woman wanted gifts.* Eurypylus was sent to fight for the Trojans by his
mother Astyoche, because her brother Priam promised to give her a golden vine.

when he went to his ship. He was unhurt—
no blows from sharp bronze spears or other wounds
from fighting hand-to-hand, the sort one gets
so frequently in battle. For Ares,   690
when he's angry, does not discriminate.'

"I spoke. Then the shade of swift Achilles
moved off with massive strides through meadows
filled with asphodel, rejoicing that I'd said
his son was such a celebrated man.

"The other shadows of the dead and gone
stood there in sorrow, all asking questions
about the ones they loved. The only one
who stood apart was the shade of Ajax,
son of Telamon, still full of anger   700
for my victory, when I'd bested him
beside our ships, in that competition
for Achilles' arms. His honoured mother
had offered them as prizes. The judges
were sons of Troy and Pallas Athena.[1]
How I wish I'd never won that contest!
Those weapons were the cause earth swallowed up
the life of Ajax, such a splendid man,
who, in his looks and actions, was the best
of all Danaans after the noble son   710
of Peleus. I called to him—my words
were meant to reassure him:

                                                    'Ajax,
    worthy son of Telamon, can't you forget,
    even when you're dead, your anger at me
    over those destructive weapons? The gods
    made them a curse against the Argives,
    when they lost you, such a tower of strength.
    Now you've been killed, Achaeans mourn your death

---

[1] . . . *Troy and Pallas Athena*: When Achilles died there was a contest for his famous
weapons. The two main claimants were Odysseus and the Greater Ajax. When Odysseus
was awarded the weapons by the judges, Ajax went berserk and later killed himself.

unceasingly, just as they do Achilles,
son of Peleus. No one is to blame   720
but Zeus, who in his terrifying rage
against the army of Danaan spearmen
brought on your death. Come over here, my lord,
so you can hear me as I talk to you.
Let your proud heart and anger now relent.'

"I finished. He did not reply, but left,
moving off toward Erebus, to join
the other shadows of the dead and gone.
For all his anger, he would have talked to me,
or I to him, but in my chest and heart   730
I wished to see more shades of those who'd died.

"Next I saw Minos, glorious son of Zeus,
sitting there, holding a golden sceptre
and passing judgments on the dead, who stood
and sat around the king, seeking justice,
throughout the spacious gates of Hades' home.

"After him I noticed huge Orion
rounding up across a field of asphodel
wild creatures he himself had hunted down
in isolated mountains. In his hand,   740
he clutched his still unbreakable bronze club.

"And I saw Tityus, son of glorious Earth,
lying on the ground. His body covered
nine acres and more.[1] Two vultures sat there,
one on either side, ripping his liver,
their beaks jabbing deep inside his guts.
His hands could not fend them off his body.
He'd assaulted Leto, Zeus' lovely wife
as she was passing through Panopeus,
with its fine dancing grounds, towards Pytho.   750

---

[1] . . . *nine acres and more*: Tityus was a giant son of Zeus (or of Uranus). Hera persuaded
Tityus to attack Leto, whose children, Apollo and Artemis, came to her help and killed
him. The measurement describing his size is unclear.

"Then I saw Tantalus in agony,
standing in a pool of water so deep
it almost reached his chin. He looked as if
he had a thirst but couldn't take a drink.
Whenever that old man bent down, so keen
to drink, the water there was swallowed up
and vanished. You could see black earth appear
around his feet. A god dried up the place.
Some high and leafy trees above his head
were in full bloom—pears and pomegranates,   760
apple trees—all with gleaming fruit—sweet figs
and luscious olives. Each time the old man
stretched out his arms to reach for them,
a wind would raise them to the shadowy clouds.[1]

"And then, in his painful torment, I saw
Sisyphus striving with both hands to raise
a massive rock. He'd brace his arms and feet,
then strain to push it uphill to the top.
But just as he was going to get that stone
across the crest, its overpowering weight   770
would make it change direction. The cruel rock
would roll back down again onto the plain.
Then he'd strain once more to push it up the slope.
His limbs dripped sweat, and dust rose from his head.[2]

"And then I noticed mighty Hercules,
or at least his image, for he himself
was with immortal gods, enjoying their feasts.[3]
Hebe with the lovely ankles is his wife,
daughter of great Zeus and Hera, goddess

---

[1] . . . to the shadowy clouds. Tantalus was a son of Zeus. His punishment comes from
some action he committed against the gods (stealing the gods' food or murdering his son
Pelops and serving him to the gods for dinner).

[2] . . . rose from his head. Sisyphus gave away the secrets of the gods and once tricked the
god of death, so that the dead could not reach the underworld.

[3] . . . enjoying their feasts. Hercules, a mortal, had the rare distinction of being admitted
to heaven. Hence, Odysseus meets an "image" of Hercules. His later mention of serving
an inferior man is a reference to the Labours of Hercules, work he had to carry out for
king Eurystheus over a twelve-year period.

of the golden sandals. Around him there
the dead were making noises, like birds
fluttering to and fro quite terrified.
And like dark night, he was glaring round him,
his unsheathed bow in hand, with an arrow
on the string, as if prepared to shoot.
The strap across his chest was frightening,
a golden belt inlaid with images—
amazing things—bears, wild boars, and lions
with glittering eyes, battles, fights, and murders,
men being killed. I hope whoever made it,   790
the one whose skill conceived that belt's design,
never made or ever makes another.
His eyes saw me and knew just who I was.
With a mournful tone he spoke to me—
his words had wings:

                              'Resourceful Odysseus,
        son of Laertes and a child of Zeus,
        are you now bearing an unhappy fate
        below the sunlight, as I, too, did once?
        I was a son of Zeus, child of Cronos,
        and yet I had to bear countless troubles,   800
        forced to carry out labours for a man
        vastly inferior to me, someone
        who kept assigning me the harshest tasks.
        Once he sent me here to bring away
        Hades' hound. There was no other challenge
        he could dream up more difficult for me
        than that one. But I carried the dog off
        and brought him back from Hades with my guides,
        Hermes and gleaming-eyed Athena.'

"With these words he returned to Hades' home.   810
But I stayed at that place a while, in case
one of those heroic men who perished
in days gone by might come. I might have seen
still more men from former times, the ones
I wished to see—Theseus and Perithous,

great children of the gods. Before I could,
a thousand tribes of those who'd died appeared,
with an astounding noise. Pale fear gripped me—
holy Persephone might send at me
a horrific monster, the Gorgon's head.[1]   820
I quickly made my way back to the ship,
told my crew to get themselves on board,
and loosen off the cables at the stern.
They went aboard at once and took their seats
along each rowing bench. A rising swell
carried our ship down Oceanus' stream.
We rowed at first, but then a fair wind blew.

[1] ... *the Gorgon's head:* The Gorgons were three terrifying sisters (the most famous being
Medusa, the only one who was not immortal, whose head, even when cut off, could turn
men to stone).

Book Twelve
The Sirens, Scylla and Charybdis,
the Cattle of the Sun

[Odysseus continues his story in Phaeacia: the ship sails from Oceanus back to Circe's island where they bury Elpenor; Circe advises Odysseus about future adventures; Odysseus and his crew leave Circe and sail past the Sirens; then they encounter Scylla and Charybdis and lose six men; the ship then sails on to Thrinacia, where the herds and flocks of Helios graze; Odysseus' men swear not to touch the animals; winds keep them on the island; desperate with hunger the crewmen round up some of the animals and kill them; they leave the island, and Zeus sends on a storm as punishment; the boat is destroyed and all of Odysseus' shipmates drown; Odysseus drifts back on a temporary raft to Charybdis, but manages to escape; he reaches Calypso's island; the tale of his past adventures concludes.]

"Our ship sailed on, away from Ocean's stream,
across the great wide sea, and reached Aeaea,
the island home and dancing grounds of Dawn.[1]
We sailed in, hauled our ship up on the beach,
then walked along the shore beside the sea.
There, waiting for bright Dawn, we fell asleep.

"As soon as rose-fingered early Dawn appeared,
I sent my comrades off to Circe's house
to fetch the body of the dead Elpenor.
Then, after quickly cutting down brush wood,   10
we buried him where the land extended
furthest out to sea. Overcome with grief,
we shed many tears. After we had burned
the dead man's corpse and armour, we piled up
a mound, raised a pillar, then planted there,
above the mound, his finely fashioned oar.

---

[1] *. . . grounds of Dawn.* This return to Aeaea, Circe's island, has puzzled commentators, because the description of it here seems to place in a very different location than earlier (in the east rather than in the north west).

"While we were occupied with all these tasks,
Circe was well aware of our return
from Hades' home. Dressed in her finery,
she quickly came to us. With her she brought   20
servants carrying bread, plenty of meat,
and bright red wine. Then the lovely goddess
stood in our midst and spoke to us:

                              'You reckless men,
    you've gone to Hades' home while still alive,
    to meet death twice, when other men die once.
    But come, eat this food and drink this wine.
    Take all day. As soon as Dawn arrives,
    you'll sail. I'll show you your course and tell you
    each sign to look for, so you'll not suffer,
    or, thanks to vicious plans of sea and land,   30
    endure great pain.'

                              "Circe finished speaking.
And our proud hearts agreed with what she'd said.
So all that day until the sun went down
we sat there eating rich supplies of meat
and drinking down sweet wine. The sun then set,
and darkness came. So we lay down and slept
beside stern cables of our ship. But Circe
took me by the hand and led me off,
some distance from the crew. She made me sit,
while she lay there on the ground beside me.   40
I told her every detail of our trip,
describing all of it from start to finish.
Then queen Circe spoke to me and said:

    'All these things have thus come to an end.
    But you must listen now to what I say—
    a god himself will be reminding you.
    First of all, you'll run into the Sirens.
    They seduce all men who come across them.
    Whoever unwittingly goes past them
    and hears the Sirens' call never gets back.   50

His wife and infant children in his home
will never stand beside him full of joy.
No. Instead, the Sirens' clear-toned song
will captivate his heart. They'll be sitting
in a meadow, surrounded by a pile,
a massive heap, of rotting human bones
encased in shriveled skin. Row on past them.
Roll some sweet wax in your hand and stuff it
in your companions' ears, so none of them
can listen. But if you're keen to hear them,   60
make your crew tie you down in your swift ship.
Stand there with hands and feet lashed to the mast.
They must attach the rope ends there as well.
Then you can hear both Sirens as they sing.
You'll enjoy their song. If you start to beg
your men, or order them, to let you go,
make sure they lash you there with still more rope.
When your crew has rowed on past the Sirens,
I cannot tell you which alternative
to follow on your route—for you yourself   70
will have to trust your heart. But I'll tell you
the options. One has overhanging rocks,
on which dark-eyed Amphitrite's great waves
smash with a roar. These cliffs the blessed gods
have called the Planctae. No birds pass through there,
not even timid doves who bring ambrosia
to father Zeus. The sheer rock precipice
snatches even these away. And then Zeus
sends out another to maintain their count.
No human ship has ever reached this place   80
and got away. Instead, waves from the sea
and deadly blasts of fire carry away
a whirling mass of timbers from the boat
and human bodies. Only one ocean ship,
most famous of them all, has made it through,
the Argo, sailing on her way from Aeetes,[1]

---

[1] . . . *from Aeetes.* The Argo, a ship named after its builder Argus, carried Jason and his companions to Colchis on their trip to capture the Golden Fleece and back again. Aeetes was king of Colchis, father of Medea.

and waves would soon have smashed that vessel, too,
against the massive rocks, had not Hera
sent her through. For Jason was her friend.
On the other route there are two cliffs.   90
One has a sharp peak jutting all the way
up to wide heaven. Around that mountain
a dark cloud sits, which never melts away.
No blue sky ever shows around the peak,
not even in summer or at harvest time.
No human being could climb up that rock
and stand on top, not even if he had
twenty hands and feet. The cliff's too smooth,
like polished stone. Half way up the rock face
there's a shadowy cave. It faces west,   100
towards Erebus. You'll steer your ship at it,
illustrious Odysseus. There's no man
powerful enough to shoot an arrow
from a hollow ship and reach that cavern.
In there lives Scylla. She has a dreadful yelp.
It's true her voice sounds like a new-born pup,
but she's a vicious monster. Nobody
would feel good seeing her, nor would a god
who crossed her path. She has a dozen feet,
all deformed, six enormously long necks,   110
with a horrific head on each of them,
and three rows of teeth packed close together,
full of murky death. Her lower body
she keeps out of sight in her hollow cave,
but sticks her heads outside the fearful hole,
and fishes there, scouring around the rock
for dolphins, swordfish, or some bigger prey,
whatever she can seize of all those beasts
moaning Amphitrite keeps nourishing
in numbers past all counting. No sailors   120
can yet boast they and their ship sailed past her
without getting hurt. Each of Scylla's heads
carries off a man, snatching him away
right off the dark-prowed ship. Then, Odysseus,
you'll see the other cliff. It's not so high.

The two are close together. You could shoot
an arrow from one cliff and hit the other.
There's a huge fig tree there with leaves in bloom.
Just below that tree divine Charybdis
sucks black water down. She spews it out   130
three times a day, and then three times a day
she gulps it down—a terrifying sight.
May you never meet her when she swallows!
Nothing can save you from destruction then,
not even Poseidon, Shaker of the Earth.
Make sure your ship stays close to Scylla's rock.
Row past there quickly. It's much better
to mourn for six companions in your ship
than to have them all wiped out together.'

"Circe paused. I answered her directly: 140

    'Goddess, please tell me this, and speak the truth—
is there some way I can get safely through,
past murderous Charybdis, and protect
me and my crew when Scylla moves to strike.'

"I spoke. The lovely goddess then replied:

    'You reckless man, you think you're dealing here
with acts of war or work? Why won't you yield
to the immortal gods? She's not human,
but a destroyer who will never die—
fearful, difficult, and fierce—not someone   150
you can fight. There's no defense against her.
The bravest thing to do is run away.
If you linger by the cliff to arm yourself,
I fear she'll jump out once more, attack you
with all her heads and snatch away six men,
just as before. Row on quickly past her,
as hard as you can go. Send out a call
to Crataiis, her mother, who bore her
to menace human beings. She'll restrain her—
Scylla's heads won't lash out at you again.   160

Next you'll reach the island of Thrinacia,
where Helios' many cattle graze,
his rich flocks, too—seven herds of cattle
and just as many lovely flocks of sheep,
with fifty in each group. They bear no young
and never die. Their herders are divine,
fair-haired nymphs Lampetie and Phaethusa.
Beautiful Neaera gave birth to them
from Helios Hyperion, god of the sun.
Once she'd raised them, their royal mother   170
sent them off to live on Thrinacia,
an island far away, where they could tend
their father's sheep and bent-horned cattle.
Now, if you leave these animals unharmed
and focus on your journey home, I think
you may get back to Ithaca, although
you'll bear misfortunes. But if you harm them,
then I foresee destruction for your ship
and crew. Even if you yourself escape,
you'll get back home in great distress and late,   180
after all your comrades have been killed.'

"Circe finished speaking. When Dawn came up
on her golden throne, the lovely goddess
left to go up island. So I returned
back to the ship and urged my comrades
to get on board and loosen off the stern ropes.
They quickly climbed into the ship, sat down
in proper order at each rowing bench,
and struck the gray sea with their oars. Fair winds
began to blow behind our dark-prowed ship,   190
filling the sail, excellent companions
sent by fair-haired Circe, fearful goddess
who possessed the power of song. We checked out
the rigging on our ship and then sat down.
The wind and helmsman kept us on our course.
Then, with an aching heart, I addressed my crew:

'Friends, it's not right that only one or two

should know the prophecies revealed to me
by the lovely goddess Circe. And so,
I'll tell you all—once we understand them,   200
we may either die or ward off Death and Fate
and then escape. She told me first of all
we should guard against the wondrous voices
of the Sirens in their flowery meadows.
She said I alone should listen to them.
But you must tie me down with cruel bonds,
so I stay where I am and cannot move,
standing upright at the mast. You must fix
the rope at both its ends onto the mast.
If I start ordering you to set me free,   210
you have to tie me down with still more rope.'

"I reviewed these things in every detail,
informing my companions. Our strong ship,
with a fair wind still driving us ahead,
came quickly to the island of the Sirens.
Then the wind died down. Everything was calm,
without a breeze. Some god had stilled the waves.
My comrades stood up, furled the sail, stowed it
in the hollow ship, and then sat at their oars,
churning the water white with polished blades   220
carved out of pine. With my sharp sword I cut
a large round chunk of wax into small bits,
then kneaded them in my strong fingers.
This pressure and the rays of Helios,
lord Hyperion, made the wax grow warm.
Once I'd plugged my comrades' ears with wax,
they tied me hand and foot onto the ship,
so I stood upright hard against the mast.
They lashed the rope ends to the mast as well,
then sat and struck the gray sea with their oars.   230
But when we were about as far away
as a man can shout, moving forward quickly,
our swift ship did not get past the Sirens,
once it came in close, without being noticed.
So they began their clear-toned cry:

240

                      'Odysseus,
you famous man, great glory of Achaeans,
come over here. Let your ship pause awhile,
so you can hear the songs we two will sing.
No man has ever rowed in his black ship
past this island and not listened to us,   240
sweet-voiced melodies sung from our lips.
That brings him joy, and he departs from here
a wiser man, for we two understand
all the things that went on there in Troy,
all Trojan and Achaean suffering,
thanks to what the gods then willed, for we know
everything that happens on this fertile earth.'

"They paused. The voice that reached me was so fine
my heart longed to listen. I told my crew
to set me free, sent them clear signals   250
with my eyebrows. But they fell to the oars
and rowed ahead. Then two of them got up,
Perimedes and Eurylochus, bound me
with more rope and lashed me even tighter.
Once they'd rowed on well beyond the Sirens,
my loyal crewmates quickly pulled out wax
I'd stuffed in each man's ears and loosed my ropes.

"But once we'd left the island far behind,
I saw giant waves and smoke. Then I heard
a crashing roar. The men were terrified.   260
The oars were snatched away, out of their hands,
and banged each other in the swirling sea.
Once they were no longer pulling hard
on their tapered oars, the boat stopped moving.
I went through the ship, cheering up the crew,
standing beside each man and speaking words
of reassurance:

                    'Friends, up to this point,
we've not been strangers to misfortunes.
Surely the bad things now are nothing worse

than when the Cyclops with his savage force   270
kept us his prisoners in his hollow cave.
But even there, thanks to my excellence,
intelligence, and planning, we escaped.
I think someday we'll be remembering
these dangers, too. But come now, all of us
should follow what I say. Stay by your oars,
and keep striking them against the surging sea.
Zeus may somehow let us escape from here
and thus avoid destruction. You, helmsman,
I'm talking, above all, to you, so hold   280
this in your heart—you control the steering
on this hollow ship. Keep us on a course
some distance from the smoke and breaking waves.
Hug the cliff, in case, before you know it,
our ship veers over to the other side,
and you've thrown us all into disaster.'

"I spoke. They quickly followed what I'd said.
I didn't speak a word of Scylla—she was
a threat for which there was no remedy—
in case my comrades, overcome with fear,   290
might stop rowing and huddle together
inside the boat. At that point I forgot
Circe's hard command, when she'd ordered me
not to arm myself. After I'd put on
my splendid armour, I took two long spears
and moved up to the foredeck of the ship,
where, it seemed to me, I could see Scylla
as soon as she appeared up on the rock
and brought disaster down on my companions.
I couldn't catch a glimpse of her at all.   300
My eyes grew weary as I searched for her
all around that misty rock. We sailed on,
up the narrow strait, groaning as we moved.
On one side lay Scylla; on the other one
divine Charybdis terrified us all,
by swallowing salt water from the sea.
When she spewed it out, she seethed and bubbled

uncontrollably, just like a cauldron
on a massive fire, while high above our heads
spray was falling on top of both the cliffs.   310
When she sucked the salt sea water down,
everything in there looked totally confused,
a dreadful roar arose around the rocks,
and underneath the dark and sandy ground
was visible. Pale fear gripped my crewmen.
When we saw Charybdis, we were afraid
we'd be destroyed. Then Scylla snatched away
six of my companions, right from the ship,
the strongest and the bravest men I had.
When I turned to watch the swift ship and crew,   320
already I could see their hands and feet,
as Scylla carried them high overhead.
They cried out and screamed, calling me by name
one final time, their hearts in agony.
Just as an angler on a jutting rock
casts out some bait with his long pole to snare
small fish and lets the horn from some field ox
sink down in the sea, then, when he snags one,
throws it quivering on shore, that's how those men
wriggled as they were raised towards the rocks.[1]   330
Then, in the entrance to her cave, Scylla
devoured the men, who still kept screaming,
stretching out their arms in my direction,
as they met their painful deaths. Of all things
my eyes have witnessed in my journeying
on pathways of the sea, the sight of them
was the most piteous I've ever seen.

"Once we'd made it past those rocks and fled,
escaping Scylla and dread Charybdis,
we reached the lovely island of the god,   340
home of those splendid broad-faced cattle
and numerous rich flocks belonging to
Helios Hyperion, god of the sun.

---

[1] *... toward the rocks*: The horn of the field ox mentioned here is, one assumes, designed
to act as a lead sinker and carry the hook into deeper water.

While I was still at sea in my black ship,
I heard the lowing cattle being penned
and bleating sheep. There fell into my heart
the speeches of Teiresias of Thebes,
the sightless prophet—Circe's words, as well,
on Aeaea. They had both strictly charged
that I should at all costs miss this island,   350
the property of Helios, who brings
such joy to men. So with a heavy heart
I spoke to my companions:

                              'Comrades,
      though you have endured a lot of trouble,
      hear what I have to say, so I can speak
      about the prophecies Teiresias made
      and Circe, too, on Aeaea. They both
      strictly charged me to avoid this island,
      which Helios owns, who gives men such joy.
      Here, she said, we face our gravest danger.   360
      So row our black ship past this island.'

"I paused. The spirit in my crew was shattered.
Then Eurylochus answered me. His words
were full of spite:

                              'You're a hard man,
      Odysseus, with more strength than other men.
      Your limbs are never weary. One would think
      you were composed entirely of iron,
      if you refuse to let your shipmates land,
      when they're worn out with work and lack of sleep.
      Here on this sea-girt island, we could make   370
      a tasty dinner. You tell us instead
      to wander on like this through the swift night.
      But harsh winds which destroy men's ships arise
      out of the night. And how could we avoid
      total disaster, if we chance to meet
      unexpected blasts from stormy South Wind
      or from blustering West Wind, the ones

most likely to completely wreck our ship,
no matter what the ruling gods may wish?
Surely we should let black night persuade us,   380
and now prepare a meal, while we stay put
alongside our swift ship. When morning comes,
we'll go on board, set off on the wide sea.'

"Eurylochus spoke. My other comrades
all agreed. So then I understood too well
some god was planning trouble. I replied—
my words had wings:

                                    'It seems, Eurylochus,
you're forcing me to stand alone. But come,
let all of you now swear this solemn oath—
if by chance we find a herd of cattle   390
or a large flock of sheep, not one of you
will be so overcome with foolishness
that you'll kill a cow or sheep. No. Instead,
you'll be content to eat the food supplies
which goddess Circe gave.'

                                    "Once I'd said this,
they swore, as I had asked, they'd never kill
those animals. When they had made the oath
and finished promising, we moved our ship
inside a hollow harbour, by a spring
whose water tasted sweet. Then my crewmen   400
disembarked and made a skilful dinner.
When everyone had eaten food and drunk
to his heart's ease, they wept as they recalled
those dear companions Scylla snatched away
out of the hollow ship and then devoured.
As they cried there, sweet sleep came over them.

"But when three-quarters of the night had passed
and the stars had shifted their positions,
cloud-gatherer Zeus stirred up a nasty wind
and an amazing storm, which hid in clouds   410

245

both land and sea alike. And from heaven
dark Night rushed down. Once rose-fingered Dawn arrived,
we dragged up our ship and made it secure
inside a hollow cave, a place nymphs used
as a fine dancing and assembly ground.
Then I called a meeting of the men and said:

> 'My friends, in our ship we have meat and drink,
> so let's not touch those cattle, just in case
> that causes trouble for us. For these cows
> and lovely sheep belong to Helios,   420
> a fearful god, who spies out all there is
> and listens in on everything as well.'

"These words of mine won over their proud hearts.
But then, South Wind kept blowing one whole month.
It never stopped. No other wind sprang up,
except those times when East or South Wind blew.
As long as the men had red wine and bread,
they didn't touch the cattle. They were keen
to stay alive. But once what we had stored
inside our ship was gone, they had to roam,   430
scouring around for game and fish and birds,
whatever came to hand. They used bent hooks
to fish, while hunger gnawed their stomachs.
At that point I went inland, up island,
to pray to the gods, hoping one of them
would show me a way home. Once I'd moved
across the island, far from my comrades,
I washed my hands in a protected spot,
a shelter from the wind, and said my prayers
to all the gods who hold Mount Olympus.   440
Then they poured sweet sleep across my eyelids.
Meanwhile Eurylochus began to give
disastrous advice to my companions:

> 'Shipmates, although you're suffering distress,
> hear me out. For wretched human beings
> all forms of death are hateful. But to die

from lack of food, to meet one's fate that way,
is worst of all. So come, let's drive away
the best of Helios' cattle, and then
we'll sacrifice to the immortal gods   450
who hold wide heaven. And if we get home,
make it to Ithaca, our native land,
for Helios Hyperion we'll build
a splendid temple, and inside we'll put
many wealthy offerings. If he's enraged
about his straight-horned cattle and desires
to wreck our ship and other gods agree,
I'd rather lose my life once and for all
choking on a wave than starving to death
on an abandoned island.'

                        "Eurylochus spoke.   460
My other comrades agreed with what he'd said.
They quickly rounded up the finest beasts
from Helios' herd, which was close by,
sleek, broad-faced animals with curving horns
grazing near the dark-prowed ship. My comrades
stood around them, praying to the gods.
They broke off tender leaves from a high oak,
for there was no white barley on the ship.[1]
After their prayers, they cut the creature's throats,
flayed them, and cut out portions of the thighs.   470
These they covered in a double layer of fat
and laid raw meat on top. They had no wine
to pour down on the flaming sacrifice,
so they used some water for libations
and roasted all the entrails in the fire.
Once the thigh parts were completely roasted
and they'd had a taste of inner organs,
they sliced up the rest and skewered it on spits.
That was the moment sweet sleep left my eyes.
I went down to our swift ship by the shore.   480
As I drew closer to our curving ship,

---

[1] ... *white barley on the ship.* The traditional sacrifice requires white barley. But since
the sailors are out of food, they have to substitute the leaves for the barley.

the sweet smell of hot fat floated round me.
I groaned and cried out to immortal gods:

'Father Zeus and you other sacred gods,
who live forever, you forced it on me,
that cruel sleep, to bring about my doom.
For my companions who remained behind
have planned something disastrous.'

"A messenger
quickly came to Helios Hyperion,
long-robed Lampetie, bringing him the news—   490
we had killed his cattle. Without delay,
he spoke to the immortals, full of rage:

'Father Zeus and you other blessed gods,
who live forever, take your vengeance now
on those companions of Odysseus,
Laertes' son, who, in their arrogance,
have killed my animals, the very ones
I always look upon with such delight
whenever I move up to starry heaven
and then turn back from there toward the earth.   500
If they don't pay me proper retribution
for those beasts, then I'll go down to Hades
and shine among the dead.'

"Cloud-gatherer Zeus
answered him and said:

'Helios, I think
you should keep on shining for immortals
and for human beings on fertile earth.
With a dazzling thunderbolt I myself
will quickly strike at that swift ship of theirs
and, in the middle of the wine-dark sea,
smash it to tiny pieces.'

"I learned of this   510

248

from fair Calypso, who said she herself
had heard it from Hermes the Messenger.

"I came down to the sea and reached the ship.
Then I bitterly attacked my crewmen,
each of them in turn, standing by the boat.
But we couldn't find a single remedy—
the cattle were already dead. The gods
immediately sent my men bad omens—
hides crept along the ground, while on the spits
the meat began to bellow, and a sound   520
like cattle lowing filled the air.

                              "For six days,
those comrades I had trusted feasted there,
eating the cattle they had rounded up,
the finest beasts in Helios' herd.
But when Zeus, son of Cronos, brought to us
the seventh day, the stormy winds died down.
We went aboard at once, put up the mast,
hoisted the white sail, and then set off,
out on the wide sea.

                        "Once we'd left that island,
no other land appeared, only sky and sea.   530
The son of Cronos sent us a black cloud,
above our hollow ship, while underneath
the sea grew dark. Our boat sailed on its course,
but not for long. All at once, West Wind whipped up
a frantic storm—the blasts of wind snapped off
both forestays on the mast, which then fell back,
and all our rigging crashed down in the hold.
In the stern part of the ship, the falling mast
struck the helmsman on his head, caving in
his skull, every bone at once. Then he fell,   540
like a diver, off the ship. His proud spirit
left his bones. Then Zeus roared out his thunder
and with a bolt of lightning struck our ship.
The blow from Zeus' lightning made our boat

shiver from stem to stern and filled it up
with sulphurous smoke. My crew fell overboard
and were carried in the waves, like cormorants,
around our blackened ship, because the god
had robbed them of their chance to get back home.

"But I kept pacing up and down the ship,   550
until the breaking seas had loosened off
both sides of the keel. Waves were holding up
the shattered ship but then snapped off the mast
right at the keel. But the ox-hide backstay
had fallen over it, and so with that
I lashed them both together, mast and keel.
I sat on these and then was carried off
by those destructive winds. But when the storms
from West Wind ceased, South Wind began to blow,
and that distressed my spirit—I worried   560
about floating back to grim Charybdis.
All night I drifted. When the sun came up,
I reached Scylla's cliff and dread Charybdis
sucking down salt water from the sea.
But I jumped up into the high fig tree
and held on there, as if I were a bat.
But there was nowhere I could plant my feet,
nor could I climb the tree—its roots were spread
far down below me, and its branches stretched
above me, out of reach, immense and long,   570
overshadowing Charybdis. I hung there,
staunch in my hope that when she spewed again,
she'd throw up keel and mast. And to my joy
they finally appeared. Just at the hour
a man gets up for dinner from assembly,
one who adjudicates the many quarrels
young men have, who then seek judgment,
that's when those timbers first came into view
out from Charybdis.[1] My hands and feet let go
and from up high I fell into the sea   580

[1] . . . *out from Charybdis*. These details suggest that Odysseus was stuck in the tree virtually all day.

250

beyond those lengthy spars. I sat on them
and used my hands to paddle my way through.
As for Scylla, the father of gods and men
would not let her catch sight of me again,
or else I'd not have managed to escape
being utterly destroyed.

                       "From that place
I drifted for nine days. On the tenth night,
the gods conducted me to Ogygia,
the island where fair-haired Calypso lives,
fearful goddess with the power of song.   590
She welcomed and took good care of me.
But why should I tell you that story now?
It was only yesterday, in your home,
I told it to you and your noble wife.
And it's an irritating thing, I think,
to re-tell a story once it's clearly told."

Book Thirteen
Odysseus Leaves Phaeacia
and Reaches Ithaca

[Odysseus ends his story; the Phaeacians collect gifts and store them on a ship; Odysseus takes his leave and goes on board, where he sleeps during the voyage to Ithaca; the Phaeacians land in Ithaca, unload the goods, place Odysseus sleeping on the shore, and leave; Poseidon complains to Zeus about the Phaeacians' transporting Odysseus safely home; Poseidon decides to turn the Phaeacian ship to stone and put up a mountain range around their city; the Phaeacians are amazed at the transformation of their ship; Alcinous recalls his father's prophecies; the Phaeacians sacrifice to Poseidon; Odysseus wakes up on Ithaca but does not recognize the place; Athena visits him in the form of a young man; she tells him he is in Ithaca; Odysseus fabricates a story about his identity; Athena transforms herself into a woman, reveals her identity, and points out the features of the island; the two of them plan how Odysseus will take his revenge on the suitors; Athena transforms his appearance so that he looks like an impoverished old beggar; she tells him to seek out the man who tends his swine; Athena leaves for Sparta to fetch Telemachus.]

Odysseus paused. All Phaeacians sat in silence,
without saying a word, spellbound in the shadowy hall.
Then Alcinous again spoke up and said to him:

> "Odysseus, since you're visiting my home,
> with its brass floors and high-pitched roof, I think
> you won't leave here and go back disappointed,
> although you've truly suffered much bad luck.
> And now I'll speak to all men present here,
> those who in this hall are always drinking
> the council's gleaming wine and enjoying   10
> the songs the minstrel sings. I tell you this.
> Clothing for our guest is packed already,
> stored in a polished chest inlaid with gold,
> as well as all the other gifts brought here
> by Phaeacia's counselors. But come now,
> let's give him a large tripod and a cauldron,

each one of us. We can repay ourselves—
we'll get the people to provide the cost.
It's too expensive for one man to give
without receiving any money back."   20

Alcinous spoke. And they agreed with what he'd said.
Then they all left to go back home and get some rest.

But as soon as rose-fingered early Dawn appeared,
they hurried to the ship and loaded on the bronze,
which strengthens men. Strong and mighty Alcinous
went in person through the ship and had the gifts
stowed below the benches, where they wouldn't hinder
any of the crewmen, as they plied their oars.
Then they went back to Alcinous' home to feast.

On their behalf, strong and mighty Alcinous   30
sacrificed a bull to Zeus, god of the dark cloud
and son of Cronos, who rules over everything.
Once they'd burned pieces of the thigh, they then enjoyed
a splendid banquet. Among them Demodocus,
the godlike minstrel honoured by his people,
sang a song of celebration. But Odysseus
kept on turning round toward the blazing sunlight,
keen to see it set—he so wanted to return.
Just as a man longs for supper, when all day long
a pair of wine-dark oxen pull a well-made plough   40
through fallow land for him, and as the sun goes down,
the sight delights him—now he can prepare a meal,
for his knees are tired when he moves—that's how
Odysseus rejoiced to see the sunlight disappear.
He spoke up at once, addressing the Phaeacians,
men who love the oar, and especially Alcinous,
saying these words:

                    "Lord Alcinous, of all men
most renowned, pour out your libations now,
and send me safely off. Farewell to you!
Now everything my dear heart once desired   50

has come about—an escort and these gifts,
marks of friendship. And may the heavenly gods
make me content with them. When I get back,
may I find my excellent wife at home,
with all my family safe. And as for you,
may you stay here and make a happy life
for the wives you married and your children.
May gods grant you success of every kind,
and may no evil things afflict your people."

Odysseus spoke. They all approved of what he'd said,   60
and ordered that their guest should be escorted off,
because he'd spoken well. Then mighty Alcinous
addressed the herald, saying:

                              "Pontonous,
        stir the mixing bowl, and serve out the wine
        to all those in the hall, so once we've prayed
        to Father Zeus, we may send off our guest,
        back to his native land."

                              Alcinous finished speaking.
Pontonous mixed wine sweet as honey, then served it round
to all of them, coming up to everyone in turn,
and, from where they sat, they poured libations   70
to all the blessed gods who hold wide heaven.
Lord Odysseus stood up, placed a two-handled cup
in Arete's hands, and spoke winged words to her:

        "Fare you well, O queen, through all your years,
        until old age and death arrive, the fate
        of every human being. I'm leaving now.
        But in this house may you have much delight
        from your own children and your people,
        and from Alcinous, the king."

                              Lord Odysseus spoke,
then moved across the threshold. Mighty Alcinous   80
dispatched a herald to conduct him to the sea

and his fast ship. Arete sent slave girls with him.
One held a freshly laundered cloak and tunic.
She told a second one to follow on behind
escorting the large trunk. Another female slave
brought red wine and bread. Once they'd come down to the ship,
beside the sea, the noble youths accompanying him
immediately took all the food and drink on board
and stowed them in the hollow ship. They spread a rug
and linen sheet on the deck inside the hollow ship,   90
at the stern, so Odysseus could sleep in peace.
He went aboard, as well, and lay down in silence.
Each man sat in proper order at his oarlock.
They loosed the cable from the perforated stone.
Once they leaned back and stirred the water with their oars,
a calming sleep fell on his eyelids, undisturbed
and very sweet, something very similar to death.
Just as four stallions yoked together charge ahead
across the plain, all running underneath the lash,
and jump high as they gallop quickly on their way,   100
that's how the stern of that ship leapt up on high,
while in her wake the dark waves of the roaring sea
were churned to a great foam, as she sped on her path,
safe and secure. Not even a wheeling hawk,
the swiftest of all flying things, could match her speed,
as she raced ahead, slicing through the ocean waves,
carrying a man whose mind was like a god's.
His heart in earlier days had endured much pain,
as he moved through men's wars and suffered on the waves.
Now he slept in peace, forgetting all his troubles.   110

When the brightest of the stars rose up, the one
which always comes to herald light from early Dawn,
the sea-faring ship sailed in close to Ithaca.
Now, in that land, Phorcys, the Old Man of the Sea,[1]
has his harbour. Two jutting headlands at its mouth
drop off on the seaward side, but on the other,

---

[1]Phorcys was an ancient god of the sea, father of a number of monsters. The title "Old Man of the Sea," the name given to Proteus in Menelaus' account of his adventures in Egypt (in Book 4), is applied here to Phorcys as well.

slope down to the cove and keep the place protected
from huge waves whipped up by stormy winds at sea.
In there well-timbered ships can ride without being moored,
once they reach that anchorage. An olive tree   120
with long pointed leaves stands at the harbour head,
and close beside it there's a pleasant shadowy cave,
sacred to the nymphs whom people call the Naiads.[1]
Mixing bowls and jars of stone are stored inside,
and bees make honey there. The cave has long stone looms
where nymphs weave cloth with a deep sea-purple dye,
an amazing thing to see. In there, too, are springs
which always flow. The cave has two entrances—
one, which faces North Wind, is the one men use
to go inside; the other one, which faces South Wind,   130
is divine—human beings may not go in there,
for the pathway is confined to the immortals.

They rowed in here, a place they knew about before.
Those rowers' arms had so much strength, half the boat,
which was moving fast, was driven up on shore.
Once they climbed out of that well-built rowing ship
onto dry land, first they took Odysseus out,
lifting him from the hollow ship still wrapped up
in the linen sheet and splendid blanket, placed him,
fast asleep, down on the sand, then carried out   140
the gifts Phaeacia's noblemen had given him,
thanks to the goodwill of great-hearted Athena,
when he was setting out for home. They put these gifts
against the trunk of the olive tree, in a pile,
some distance from the path, in case someone came by,
before Odysseus could wake up, stumbled on them,
and robbed him. Then they set off, back to Phaeacia.

But the Shaker of the Earth had not forgotten
those threats he'd once made against godlike Odysseus.
So he asked Zeus what plan he had in mind:

[1] . . . the Naiads: the Naiads are the nymph goddesses of fresh water, one of three classes
of water nymphs (the others being the Nereids, nymphs of the sea, and the Oceanids,
nymphs of the Ocean).

the immortal gods will honour me no more,
for these men pay me no respect at all,
these Phaeacians, who, as you well know,
are my descendants.[1] For I clearly said
Odysseus should suffer much misfortune
before he made it home. I'd not rob him
of his return completely, once you'd made
that promise and confirmed it with a nod.
But these men carried him, while still asleep,
over the sea in their swift ship, set him   160
in Ithaca, and gave him countless gifts—
bronze and gold and piles of woven clothing,
more than Odysseus ever would have got
at Troy, if he'd come safely back, bringing
his fair share of the trophies with him."

Cloud-gatherer Zeus then gave Poseidon this reply:

"Mighty Earthshaker, what strange things you say!
The gods aren't treating you with disrespect.
To heap dishonour on the oldest and the best
would be hard to bear. But if any man,   170
seduced by his own force and power,
fails to honour you somehow, it's up to you
to take vengeance later. Do what you want,
what gives your heart delight."

Earthshaker Poseidon
then answered Zeus:

"Lord of the Dark Cloud,
I would have quickly done as you've just said,
but I was afraid you might be angry,
and that I wanted to avoid. But now,
I wish to strike at those Phaeacians,
at their splendid ship, as it sails back home,   180

---

[1] ... *my descendants*: The Phaeacians, according to legend, stem from Pheax, a son of
Poseidon, or from Nausithous, father of Alcinous, also a son of Poseidon.

after its trip across the misty seas,
so they will stop and never more provide
an escort carrying human beings.
Then all around their city I'll throw up
a massive mountain range."

Cloud-gatherer Zeus
then answered him and said:

"Brother, listen now
to what my heart thinks best—when all of them
are in the city looking out, as that boat
speeds on her way, then turn her into stone
close to the shore, a rock that looks just like   190
some fast ship, so all men will be amazed.
Then raise a massive mountain round their town."

When Earthshaker Poseidon heard these words, he left
and went to Scheria, home of the Phaeacians.
There he waited. As their sea-faring ship approached,
moving quickly on her course, Earthshaker came up
and turned it into stone. With the palm of his hand
he hit it once and from below froze it in place.
Then Poseidon left. The long-oared Phaeacians,
men famous for their ships, spoke to one another—   200
their words had wings. Looking at the man beside him,
one of them would say:

"Who has fixed our swift ship
out at sea as she was racing homeward,
and in plain sight of all?"

That's what they said.
But they didn't understand why this had happened.
Then Alcinous addressed them all and said:

"Alas!
The prophecies my father used to make
so long ago have come to pass. He'd say

Poseidon would get angry with us,
because we conduct all men in safety.   210
He claimed that one day, as a splendid ship
of the Phaeacians was returning home,
after a convoy on the misty seas,
Poseidon would strike her and then throw up
a huge mountain range around our city.
That's what the old man said. And now all this
is taking place. But come, let all of you
attend to what I say. You must now stop
escorting mortal men when any man
comes to our city. And let's sacrifice   220
twelve choice bulls as offerings to Poseidon,
so he'll take pity and not ring our city
with a lofty mountain range."

                         Alcinous spoke.
They were all afraid, so they prepared the bulls.
Then the Phaeacian counselors and leaders,
standing by the altar, prayed to lord Poseidon.

Meanwhile, Odysseus, asleep in his own land,
woke up. He didn't recognize just where he was.
He'd been away so long, and Pallas Athena,
Zeus' daughter, had shed a mist around him,   230
to make him hard for people to identify,
so she could tell him everything, while his wife,
his townsfolk, and his friends would not know who he was,
until the suitors' crimes had all been paid in full.
And so all things seemed unfamiliar to their king,
the long straight paths, the harbour with safe anchorage,
the sheer-faced cliffs, the trees in rich full bloom.
So he jumped up and looked out at his native land.
He groaned aloud and struck his thighs with both his palms,
then expressed his grief, saying:

                      "Where am I now?   240
Whose country have I come to this time?
Are they violent, unjust, and cruel,

259

or do they welcome strangers? Do their minds
respect the gods? And all this treasure here,
where do I take that? Where do I go next?
I wish I'd stayed with the Phaeacians there.
I'd have visited another mighty king
who would've welcomed me, then sent me off
on my way home. I've no idea now
where to put this wealth. I won't leave it here,   250
in case someone robs me and removes it
as his spoils. Alas! All those Phaeacians,
those counselors and leaders, weren't so wise
or just—they led me to a foreign land.
They said they'd bring me to bright Ithaca,
but that's not what they've done. I pray that Zeus,
god of suppliants, who watches everyone
and punishes the man who goes astray,
will pay them back. But come, I'll count these gifts
and check them out, just in case these men   260
in their hollow ship have carried away
some property of mine."

                        After saying this,
Odysseus began to count the lovely tripods,
cauldrons, gold, and splendid clothing. It was all there.
Then, overwhelmed with longing for his native land,
he wandered on the shore beside the crashing sea,
with many cries of sorrow. Then Athena came,
moving close to him in the form of a young man,
someone who herded sheep, but with a refined air
that marks the sons of kings. She wore a well-made cloak,   270
a double fold across her shoulders, and sandals
on her shining feet. In her hand she gripped a spear.
Odysseus, happy to catch sight of her, came up
and spoke to her—his words had wings:

                              "My friend,
since you're the first one I've encountered here,
my greetings to you, and may you meet me
with no evil in your mind. Save these goods,

and rescue me. For I'm entreating you,
the way I would a god, and I've come here
begging as a dear friend at your knee.   280
Tell me the truth, so I can understand—
What country is this? Who are these people?
Is it some sunny island or a headland
of the fertile mainland reaching out to sea?"

Athena, goddess with the gleaming eyes, replied:

          "Stranger, you're a fool, or else you've come
          from somewhere far away, if you must ask
          about this land. It's name is not unknown—
          not at all—many men have heard of it,
          all those who live in regions of the dawn   290
          and rising sun, as well as all who dwell
          towards the gloomy darkness in the west—
          a rugged place, not fit for herding horses,
          yet not too poor, although not very wide.
          There are countless crops and wine-bearing grapes.
          There's no lack of rain or heavy dew,
          a fine land for raising goats and cattle.
          There are all sorts of trees and watering holes
          that last throughout the year. And so, stranger,
          the name of Ithaca is even known in Troy,   300
          a long way from Achaean land, they say."

Athena spoke, and much-enduring lord Odysseus
felt great joy, happy to learn of his ancestral lands
from what Pallas Athena said, daughter of Zeus,
who bears the aegis. So he spoke winged words to her.
He didn't tell the truth, but left some things unsaid,
always thinking up sly thoughts inside his chest:

          "I've heard of Ithaca, even in wide Crete,
          far across the sea. Now I'm here in person,
          with these goods of mine. When I ran away,   310
          I left even more there with my children.
          I killed a dear son of Idomeneus,

261

swift-footed Orsilochus—in spacious Crete
he was the fastest runner of all those
who work to earn their bread.[1] He wished
to steal away the spoils I'd won at Troy,
for which my heart had gone through so much pain,
suffering men's wars and dangers on the sea,
because I wouldn't gratify his father
and serve as his attendant there in Troy,   320
but led another group of my own men.
As he was coming home, back from the fields,
I lay in wait for him with my companions,
close to the road. There with my bronze-tipped spear
I struck him. Black night concealed the heavens,
and no one noticed us or was aware
I took his life. Once my sharp bronze killed him,
I ran off to a ship without delay,
offered prizes to some fine Phoenicians,
as much as they could wish, entreating them,   330
begging them to take me off to Pylos,
land me there, or else to lovely Elis,
where Epeians rule. Much against their will,
the power of the winds drove them off course.
They didn't wish to cheat me, but were blown
away from there and sailed in here at night.
We quickly rowed into this anchorage.
Although we needed food, we never thought
of dinner—we all lay down where we were.
I was so tired, sweet sleep fell over me.   340
They took my goods out of the hollow ship
and piled them where I lay down in the sand.
Then they went on board and sailed away
for bustling Sidon, leaving me behind
with all these troubles in my heart."

                                                   Odysseus finished.
Bright-eyed Athena smiled and stroked him with her hand.
Then she changed herself into a lovely woman,

---

[1] . . . to earn their bread: In the *Iliad* Idomeneus, leader of the forces from Crete, is a
major ally and a senior leader among the Achaean troops fighting against the Trojans.

tall and very skilled in making splendid things.
She spoke to him—her words had wings:

                           "Any man
    or even a god who ran into you   350
    would have to be a cunning charlatan
    to surpass your various kinds of trickery.
    You're bold, with subtle plans, and love
    deceit. Although you're now in your own land,
    it doesn't look as if you're going to stop
    your lies or making up those artful stories,
    which you love from the bottom of your heart.
    But come, let's no longer speak of this,
    for we both understand what shrewdness means.
    Of all men you're the best in making plans   360
    and giving speeches, and among all gods
    I'm well known for subtlety and wisdom.
    Still, you failed to recognize Pallas Athena,
    daughter of Zeus, who's always at your side,
    looking out for you in every crisis.
    Yes, I made all those Phaeacians love you.
    Now I've come to weave a scheme with you
    and hide these goods Phaeacian noblemen
    gave you as you were setting out for home,
    thanks to my plans and what I had in mind.   370
    I'll tell you what Fate has in store for you.
    You'll find harsh troubles in your well-built home.
    Be patient, for you must endure them all.
    Don't tell anyone, no man or woman,
    you've returned from wandering around.
    Instead, keep silent. Bear the many pains,
    and, when men act savagely, do nothing."

Resourceful Odysseus then answered her and said:

    "Goddess, it's difficult for any man
    to recognize you when he meets you,   380
    even if he's really wise, for you appear
    in any shape you wish. But I know well

that in years past you've been kind to me,
when we sons of Achaea fought in Troy.
But when we'd ransacked Priam's lofty city
and sailed off in our ships and then some god
scattered the Achaeans, I never saw you,
daughter of Zeus. I didn't notice you
coming aboard our ship to keep me safe
from danger. So I kept on wandering,   390
my heart always divided in my chest,
until the gods delivered me from trouble.
Then, in the rich land of the Phaeacians,
your words encouraged me, and you yourself
led me into their city. Now I beg you,
in your father's name, for I don't believe
I've come back to sunny Ithaca. No.
I'm footloose in some other country,
and you're attempting to confuse my mind.
So tell me truly if I have arrived   400
in my dear native land."

Then Athena,
the bright-eyed goddess, answered him:

"That heart in your chest
always thinks this way. And that's the reason
I can't leave you in distress. You're so polite,
intelligent, and cautious. Another man
who'd just come back from wandering around
would've been eager to rush home to see
his wife and children. But you're not keen
to learn about or hear of anything,
before you can observe your wife yourself.   410
She's still living in her home, as before—
her nights and days always end in sorrow,
and she weeps. As for me, I had no doubts,
for my heart always knew you'd get back home,
although your comrades would all be destroyed.
But you should know I had no wish to fight
against Poseidon, my father's brother,

who bears anger in his heart against you,
enraged that you destroyed his dear son's eye.
But come, I'll demonstrate to you this land   420
is Ithaca, so you'll be reassured.
This anchorage here belongs to Phorcys,
the Old Man of the Sea. At the harbour head
stands the long-leafed olive tree. Beside it
is the pleasant, shadowy cave, sacred
to those nymphs they call the Naiads.
This, you must know, is the arching cavern
where you made many sacrificial gifts
to those same nymphs to grant your wishes.
And there is forested Mount Neriton."   430

As the goddess said these words, she dispersed the mist.
Once the land was visible, lord Odysseus,
who had endured so much, overjoyed to see it,
kissed the fertile ground. Then, stretching out his arms
towards the nymphs, he made this prayer:

                     "You Naiad nymphs,
Zeus' daughters, I thought I'd never catch
a glimpse of you again. Now I greet you
with a loving prayer. I'll give gifts, as well,
as I have done for you in earlier days,
if Zeus' daughter who awards the spoils   440
will in her goodness let me stay alive
and help my dear son grow into a man."

Athena, the bright-eyed goddess, then said to him:

"Be brave, and don't weigh down your heart with this.
Now, let's not delay, but put away these goods
in some hidden corner of this sacred cave,
where they'll stay safely stored inside for you.
And then let's think about how all these things
may turn out for the best."

                     After saying this,

the goddess went into the shadowy cave
and looked around for hiding places. Odysseus
brought in all the treasures—enduring bronze and gold
and finely woven clothes, gifts from the Phaeacians.
He stored these carefully, and Pallas Athena,
daughter of aegis-bearing Zeus, set a rock in place
to block the entranceway.

      Then the two of them
sat down by the trunk of the sacred olive tree
to think of ways to kill those arrogant suitors.
Bright-eyed goddess Athena was the first to speak:

> "Resourceful Odysseus, Laertes' son   460
> and child of Zeus, think how your hands may catch
> these shameless suitors, who for three years now
> have been lording it inside your palace,
> wooing your godlike wife and offering her
> their marriage gifts. She longs for your return.
> Although her heart is sad, she feeds their hopes,
> by giving each man words of reassurance.
> But her mind is full of other things."

Resourceful Odysseus then answered her and said:

> "Goddess, if you had not told me all this,   470
> I would have shared the fate of Agamemnon,
> son of Atreus, and died in my own home.
> Come, weave a plan so I can pay them back.
> Stand in person by my side, and fill me
> with indomitable courage, as you did
> when we loosed the bright diadem of Troy.
> O goddess with the gleaming eyes,
> if you are with me now as eagerly
> as you were then, with your aid I'd fight
> three hundred men, if you, mighty goddess,   480
> are willing in your heart to help me."

Bright-eyed goddess Athena then answered him:

"You can be sure I'll stand beside you.
I won't forget you when the trouble starts.
I think the brains and blood of many suitors
who consume your livelihood will spatter
the wide earth. But come, I'll transform you,
so you'll be unrecognizable to all.
I'll wrinkle fine skin on your supple limbs,
remove the dark hair on your head, and then   490
dress you in rags which would make you shudder
to see clothing anyone. And your eyes,
so striking up to now, I'll make them dim.
To all those suitors you'll appear disgusting,
and to the wife and son you left at home.
You must go first of all to see the swineherd,
who tends your pigs. He's well disposed to you
and loves your son and wise Penelope.
You'll find him keeping his swine company
where they feed by Corax Rock, near the spring   500
of Arethusa, drinking its dark water
and eating lots of acorns, which make pigs
grow rich in fat. Stay there and sit with him.
And ask him questions about everything.
I'll go to Sparta, land of lovely women,
and there, Odysseus, I'll summon back
your dear son, Telemachus, who has gone
to spacious Lacedaemon, to the home
of Menelaus, to find out news of you,
to learn if you are still alive somewhere."   510

Resourceful Odysseus then answered her and said:

"Why did you not tell him, since in your mind
you know all things? What did you intend—
that he'd experience hardships on his trip
across the restless seas, while other men
were eating up his livelihood?"

                                        Athena,
goddess with the gleaming eyes, then said to him:

267

"Don't let your heart get too concerned with him.
I sent him off myself, so he might earn
a well-known reputation going there.   520
He's not in trouble, but sits there in peace,
in the home of the son of Atreus,
with countless fine things set before him.
It's true some young men out in a black ship
are lying in ambush, keen to murder him
before he gets back to his native land,
but I don't think that's what will come about.
Before that happens, earth will cover up
the many suitors who consume your goods."

As she said this, Athena touched him with her staff.   530
She wrinkled the fair skin on his supple limbs
and took the dark hair from his head. His arms and legs
she covered with an old man's ancient flesh and dimmed
his eyes, which had been so beautiful before.
She dressed him in different clothes—a ragged cloak,
a dirty tunic, ripped and disheveled, stained
with stinking smoke. Then she threw around him
a large hairless hide from a swift deer and gave him
a staff and a tattered leather pouch, full of holes
and with a twisted strap.

             When the two of them   540
had made their plans, they parted, and Athena went
to Lacedaemon to bring back Odysseus' son.

Book Fourteen
Odysseus Meets Eumaeus

[Odysseus leaves the harbour and moves inland to the farm of Eumaeus, the swineherd; Eumaeus welcomes Odysseus and prepares a meal for him; Eumaeus talks about his absent master; Odysseus assures Eumaeus that his master will return, but Eumaeus does not believe him; Odysseus tells Eumaeus a long made-up story about his identity and his adventures in Egypt and elsewhere, telling him he heard news of Odysseus' return; Eumaeus still does not believe him; the other swineherds arrive; Eumaeus prepares a sacrifice and another meal; Odysseus tells another story about an incident in the Trojan War; Eumaeus prepares a bed for Odysseus, then goes outside to guard the boars.]

Odysseus left the harbour, taking the rough path
into the woods and across the hills, to the place
where Athena told him he would meet the swineherd,
who was, of all the servants lord Odysseus had,
the one who took best care of his possessions.
He found him sitting in the front part of his house,
a built-up courtyard with a panoramic view,
a large, fine place, with cleared land all around.
The swineherd built it by himself to house the pigs,
property belonging to his absent master.   10
He hadn't told his mistress or old man Laertes.
He'd made it from huge stones, with a thorn hedge on top
and surrounded on the outside with close-set stakes
facing both ways, made by splitting oaks apart
to leave the dark heart of the wood. Inside the yard,
to house the pigs, he'd packed twelve sties together.
In each one fifty wallowing swine were penned,
sows for breeding. The boars, far fewer of them,
stayed outside. The feasting of the noble suitors
kept their numbers low, for the swineherd always sent   20
the finest of all fattened hogs for them to eat.
Three hundred and sixty boars were there—four dogs,
fierce as wild animals, always lay beside them.
These the swineherd, a splendid man, had raised himself.

He was trimming off a piece of coloured ox-hide,
shaping sandals for his feet. Three of his fellows
had gone off, herding pigs in different directions.
He'd had to send a fourth man to the city
with a boar to be butchered for the suitors,
so they could eat meat to their heart's content.   30

All of a sudden the dogs observed Odysseus.
They howled and ran at him, barking furiously.
Odysseus was alert enough to drop his staff
and sit. Still, he'd have been severely mauled
in his own farmyard, but the swineherd ran up fast
behind them, dropping the leather in his hands.
Charging through the gate and shouting at his dogs,
he scattered them in a hail of stones here and there.
Then he spoke out to his master:

                                  "Old man,
those dogs would've ripped at you in no time,   40
and then you'd have heaped the blame on me.
Well, I've got other troubles from the gods,
things to grieve about. For as I stay here,
raising fat pigs for other men to eat,
I'm full of sorrow for my noble master,
who's probably going hungry somewhere,
as he wanders through the lands and cities
where men speak a foreign tongue, if, in fact,
he's still alive and looking at the sunlight.
But follow me, old man. Come in the hut.   50
When you've had enough to eat and drink
and your heart's satisfied, you can tell me
where you come from, what troubles you've endured."

With these words, the loyal swineherd went inside the hut,
brought Odysseus in, and invited him to sit,
after piling up some leafy twigs and, over them,
spreading out the shaggy skin of a wild goat,
the large and hairy hide which covered his own bed.
Odysseus was glad to get this hospitality,

so he addressed him, saying:

> "Stranger,   60
> may Zeus and other gods who live forever
> give you what you truly want—you've welcomed me
> with such an open heart."

Then, swineherd Eumaeus,
you answered him and said:[1]

> "It would be wrong,
> stranger, for me to disrespect a guest,
> even if one worse off than you arrived,
> for all guests and beggars come from Zeus,
> and any gift from people like ourselves,
> though small, is welcome. It's the fate of slaves
> always to fear young masters who control them.   70
> The gods are holding up the journey home
> of the man who would've loved me kindly
> and given me possessions of my own,
> a home, a plot of land, a wedded wife
> worthy of being wooed by many suitors,
> the sorts of things a generous master gives
> a servant who has toiled so hard for him,
> whose work the gods have helped to thrive and grow,
> the way the tasks I put my mind to here
> have prospered. If my master was at home   80
> and growing old, he would've given me
> so many things. But he has perished.
> How I wish all of Helen's relatives
> had died, brought to their knees, since she
> loosed the knees of so many warriors.
> He went to Troy, famous for its horses,
> to carry out revenge for Agamemnon
> by fighting Trojans."

---

[1] *. . . you then answered him and said*: Here the narrator makes an unexpected shift and addresses one of the characters in person ("you"), suggesting a certain closeness between the narrator and the character. While this is not common in Homer, it does occur several times (e.g., with Menelaus in the *Iliad*).

After saying this,
he quickly cinched a belt around his tunic,
went out to the pig pens where the swine were held,   90
picked out two from there, brought them in, and killed them.
He singed and cut them up, then skewered them on spits.
Once he'd roasted them completely, he picked them up
and, without taking out the spits, carried them still hot
over to Odysseus. Then he sprinkled over them
white barley meal. In a bowl carved out of ivy wood
he mixed wine sweet as honey. Then he sat down
opposite Odysseus, inviting him to dine:

> "Eat now, stranger, what a servant offers,
> meat from a young pig, for the suitors take   100
> the fatted hogs. Their hearts have no pity
> and don't ever think about gods' anger.
> The truth is this—blessed gods don't love
> men's reckless acts. No. They honour justice
> and men's righteousness. Even enemies
> with cruel intentions can invade the lands
> of someone else, and Zeus awards them spoils.
> They fill their ships and then sail off for home.
> And even in the hearts of men like these
> falls a great fear of vengeance from the gods.   110
> But these suitors here, I think, know something—
> they've heard a voice from one of the gods
> about my master's painful death. That's why
> they don't want to have a righteous courtship
> or go back to their own homes. No. Instead,
> without a care they waste our property
> in all their insolence, sparing nothing.
> Every day and night Zeus sends, they kill
> our animals, and not just one or two,
> and, with their arrogance, they draw our wine,   120
> taking what they want and even more.
> My master used to be a man of substance,
> beyond all measure. No warrior hero
> on the dark mainland or Ithaca itself
> possessed as much. Twenty men combined

did not have so much wealth. I'll tell you this—
on the mainland he's got twelve cattle herds,
as many flocks of sheep and droves of pigs
and wide-ranging herds of goats, all of these
tended by foreign herdsmen or his own.   130
And here, on the edges of this island,
graze wandering herds of goats, eleven in all,
with loyal servants keeping watch on them.
To serve the suitors, every one of them
keeps driving in a creature from his flock,
the fattest one which seems to him the best.
That always happens, each and every day.
As for me, I guard and raise these pigs.
I choose with care and then deliver them
the finest of the boars."

                                 Eumaeus finished.   140
Meanwhile Odysseus eagerly devoured the meat
and drank the wine in silence. He was ravenous.
He was also sowing troubles for the suitors.
Once he'd eaten his heart's fill and had enough,
Eumaeus filled the bowl from which he drank himself
and gave it to him full of wine. Odysseus took it,
happy in his heart, and spoke winged words to him:

        "My friend, who was the man who used his wealth
to purchase you? Was he powerful and rich,
as you've just said? You claim he was destroyed   150
helping Agamemnon get his revenge.
Tell me. I may know him, a man like that.
Zeus and the rest of the immortal gods
know if I've seen him or heard any news.
For I've been traveling a lot."

                         Then Eumaeus,
a worthy man, answered him and said:

                         "Old man,
no wanderer who came with news of him

could convince his wife or his dear son.
Men who roam about, when they need a meal,
have no desire to speak the truth—they lie.   160
Whoever moves around and reaches here,
this land of Ithaca, goes to my mistress
with some made-up tale. She receives him well,
with hospitality, and questions him
about each detail. Then she starts to grieve,
and tears fall from her eyes, as is fitting
when a woman's husband dies far away.
You too, old man, would make up a story
quickly enough, if someone offered you
a cloak and tunic and some clothes to wear.   170
But by this time swift birds and dogs have ripped
the flesh from off his bones, and his spirit's
slipped away. Or else in the sea the fish
have eaten him, and his bones now lie
on shore somewhere, buried in deep sand.
Anyway, he died out there. From now on,
it's the fate of all his friends to grieve,
especially me—however far I travel,
I'll never come across another man
who'd match him as a gentle master,   180
not even if I went back home again
to where my mother and my father live,
where I was born, where they reared me themselves.
I don't mourn for them so much, though I yearn
to see them again with my own eyes
and be in my own native land once more.
What grips me is a longing for Odysseus,
who is gone. Even though he is not here,
stranger, I speak his name with full respect.
His love for me was great, and in his heart   190
he cared. So although he may be absent,
I call him my dear master."

                    Resourceful lord Odysseus
then answered him and said:

            "My friend,
since you're so resolved in your denials,
when you declare he'll not come home again,
and your heart always clings to this belief,
I won't just tell you Odysseus will be back—
no, I'll take an oath on it. When he comes,
when he gets back home, give me my reward
for my good news—let me have fine clothing,   200
a cloak and tunic. Until that moment,
there's nothing I'll accept, despite my need.
For just as I despise the gates of Hades,
I hate the man who, in his poverty,
tells stories which are lies. Now let Zeus,
the first of gods, this welcoming table,
and the hearth of excellent Odysseus,
which I have reached, let them bear witness—
all these things will happen the way I say.
Odysseus will come here within a month,   210
between the waning and the rising moons.
He'll get back home and take out his revenge
on anyone here who has not honoured
his wife and noble son."

                    Then, swineherd Eumaeus,
you answered him and said:

                              "Old man,
I won't be rewarding you for that good news.
Odysseus won't be coming back. Drink up.
Relax. Now, let's talk of something else.
I don't want to remember all those things.
The heart here in my chest gets full of grief,   220
when someone mentions my good master.
So let's forget about your oath. I wish
Odysseus would come home—that's what I want.
So does Penelope, Laertes, too,
the old man, and noble Telemachus.
Right now I'm always grieving for the boy,
the child Odysseus had, Telemachus.

The gods brought him up just like a sapling,
and, as a man, I thought he'd be a match
for his dear father, with a splendid shape   230
and handsome. But one of the immortals
warped his better judgment—perhaps it was
some human being. For he's gone on a trip
to sacred Pylos to find out some news
about his father. Now noble suitors
lie in wait for him as he comes home,
and so the race of noble Arcesius
will die without a name in Ithaca.[1]
But let's just let him be—they may get him,
or he may escape, if the son of Cronos   240
holds out his hand to guard him. But come now,
old man, tell me about your troubles.
Give me the truth, so I clearly understand—
Who are you among men? Where are you from?
Where are your city and your parents?
On what kind of ship did you get here?
How did sailors bring you to Ithaca?
Who did they claim they were? For I don't think
you reached this place on foot."

           Resourceful Odysseus
then answered him and said:

                        "All right, then,   250
I'll tell you the truth of what you've asked me.
I wish we two had food and honey wine
to last a while, so we could feast in peace
inside your hut, while others did the work.
I could easily go on for one whole year
and never finish talking of those things
my heart has suffered, all those torments
I've endured, thanks to what the gods have willed.
I claim my family comes from spacious Crete.

---

[1] . . . *without a name in Ithaca*: Arcesius is the name of the father of Laertes and thus of
Odysseus' paternal grandfather.

I'm a rich man's child, and in his house   260
many other sons were born and raised,
his legal children from his lawful wife.
My mother was a purchased concubine.
Still, Castor, son of Hylax, the man
I claim as my own father, honoured me,
just as he did his true-born sons. Back then,
since he had wealth and land and worthy sons,
the Cretans in the country looked on him
as if he were a god. But lethal Fates
took him to Hades' home, and his proud sons   270
divided up his goods by drawing lots.
They gave me a really tiny portion
and assigned a house. But I won a wife
from people who had many rich estates,
thanks to my courage—for I was no fool,
nor was I coward. Now all that strength
has gone. A host of troubles wears me down.
But by examining the husk, I think,
you can assess the plant. Back then, Ares
and Athena gave me strength and courage,   280
the power to break ranks of men apart.
When I picked the finest troops for ambush
devising perils for my enemies,
my proud spirit never gave me any sense
that I might die. I always jumped out first,
and my spear killed whatever enemy
ran off in front of me. That's what I was like
when it came to war. But I got no joy
from working on the land or household chores,
like raising lovely children. No. Instead,   290
I was always fond of ships with oars
and wars with polished shields and arrows,
deadly things, so horrible to others.
I think I loved those things because a god
somehow set them in my heart. Different men
find their delight in different kinds of work.
Before Achaea's sons set foot in Troy,
I'd led warriors and fast ships nine times

against soldiers from foreign lands and won
enormous quantities of loot. I'd pick out
what pleased me and then later get much more,
when we drew lots. Soon my house grew rich,
and Cretans honoured and respected me.
But when far-seeing Zeus planned that fatal trip
which loosed the knees of many warriors,
they asked me and famous Idomeneus
to lead their ships to Troy. There was no way
one could refuse—the people's voice insisted.
So we Achaean sons fought there nine years,
and ransacked Priam's city in the tenth. 310
We set out for home, but then some god
scattered the Achaeans. And Counselor Zeus
devised some difficulties just for me,
to make me miserable. I stayed at home,
enjoying my children, the wife I'd married,
and my wealth only for a single month.
Then my heart urged me to outfit some ships
and sail to Egypt with my noble comrades.
I manned nine ships. The fleet was soon prepared.
My loyal companions feasted for six days— 320
I gave them many beasts to sacrifice,
as offerings to the gods and to prepare
a banquet for themselves. On the seventh day,
we left wide Crete. North Wind provided us
a stiff and welcome breeze, so we sailed on
quite easily, like drifting down a stream.
None of my ships was harmed, no one got sick
or injured, and we stayed in our seats,
while wind and helmsman held us on our course.
The fifth day we reached Egypt's mighty river, 330
where I moored my curving ships. Then I told
my loyal comrades to stay there with the ships,
keeping watch on them, while I sent out scouts
to find some places we could use as lookouts.
But my crew, overcome with arrogance,
and trusting their own might, at once began
to plunder the Egyptians' finest fields.

They took their women and small children, too,
and killed the men. Shouts soon reached the city,
and, once they heard the noise, Egyptians came,   340
as daylight first appeared. The entire plain
filled up with chariots and infantry,
all flashing bronze. Zeus, who hurls the lightning,
threw a nasty panic in my comrades,
so no one dared to stay and face the fight.
We were badly threatened from all quarters.
They killed many of our men with their sharp bronze,
and took some alive, so they could force men
to do their work for them. Then Zeus himself
put an idea in my heart—but still,   350
I wish I'd died and met my fate right there,
in Egypt, since all sorts of troubles still
lay waiting for me—I at once removed
the finely crafted helmet from my head
and the shield slung round my shoulders. My hand
let go my spear. I ran out straight ahead,
to the chariot of the king, clutched his knee,
and kissed it. Because he pitied me,
he saved my life. He set me in his chariot,
and, as I wept, he took me to his home.   360
Many of his men, armed with their ash spears,
charged at me—their anger was so great,
they were keen to slaughter me. But the king
restrained them—he wanted to respect
the rage of Zeus, the god of strangers,
who is especially irked at wicked deeds.
I stayed there seven years and gathered up
a great deal of wealth from those Egyptians,
for they all gave me gifts. When the eighth year
came wheeling in, a Phoenician man arrived,   370
a greedy rogue who understood deceit.
He'd already brought men lots of trouble.
Well, he won me over with his cunning
and took me with him, until we reached
his house and his possessions in Phoenicia.
I stayed there with him an entire year.

279

But as the days and months kept passing by
and yearly seasons rolled around once more,
he put me on a sea-going ship to Libya,
making up a story for me of some scheme   380
that I'd be carrying a cargo with him,
whereas, in fact, once we were there, he meant
to sell me off for an enormous profit.
Though I suspected something, I had to go
aboard the ship with him. North Wind blew
a fresh and welcome breeze, and we sailed off,
a mid-sea course on the windward side of Crete.[1]
Then Zeus planned the destruction of his men.
When we'd sailed past Crete, we saw land no more,
only sky and sea. Then the son of Cronos   390
sent a black cloud above our hollow ship.
Underneath the sea grew dark. All at once,
Zeus thundered and then hurled a lightning flash
down on our ship, which shook from stem to stern
and filled with sulphurous smoke, as Zeus' bolt
came crashing down. All the crew fell overboard
and floated on the waves, like cormorants,
by our black ship—the god then took away
the day of their return. As for me,
though anguish filled my heart, Zeus himself   400
set my hands on the colossal main mast
from our black-prowed ship, so once again
I could escape destruction. I hung on,
and was carried off by dreadful winds
for nine full days. On the tenth dark night,
a huge rolling wave threw me up on shore
in Thesprotian land, and there the king,
Pheidon, ruler of the Thesprotians,
welcomed me, without demanding ransom.[2]
When I'd been overcome with weariness   410
and freezing wind, his dear son had met me,

---

[1] ... *windward side of Crete.* This seems to mean that the ship passed along the northern
coast of Crete, but the precise meaning is disputed.

[2] ... *without demanding ransom.* The Thesprotians lived in southern Epirus, a coastal
region in north-west Greece, nowadays on the border with Albania.

helped me stand again, and brought me home,
to his father's palace. He gave me clothes—
a tunic and a cloak. There I heard reports
about Odysseus. For king Pheidon said
he'd welcomed him with entertainments,
as he was returning to his native land.
He showed me what Odysseus had gathered,
all the bronze and gold and well-worked iron,
so many riches stored in Pheidon's home,   420
they'd feed ten generations after him.
Odysseus, he said, had gone to Dodona,
to hear from the massive towering oak tree,
sacred to the god, what Zeus had willed
about his own return to that rich land
of Ithaca, after being away so long—
whether he should do so openly or not.[1]
As he poured libations in his house,
he swore to me a ship had been hauled down
and a crew prepared to take Odysseus   430
to his native land. However, before that,
he sent me off, since, as it so happened,
a ship with a crew of Thesprotians,
full of corn, was sailing to Dulichium.
He told them to take me there, treating me
with all due kindness, and deliver me
to king Acastus. But those sailors' hearts
were more attracted to a nasty scheme
concerning me—so I would be reduced
to utter wretchedness. Thus, when the ship   440
had sailed some distance from the land, they tried
from that day forward to make me their slave.
They ripped away my clothes, cloak and tunic,
and dressed me differently, a ragged cloak
and filthy tunic ripped to bits, these here—
the ones you see before your very eyes.

---

[1] ... *openly or not.* Dodona was a very ancient shrine in the interior of Epirus, sacred to
Zeus and Dione. The centre of the oracle was an oak tree where doves nested, and
interpretations were made of the noises coming from the leaves of the tree, the doves,
and brass ornaments hung in the branches.

They reached the fields of sunny Ithaca
that evening. Inside that well-decked ship
they tied me up with tightly twisted rope
and went ashore, in a rush to eat a meal   450
beside the sea. But the gods themselves
with ease untied my bonds, and so I wrapped
my rags around my head and slipped away
down a smooth plank, chest first into the sea.
Then with both arms I paddled and swam off.
I left the water far away from them
and moved inland, where leafy bushes grew,
and lay crouching down. They began to shout
and wandered here and there. But then they thought
there was no point in searching any more.   460
So they went back on board their hollow ship.
The gods themselves concealed me easily
and led me on my way. They brought me here,
to the farmyard of a man who understands.
My fate, I think, is to continue living."

Then, swineherd Eumaeus, you answered him and said:

"Stranger, you're unlucky. The tale you tell
has really touched my heart, all those things
you've suffered, all the places where you roamed.
But I don't think it's all just as you said,   470
and what you mentioned of Odysseus
does not convince me. Given who you are,
why must you tell such pointless falsehoods?
I know well that in my master's journey home
he was totally despised by all the gods.
That's why they didn't kill him over there,
among the Trojans or in his comrades' arms,
when he was done with war. All Achaeans then
would have made him a tomb—and for his son
he would've won great fame in days to come.   480
Now the spirits of the storm have snatched him,
and there's no glory. And as for me, I live
here among the pigs, far away from men.

282

I don't go to the city, unless I'm called
to travel there by wise Penelope,
when a message reaches her from somewhere.
Then people sit around the man who's come
and ask him questions about everything,
both those who are grieving for their ruler,
who's been away so long, and other men   490
who're happy to consume his livelihood
without paying anything. I don't like
to investigate it or ask questions,
not since the day a man from Aetolia
tricked me with his story. He'd killed a man.
After moving around in many lands,
he reached my home. I gave him a fine welcome.
He said he'd seen Odysseus with Cretans
in Idomeneus' home, mending his ships,
which had been damaged in some storms. He claimed   500
he'd return by summer or harvest time,
with his fine comrades and many treasures.
And so you, you long-suffering old man,
since a spirit led you to me, shouldn't try
to cheer me up or secure my favour
by telling falsehoods. That's not the reason
I show you respect and give you welcome,
but because I pity you and fear Zeus,
god of strangers."

        Then resourceful Odysseus
answered Eumaeus with these words:

                "The heart in your chest   510
is really hard to sway. That oath I swore,
even that action didn't influence you
or win you over. But come now, let's make
this promise—the gods who hold Olympus
will stand as witnesses for both of us
in days to come—if your master does get back
to his own home, you'll give me some clothing,
a cloak and tunic, and then send me off

to Dulichium, as my heart desires,
and if your master doesn't come the way   520
I say he will, then set your men on me
and have them throw me off a towering cliff,
so some other beggar will be careful
to avoid deception."

The splendid swineherd
then said in reply:

"Yes, stranger, what a way for me
to gather fame and fortune among men,
both now and in the future, to kill you,
steal your precious life, after bringing you
to my own hut and entertaining you!
I could later pray to Zeus, Cronos' son,   530
with a sincere heart. Now it's time to eat.
I hope my comrades get here quickly,
so we can make a tasty meal here in the hut."

As these two were talking like this to each other,
the other herdsmen came in with their swine.
They shut the sows up in their customary pens,
so they could sleep. The pigs gave out amazing squeals,
as they were herded in. Then the trusty swineherd
called out to his companions:

"Bring a boar in here,
the best there is, so I can butcher it   540
for this stranger from another country.
We too will get some benefit from it,
seeing that we've worked hard for such a long time
and gone through troubles for these white-tusked pigs,
while others gorge themselves on our hard work
without paying anything."

Once he'd said this,
with his sharp bronze axe he chopped up wood for kindling,
while others led in a big fat boar, five years old,

284

and stood him by the hearth. The swineherd's heart was sound,
and he did not forget the gods. So he began   550
by throwing in the fire some bristles from the head
of the white-tusked boar and praying to all the gods
that wise Odysseus would come back to his own home.
Then he raised his arm, and with a club made out of oak,
which he'd left lying beside him, he struck the boar.
Life left the beast. Then the others slit its throat,
singed its bristles, and quickly carved it up.
At first, the swineherd offered pieces of the meat
from all the limbs, set in layers of rich fat.
After sprinkling barley meal all over these,   560
he threw them in the fire. They sliced up the rest,
put it on spits, cooked it with care, drew it all off,
and set heaps of meat on platters. The swineherd,
whose heart always concerned itself with what was fair,
stood up to carve, and as he served up all the meat,
he split it into seven portions. Saying a prayer,
he set one aside for Hermes, son of Maia,
and for the nymphs. The rest he gave to each of them,
honouring Odysseus with a long cut from the back
of the white-tusked boar. That pleased his master's heart.   570
So resourceful Odysseus spoke to him and said:

> "Eumaeus, may father Zeus treat you as well
> as you are treating me with this boar's chine,
> the very finest cut of meat, even though
> I'm just a beggar."

                    Then, swineherd Eumaeus,
you replied by saying:

>   "Eat up, god-guided stranger,
> and enjoy the kind of food we offer.
> A god gives some things and holds others back,
> as his heart prompts, for he can do all things."

Eumaeus spoke and offered to eternal gods   580
the first pieces he had cut. He poured gleaming wine

285

as a libation, passed it over to Odysseus,
sacker of cities, then sat to eat his portion.
Mesaulius served the bread, a servant
Eumaeus purchased on his own, when his master
was away. He'd not informed his mistress
or old man Laertes. He'd acquired the slave
from Taphians, using resources of his own.[1]
So they stretched out their hands to the generous meal
set out in front of them. Once they'd had their fill   590
of food and drink, and their hearts were quite content,
Mesaulius took away their food. They'd eaten
so much bread and meat, they were keen to get some rest.

Night came on, bringing storms. There was no moon.
And Zeus sent blustery West Wind blowing in with rain,
a steady downpour all night long. Odysseus
spoke to them, trying to test Eumaeus, to see if,
given all the hospitality he'd shown,
he'd take off his cloak and give it to Odysseus,
or would urge one of his comrades to give up his.   600

> "Eumaeus and the rest of you, his work mates,
> hear me now—I wish to tell a story,
> prompted by this wine, which can confuse our wits.
> Wine can make a man, even though he's wise,
> sing out loud, or giggle softly to himself,
> or leap up and dance. It can bring out words
> which were better left unsaid. But still,
> since I've begun to speak, I'll hide nothing.
> I wish I were as young, my strength as firm,
> as when we were setting up an ambush   610
> and guiding men to it below Troy's walls.
> Our leaders were Odysseus and Menelaus,
> son of Atreus—and along with them,
> I was third in command, on their orders.
> When we reached the steep walls of the city,

---

[1] . . . *resources of his own*: the Taphians lived on a cluster of islands in the Ionian Sea. In Book 1 of the *Odyssey*, when Athena visits Telemachus in Ithaca (1.138), she takes on the form of Mentes, king of the Taphians.

we lay down in thick bushes round the place,
swampy reeds, crouched down behind our weapons.
A nasty night came on. North Wind dropped off,
and it was freezing cold. Snow fell on us,
like frost from high above, bitterly cold.   620
Our shields were caked with ice. Now, the others
all wore cloaks and tunics, and could rest there
quite easily, their shields across their shoulders.
But when I'd set out, like a fool I'd left
my cloak behind with my companions.
Not thinking I'd feel the cold without it,
I'd just brought my shield and shining doublet.
Well, when it was the third watch of the night
and the stars had shifted their positions,
I spoke to Odysseus, who was close by.   630
When my elbow nudged him, he was all ears,
instantly prepared to listen:

    'Resourceful Odysseus, Laertes' son,
    and child of Zeus, I won't be here for long,
    not among the living. Instead, this cold
    will kill me off. I don't have a cloak.
    Some spirit deluded me, made me come
    with just a tunic. Now there's no way out.'

"That's what I said. In his heart he had a plan—
that's the kind of man he was for scheming   640
or for fighting war. With a quiet whisper,
he spoke to me:

               'Keep silent for the moment,
    in case one of our Achaeans hears you.'

"Then he propped his head up on his elbow,
and spoke out, saying:

               'Listen to me, friends.
    As I slept, a dream sent from the gods
    came to me. We've moved a long way forward,

too far from our ships. I wish some man
would tell Agamemnon, son of Atreus,
shepherd of his people, in the hope   650
he'd tell more men to come out from the fleet.'

"Once he'd said this, Thoas jumped up quickly,
Andraemon's son. He threw off his purple cloak
and started running to the ships. Well then,
I was happy to lie down in his cloak.
Then Dawn appeared on her golden throne.
I wish I were as young as I was then,
and my strength as firm. Then in this farmyard,
some swineherd would give me a cloak to wear,
from kindness and respect for a brave man.   660
But now, with filthy clothing on my skin,
I receive no honours."

                                        Then, swineherd Eumaeus,
you answered him and said:

                                "Old man, that story
you just told us is all right—you've spoken
to the point and made your wishes clear.
You won't lack clothes or any other thing
which a long-suffering suppliant should get
from those he meets, for tonight at least.
When morning comes you'll have to dance around
in those rags of yours. We don't have many cloaks   670
or other tunics here. We've each got only one.
But when Odysseus' dear son arrives,
he'll give you clothes himself, a cloak and tunic,
and send you where your heart desires to go."

After saying this, he jumped up and placed a bed
for Odysseus near the fire. On the bed he threw
some skins from sheep and goats. Odysseus lay down there.
Eumaeus covered him with a huge thick cloak,
which he kept there as a change of clothing,
something to wear whenever a great storm blew.   680

So Odysseus went to sleep there, and the young men
slept around him. But Eumaeus had no wish
to have his bed inside and sleep so far away
from all his boars. So he prepared to go outside.
Odysseus was pleased he took so many troubles
with his master's goods while he was far away.
First, Eumaeus slung his sharp sword from his shoulder
and wrapped a really thick cloak all around him,
to keep out the wind. Then he took a massive fleece
from a well-fed goat and grabbed a pointed spear   690
to fight off dogs and men. Then he left the hut,
going to lie down and rest where the white-tusked boars
slept beneath a hollow rock, sheltered from North Wind.

Book Fifteen
Telemachus Returns to Ithaca

[Pallas Athena visits Sparta to urge Telemachus to return home, tells him to visit Eumaeus, the swineherd, when he gets back; Telemachus tells Menelaus he'd like to leave; Menelaus and Helen give gifts and a farewell banquet; they receive a favourable omen before leaving; Helen interprets the omen; Telemachus and Peisistratus leave Sparta and reach Pylos; Telemachus asks Peisistratus to leave him at his ship, so that Nestor won't delay his return; Peisistratus agrees; a stranger arrives, Theoclymenus, a descendant of the prophet Melampus, and asks for passage on Telemachus' ship; Telemachus agrees, and they sail for Ithaca; Odysseus and Eumaeus feast in the hut; Odysseus asks Eumaeus about his parents, and Eumaeus tells him; Eumaeus tells the story of how he got to Ithaca and was sold to Laertes; Telemachus lands in Ithaca and tells the crew to take the ship on without him; Theoclymenus interprets a bird omen; Telemachus walks to Eumaeus' farmyard.]

Then Pallas Athena went to spacious Lacedaemon,
to remind the noble son of glorious Odysseus
about going home and to urge him to return.
She found Telemachus and Nestor's noble son
lying on the portico, resting in their beds,
inside the palace of splendid Menelaus.
Gentle sleep had overpowered Nestor's son,
but for Telemachus no sweet sleep had come,
because in his heart all through that immortal night
anxious thoughts about his father kept him awake.   10
Bright-eyed Athena stood beside him and spoke out:

> "Telemachus, it's not good to wander
> any longer from your home, abandoning
> your property and leaving in your house
> such overbearing men, who may divide
> and use up all your goods. Then this journey
> you have undertaken will be pointless.
> As quickly as you can urge Menelaus,
> expert at war shouts, to let you go back,

so you can find your noble mother there,   20
still at home. Her father and her brothers
are already telling her to marry
Eurymachus—he gives more courting gifts
than any other suitor, and now he's going
to offer even more as wedding gifts.
Take care she doesn't carry from the house
some property, without your knowing it.
You understand what sort of spirit lies
inside a woman's chest. She wants to enrich
the household of the man who marries her   30
and no longer thinks about her children
or her previous husband whom she loved.
Now he's dead, she doesn't ask about him.
You should go yourself and entrust your goods
to the female slave you esteem the most,
until the gods show you a splendid bride.
I'll tell you something else—take it to heart.
The bravest of the suitors lie in wait,
enough to set an ambush, in the straits
between Ithaca and rugged Samos.   40
Before you get back to your native land,
they want to murder you. But in my view,
that won't be happening. Before it does,
the earth will cover many of those suitors,
who are consuming all your livelihood.
You must steer your well-built ship on a course
far from the islands, and keep on sailing
day and night. One of the immortal gods
who's watching over and protecting you
will send you following winds. And then,   50
at the first place you reach in Ithaca,
send your companions and the ship ahead,
on to the city—you yourself should go
to see the swineherd, the man who tends your pigs.
He's very well disposed towards you.
Spend the night with him. And then tell him
to go into the city and bring news
to wise Penelope that you are safe

and have returned from Pylos."

                           Athena spoke.
Then she left, going back to high Olympus.   60
With his foot Telemachus nudged Nestor's son
and roused him from sweet sleep. Then he spoke to him:

    "Wake up, Peisistratus, son of Nestor.
    Bring up your well-shod horses, then yoke them
    to the chariot, and we'll be on our way."

Peisistratus, Nestor's son, then answered him:

    "No matter how keen you may be to leave,
    Telemachus, there's no way we can ride
    in this dark night. Dawn will soon be here.
    So wait until warrior Menelaus,   70
    son of Atreus, that famous spearman,
    brings gifts and puts them in the chariot,
    then sends us off with a kind farewell speech.
    A guest remembers all his life the man
    who gave him hospitality and kindness."

He spoke. Soon Dawn arrived on her golden throne.
Then Menelaus, expert in battle shouts,
rose up from bed beside his fair-haired Helen
and came to see the two. When he noticed him,
Odysseus' dear son rushed to put on a bright tunic,   80
slung a thick cloak across his hefty shoulders,
and went out. He came up to Menelaus
and spoke to him, saying:

                     "Menelaus,
    son of Atreus and cherished of Zeus,
    leader of your people, send me back now
    to my native land, for my heart is keen
    to get back home."

              Then Menelaus,

expert at war cries, answered him:

> "Telemachus,
> I'll not hold you back a long time here,
> not if you're eager to return. I'd blame   90
> another man who, as a host, provides
> too much hospitality or not enough.
> It's far better to show moderation.
> It's bad when someone doesn't want to leave
> to be too quick to send him on his way,
> but just as bad is holding someone back
> when he's ready to depart. For a host
> should welcome any guest in front of him
> and send away the one who wants to go.
> But stay until I bring some fine gifts here   100
> and set them in your chariot, where your eyes
> can see them, and I can tell the women
> to prepare a meal inside the palace
> from the plentiful supply of food there.
> For a traveler to feast before he leaves
> to journey on the wide unbounded earth
> brings double benefits—it gives him help
> and gives me fame and honour. If you wish
> to go through Hellas and middle Argos,
> then I'll accompany you in person.[1]   110
> I'll have some horses harnessed for you,
> and I'll guide you to men's cities there.
> Not one of them will send us from their town
> without offering some gift for us to take,
> a beautiful bronze tripod or a cauldron,
> a pair of mules or goblet made of gold."

Prudent Telemachus then answered him and said:

> "Menelaus, son of Atreus,
> child of Zeus, and leader of your people,

---

[1] *... accompany you in person.* This invitation from Menelaus seems to involve a detour on the journey back so as to include a trip through the northern Peloponnese. However, the terms Hellas and Argos in Homer are often very imprecise and ambiguous.

293

I wish to get back home without delay—   120
when I went away I didn't leave behind
anyone to protect my property.
As I keep searching for my noble father,
I hope I don't get killed or in my palace
have any fine possessions stolen."

When Menelaus, skilled in war cries, heard these words,
he quickly told his wife and her attendants
to use some of the abundant food they stored
to prepare a banquet. Then Etoneus,
son of Boethous, came up to Menelaus—   130
he lived close by and had just got out of bed.
Menelaus, skilled at war shouts, ordered him
to get a fire started and to roast some meat.
Once Etoneus heard, he did what he'd been asked.
Menelaus went down to his fragrant storage room—
not by himself, for Helen and Megapenthes
went along as well. Once they reached the places
where his treasures lay, the son of Atreus
picked up a two-handled cup and told his son,
Megapenthes, to take a silver mixing bowl.   140
Helen went up to the storage chests which held
the richly woven garments she herself had made.
Then Helen, goddess among women, picked out one,
the largest and most beautifully embroidered—
it lay below the others, shining like a star.
Helen carried off this robe, and they returned,
back through the house, until they reached Telemachus.
Fair-haired Menelaus then spoke to him:

                              "Telemachus,
may Zeus, Hera's loud-thundering husband,
accomplish your return, as your heart desires.   150
Of all the treasured gifts stored in my home,
I'll give you the one with highest value
and the loveliest—I'll present to you
this finely crafted mixing bowl. It's made
entirely of silver and its rims

are plated gold. Hephaestus crafted it.
Warrior Phaedimus, the Sidonian king,
presented it to me on my way home,
when his house gave me shelter. Now I'd like
to send it back with you."

Menelaus spoke.

Then Atreus' warrior son handed Telemachus
the two-handled cup, and mighty Megapenthes
brought in the mixing bowl of shining silver
and set it down before him. Fair-cheeked Helen,
standing beside him with the garment in her hands,
spoke to Telemachus and said:

"My dear child,

I'm giving you this gift as a reminder
of Helen, something made by her own hands.
Your bride can wear it on her wedding day,
a moment to look forward to. Until then,   170
let it remain in your dear mother's room.
As for you, I wish you a joyful journey
back to your well-built home and native land."

With these words, Helen placed the garment in his hands.
Telemachus accepted it with pleasure.
Noble Peisistratus took the gifts and packed them
in a box inside the chariot, gazing at them
with wonder in his heart. Fair-haired Menelaus
then led them to the house, where they sat down
on stools and chairs. A female servant carried in   180
a beautiful gold jug and poured some water out
into a silver basin, so they could rinse their hands,
then placed a polished table right beside them.
The worthy housekeeper carried in some bread
and set it down before them, then lots of meat,
giving freely from the food she had in store.
Standing near them, Etoneus carved the meat
and handed out the portions, while Megapenthes,
son of splendid Menelaus, poured the wine.

Then their hands reached for the food spread out before them.   190
Once they'd had food and drink to their heart's content,
Telemachus and the noble son of Nestor
yoked the horses, climbed in the ornate chariot,
and drove from the portico through the echoing gate.
Fair-haired Menelaus went out after them.
His right hand held a gold cup full of honey wine,
so they might pour libations before setting out.
Standing there beside the horses, Menelaus
made a pledge to both of them and said:

                               "Farewell,
young men. Make sure you greet Nestor for me,   200
shepherd of his people. Over in Troy,
when we sons of Achaea went to war,
he truly was a gentle father to me."

Prudent Telemachus then replied and said:

"Zeus-fostered king, we will indeed tell him
all the things you ask, once we get there.
How I wish when I returned to Ithaca
I'd come across Odysseus in his home,
so I could tell him how, when I left here,
I'd met with every hospitality   210
and taken many splendid gifts away."

As he said these words, a bird flew over them,
to the right—an eagle clutching in its talons
a huge white goose, a tame one from some farm.
A crowd of men and women chased behind it,
shouting as they ran. The bird came close to them,
then veered off to the right before the horses.
When they saw that, they were happy—in all their chests
the spirits filled with joy. Then the son of Nestor,
Peisistratus, was the first of them to speak: 220

"Menelaus, leader of your people,
cherished by Zeus, tell us about this sign—

whether god sent it to the two of us
or just to you alone."

                    Peisistratus spoke.
War-loving Menelaus thought it over—
How should he understand the omen properly
and then provide the correct interpretation?
But before he said a word, long-robed Helen spoke
and said these words:

                    "Listen to me.
I will prophesy what the immortals   230
have set into my heart, what I believe
will happen. Just as this eagle came here
from mountains where it and its young were born
and snatched up this goose bred in the household,
that's how Odysseus, after all his suffering
and his many wanderings, will come home
and take revenge. Or he's already home,
sowing destruction for all the suitors."

Wise Telemachus then answered her and said:

                    "Now may Zeus, loud-thundering mate of Hera,   240
bring that about. If so, I'll pray to you
as to a god."

                    Telemachus said this,
then flicked the horses with his whip. They sped off quickly,
keen to move on through the city toward the plain.
All day long the yoke around their shoulders rattled.
Then the sun went down, and all the roads grew dark.
They came to Pherae, to Diocles' house,
the son of Ortilochus, Alpheus' child.
Diocles welcomed them with hospitality
the way one should with strangers. There they spent the night.   250

As soon as rose-fingered early Dawn appeared,
they yoked the horses, climbed in the ornate chariot,

then drove out from the echoing portico and gate.
Peisistratus touched the horses with his whip,
and they sped on willingly. They quickly reached
the steep citadel of Pylos. Telemachus
then addressed the son of Nestor:

                    "Peisistratus,
will you promise to do something for me,
and see it through just as I tell you?
We can claim that we've always been friends,   260
because our fathers were good friends, as well,
and we are the same age. This trip of ours
will make our hearts united even more.
So, child of Zeus, don't take me past my ship
but leave me there, in case old man Nestor
keeps me in his house against my will,
wishing to show me hospitality,
when I must now get home with all due speed."

Telemachus spoke. In his heart Nestor's son
considered how he might make such a promise   270
and see it through to its conclusion. As he thought,
he did what seemed to him the better option—
he turned the horses to the swift ship by the shore,
took out the lovely gifts, the clothing and the gold,
which Menelaus had given Telemachus,
stowed them in the stern, then urged him onward—
his words had wings:

                    "Move quickly now.
Climb in your ship, and tell all your comrades
to do so, too, before I get back home
and let old Nestor know what's happening.   280
For in my heart and mind I know too well
he likes things done his way—he won't let you go
but come in person here to call you back.
I tell you, he won't go back without you.
In any case, he's sure to be upset."

Once he'd said this, Peisistratus drove his horses,
creatures with lovely manes, quickly back to Pylos.
He soon reached the palace. Meanwhile, Telemachus
urged his companions on, saying to them:

> "Comrades, put all the stuff in our black ship.   290
> Let's get ourselves on board, so we can sail."

Once he spoke, they all heard him and obeyed at once.
Soon they were aboard, sitting at their oarlocks.
At the ship's stern, Telemachus was busy
praying to Athena and offering sacrifice.
Then a man approached, someone from far away,
fleeing from Argos because he'd killed a man.
He was prophet, descended from Melampus,
who many years ago had lived in Pylos,
a sheep-breeding land. He'd been a wealthy man,   300
living in a rich house among the Pylians.
But then Melampus went into a foreign land,
fleeing his country and great-hearted Neleus,
the most illustrious of all living men,
who for one whole year had taken his wealth by force,
while Melampus lay tied up in savage bondage
in Phylacus' palace, suffering harsh cruelty,[1]
all for the sake of Neleus' daughter
and thanks to the terrible blindness in his heart
which the goddess Erinys, who strikes down families,   310
had fixed on him. But then he got away from Fate
and drove the bellowing herd from Phylace
to Pylos. Thus, he managed to obtain revenge
for the disgraceful acts of noble Neleus
and led the daughter home to be his brother's wife.
But he went off to Argos, where horses graze,
a land of strangers. He was destined to live there,

---

[1] *. . . harsh cruelty*. This passages gives yet another reference the story of Melampus (see
previous references at 11.320 and 11.352), the prophet who could communicate with animals.
His brother fell in love with Neleus' daughter. Neleus said that whoever could steal the cattle
of Phylacus could have the daughter. Melampus was caught trying to help his brother and
imprisoned by Phylacus, but his prophetic powers persuaded Phylacus to release him and give
him the cattle. These he brought back to Neleus and thus won the daughter for his brother.

ruling many Argives. Then he took a wife,
built a high-roofed house, and fathered two strong sons,
Antiphates and Mantius. Antiphates   320
fathered brave Oicles, who then produced
Amphiaraus, a man who could rouse people up,
and whom Apollo and aegis-bearing Zeus
loved in all sorts of ways. But he failed to reach old age—
he died in Thebes, thanks to a woman's need for gifts.[1]
He had two sons—Alcmaeon and Amphilocus.
And Mantius fathered Cleitus and Polypheides.
Cleitus was so beautiful he was snatched away
by Dawn on her golden throne, so he might live
with the immortal gods, and then Apollo   330
made high-minded Polypheides his prophet,
the best of men, after Amphiaraus perished.
He was angry with his father and moved away
to Hyperesia, where he lived and prophesied
to all. His son's name was Theoclymenus—
he was the one who now approached Telemachus,
as he poured out libations by his swift black ship
and prayed. Standing by him, Theoclymenus spoke—
his words had wings:

> "Friend, since I've met you here
> while making sacrifice, I'm asking you,   340
> for the sake of your offerings and the god
> and by your comrades' lives and by your own,
> answer what I ask, and tell me the truth,
> concealing nothing. Among men who are you?
> Where is your city and your parents?"

Shrewd Telemachus then answered him and said:

> "All right, stranger, I will speak candidly.
> I am from Ithaca by birth. My father
> is Odysseus, as surely as he was alive,

---

[1] . . . *woman's need for gifts.* Amphiaraus was married to Eriphyle, who was bribed
with a gold necklace to persuade her husband to join a military expedition against
Thebes. He died in the fighting.

but now he's died by some pitiful fate.   350
That's why I got this crew and this black ship
and came to find news about my father
who's been absent for so long."

Noble Theoclymenus
then said in reply:

"I, too, have run away,
leaving my own country. I killed a man,
one of my family. Many relatives of his
live in horse-nurturing Argos—they rule
Achaeans there and have enormous power.
I'm fleeing to prevent them killing me,
a dark fate. So now it's my destiny,   360
I think, to roam around among mankind.
Let me board your ship—I'm a fugitive,
and I'm begging you, so they won't kill me.
I think they're on my track."

Prudent Telemachus
then answered him and said:

"If you're keen to come,
there's no way I'd stop you boarding my trim ship.
So come with us. You'll find a welcome here,
as much as we possess."

As he said these words,
he took the bronze spear Theoclymenus held,
set it lengthwise on the deck of the curved ship,   370
and then himself climbed in the ocean-going boat.
He had Theoclymenus sit by him in the stern.
The crewmen loosed the cables. Then Telemachus
called his comrades, urging them to hoist the tackle.
They hurried to obey, lifting up the mast of fir
and setting it in place in its hollow socket.
They tightened forestays, and then hoisted a white sail
on twisted ox-hide ropes. Bright-eyed Athena

send favouring winds blowing stiffly through the air,
so the ship could complete its voyage quickly   380
over salt waters of the sea. So they sailed on
past Crouni and Calchis, with its lovely streams.
Then the sun went down, and all the routes grew dark.
They made for Pheae, driven on by winds from Zeus,
and for fair Elis, where Epeians rule. From there,
Telemachus steered them past the jagged islands,
wondering if he'd get caught or escape being killed.

Meanwhile, Odysseus and the faithful swineherd
were eating in the hut, with the other men as well.
When they'd had food and drink to their heart's content,   390
Odysseus spoke to them, testing the swineherd,
to see if he would keep up his kindly welcome
and ask him to go on staying at the farm
or if he would send him off towards the city:

> "Eumaeus and all the rest of you,
> listen to me now. Tomorrow morning
> I'd like to wander off and beg in town,
> so I won't exhaust you and your comrades.
> So give me good advice, then send me off
> with a fine guide who can conduct me there.   400
> I'll have to wander round the city by myself,
> hoping to get a cup and piece of bread.
> Then I could go to lord Odysseus' home
> and give some news to wise Penelope
> and mingle with those arrogant suitors.
> They might give me a meal—they've lots of food.
> If so, I could serve them well in what they want.
> Let me tell you. Pay attention now and listen.
> Thanks to Hermes the Messenger, the one
> who places grace and fame on all men's work,   410
> no other man can match the way I serve
> in splitting dry wood and building a good fire,
> roasting and carving meat, and serving wine,
> all those actions performed by lesser men
> when they are servants to nobility."

Then, swineherd Eumaeus, you were most upset
and spoke out to Odysseus:

>   "Why, stranger,
> is your heart so full of this idea?
> You must have a strong desire to die,
> if you intend to go among the suitors,   420
> that crowd whose pride and violence extend
> right up to iron heaven. Their servants
> are not like you. No. The ones who serve them
> are young men, well dressed in cloaks and tunics,
> their heads and faces always sleek with oil.
> They keep well-polished tables loaded down
> with bread and meat and wine. So stay here.
> No one in this place finds you a bother—
> I don't, nor do the others here with me.
> When the dear son of Odysseus comes,   430
> he'll give you clothing, a cloak and tunic,
> and send you where your heart and spirit urge."

Then much-enduring lord Odysseus answered him:

> "Eumaeus, I hope father Zeus likes you
> as much as I do—you've brought to an end
> my wanderings and painful hardships.
> Nothing's more miserable for human beings
> than wandering round, but men put up with
> wretched troubles for their stomach's sake,
> when they have to face the pain and sorrow   440
> their roaming brings. Now, since you keep me here,
> telling me to wait for your young master,
> tell me of noble Odysseus' mother
> and his father, too. When he went away,
> he left him just as he was growing old.
> Are they still living in the sunshine here
> or have they died and gone to Hades' home?"

Then the swineherd, a splendid fellow, answered him:

"Well, stranger, I'll tell you the honest truth.
Laertes is still living, but all the time   450
inside his home he keeps praying to Zeus
the spirit in his limbs will fade away.
He grieves excessively for his own son,
who's gone, and for the wife he married,
a wise lady, whose death, above all else,
really troubled him and made him old
before his time. She died a wretched death
grieving for her splendid son. May no man
who lives here as my friend and treats me well
die the way she did! While she was alive,   460
though she was sad, it was a pleasure for me
to ask about her, to find out how she was,
because she personally brought me up,
together with long-robed Ctimene,
her fine daughter, the youngest child she bore.
I was raised with her, though with less honour.
When we both reached our young maturity,
that time we long for, they sent her to Same
to be married and got countless wedding gifts.
She dressed me in fine clothes, cloak and tunic,   470
and gave me sandals to tie on my feet,
then sent me out into the fields. In her heart
she was especially fond of me. But now,
I lack all this, though personally for me
the sacred gods prosper the work I do.
From that I've had food and drink and helped out
those who have a claim on my attention.
But now bad times have fallen on the house
with those overbearing men, I don't hear
anything good, whether in word or deed,   480
about my lady, although servants have
a powerful longing to talk face to face
with their mistress and find out everything,
to eat and drink and then take something back
into the fields—such things warm servants' hearts."

Resourceful Odysseus then answered him and said:

"Well, swineherd Eumaeus, you were just a child
when you wandered far off from your parents
and your native land. Come now, tell me this—
and speak candidly—was the place ransacked,   490
that populated city with broad streets
where your lady mother and your father lived,
or were you alone with sheep or cattle?
Did hostile people take you in their ships
and bring you here to sell you to the master
of this palace, who paid a decent price?"

The swineherd, an outstanding fellow, then replied:

"Stranger, since you ask me questions about this,
stay quiet, enjoy yourself, drink your wine,
as you sit there, and listen to my tale.   500
These nights go on forever. There's a time
to sleep, and there's a time to take delight
in hearing stories. You don't need to rest
before you're ready, and too much sleep
can leave one weary. As for the others,
if any man's heart and spirit tell him,
let him go outside and sleep. Then at dawn
he can eat and walk behind our master's swine.
We two will drink and feast here in the hut
and enjoy each other's wretched troubles,   510
as we recall them. For once they're over,
a man who's done a lot of wandering
and suffered much gets pleasure from his woes.
So now I'll give you answers to those questions.
There's an island you may have heard about
beyond Ogygia—it's called Syrie,
where Sun changes his course. The land is good.
Though not too many people live on it,
there're many herds and flocks, plenty of wine,
and lots of wheat. Famine never comes there,   520
no dreadful sickness falls on poor mortal men.
Inside the city, when tribes of men get old,
Apollo comes there with his silver bow

and Artemis as well. He attacks them
with his gentle arrows and kills them off.
There are two cities there, with all the land
divided up between them. My father
ruled both of them as king. He was Ctesius,
Ormenus' son, like an immortal god.
Phoenicians came there, famous sailing men,   530
greedy rogues, who carried countless trinkets
in their black ship. Now, in my father's house
lived a tall, beautiful Phoenician woman,
skilled in making lovely things. Those Phoenicians,
truly crafty men, seduced her. First of all,
while she was doing laundry, one of them
had sex with her beside the hollow ship—
love like that distracts the minds of women,
even the virtuous ones. When he asked her
who she was and where she came from, she said,   540
pointing to my father's high-roofed house:

    'I claim to come from Sidon, rich in bronze.
    I'm a daughter of Arybas, whose wealth
    was like a flood. But then I was taken
    by Taphian pirates, as I was coming
    from the fields. They brought me to this place
    and sold me to the household of that man,
    who paid an excellent price.'

                    "Then the man
who'd slept with her in secret said to her:

    'Would you come back home again with us,   550
    to see your father's and mother's lofty home
    and them, as well? Yes, they're still alive
    and people say they're wealthy.'

"Then the woman answered him and said:

    'I might come, if you sailors were willing
    to promise me on oath to take me home

safe and sound.'

"When she'd said that,
they all took the oath, as she'd requested.
When they'd sworn and finished promising,
the woman spoke to them again and said: 560

'Now, keep silent. None of your company
must talk to me, if you meet me in the street
or maybe at the springs, in case someone
runs to tell the old king in the palace.
If he gets suspicious, he'll tie me up
in cruel bondage and then plan your death.
Keep what I'm saying in mind, and finish off
your trading quickly. When your ship is full,
your goods on board, send me a message
at the palace right away. I'll bring gold,   570
whatever I can lay my hands on there.
And there's something else I'd like to offer
to pay my passage. Inside the palace
my master has a child. I am his nurse.
Quite an impish boy—when we're outside
he runs beside me. I'll bring him on board.
He'll earn you an enormous sum of money,
wherever you run into foreigners.'

"She said this, then left for the fine palace.
The men stayed there with us for one whole year,   580
and by trading filled their hollow ship with goods.
When the deep boat was loaded to return,
they sent a messenger to tell the woman.
The man, a shrewd one, reached my father's house
with a gold necklace strung with amber beads.
In the hall servants and my noble mother
were handling and inspecting it, haggling
about the price. He nodded at the woman,
without saying a word. After that signal,
he went back to his hollow ship. So then,   590
she took my hand and led me from the house.

307

In the front hall she found cups and tables
left by those who had been feasting there,
men who were attendants on my father.
They'd just gone out to a council meeting
where they held public debates. On the spot
she stuffed three goblets in her bosom
and walked out with them. I followed her,
without thinking a thing. The sun went down,
and all the roads grew dark. But we rushed on   600
and came to the fine harbour where we found
the swift ship which belonged to those Phoenicians.
They put us both on board, climbed in themselves,
and sailed away along the watery road.
Zeus sent a favouring wind. We sailed six days,
moving day and night. When Zeus, Cronos' son,
brought us the seventh day, archer Artemis
struck the woman, and she fell with a thud
down in the hold, just like a sea bird's fall.
They threw her overboard to make a meal   610
for seals and fish. But I was left heart-sick.
The winds and waters carried them along
and brought them to Ithaca, where Laertes
purchased me with his own money. That how
I came to see this land with my own eyes."

Odysseus, born from Zeus, then answered him and said:

"Eumaeus, by telling me these things,
you've really stirred the heart here in my chest,
all those ordeals your spirit has endured.
But with the bad things Zeus has given you   620
he's put some good—you've undergone much pain,
but you did come to a kind man's house.
With a good heart, he gives you food and drink,
and the life you lead is good. As for me,
I've reached here only after wandering
through many cities of men."

                                    So the two men

kept talking to each other. Then they fell asleep.
But they didn't sleep for long, only for a while,
since Dawn soon reached there on her golden throne.

As Telemachus' comrades were approaching land,   630
they furled the sail and quickly lowered the mast.
Then, with their oars they rowed into an anchorage,
tossed out mooring stones, and lashed the cables at the stern.
They themselves then disembarked in the crashing surf,
to prepare a meal and mix the gleaming wine.
When they'd had food and drink to their heart's content,
prudent Telemachus was the first to speak:

> "You men row the black ship to the city,
> while I check on the fields and herdsmen.
> I'll come to the city in the evening,   640
> after I've looked over my estates.
> In the morning I'll lay out a banquet
> as payment to you for the journey,
> a splendid meal of meat and sweetened wine."

Then godlike Theoclymenus spoke up and said:

> "Where do I go, dear lad? Of those who rule
> in rocky Ithaca, whose house do I go to—
> directly to your and your mother's home?"

Prudent Telemachus then answered him and said:

> "In different circumstances, I'd tell you   650
> to visit our house—there is no lack
> of welcome there for strangers. But for you
> it would be worse, because I'll not be there,
> and my mother will not see you. It's rare
> for her to show up among the suitors
> in the house—she stays away from them
> and does her weaving in an upper room.
> But I'll mention another man to you
> and you can visit him—Eurymachus,

309

the illustrious son of wise Polybus, 660
whom men of Ithaca see as a god.
He's the best man by far and really keen
to marry my mother and then possess
the royal prerogatives of Odysseus.
But Olympian Zeus, who lives in heaven,
knows if, before that wedding day arrives,
he'll bring about a day of reckoning."

As he said this, a bird flew past on the right,
a hawk, Apollo's swift messenger. In its talons
it held a dove, which it was plucking, and feathers 670
fell on the ground halfway between Telemachus
and his ship. Theoclymenus called him aside,
away from his companions, grasped his hand, and spoke:

"Telemachus, this bird flying to our right
has not come without being prompted by some god.
I knew when I saw it darting forward
it was an omen. In the land of Ithaca
no family is more royal than yours is.
No. You'll be powerful for ever."

Prudent Telemachus then answered him and said: 680

"Stranger, I hope that prophecy of yours
may be fulfilled. If so, you'll quickly hear
of many gifts and kindnesses from me,
so any man you meet will call you happy."

Then he spoke to Peiraeus, a faithful comrade:

"Peiraeus, son of Clytius, of all those
who came with me on the trip to Pylos
you're the one who is especially loyal.
So now conduct this stranger to your home,
take care to welcome him with honour, 690
until I get there."

Peiraeus, a famous spearman,
then answered him and said:

"Telemachus,
if you stay for a long time in these parts,
I will entertain him. He will not lack
anything that's appropriate for guests."

After saying this, he went on board the ship,
and told the crew to get in and loose the cables.
They boarded quickly and sat down at their benches.

Telemachus tied sturdy sandals on his feet,
then from the deck picked up his powerful spear   700
with a sharp bronze point. The crew untied stern cables
and then pushed out to sea, sailing to the city,
as Telemachus, godlike Odysseus' dear son,
had ordered them to do, while he strode quickly off,
his feet carrying him onward, until he reached
the farmyard and the pigs in countless numbers,
among whom the worthy swineherd lay asleep,
always thinking gentle thoughts about his master.

Book Sixteen

Odysseus Reveals Himself to Telemachus

[Telemachus arrives at Eumaeus' farm; Eumaeus is overjoyed to see
Telemachus back from his voyage; Telemachus, Eumaeus, and Odysseus
(in disguise) talk together; Telemachus sends Eumaeus off to tell
Penelope of his safe return; Athena tells Odysseus to reveal himself to his
son and transforms his appearance; Telemachus and Odysseus are
reunited; Telemachus and Odysseus discuss strategies for dealing with
the suitors; Odysseus gives Telemachus instructions about hiding
weapons and behaving in front of the suitors; a herald from Telemachus'
crew announces to Penelope and others the news of his return from
Pylos; the suitors are upset and discuss what to do; Penelope appears
before the suitors and upbraids Antinous for his behaviour; Antinous
replies; Eumaeus returns to Odysseus and Telemachus in the hut; Athena
transforms Odysseus into an old beggar once again; Odysseus, Eumaeus,
and Telemachus eat a meal and go to sleep.]

Meanwhile at dawn Odysseus and the loyal swineherd,
once they'd sent the herdsmen out with droves of pigs,
made a fire in the hut and prepared their breakfast.
As Telemachus came closer, the yelping dogs
stopped barking and fawned around him. Lord Odysseus
noticed what the dogs were doing and heard his footsteps.
At once he spoke out to Eumaeus—his words had wings:

> "Eumaeus, some comrade of yours is coming,
> or someone else you know. The dogs aren't barking
> and are acting friendly. I hear footsteps."   10

He'd hardly finished speaking when his own dear son
stood in the doorway. The swineherd, amazed, jumped up—
the bowls he was using to mix the gleaming wine
fell from his hands. He went up to greet his master,
kissed his head, both his handsome eyes, his two hands,
then burst into tears. Just as a loving father
welcomes his dear son after a nine-year absence,
when he comes from a foreign land, an only son,

his favourite, for whom he's undergone much sorrow,
that's how the loyal swineherd hugged Telemachus   20
and kissed him often, as if he'd escaped his death.
And through his tears he spoke winged words to him:

> "You've come, Telemachus, you sweet light.
> I thought I'd never see you any more,
> once you went off in that ship to Pylos.
> Come in now, dear boy, so that my heart
> can rejoice to see you here in my home,
> now you've just returned from distant places.
> You don't often visit farm and herdsmen—
> your life is in the city. Your heart, I think,   30
> must like to watch that hateful bunch of suitors."

Shrewd Telemachus then answered him and said:

> "If you say so, old friend. I've come here now
> on your account, to see you face to face
> and to hear you talk about my mother.
> Is she still living in the palace halls,
> or has some other man now married her?
> Is no one sleeping in Odysseus' bed?
> Is it all covered in disgusting cobwebs?"

The swineherd, that outstanding man, then answered him: 40

> "Yes indeed, she still lives in your palace,
> with a faithful heart, but always grieving,
> wasting days and nights away with weeping."

Once he'd said this, he took Telemachus' bronze spear,
and let him enter. He crossed the stone threshold.
As he approached, Odysseus, his father, got up
to offer him his seat, but from across the room
Telemachus stopped him and said:

> "Stay put, stranger.
> We'll find a chair in the hut somewhere else.

313

Here's a man who'll get one for us."

He spoke. Odysseus went back and sat down again.
Eumaeus piled up green brushwood on the floor
and spread a fleece on top. Odysseus' dear son
sat down there. The swineherd then set out before them
platters of roast meat, left over from the meal
they'd had the day before, and quickly heaped up
baskets full of bread. In a wooden bowl he mixed
wine sweet as honey, and then sat down himself,
opposite godlike Odysseus. Their hands reached out
to the fine meal prepared and spread before them.   60
When they'd had food and drink to their heart's content,
Telemachus then said to the splendid swineherd:

"Old friend, where does this stranger come from?
How did sailors bring him to Ithaca?
Who do they claim to be? For I don't think
there's any way he could get here on foot."

Then, swineherd Eumaeus, you answered him and said:

"My child, I'll tell you nothing but the truth.
He claims that he was born in spacious Crete
and says he has been roaming all around,   70
wandering through many human cities.
That how some god has spun a fate for him.
He's just fled from a ship of Thesprotians
and come here to my farm. I give him to you.
Do as you wish. He's a suppliant, he says."

Shrewd Telemachus then answered him and said:

"Eumaeus, I'm really distressed at heart
by what you've said. How can I welcome
this guest into my home? I myself am young—
I don't believe my hands are strong enough   80
to fight a man who acts with violence
against me first. As for my mother,

314

in her chest the heart is quite divided,
whether to stay with me and tend the house,
out of respect for what the people say
and for her husband's bed, or to go now
with the finest man of those Achaeans
who've been courting her within the halls,
the one who offers the most marriage gifts.
But anyway, now this stranger's come here,   90
to your home, I'll dress him in fine clothing,
cloak and tunic, and give a two-edged sword
and sandals for his feet. I'll send him off
wherever his heart and spirit prompt him.
If you wish, you can keep him at this farm
and care for him. I'll send some clothing here
and all the food he'll eat, so he won't ruin
you and your comrades. But I won't permit him
to go there and mingle with the suitors—
they are far too full of arrogant pride   100
and might make fun of him, which would bring me
deadly sorrow. It's difficult for one man,
even if he's powerful, to do much
with so many more. They are far stronger."

Then lord Odysseus, who had endured so much,
said to Telemachus:

          "Friend, surely it's all right
for me to answer, and my heart is torn
as I hear you talk—these suitors think up
such presumptuous actions in your palace
and flout your will, though you're a decent man.   110
Tell me, do you agree with this oppression?
Do the people of the country hate you
and follow what some god is telling them?
Do you think the blame rests with your kinsmen,
whom a man relies on when there's fighting,
even if a major quarrel should arise?
With my heart the way it is, how I wish
I were either as young as you, the son

of brave Odysseus, or the man himself
returning from his travels—there's still room   120
for us to hope for that—then, if I came
to the halls of Laertes' son, Odysseus,
and didn't bring destruction on them all,
let a stranger slice this head off my neck.
If I, acting all alone, was overwhelmed
by their greater numbers, I'd rather die,
killed in my own home, than continue watching
such disgraceful acts—guests treated badly,
women servants shamelessly being dragged
through the fine palace, wine drawn and wasted,   130
and all the time food eaten needlessly,
acts which go on and on, without an end."

Shrewd Telemachus then answered him and said:

"Well, stranger, I'll speak candidly to you.
The people are not all angry with me,
nor do they bear a grudge. And I don't blame
my kinsmen, the ones a man relies on
in a fight, even if a great quarrel comes.
The son of Cronos has made our family
follow a single line. It goes like this—   140
Arcisius fathered a single son,
Laertes, and he, too, was the father
of only a single son, Odysseus,
and Odysseus fathered me, his only son,
then left me by myself in his own hall.
He got no joy of me. And that's why now
countless hostile men are in our home.
All those lords with power in the islands—
Dulicium, Same, wooded Zacynthus—
and those who rule in rocky Ithaca,   150
all of them are trying to court my mother
and destroy my home. She does not turn down
the hateful marriage, but cannot decide

to bring these matters to an end.[1] And so,
with their feasting they consume my household,
and they'll soon be the ruin of me, too.
But all this lies in the lap of the gods.
Old friend, you must go quickly and report
to wise Penelope that I've returned,
I'm safely home from Pylos. I'll stay here,   160
until you've given the news to her alone
and come back here. No other Achaean
must learn about it, for many of them
are planning nasty things against me."

Then, swineherd Eumaeus, you answered him and said:

"I know what you're saying—I understand.
You're speaking to a man who thinks things through.
But come, tell me this, and be frank with me.
On this trip should I go to Laertes
with the news? The poor man's miserable.   170
For a while, though suffering great distress
about Odysseus, he'd supervise the fields
and in his home eat and drink with servants,
as the heart inside his chest would urge him.
But now, since the time you left for Pylos,
people say he no longer eats and drinks
the way he used to or inspects the fields,
but sits there groaning and wailing, in tears,
with his flesh shriveling around his bones."

Shrewd Telemachus then answered him and said: 180

"That's more distressing, but nevertheless,
though it makes us sad, we'll leave him alone.

[1] *. . . matters to an end*: The exact political status of the suitors is ambiguous and in places
confusing. Sometimes, as here, they are called the chief leaders or rulers of the islands
or those with ruling power in Ithaca. They all appear to live in Ithaca and visit the palace
during the day. However, the islands listed here are sometimes described as under
Odysseus' control. What does seem clear is that the suitors have political importance as
noblemen, as the most important leaders, whatever the precise arrangements between
them and the royal family of Odysseus in Ithaca.

If mortal men could somehow get all things
simply by wishing, we would first of all
select the day my father gets back home.
But after you've delivered your message,
then come back here. Don't go wandering
around the fields looking for Laertes.
Instead, tell my mother to send her maid,
the housekeeper, quickly and in secret.   190
She can report the news to the old man."

His words spurred on the swineherd. He took his sandals,
tied them on his feet, and set off for the city.

Now, it did not escape the notice of Athena
that swineherd Eumaeus was going from the farm.
She approached the hut, appearing like a woman,
beautiful, tall, and skilled in making lovely things.
She stood just outside the entrance to the farm
and was visible to no one but Odysseus.
Telemachus did not see her face to face   200
or notice she was there. For when gods appear,
there's no way their form is perceptible to all.
But Odysseus saw her. So did the dogs, as well.
But they didn't bark. Instead, they crept away,
whimpering in fear, to the far side of the hut.
She signaled with her eyebrows. Lord Odysseus
noticed and went out of the hut, past the large wall
around the yard, and stood in front of her.
Then Athena spoke to him:

                              "Son of Laertes,
resourceful Odysseus, sprung from Zeus,   210
Now is the time to speak to your own son—
make yourself known and don't conceal the facts,
so you two can plan the suitors' lethal fate,
then go together to the famous city.
I won't be absent from you very long—
I'm eager for the battle."

As she said this, Athena
touched Odysseus with her golden wand. To start with,
she placed a well-washed cloak around his body,
then made him taller and restored his youthful looks.
His skin grew dark once more, his countenance filled out,   220
and the beard around his chin turned black again.
Once she'd done this, Athena left. But Odysseus
returned into the hut. His dear son was amazed.
He turned his eyes away, afraid it was a god,
and spoke to him—his words had wings:

                    "Stranger,
you look different to me than you did before—
you're wearing different clothes, your skin has changed.
You're one of the gods who hold wide heaven.
If so, be gracious, so we can give you
pleasing offerings, well-crafted gifts of gold.   230
But spare us."

               Long-suffering lord Odysseus
then answered him and said:

                "I'm not one of the gods.
Why do you compare me to immortals?
But I am your father, on whose account
you grieve and suffer so much trouble,
having to endure men's acts of violence."

He spoke, then kissed his son. A tear ran down his cheek
onto the ground—till then he'd held himself in check.
But Telemachus, who could not yet believe
it was his father, spoke to him again, saying: 240

"You cannot be Odysseus, my father.
No. Some spirit has cast a spell on me,
to make me lament and grieve even more.
There's no way a mortal man could plan this
with his own wits, unless some god himself
came by, who could, if he so desired,

319

make him young or old quite easily.
Not long ago you wore filthy clothing
and were an old man. But now you're like
the gods who hold wide heaven."

Then resourceful Odysseus answered him and said:

"Telemachus, it's not appropriate for you
to be overly surprised your father
is back home or to be too astonished.
You can rest assured—no other Odysseus
will ever be arriving. I am here.
I've endured a lot in many wanderings,
and now, in the twentieth year, I've come back
to my native land. This present business,
you should know, is forager Athena's work.
She's made me look like this—it's what she wants,
and she has power—in one moment,
like a beggar, and in another one,
a young man with fine clothes around his body.
It's easy for the gods who hold wide heaven
to glorify or else debase a man."

Once he'd said this, he sat down, and Telemachus
embraced his noble father, cried out, and shed tears.
A desire to lament arose in both of them—
they wailed aloud, as insistently as birds,
like sea eagles or hawks with curving talons
whose young have been carried off by country folk
before they're fully fledged. That's how both men then
let tears of pity fall from underneath their eyelids.
And now light from the sun would've gone down on them,
as they wept, if Telemachus had not spoken.
He suddenly addressed his father:

                      "In what kind of ship,
        dear father, did sailors bring you here,
        to Ithaca? Who did they say they were?
        For I don't think you made it here on foot."

Noble long-suffering Odysseus answered him:

"All right, my child, I'll tell you the truth.
Phaeacians, those famous sailors, brought me.
They escort other men, as well, all those
who visit them. And I remained asleep
as they transported me across the sea
in their swift ship and set me here in Ithaca.
They gave me splendid gifts of bronze and gold
and woven clothing. Now, thanks to the gods,
these things are stored away in caves. I've come   290
at Athena's bidding, so we may plan
destruction for our enemies. But come now,
tell me about the number of the suitors,
so I know how many men there are
and what they're like. Then, once my noble heart
has thought it over, I'll make up my mind,
whether we two are powerful enough
to take them on alone, without assistance,
or whether we should seek out other men."

Shrewd Telemachus answered him and said: 300

                          "Father,
I've always heard about your great renown,
a mighty warrior—your hands are very strong,
your plans intelligent. But what you say
is far too big a task. I'm astonished.
Two men cannot fight against so many—
and they are powerful. In an exact count,
there are not just ten suitors or twice ten,
but many more. Here, you can soon add up
their numbers—from Dulichium there are
fifty-two hand-picked young men, six servants   310
in their retinue, from Same twenty-four,
from Zacynthus twenty young Achaeans,
and from Ithaca itself twelve young men,
all nobility. Medon, the herald,
is with them, as is the godlike minstrel,

321

and two attendants skilled in carving meat.
If we move against all these men inside,
I fear revenge may bring a bitter fate,
now you've come home. So you should consider
whether you can think of anyone who'll help,   320
someone prepared to stand by both of us
and fight with all his heart."

                         Then lord Odysseus,
who had endured so much, answered him and said:

        "All right, I'll tell you. Pay attention now,
and listen. Do you believe Athena,
along with Father Zeus, will be enough
for the two of us, or should I think about
someone else to help us?"

                    Shrewd Telemachus
then said in reply:

                         "Those two allies you mention
are excellent. They sit high in the clouds,   330
ruling others, men and immortal gods."

Long-suffering lord Odysseus answered him and said:

        "The two of them won't stand apart for long
from the great fight—we can be sure of that—
when Ares' warlike spirit in my halls
is put to the test between these suitors
and ourselves. But for now, when Dawn arrives,
go to the house, join those arrogant suitors.
The swineherd will bring me to the city
later on. I'll be looking like a beggar,   340
old and wretched. If they're abusive to me,
let that dear heart in your chest endure it,
while I'm being badly treated, even if
they drag me by my feet throughout the house
and out the door or throw things and hit me.

322

Keep looking on, and hold yourself in check.
You can tell them to stop their foolishness,
but seek to win them over with nice words,
even though you'll surely not convince them,
because the day they meet their fate has come.   350
I'll tell you something else—keep it in mind.
When wise Athena puts it in my mind,
I'll nod my head to you. When you see that,
take all the weapons of war lying there,
in the hall, and put them in a secret place,
all of them, in the lofty storage room.
When the suitors notice they've gone missing
and ask about them, you must deceive them
with reassuring words:

       'I've placed them
 well beyond the smoke, since they're no longer   360
 like the weapons Odysseus left behind
 when he went off to Troy. They're all tarnished—
 the fire has breathed on them too many times.
 Beyond that, the son of Cronos has put
 a greater worry in my heart that you,
 after too much wine, may start up a fight
 amongst yourselves and then hurt each other,
 dishonouring your courtship and the feast.
 For iron attracts a man all on its own.'

"But leave behind a pair of swords, two spears,   370
and two ox-hide shields, for the two of us
to grab up when we make a rush at them,
while Pallas Athena and Counselor Zeus
will keep the suitors' minds preoccupied.
I'll tell you something else—keep it in mind.
If you are my son and truly of our blood,
let no one hear Odysseus is back home.
Don't let Laertes know or the swineherd,
or any servants, or Penelope herself.
You and I alone will investigate   380
how the women feel, and we'll check out

some of the serving men, to discover
if any of them fears and honours us
in his heart—and the ones with no respect,
who discredit you for being the man you are.”

Then his splendid son answered him and said:

"Father,
I think you'll later come to recognize
my spirit, for no timidity of mind
possesses me. But still, I do not think
your plan will benefit the two of us.   390
I'd ask you to consider this—you'll spend
a long time simply testing every man,
as you visit the farms, while those others,
in their proud way, relax inside your halls
and consume your goods without restraint.
But I'd suggest you learn about the women,
those disgracing you and the guiltless ones.
As for men on the estates, I'd prefer
we didn't test them. We can deal with that
at a later time, if you truly recognize   400
some sign from Zeus, who bears the aegis.”

So the two men talked about these things together.

Meanwhile, the well-built ship which brought Telemachus
from Pylos with all his comrades had reached Ithaca.
Once they'd come inside the deep water harbour,
they hauled the black ship up on shore. Eager servants
carried off their weapons and without delay
took the splendid gifts to Clytius' home.
They also sent a herald to Odysseus' house,
to report to wise Penelope, telling her   410
Telemachus had gone to visit the estates
and had told the ship to sail off for the city,
in case the noble queen might get sick at heart
and shed some tears. This herald and the swineherd met
because they'd both been sent off with the same report

324

to tell the queen. When they reached the royal palace,
the herald spoke out in front of female servants:

"My queen, your dear son has just returned."

But the swineherd came up close to Penelope
and gave her all the details her dear son   420
had ordered him to say. Once he'd told her
every item he'd been asked to mention to her,
he went off, leaving the courtyard and the hall,
back to his pigs. The suitors were unhappy,
their hearts dismayed, and they departed from the hall,
past the large courtyard wall. There, before the gates,
they sat down. The first one of them to say something
was Eurymachus, son of Polybus:

"O my friends,
to tell the truth, in his great arrogance
Telemachus has carried out his trip,   430
a great achievement. We never thought
he would complete it. So come on now,
let's launch a black ship, the best one we have,
collect some sailors, a crew of rowers,
so they can quickly carry a report
to those other men to go home at once."[1]

No sooner had he said all this, than Amphinomus,
turning in his place, saw a ship in the deep harbour.
Men were bringing down the sail, others holding oars.
With a hearty laugh, he then addressed his comrades: 440

"Don't bother with a message any more.
Here they are back home. Either some god
gave them news, or they saw his ship themselves,
as it sailed past, but couldn't catch it."

He spoke. They all got up and went to the sea shore,

---

[1] *. . . to go home at once.* The "other men" are the ones waiting in the islands to ambush
Telemachus on his voyage home. They may still unaware that he has slipped past them.

then quickly dragged the black ship up onto dry ground,
while eager attendants carried off their weapons.
They themselves went to the meeting place together.
No one else was allowed to sit there with them,
no old or younger men. Then Antinous addressed them,   450
son of Eupeithes:

                       "Well, this is bad news—
the gods have delivered the man from harm.
Our lookouts sat each day on windy heights,
always in successive shifts. At sunset,
we never spent the night on shore, but sailed
over the sea in our swift ship, waiting
for sacred Dawn, as we set our ambush
for Telemachus, so we could capture
and then kill him. Meanwhile, some god
has brought him home. But let's think about   460
a sad end for Telemachus right here
and ensure he doesn't get away from us.
For as long as he's alive, I don't think
we'll be successful in what we're doing.
He himself is clever, shrewd in counsel,
and now people don't regard us well at all.
So come now, before he calls Achaeans
to assembly. I don't think he will give up.
He'll get angry and stand up to proclaim
to everyone how we planned to kill him   470
and how we didn't get him. The people
will resent us, once they learn about
our nasty acts. Take care they do not harm us
and force us out, away from our own land,
until we reach a foreign country. And so,
let's move first—capture him out in the fields,
far from the city, or else on the road.
We ourselves will keep the property he owns,
his wealth, too, and share it appropriately
among us. As for possession of the house,   480
that's something we should give his mother
and the man who marries her. However,

326

if what I've been saying displeases you,
and you'd prefer he should remain alive,
retaining all the riches of his fathers,
then let's not keep on gathering in this place,
consuming his supply of pleasant things.
Instead, let each man carry on his courtship
from his own home, seeking to prevail with gifts.
Then she can marry the one who offers most   490
and comes to her as her destined husband."

He finished. They all sat quiet, not saying a thing.
Then Amphinomus spoke out and addressed them,
splendid son of lord Nisus, Areteias' son—
leader of the suitors from Dulichium,
land rich in grass and wheat. Penelope found him
especially pleasant because of how he talked,
for he understood things well. With good intentions,
he spoke to them and said:

                        "My friends,
I wouldn't want to slay Telemachus.   500
It's reprehensible to kill someone
of royal blood. But first let's ask the gods
for their advice. If great Zeus' oracles
approve the act, I myself will kill him
and tell all other men to do so, too.
But if the gods decline, I say we stop."

Amphinomus finished. They agreed with what he'd said.
So they immediately got up and went away
to Odysseus' house. Once they reached the palace,
they sat down on the polished chairs. By that point,   510
wise Penelope had thought of something else—
to put in an appearance before the suitors,
despite their arrogance, because she'd heard about
the destruction of her son there in the hall.
The herald Medon, who'd heard their plans, had told her.
So she set off on her way toward the hall,
accompanied by her attendant women.

327

As soon as the noble lady reached the suitors,
she stood beside the door post of the well-built room
and, holding a bright veil across her countenance,
addressed Antinous, reprimanding him:

"Antinous, though you're an arrogant man
and come up with devious schemes, people say
you are the best among those men your age
at offering advice and making speeches.
But you don't seem to be a man like that.
You madman, why devise a fatal plan
to kill Telemachus and disregard
the things involved with being a suppliant,
who has Zeus as witness? It's impiety
to plan evil things for one another.
Do you not know your father came here
a fugitive, afraid of his own people?
They were extremely angry with him,
because he'd joined with Taphian pirates
to cause trouble for the Thesprotians,
who were allied with us. Those men wished
to kill him, rip out his heart, and devour
his huge and pleasant livelihood. But then,
Odysseus restrained them, kept them in check,
for all their eagerness. Now you eat up
that man's home without paying anything,
court his wife, attempt to kill his son,
and cause me much distress. So stop all this,
I tell you, and order other suitors
to do the same."

Then Eurymachus,
son of Polybus, answered her:

"Wise Penelope,
daughter of Icarius, cheer up. Don't let
these things concern your heart. No man living
and no man born and no one yet to be
will lay hands on your son Telemachus,

not while I'm alive, gazing on the earth.
I tell you this—and it will truly happen—
that man's black blood will quickly saturate
my spear, for Odysseus, sacker of cities,
also set me on his knees many times
and put roast meat into my hands and held
red wine up for me. Thus, Telemachus
is far the dearest of all men to me.
I say to him—don't be afraid of death,   560
not from the suitors, but there's no way out
when death comes from the gods."

He said these words to ease her mood, while he himself
was planning her son's death. But Penelope
went to her bright room upstairs and wept there
for Odysseus, her dear husband, until sweet sleep,
cast by bright-eyed Athena, spread across her eyelids.

At evening the fine swineherd came to Odysseus
and to his son, busy getting dinner ready.
They'd killed a boar, one year old. Then Athena   570
approached Odysseus, Laertes' son, and touched him
with her wand and made him an old man once again.
She put shabby clothes around his body, just in case
the swineherd, by looking up, would recognize him
and then go off to tell faithful Penelope,
and thus fail to keep the secret in his heart.
Telemachus addressed the swineherd first and said:

> "Good Eumaeus, you've come. What news is there
> in the city? Are those arrogant suitors
> back in the house already from their ambush,   580
> or are they still out there watching for me
> as I travel on my journey homeward?"

Then, swineherd Eumaeus, you answered him and said:

> "I didn't bother to make enquiries
> or ask about such things on my travels

through the town. Once I'd given my report,
my heart told me to get myself back here
as fast as possible. A swift messenger,
who came from your companions, met me,
a herald. Your mother first got the report   590
from him. But I found out something else,
which I saw with my own eyes. As I walked
above the city, by the hill of Hermes,
I saw a fast ship coming in our harbour,
with lots of men aboard and loaded down
with shields and two-edged spears. I thought
it could be them, but I'm not certain."

Eumaeus finished. Telemachus with a smile,
full of confidence and strength, allowed his eyes
to glance over to his father, avoiding contact   600
with the swineherd. Then, once they'd finished working
and dinner was prepared, they dined. Their hearts
did not lack a thing—they shared the meal as equals.
When they'd had food and drink to their heart's content,
they thought of rest, and so they took the gift of sleep.

Book Seventeen
Odysseus Goes to the Palace as a Beggar

[Telemachus leaves Eumaeus and Odysseus at the farm, telling the
swineherd that the beggar (Odysseus) must go to the city; Telemachus is
welcomed in the palace by Eurycleia and his mother; Telemachus joins
the suitors; Peiraeus leads in Theoclymenus; Theoclymenus and
Telemachus dine with Penelope; Telemachus tells Penelope about his
journey; Theoclymenus makes a prophecy of Odysseus' return; Eumaeus
and Odysseus leave the farm for the city; they meet Melanthius, the goat
herder, on the way, who insults them; Eumaeus and Odysseus arrive at
the palace, meet Odysseus' old dog, Argus, who recognizes him and dies;
Eumaeus enters the palace and joins Telemachus at dinner; Odysseus sits
by the entrance way; Telemachus offers food to the disguised Odysseus,
who then starts begging from the suitors; Melanthius and Antinous
insult Eumaeus and Odysseus; Odysseus tells Antinous his story, they
trade insults, and Antinous throws a foot stool at Odysseus and hits him;
Penelope summons Eumaeus to her, asks him to call the disguised beggar
to her; Odysseus tell Eumaeus that he'll meet Penelope in the evening,
not now; Eumaeus tells Penelope, talks to Telemachus, and returns to the
farm, leaving the feast still in progress.]

As soon as rose-fingered early Dawn appeared,
Telemachus, dear son of god-like Odysseus,
tied some fine sandals on his feet, took a strong spear,
well suited to his grip, and, as he headed off
towards the city, spoke out to the swineherd:

> "Old friend, I'm leaving for the city,
> so my mother can observe me. I don't think
> her dreadful grieving and her sorry tears
> will stop until she sees me for herself.
> So I'm telling you to do as follows—   10
> take this wretched stranger to the city.
> Once there, he can beg food from anyone
> who'll offer him some bread and cups of water.
> I can't take on the weight of everyone,
> not when I have these sorrows in my heart.

As for the stranger, if he's very angry,
things will be worse for him. Those are the facts,
and I do like to speak the truth."

                                        Odysseus,
that resourceful man, then answered him and said:

    "Friend, I myself am not all that eager   20
    to be held back here. For a beggar man
    it's better to ask people for a meal
    in the city instead of in the fields.
    Whoever's willing will give me something.
    At my age it's not appropriate for me
    to stay any longer in the farmyard,
    obeying everything a master orders.
    No. So be on your way. This man here,
    who you give orders to, will take me there,
    as soon as I've warmed up beside the fire   30
    and the sun get hot. These clothes I'm wearing
    are miserably bad, and I'm afraid
    the morning frost may be too much for me—
    you say the city is a long way off."

Odysseus finished. Telemachus walked away,
across the farmyard, moving with rapid strides.
He was sowing seeds of trouble for the suitors.
As he entered the beautifully furnished house,
he carried in his spear and set it in its place,
against a looming pillar. Then he moved inside,   40
across the stone threshold. His nurse Eurycleia
saw him well before the others, while spreading fleeces
on the finely crafted chairs. She burst out crying,
rushed straight up to him, while there gathered round them
other female servants of stout-hearted Odysseus.
They kissed his head and shoulders in loving welcome.
Then from her chamber wise Penelope emerged,
looking like Artemis or golden Aphrodite.
She embraced the son she loved, while shedding tears,
and kissed his head and both his beautiful eyes.   50

Through her tears, she spoke to him—her words had wings:

> "You've come, Telemachus, you sweet light.
> I thought I'd never see you any more,
> when you secretly went off to Pylos
> in your ship, against my wishes, seeking
> some report of your dear father. So come,
> describe for me how you ran into him."

Shrewd Telemachus then answered her and said:

> "Mother, don't encourage me to grieve,
> or get the heart inside my chest stirred up.   60
> I've just escaped being utterly destroyed.
> But have a bath, and pick fresh clothing
> for your body. Then, with your attendants
> go to the room upstairs, and promise
> all the gods you'll offer perfect sacrifices,
> if Zeus will somehow bring to fulfilment
> actions which will give us retribution.
> I'll go to the place where we assemble,
> so I can call upon a stranger, a man
> who came with me on my trip from Pylos.   70
> I sent him ahead with my noble comrades,
> telling Peiraeus to take him to his home,
> to treat him kindly, and to honour him,
> until the time I got there."

Telemachus finished.
Penelope was quiet—no winged words flew from her.
She bathed herself and took fresh clothing for her body.
Then she promised she'd offer perfect sacrifice
to all the gods, if Zeus would somehow bring about
those actions which would give them retribution.
Telemachus walked through the hall, gripping his spear.   80
Two swift dogs went with him. Athena poured on him
such marvelous grace that, as he moved along,
all people gazed at him. The arrogant suitors
thronged around him, making gentle conversation,

but deep in their hearts they were planning trouble.
He avoided the main crowd of them and took a seat
where Mentor and Antiphus and Halitherses sat,
companions of his father's from many years ago.
They asked him all kinds of questions. Then Peiraeus,
the well-known spearman, approached, leading the stranger   90
through the city to the place where they assembled.[1]
Telemachus did not turn his back for very long
upon the stranger, but went up to him. Peiraeus
was the first to speak:

> "Telemachus,
> send some women quickly to my home,
> so I may have those gifts sent here to you
> which Menelaus gave you."

Shrewd Telemachus then answered him and said:

> "Peiraeus,
> we don't know how these matters will turn out.
> If these overbearing suitors kill me   100
> in my own halls in secret and divide
> all my father's goods amongst themselves,
> I'd prefer you keep those gifts yourself—
> enjoy them—rather than any of those men.
> But if I sow a lethal fate for them,
> then bring them to the house, and be happy
> with me, for I will be rejoicing."

As he said this, he led the long-suffering stranger
towards the house. When they reached the stately palace,
they put their cloaks down on the seats and armchairs,   110
then went into the polished tubs to have a bath.
After the attending women had washed both men,
rubbed them down with oil, and wrapped around them
woolen cloaks and tunics, they came out from the bath

---

[1] . . . *place where they assembled*: The "stranger" being led to the city is the prophet
Theoclymenus, who earlier (in Book 16) asked Telemachus to take him to Ithaca.

and sat down on the chairs. A servant brought in water
in a lovely golden pitcher and poured it out
in a silver basin, so they could wash their hands.
Beside them she then set up a polished table.
The worthy housekeeper brought bread and set it out,
then added lots of meat, giving freely from her stores.   120
Telemachus' mother sat across from him,
by the door post of the hall, leaning from her seat
to spin fine threads of yarn. They stretched out their hands
to take the fine food prepared and set before them.
When they'd had food and drink to their heart's content,
the first to speak to them was wise Penelope:

> "Telemachus, once I've gone up to my room,
> I'll lie down in bed, which has become for me
> a place where I lament, always wet with tears,
> ever since Odysseus went to Troy   130
> with Atreus' sons. Yet you don't dare
> to tell me clearly of your father's trip,
> even before the haughty suitors come
> into the house, no word of what you learned."

Shrewd Telemachus then answered her and said:

> "All right then, mother, I'll tell you the truth.
> We went to Pylos and reached Nestor,
> shepherd of his people. He welcomed us
> in his lofty home with hospitality
> and kindness, as a father for a son   140
> who's just returned from far-off places
> after many years—that's how Nestor
> and his splendid sons looked after me
> with loving care. But of brave Odysseus,
> alive or dead, he told me he'd heard nothing
> from any man on earth. He sent me off
> with horses and a well-built chariot
> to that famous spearman Menelaus,
> son of Atreus. There I saw Argive Helen,
> for whom many Trojans and Achaeans   150

335

struggled hard, because that's what gods had willed.
Menelaus, skilled at war shouts, at once
asked me why I'd come to lovely Sparta,
what I was looking for. I told him the truth,
all the details. He answered me and said:

    'That's disgraceful! They want to lie down
in the bed of a courageous warrior,
when they themselves are cowards—just as if
a doe has put two new-born suckling fawns
in a mighty lion's thicket, so they can sleep,   160
and roams mountain slopes and grassy valleys
seeking pasture, and then the lion comes
back to that lair and brings a dismal fate
for both of them—that's how Odysseus
will bring those men to their disastrous end.
By Father Zeus, Athena, and Apollo,
how I wish he could be as he was once
in well-built Lesbos, in a wrestling match,
when he stood and fought Philomeleides,
threw him decisively, and all Achaeans   170
felt great joy—if he were that sort of man,
Odysseus might well mingle with the suitors,
and they'd all meet death, a bitter courtship.
But as for these things you're asking me about,
begging me to speak, I'll not evade them
or lead you astray. No. I won't conceal
or bury a single word that I was told
by that infallible Old Man of the Sea.
He said that he had seen Odysseus
on an island, suffering great distress   180
in nymph Calypso's home—she keeps him there
by force. He can't get to his native land
because he has no ship available,
no oars, and no companions, men who might
transport him on the broad back of the sea.'

"That's what famous spearman Menelaus said,
the son of Atreus. When I was finished,

I came home, and the immortals gave me
favourable winds which quickly carried me
back to my native land."

                               Telemachus' words   190
stirred the heart within her chest. Then among the group
Theoclymenus, a godlike man, spoke out:

> "Noble wife of Laertes' son, Odysseus,
> Menelaus has no certain knowledge.
> You should attend to what I have to say,
> for I will make a truthful prophecy
> and not conceal a thing. Now, let Zeus,
> first among the gods, act as my witness,
> and this table welcoming your guests,
> and the hearth of excellent Odysseus,   200
> which I've reached, that Odysseus is, in fact,
> already in his native land, sitting still
> or moving, learning of these wicked acts.
> He's sowing trouble for every suitor.
> That's how I interpret that bird omen
> I saw, while sitting on the well-decked ship—
> that's what I said then to Telemachus."

Wise Penelope then answered him and said:

> "Ah stranger, I wish what you've just said
> might come about. Then you'd quickly learn   210
> how kind we are, how many gifts I'd give—
> anyone you met would call you blessed."

Thus they talked to one another of these things.

Meanwhile, outside in front of Odysseus' palace,
the suitors were enjoying themselves, throwing discus
and tossing javelins on a level piece of ground,
as was their custom, displaying their arrogance.
But when it was time for dinner and the sheep arrived,
coming from the fields in all directions, with those

who used to lead them there, Medon spoke to them.
He was the herald they liked more than all the rest,
and he was present with them when they feasted:

> "Young men, now you've entertained your hearts
> with tests of skill, so come inside the house,
> and we'll prepare a meal. There's nothing wrong
> with eating when it's time to have some food."

Medon spoke. Agreeing with what he'd said, they stood up
and moved away. When they reached the stately home,
they set their cloaks down on the seats and armchairs.
Men sacrificed huge sheep and goats with lots of fat. 230
They killed a heifer from the herd, plump hogs as well,
as they prepared the meal.

Meanwhile Odysseus

and the loyal swineherd were hastening to leave,
moving from the fields into the city. Eumaeus,
that outstanding man, was the first to speak. He said:

> "Stranger, since you're keen to reach the city,
> as my master ordered, and get there today—
> myself, I'd rather leave you at the farm
> to guard the place, but I respect and fear him,
> for he may reprimand me afterwards, 240
> and a master's punishment can be severe—
> so come now, let's be off. Most of the day
> has already passed, and as evening comes
> you'll quickly sense it's getting colder."

Resourceful Odysseus then answered him and said:

> "I see that. I know. You're talking to a man
> who understands. So let's be setting out.
> You yourself can lead me the whole way.
> But if you've got a pole somewhere that's cut
> for you to lean on, then give it me. 250
> For you did say the road is slippery."

Odysseus finished, then threw around his shoulders
his ragged bag full of holes, with a twisted strap.
Eumaeus gave him a staff he liked, and then
the two of them set off. The dogs and herdsmen
stayed behind to guard the farmyard. The swineherd
led his master to the city, like a beggar,
leaning on a stick, an old and miserable man,
with his body wrapped in wretched clothing.
But as they walked along the rugged pathway,   260
getting near the city, they reached a well-made spring,
with a steady flow, where townsfolk drew their water,
built by Ithacus, Neritus, and Polyctor.[1]
Around it was a poplar grove, fed by its waters.
They grew on all sides of the spring. Cold water flowed
down from a rock above, and on the top of that
an altar had been dedicated to the nymphs,
where all the people passing by made offerings.
Here Melanthius, son of Dolius, met them—
he was driving on some goats, the finest ones   270
in all the herds, to serve as dinner for the suitors.
Two herdsmen followed with him. When he saw them,
Melanthius started yelling insults. What he said
was shameful and abusive—it stirred Odysseus' heart.

> "Now here we have a truly filthy man
> leading on another filthy scoundrel.
> As always, god matches like with like.
> You miserable swineherd, where are you going
> with this disgusting pig, this beggar man,
> a tedious bore who'll interrupt our feasts?   280
> He'll scratch his shoulders on many doorposts,
> begging scraps—no need for sword or cauldron.[2]
> If you'd let me have him guard my farmyard,
> clean out the pens, and carry tender shoots

---

[1] . . . *and Polyctor.* Ithacus, Neritus, and Polyctor were the ancient founders of
Cephallenia and Ithaca.

[2] *. . . sword or cauldron.* Melanthius is mocking the beggar's status. All he wants is scraps
of food, so the traditional trophies sought by and awarded to successful warriors (swords
and cauldrons) are irrelevant to him.

to my young goats, then he could drink down whey
and put some muscle on those thighs of his.
But since he's picked up his thieving habits,
he won't want to get too close to real work.
No. He'd rather creep around the country
and beg food to fill his bottomless gut.   290
I'll tell you something—and this will happen—
if he reaches godlike Odysseus' home,
many a footstool hurled by real men
will hit his ribs and all parts of his head,
as he's tossed around throughout the house."

Melanthius finished, and as he moved on past them,
in his stupidity he kicked Odysseus on the hip.
But that didn't push Odysseus off the pathway.
He stood there without budging. He was wondering
whether he should charge and kill him with his staff,   300
or grab him by the waist, lift him up, and smash his head
down on the ground. But he hung on, controlling
what was in his heart. Eumaeus looked at the man,
scolded him, then, lifting up his hands in prayer,
he cried aloud:

      "Fountain nymphs, daughters of Zeus,
if for your sake Odysseus ever burned
pieces of thigh from lambs or from young goats,
richly wrapped in fat, grant this prayer for me—
let my master come, guided by some god.
Then he would scatter this presumption,   310
which you now, in your arrogance, display,
always roaming down into the city,
while wicked herdsmen are destroying the flock."

Then Melanthius the goatherd answered him:

      "Dear me, the things this crafty mongrel says!
I'll take him someday on a trim black ship
far from Ithaca—he can make me very rich.
How I wish Apollo with his silver bow

would strike Telemachus in his own house
this very day, or that he'd be overwhelmed   320
by those suitors, since the day Odysseus
will be returning home has been wiped out
in some land far away."

             Melanthius said this
and left them there, as they walked slowly onward.
He strode ahead and quickly reached the royal palace.
He went in at once and sat among the suitors,
opposite Eurymachus, who was fond of him
more than the others were. Those serving at the meal
laid down a portion of the meat in front of him.
The respected housekeeper brought in the bread   330
and placed it there for him to eat.

             Meanwhile Odysseus
and the loyal swineherd paused as they came closer.
Around them rang the music of the hollow lyre,
for Phemius was striking up a song to sing
before the suitors. Odysseus grabbed the swineherd
by the hand and said to him:

                  "Eumaeus,
this place surely is the splendid palace
belonging to Odysseus. It's easy
to recognize, even when one sees it
among many others, for here there is   340
building after building, and this courtyard—
it's finished off with walls and coping stones,
and there's a double gateway well fenced in.
No man could criticize a house like this.
I notice many men are feasting here—
smoke from cooked meat is rising from the house,
and a lyre is playing. A god made that
as our companion at a banquet."

Then, swineherd Eumaeus, you answered him and said:

341

"You recognized it easily enough—   350
for in other things you're quite perceptive.
But come, let's consider how this business
will be carried out. Either you go first
and move inside the finely furnished house
to join the suitors, while I stay outside,
or, if you wish, stay here. I'll go ahead.
But don't hang around for long, just in case
someone sees you here outside and hits you
or throws something. You should consider that,
I tell you."

        Long-suffering lord Odysseus   360
then said to Eumaeus:

           "I know. I see that.
You're talking to a man who understands.
But you go on ahead. I'll stay out here.
Having objects thrown at me or being hit
is nothing new. My heart can bear all that,
since I've put up with many hardships
in war and on the waves. So let all this
be added in with those. There is no way
someone can hide a ravenous stomach—
that torment which brings men so many troubles.   370
Because of it, they launch their well-built ships
and transport evil to their enemies
across the restless sea."

          And so these two men
talked to each other about these things. Then a dog
lying there raised its head and pricked up its ears.
It was Argus, brave Odysseus' hunting dog,
whom he himself had brought up many years ago.
But before he could enjoy being with his dog,
he left for sacred Troy. In earlier days, young men
would take the dog to hunt wild goats, deer, and rabbits,   380
but now, with his master gone, he lay neglected
in the piles of dung left there by mules and cattle,

heaped up before the doors until Odysseus' servants
took it as manure for some large field. Argus lay there,
covered in fleas. Then, when he saw Odysseus,
who was coming closer, Argus wagged his tail
and dropped his ears. But he no longer had the strength
to approach his master. Odysseus looked away
and brushed aside a tear—he did so casually
to hide it from Eumaeus. Then he questioned him: 390

    "Eumaeus, it's strange this dog is lying here,
in the dung. He has a handsome body.
I'm not sure if his speed once matched his looks
or if he's like those table dogs men have,
ones their masters raise and keep for show."

Then, swineherd Eumaeus, you answered him and said:

    "Yes, this dog belongs to a man who died
somewhere far away. If he had the form
and acted as he did when Odysseus
left him and went to Troy, you'd quickly see   400
his speed and strength, and then you'd be amazed.
No wild animal he chased escaped him
in deep thick woods, for he could track a scent.
He's in a bad way now. His master's dead
in some foreign land, and careless women
don't look after him. For when their masters
no longer exercise their power, slaves
have no desire to do their proper work.
Far-seeing Zeus steals half the value of a man
the day he's taken and becomes a slave."   410

This said, Eumaeus went inside the stately palace,
straight into the hall to join the noble suitors.
But once he'd seen Odysseus after nineteen years,
the dark finality of death at once seized Argus.

As the swineherd Eumaeus came inside the house,
godlike Telemachus was the first to see him,

well before the others. He quickly summoned him
by nodding. Eumaeus looked around, then picked up
a stool lying where a servant usually sat
to carve large amounts of meat to serve the suitors,
when they feasted in the house. He took this stool,
placed it by Telemachus' table, facing him,
and then sat down. Meanwhile, a herald brought him
a portion of the meat, set it in front of him,
and lifted some bread for him out of the basket.
Odysseus came into the house behind Eumaeus,
looking like an old and miserable beggar,
leaning on his staff, his body dressed in rags.
He sat on the ash wood threshold in the doorway,
propping his back against a post of cypress wood,
which a craftsman had once planed with skill
and set in true alignment. Then Telemachus
called the swineherd to him and, taking a whole loaf
from the fine basket and as much meat as he could hold
in both his hands, he spoke to him, saying:

"Take this food, and give it to the stranger.
Tell him he can move among the suitors
and beg from each of them in person.
When a man's in need, they say that shame
is not a good companion."

                                    Telemachus spoke.
Once he'd heard these words, Eumaeus went and stood
beside Odysseus, then spoke—his words had wings:

"Stranger, Telemachus gives you this food
and invites you to move around and beg
among the suitors, each in turn. He says,
when one's in need, it's no good being ashamed."

Resourceful Odysseus then answered him and said:

"May lord Zeus, I pray, grant Telemachus
be blessed among all men, get everything

he may desire in his heart."

Once he'd said this, 450
he took the food in his two hands and set it down
right there at his feet, on his tattered bag, and ate,
while the minstrel sang his song throughout the hall.
When he'd eaten and the godlike singer finished,
the suitors were making an uproar in the room.
But Athena approached Odysseus, Laertes' son,
and urged him to collect bread from the suitors,
so he might find out those who did respect the law
and those who flouted their traditions. Even so,
she wouldn't let any man escape destruction. 460
Odysseus then moved off to beg for scraps of bread,
holding out his hand to each of them on every side,
starting on the right, as if he'd been a beggar
for years and years. They pitied him, gave him bread,
and wondered about him, asking one another
who he was and where he came from. Then the goatherd,
Melanthius, spoke out to them:

"Listen to me,
those of you courting the glorious queen,
about this stranger. I've seen him before.
The swineherd was the one who brought him here. 470
I don't know his identity for sure
or the family he claims to come from."

Once he'd said this, Antinous turned on Eumaeus,
to reprimand him:

"You really are a man
who cares for pigs—why bring this fellow here
into the city? As far as vagrants go,
don't we have enough apart from him,
greedy beggars who disrupt our banquets?
Do you think too few of them come here
and waste away your master's livelihood, 480
so you invite this man to come as well?"

Then, swineherd Eumaeus, you answered him and said:

> "Antinous, you may be a noble man,
> but what you've said is not a worthy speech.
> Who looks for strangers from another land
> and then in person asks them to come in,
> unless they're workers in a public space—
> prophets, healers of disease, house builders,
> or inspired minstrels, who sing for our delight?
> Such men are summoned to where people live   490
> all around the boundless earth. But no one
> invites a beggar to consume his goods.
> You are abusive to Odysseus' slaves,
> more so than any of the other suitors,
> especially to me. But I don't care,
> not while faithful Penelope lives here,
> in these halls, and godlike Telemachus."

Then prudent Telemachus replied and said:

> "Be quiet. For my sake don't reply to him
> with a long speech. It's Antinous' habit   500
> always to offer nasty provocation,
> to start a quarrel with abusive words.
> He urges other men to do the same."

That said, he spoke to Antinous—his words had wings:

> "Antinous, you really do care for me,
> like a father for his son, when you tell me
> with your forceful words to drive this stranger
> from the house. May god forbid such action.
> Take some food and give it him yourself—
> I don't mind. In fact, I'm asking you to do it.   510
> You need not worry about my mother
> or any of the servants in this house
> belonging to godlike Odysseus. But still,
> no thought like this could be inside your chest—
> you'd much prefer to stuff yourself with food

than give it to another man."

Antinous
then answered him and said:

"Telemachus,
you're a braggart and won't control your rage.
What are you saying? If every suitor
offered him as much as I will, this house   520
would make him keep his distance for three months."

As he said this, he picked up a stool standing there,
where he used to rest his shining feet while feasting,
raised it from below the table, and brandished it.
But all the other suitors offered something,
and so the beggar's bag was filled with meat and bread.
Odysseus was soon going to retrace his steps
back to the doorway and sound out the Achaeans
with impunity, but he stopped by Antinous,
and spoke to him, saying:

"My friend, give something.   530
You don't seem to me the worst Achaean,
but the very best. You look like a king.
So you should give a bigger piece of bread
than these others. I'd publicize your fame
across the boundless earth. For once I, too,
lived among men in my home, a rich man
with a happy life. There were many times
I'd give presents to some sort of vagabond,
no matter who he was or what he needed
when he came. I had countless servants, too,   540
and many other things that people have
when they live well and are considered wealthy.
But Zeus, son of Cronos, destroyed all that.
That's what he wanted, I suppose. He sent me
with some wandering pirates off to Egypt,
a lengthy voyage, to do away with me.
I moored my curving ships in Egypt's river,

and told my loyal comrades to stay there
with the ships and guard them. I sent out scouts
to go up to the lookouts. But the crew,   550
giving way to impulse and counting on
their strength, quickly started to destroy
the attractive farms of the Egyptians,
carrying off the women and young children,
while slaughtering the men. The cry went up,
and soon it reached the city. Hearing noise,
the people came as soon as dawn appeared—
the entire plain was filled with men on foot
and in their chariots and with gleaming bronze.
Then Zeus, who hurls the thunderbolt, threw down   560
a dreadful panic on my comrades. None of them
dared stand and face up to the enemy.
Disaster loomed for us from every side.
With their sharp bronze they killed a lot of us,
but others they led off while still alive
so they could be compelled to work for them.
They gave me to a stranger they had met,
bound for Cyprus, Dmetor, son of Iasus,
a powerful man who was king of Cyprus.
From there I reached this place in great distress."   570

Then Antinous answered him and said:

                              "What god
sent this nuisance to interrupt our feast?
Go away from my table—over there,
in the middle, or you'll soon find yourself
in a harsher place than Cyprus or in Egypt.
You're an insolent and shameless beggar—
you come up to every man, one by one,
and they give you things without holding back,
for there's no check or scruple when one gives
from someone else's goods, and each of them   580
has plenty of supplies in front of him."

Resourceful Odysseus then moved back and replied:

"Well now, it seems as if that mind of yours
doesn't match your looks—you'd refuse to give
even a grain of salt from your own house
to a follower of yours, and now you sit
in someone else's house and do not dare
to take some bread and offer it to me.
And yet there's plenty right in front of you."

Odysseus finished. Antinous in his heart   590
was even angrier than before. He glared at him,
then, with a scowl, replied—his words had wings:

"I no longer think you'll leave this hall unharmed,
now that you've begun to babble insults."

As he said this, he grabbed the stool and threw it.
It hit the bottom of Odysseus' right shoulder,
where it joins the back. But he stood firm, like a rock—
what Antinous had thrown didn't make him stagger.
He shook his head in silence, making cruel plans
deep in his heart. He went back to the door, sat there,   600
set down his well-filled bag, and addressed the suitors:

"Listen to me, you suitors of the splendid queen,
so I can say what the heart in my chest prompts.
There's no pain in a man's heart, no grieving,
when he's hit fighting for his own possessions,
for cattle or white sheep. But Antinous
struck me because of my wretched belly,
that curse which gives men all kinds of trouble.
So if beggars have their gods and Furies,
may Antinous come to a fatal end,   610
before his wedding day."

Then Antinous, Eupeithes' son,
gave him this reply:

"Sit still and eat, stranger,
or go somewhere else, just in case young men

349

drag you by your hands and feet all through the house
for what you say, scraping your whole body."

He finished. But all those proud men were furious,
and one of the arrogant young men spoke out:

> "Antinous, it was wrong of you to hit
> a wretched vagrant. And you may be doomed,
> if somehow he's a god come down from heaven.   620
> For, in fact, gods make themselves appear
> like foreign strangers, assuming many shapes
> and haunting cities, to investigate
> men's pride and their obedience to the laws."

That's what the suitors said. However, Antinous
paid no attention to their words. Telemachus,
having seen the blow, felt pain growing in his heart.
But his eyelids shed no tears upon the ground.
No. He shook his head in silence and kept planning
dark schemes in his heart. But when wise Penelope   630
heard about the stranger being hit inside the hall,
she spoke to her attendant women, saying:

> "How I wish that he, too, might be struck
> by Apollo, that celebrated archer."

Then housekeeper Eurynome said to her:

> "Oh, if only our prayers could be fulfilled,
> not one of them would see Dawn's lovely throne."

Wise Penelope then answered her:

>   "Good nurse,
> they're all enemies hatching evil plans,
> but Antinous, more than any of them,   640
> is like black fate. Some unhappy stranger
> roams through the house, begging from the men.
> His own need drives him to it. The others,

all of them, gave him gifts and filled his bag,
but Antinous threw a footstool at him
and struck him under his right shoulder."

So Penelope talked with her serving women,
sitting in her room, while lord Odysseus ate.
Then she called out to the loyal swineherd, saying:

> "Good Eumaeus, go and ask the stranger   650
> to come here, so I can greet him warmly
> and ask if he perhaps has heard about
> my brave Odysseus, or caught sight of him
> with his own eyes. He looks like a man
> who's spent a long time wandering around."

Then, swineherd Eumaeus, you answered her and said:

> "I wish the Achaeans would keep quiet,
> my queen, for he tells the kind of stories
> which enchant one's heart. I had him with me
> for three nights, and for three days I kept him   660
> in my hut. He came to me first of all,
> while he was fleeing in secret from a ship.
> But he never finished what he had to say
> of his misfortunes. Just as any man
> looks at a minstrel who sings enticing songs
> to mortal men, ones the gods have taught him,
> and there's no end to their desire to hear,
> whenever he may sing, that's how this man
> enchanted me, as he sat in my home.
> He claims he's a friend of Odysseus' father,   670
> from Crete, where the race of Minos lives,
> He's come here from there, enduring troubles,
> as he keeps wandering from place to place.
> He insists he's heard about Odysseus—
> he's close by, still alive in the rich land
> of Thesprotians—with many treasures
> which he's going to bring back home."

Wise Penelope

then answered him:

"Go and call him here—
he can tell me for himself. And let the men
keep sitting in the hall or at the door   680
enjoying themselves—their hearts are cheerful.
Their own possessions lie untouched at home,
sweet wine and bread, which their servants eat.
But they fill up our house day after day,
butchering our cattle, fat sheep, and goats,
carousing and drinking our gleaming wine,
without restraint. So much is wasted.
There's no one like Odysseus here who'll guard
our house from ruin. If Odysseus came,
got back to his native land, he and his son   690
would quickly take their vengeance on these men
for their violent ways."

As Penelope said this,
Telemachus gave a mighty sneeze—it echoed
through the house. Penelope laughed and quickly spoke
these winged words to Eumaeus:

"Go call the stranger.
Bring him here in front of me. Did you not see
my son sneezing at everything I said?
So the complete destruction of the suitors
will not go unfulfilled—for all of them—
not one will escape his fatal destiny.[1]   700
I'll tell you something else. Lay it to heart.
If I see he tells me the entire truth,
I'll dress him in fine clothes, cloak and tunic."

Penelope finished. Once Eumaeus heard her,
he went off and, standing beside Odysseus,
spoke to him—his words had wings:

---

[1] . . . *fatal destiny*: sneezes can be viewed as omens, hence Penelope's prophetic tone

"Honoured stranger,
wise Penelope is summoning you,
Telemachus' mother. For her heart,
in spite of bearing much anxiety,
is telling her to ask about her husband.   710
If she knows that everything you say
is true, she'll give you a cloak and tunic,
things you really need. And as for food,
you can beg for it throughout the country
and fill your stomach. Whoever wants to
will give it to you."

                    Long-suffering lord Odysseus
then answered him:

                    "Eumaeus, I'll tell the truth,
all the details, to wise Penelope,
daughter of Icarius, and quickly, too.
For I know Odysseus well—both of us   720
have had the same misfortunes. But I fear
this abusive crowd of suitors, whose pride
and violence reach up to iron heaven.
Just now, as I was moving through the house,
doing nothing wrong, this man struck me
and caused me pain. Meanwhile Telemachus
couldn't do a thing to stop him, nor could
any other man. So tell Penelope,
for all her eagerness, to wait right now,
there in the hall, until the sun goes down.   730
Let her ask me then about her husband
and the day of his return. And let me sit
close to the fire, for the clothes I have
are pitiful, as you know for yourself,
since I came to you first of all for help."

Odysseus finished. Once he'd listened to him,
the swineherd went away. As he crossed the threshold,
Penelope addressed him:

                    "You haven't brought him,
Eumaeus. What does the vagrant mean by this?
Is he somehow too afraid of something,   740
or is there some other reason he's ashamed?
He's a bad beggar if he feels disgraced."

Then, swineherd Eumaeus, you answered her and said:

        "What he said made sense—what any other man
would think if he was planning to avoid
the insolence of those presumptuous men.
He says you should wait around till sunset.
And, my queen, it would be far more fitting
for you to talk in person to the stranger,
to hear for yourself what he has to say."   750

Wise Penelope then answered him and said:

        "The stranger is not stupid. For he thinks
about those things that well may happen.
I don't believe there are any mortal men
who are as high handed as these suitors are,
the way they plan their wicked foolishness."

Penelope spoke. Once he'd told her everything,
the loyal swineherd joined the crowd of suitors.
He quickly spoke winged words to Telemachus,
holding his head close to him, so others couldn't hear: 760

        "Friend, I'm going to leave and guard the swine
and other things, your livelihood and mine.
You take charge of all the problems here.
First and foremost, protect yourself. Your heart
must stay alert, so you don't suffer harm.
Many Achaeans are hatching evil plans—
may Zeus destroy them before they harm us."

Shrewd Telemachus then answered him and said:

"It will happen, old friend. Now, you should eat
before you leave. Come here in the morning,
and bring fine animals for sacrifice.
Everything going on here is my concern,
mine and the immortals."

                            Telemachus spoke.
The swineherd sat down on the polished chair again.
Once he'd filled his heart with food and drink, he left,
returning to his pigs, through the courtyard and the hall
full of banqueters, who were enjoying themselves
with dance and song, for evening had already come.

Book Eighteen
Odysseus and Irus the Beggar

[Irus the beggar arrives at the palace and starts abusing Odysseus; the
suitors encourage them to fight; in the scrap Odysseus knocks Irus out;
Odysseus warns Amphinomus of trouble ahead; Athena makes Penelope
want to appear before the suitors; Athena puts Penelope to sleep and
makes her more beautiful; Penelope wakes up and goes downstairs to
mix with the suitors; Telemachus and Penelope talk about the stranger;
Penelope encourages the suitors to bring presents for her, and they do
so; Odysseus talks to the female servants, criticizing them for assisting
the suitors; Odysseus holds up the lamps for the suitors at their feast;
Eurymachus makes fun of Odysseus, and Odysseus give him a heated
reply; Eurymachus throws a stool at Odysseus but misses and hits the
wine steward; Telemachus and Amphinomus restore order; the suitors
continue feasting and then leave.]

Then a vagrant from the community arrived,
who used to beg through all the town of Ithaca,
a man celebrated for his gluttonous stomach,
with an incessant appetite for food and drink.
He looked huge, but had little energy or strength.
He was called Arnaeus—his honoured mother
had given him that name when he was born, but now
all young men called him Irus, because he ran around
carrying messages for anyone who asked him.[1]
At this point he arrived and tried to drive Odysseus   10
away from his own home by shouting out abuse—
his words had wings:

>   "Get out of the door, old man,
> or you'll be dragged off by your feet. Don't you see
> how they're all winking at me, telling me
> to pull you out? As far as I'm concerned,
> I'd be ashamed to do it. So get up,
> or else we'll fight this quarrel with our fists."

---

[1] *. . . for anyone who asked him.* The name Irus is probably a masculine version of Iris,
the name of the goddess who carries messages for the gods.

Resourceful Odysseus frowned, looked at him, and said:

> "My good man, I'm not doing you any harm
> or shouting insults at you. Nor do I care   20
> if someone gives you something, even if
> he takes a generous portion. This doorway
> has room for both of us, and there's no need
> to begrudge what someone else may get.
> You seem to be a vagrant, just like me—
> gods are supposed to give us happiness.
> But don't provoke me too much with your fists,
> in case you make me angry. Though I'm old,
> I might stain your lips and chest with blood.
> If so, I'd enjoy more peace tomorrow,   30
> for I don't think you'd come a second time
> to Odysseus' home, son of Laertes."

That made the beggar Irus angry, so he said:

> "Well, see how nicely this filthy beggar talks,
> like an old woman from the baking ovens.
> But I'll make trouble for him. I'll punch him
> with both fists on the jaw, smash all his teeth
> onto the ground, and treat him like a sow
> who's been devouring the crop. Come now,
> tighten your belt, so all these people here   40
> may recognize that we're about to fight.
> How can you go against a younger man?"

So as their tempers heated up, they both grew angry
on the polished threshold by the lofty doors.
Strong and powerful Antinous observed them there,
and, laughing cheerfully, shouted to the suitors:

> "My friends, here's something we've not seen before.
> Some god has sent this house such entertainment!
> Irus and the stranger are quarreling—
> they're going to fight each other with their fists.   50
> Let's get them started right away!"

Antinous' words

made them all jump up laughing. They gathered there,
around the shabby beggars. Then Eupeithes' son,
Antinous, said to them:

> "Listen to me,
> you brave suitors. I've something to suggest.
> We've got goats' bellies lying by the fire,
> stuffed full of fat and blood, our dinner meal.
> Whichever of these two men wins this fight
> and proves the better man, let him stand up
> and take the one he wishes for himself.   60
> And he will always eat his meals with us.
> Nor will we allow another beggar
> to come into our group and ask for food."

Antinous finished. They were pleased with what he said.
Then, resourceful Odysseus with his crafty mind
spoke to them:

> "Friends, there's no way an older man
> weighed down with grief can fight a younger man.
> But that trouble-making stomach of mine
> urges me to do it, so he may beat me
> with his blows. But come now, let all of you   70
> swear a binding oath that not one of you
> supporting Irus will use his heavy fists
> to strike at me unfairly, and by force
> overpower me on Irus' behalf."

Odysseus spoke. They all promised, as he'd asked.
After they had sworn and finished with the oath,
Telemachus spoke up with strength and confidence,
so all could hear:

> "Stranger, if your proud spirit
> and your heart urge you on to beat this man,
> don't fear a single one of these Achaeans.   80
> Whoever strikes at you will have to fight

with many more as well. I am your host,
and the two princes here agree with me,
Antinous and Eurymachus, both men
who understand things well."

                      Telemachus spoke,
and everyone endorsed his words. Then Odysseus,
while hitching up the rags around his private parts,
exposed his fine large thighs, and they could also see
his wide shoulders and his chest and powerful arms.
Athena came up close beside that shepherd of his people   90
and enlarged his limbs. Each suitor, quite astonished,
would glance at the man beside him and then mutter
words like these:

                "Irus will soon be in trouble,
    something he brought on himself—he won't be
    Irus any more, judging from the thighs
    that old man shows under those rags of his."

That's how they talked. Irus' heart was badly shaken.
But the servants girded up his clothes and led him up.
He was afraid—his flesh quivering on every limb—
but they forced him forward. Antinous sneered at him,   100
addressing him right to his face:

                  "You bragging fool,
    if you're afraid and tremble at this man,
    you should not exist or ever have been born.
    He's a old man worn down by misfortunes
    that have overcome him. I'll tell you this,
    and what I say will happen—if this man
    beats you and proves himself the better man,
    I'll throw you in a black ship, then take you
    over to the mainland to king Echetus,
    who tortures everyone. With pitiless bronze   110
    he'll cut off your nose and ears, then slice away
    your cock and balls and throw them to the dogs,

raw meat for them rip to pieces."[1]

Antinous spoke. An even greater trembling seized
the beggar's legs, as they led him to the middle.
Both men raised their fists. At that point lord Odysseus,
who had endured so much, was of two minds—Should he
hit Irus so his life would leave him where he fell,
or should he strike him a less punishing blow
and stretch him on the ground? As he thought about it,   120
this seemed the better choice—to hit him with less force,
so Achaeans wouldn't look at him too closely.
Once their fists were up, Irus hit Odysseus
on his right shoulder, but Odysseus then struck him
on the neck, below his ear, and crushed the bones.
Immediately red blood came flowing from his mouth.
He fell down moaning in the dirt, grinding his teeth.
His feet kept kicking at the ground. The noble suitors
threw up their hands and almost died of laughter.
Odysseus grabbed Irus by the foot and dragged him   130
through the doorway until he reached the courtyard
and the portico gate. There he left him, leaning
against the courtyard wall with his stick in his hands.
Odysseus then addressed him—his words had wings:

> "Sit there and scare away the pigs and dogs.
> And do not, in your miserable state,
> try to boss around strangers and beggars,
> in case you end up in even worse distress."

As he spoke, he threw his tattered bag full of holes
across his shoulders, hanging by a twisted strap.   140
Then he went back into the doorway and sat down.
The suitors moved inside, laughing uproariously,
and threw him words of greeting as they went.
One of the arrogant young men said something like:

> "May Zeus and the other eternal gods

[1] . . . *tortures everyone.* Echetus was king of Epirus and notorious for his extreme cruelty. He is reputed to have driven bronze spikes into his daughter's eyes.

give you, stranger, the thing you most desire,
what fills your heart—since you've now stopped
this greedy vagrant begging in this place.
We'll soon take him over to the mainland,
to king Echetus, who mutilates all men."   150

That's how they talked. Lord Odysseus was happy
at such welcome words. Then Antinous set down by him
the huge goat stomach stuffed with blood and fat,
and Amphinomus picked two loaves from the basket,
placed them before Odysseus, and then toasted him
with a golden cup, saying:

                    "Greetings, honoured stranger,
          though right now you've got many miseries,
          may happiness be yours in future days."

Then resourceful Odysseus answered him and said:

          "Amphinomus, you seem to be a man   160
          with true intelligence. Your father, too,
          had the same quality. I've heard about
          his noble name—Nisus of Dulichium,
          a brave and wealthy man. And people say
          you come from him, and you do seem discreet.
          So I'll tell you something. You should note this
          and listen. Of all the things that breathe
          and move along the ground, Earth does not raise
          anything more insignificant than man.
          He thinks he'll never suffer any harm   170
          in days to come, as long as gods provide
          prosperity and his knees stay supple.
          But when blessed gods bring on misfortunes,
          he bears those, too, though much against his will.
          The father of gods and men brings men the days
          which shape the spirit of earth's inhabitants.
          Among men I was set to be successful, too,
          but, yielding to my strength and power,
          I did many reckless things. I trusted

361

my father and my family. So no man   180
should ever practise any lawlessness.
He should hold his gifts from gods in silence,
whatever they give. I see suitors here
planning desperate acts, wasting the wealth
and dishonouring the wife of a man who,
I think, will not remain away for long,
not from his family and his native land.
He is close by. May some god lead you home,
and may you not have to confront the man
whenever he comes back to his own place.   190
For I don't believe, once he comes here,
under his own roof, he and the suitors
will separate without some blood being spilled."

Odysseus spoke, and after pouring a libation,
drank some honey wine, then handed the cup back
to the leader of the people. Amphinomus
went through the house, head bowed, with foreboding
in his heart, for he had a sense of troubles
yet in store. Still, he did not escape his fate.
Athena had bound even him to be destroyed   200
by a spear in the strong hand of Telemachus.
He sat back down on the chair from which he'd risen.

Then goddess Athena with the gleaming eyes
put an idea in the mind of wise Penelope,
Icarius' daughter—to appear before the suitors,
so she might really get their hearts excited
and win more honour from her son and husband
than she'd had before. With an unnatural laugh
she spoke out and said:[1]

>   "Eurynome, though my heart
> was never keen before to show myself   210
> to these suitors, it is so now, disgraceful

---

[1] ... *than she had before.* This entire incident (lines 203 to 380) has been the subject of
much scholarly discussion, especially concerning Penelope's motivation and the style of
the writing, since it seems an unnecessary and awkward interruption.

though they are. And I've got words to say
to my own son—it would be better for him
not to mingle with those arrogant suitors.
They may say nice things, but they're making plans
for nasty schemes in future."

                    Then her housekeeper,
Eurynome, answered her and said:

                              "Indeed, my child,
all these things you say make sense. So you must go
and say that to your son. Do not hide it.
But first of all, you should wash your body   220
and put ointment on your face. Don't leave here
showing both cheeks stained with tears like this.
It's wrong to go on suffering grief for ever
and never stop. Your son is old enough
to grow a beard—and you prayed very hard
to gods that you would see him reach that age."

Then wise Penelope replied and said:

          "Eurynome, although you care for me,
don't tell me I should rinse my body off
or rub my skin with oil. Gods on Olympus   230
have ravaged all my beauty, since the day
Odysseus went off in his hollow ships.
But tell Hippodameia and Autonoe
to come in here—they can stand beside me
in the hall. For I won't go in there alone
among the men. I'd be ashamed."

                    Once Penelope said this,
the old woman went through the chamber to instruct
the women and urge them to appear. Then once again,
Athena, bright-eyed goddess, thought of something else.
She poured sweet sleep over Icarius' daughter,   240
who leaned back and fell asleep. Lying on the couch,
all her limbs relaxed. Meanwhile, the lovely goddess

gave her immortal gifts, so those Achaean men
would be enchanted with her. First, with an ointment
made from ambrosia she cleaned her lovely face,
like the balm well-crowned Cytherea rubs on herself
when she goes to the joyful dancing of the Graces.[1]
She made her taller, too, and changed her figure,
so it looked more regal. Then she made her whiter
than fresh-cut ivory. After she'd done all this,   250
the lovely goddess left, and white-armed servants came,
chattering as they moved there from their chambers.
Sweet sleep then released Penelope. With her hands
she rubbed her cheeks and said:

> "In spite of heavy pain,
> a deep sweet sleep has held me in its arms.
> I wish pure Artemis would quickly bring
> a gentle death to me right now, so I
> no longer waste my life away, mourning
> in my heart and craving my dear husband,
> a man with every form of excellence,   260
> the finest of Achaeans."

> Once she'd said this,
she moved down from her shining upper chambers.
She was not alone—two attendants went with her.
When the noble lady reached the suitors, she stood
beside a pillar holding up the well-made roof,
with a bright veil before her face. Loyal servants
stood with her, one on either side. The suitors
in their hearts felt immediately overwhelmed
with sexual desire, and their legs grew weak.
Each of them prayed that he could go to bed with her.   270
But she addressed her dear son Telemachus:

> "Telemachus, your wit and understanding
> are not as steady as they used to be.
> While still a child, the way you used to think
> was more astute. But now you're fully grown,

[1] *Cytherea*: a common name for Aphrodite, goddess of sexual desire.

on the verge of being a man, and anyone
from somewhere far away who looked at you
and only saw your beauty and your size
might well observe that you're a rich man's son.
Yet your mind and thoughts are no longer wise.   280
What sort of actions are going on in here,
in this house, when you allow a stranger
to be mistreated in this way? And now,
what if this stranger, sitting in our home,
should suffer harm from such severe abuse?
You'd be disgraced among all men and shamed."

Shrewd Telemachus then answered her and said:

"Mother, I don't take issue with you now
for being angry. I know about these things.
My heart understands them, all the details,   290
good and bad. I was still a child before.
But I can't think through everything correctly,
with these men sitting round me on all sides—
they strike at me and hatch their wicked plans.
And I've no one here to guard me. But still,
this battle between Irus and the stranger
did not turn out the way the suitors wished.
The stranger's strength made him the better man.
By Father Zeus, Athena, and Apollo,
I wish these suitors now inside our home   300
could be overpowered, just as Irus was,
their heads drooping down inside the courtyard
and inside the hall, with each man's limbs
gone limp—that's how Irus is now sitting
beside the courtyard gate, nodding his head,
like some drunken fool. He can't stand upright
or wander home, wherever his home is,
because his precious limbs have all gone slack."

As they were talking to each other in this way,
Eurymachus spoke to Penelope and said: 310

365

"Daughter of Icarius, wise Penelope,
if all the Argives in Iasian Argos
could see you, more suitors would be feasting
in your home from tomorrow on, since you
excel all women for your form, your stature,
and for the wisdom you have in your heart."[1]

Wise Penelope then answered him:

                              "Eurymachus,
what's excellent about my form and beauty
the gods destroyed when Argives left for Troy
and Odysseus, my husband, went with them.   320
If he would come and organize my life,
then I'd be more beautiful and famous.
But now I'm grieving. A god has sent me
so much trouble! You know, when he went off
and left his native land, he held the wrist
on my right hand and said:

                              'Wife,
I don't believe all well-armed Achaeans
will make it safely back from Troy unharmed.
For Trojans, people say, are fighting men,
who can hurl their spears and draw their arrows   330
and control swift-footed horses, those things
which soon decide the outcome of the fight
in an impartial war. So I don't know
if god will get me back or I'll be killed
over there in Troy. So you must care for
everything back here. When I'm away,
think of father and mother in the home,
the way you do right now, but even more.
But when you see our son has grown a beard,
then marry who you wish, and leave the house.'   340

"That's what he said. Now it's all happening.

---

[1] *. . . in your heart:* Iasian Argos seems to be a reference to a wide geographical area, either the
whole of the Peloponnese or all Greek settlements generally.

The night will come when some hateful marriage
will be my lot, now that I've been cursed,
for Zeus has taken away my happiness,
and painful grief has come into my heart,
into my spirit. The way you men behave
was not appropriate for suitors in the past.
Those who wish to court a noble lady,
daughter of a wealthy man, and compete
against each other, bring in their cattle,   350
their own rich flocks, to feast the lady's friends.
They give splendid presents and don't consume
another's livelihood and pay him nothing."

Penelope finished. Long-suffering lord Odysseus
was pleased that she was getting them to give her gifts,
charming them with soothing words, her mind on other things.

Then Antinous, Eupeithes' son, spoke to her:

"Daughter of Icarius, wise Penelope,
if one of the Achaeans wants to bring
a gift in here, you should accept it.   360
It's not good if you refuse a present.
But we'll not be going back to our estates
or any other place, until you marry
whoever is the best of the Achaeans."

Antinous spoke. His comments pleased the suitors.
Each man sent a herald out to fetch some gifts.
One of them brought back, at Antinous' request,
a large and lovely robe with rich embroidery.
It had golden brooches on it, twelve in all,
fitted with graceful curving clasps. Another man   370
brought in a chain made of gold for Eurymachus,
a finely crafted work strung with amber beads,
bright as the sun. Two attendants carried back
some earrings for Eurydamas, with three droplets
in a stylish shining cluster. For lord Peisander,
Polyctor's son, an attendant brought a necklace,

367

a splendid piece of jewelry. All Achaeans
presented her with some gorgeous gift or other.
Noble Penelope then left and went upstairs.
Her servants carried up the lovely gifts for her.   380
Then the suitors turned to joyful songs and dances,
enjoying themselves, waiting for evening to arrive.
And as they entertained themselves, black evening came.
They then set up three braziers in the hall for light.
They put dry kindling round them, hard seasoned wood,
freshly split by axe. They set torches in between,
and brave Odysseus' servants held up the blazing flames.
Then Odysseus, born from Zeus, man of many schemes,
addressed those slaves in person, saying:

                              "Servants of Odysseus,
          your master, who's been gone away so long,   390
          go to the rooms the honoured queen lives in,
          and twist the yarn beside her. Sit down there,
          and make her happy, by staying in the room
          or combing wool by hand. As for these lamps,
          I'll keep providing light for all these men.
          Even if they wish to stay for fair-throned Dawn,
          they cannot not wear me down, for I'm a man
          who can endure much suffering."

                                        Odysseus spoke.
The servants looked at one another and burst out laughing.
Then fair-cheeked Melantho chastised him shamefully,   400
a child of Dolius, but Penelope had raised her,
treating her as her own daughter, providing toys,
whatever she desired. And yet, in spite of this,
her heart was never sorry for Penelope,
for she loved Eurymachus and had sex with him.
Now in abusive language she rebuked Odysseus:

          "You idiotic stranger, you're a man
          whose mind has had all sense knocked out of it.
          You've no wish to go into the blacksmith's home
          or a public house somewhere to get some sleep.   410

368

No. You're here, and you babble all the time.
Around these many men, you're far too brash.
There's no fear in your heart. In fact, it's wine
that's seized your wits, or else your mind
has always been that way and forces you
to prattle uselessly. Are you playing the fool
because you overcame that beggar Irus?
Take care another man, better than him,
doesn't quickly come to stand against you.
His heavy fists will punch you in the head,   420
stain you with lots of blood, and shove you out,
send you packing from this house."

       With an angry frown,
wily Odysseus then answered her and said:

  "You bitch! Now I'll go and tell Telemachus
  the way you talk, so he can cut you up,
  limb from limb, right here."

       Once Odysseus spoke,
his words alarmed the women, and they scattered,
moving off and fleeing through the hall. Each of them
felt her limbs grow slack with fear—they all believed
he was telling them the truth. Then Odysseus stood   430
beside the flaming braziers, keeping them alight.
He looked at all the men. But in his chest his heart
was making other plans, which he would act upon.

There was no way Athena would allow the suitors,
those arrogant men, to stop behaving badly,
so that still more pain would sink into the heart
of Laertes' son, Odysseus. So Eurymachus,
son of Polybus, began to shout to them,
insulting Odysseus, to make his comrades laugh.

  "Listen to me, those of you who're courting   440
  the splendid queen, so I may speak to you
  of what the heart inside my chest is urging.

369

The gods were not unwilling this man came
into Odysseus' home. In fact, I think
the torch light emanates from his own head
because he's got no hair up there at all."[1]

Once he'd said this, he then spoke to Odysseus,
destroyer of cities:

"Stranger, how'd you like to work?
What if I hired you for some distant farm—
I guarantee I'd pay you—gathering stones   450
to build up walls and planting lofty trees?
I'd bring some food there for you all year round,
clothe you, and get some sandals for your feet.
But since you've only learned to misbehave,
you won't want to acquaint yourself with work.
No. You'd prefer to beg throughout the land,
collecting food for your voracious gut."

Resourceful Odysseus then answered him and said:

"Eurymachus, I wish the two of us
could have a contest working in the spring,   460
when long days come, both mowing down the grass.
I'd have a curved scythe in my hands, and you
with one just like it. Then we'd test ourselves,
in lush grass, with no food to eat till dusk.
If we had oxen there, the best there are,
huge tawny beasts, both well fed on grass,
with strength that never tires, and in a field
measuring four acres and containing soil
which turns under the plough, then you'd see
if I could cut a straight unbroken furrow.   470
If this very day Cronos' son stirred up
a battle somewhere and I had a shield,
two spears, and a helmet all of bronze,
well fitted to my temples, then you'd see

---

[1] ... *there at all.* He means Odysseus must be radiating light (hence must be divine or getting divine help) because he has no hair on his head which might burn to produce a flame.

how I'd join in with fighters in the front.
And you'd not chatter on, insulting me
about my stomach. But you're much too proud,
and your mind's unfeeling. You really think
you're an important man, with real power,
because you mingle with a few weak men.   480
But if Odysseus returned, got back here
to his native land, those doors over there,
although they're really wide, would quickly seem
too narrow for you as you fled outside."

Odysseus finished. Eurymachus in his heart
grew even angrier, and, with scowl, he spoke—
his words had wings:

                    "You miserable man,
I'll bring you trouble soon enough. You talk
brashly in this way among so many men,
no fear in your heart! Wine has seized your wits,   490
or else your mind has always been like this,
and prattles vainly on. Have you gone mad
because you beat that beggar Irus?"

As he said this, he picked up a stool. But Odysseus
sat down beside the knee of Amphinomus
from Dulichium, in fear of Eurymachus.
So Eurymachus struck a person serving wine
on his right hand. The wine jug fell and hit the ground
with a resounding clang, and the server groaned,
then toppled backwards in the dirt. The suitors   500
broke into an uproar in the shadowy halls,
and one man, glancing at the person next to him,
said something like these words:

                    "How I wish
that wandering stranger there had perished
somewhere else before he reached this place.
He'd not be making such a fuss among us.
Now we're brawling over beggars. This meal,

the splendid feast, will bring us no delight,
now that this trouble's got the upper hand."

Telemachus then spoke to them with royal authority: 510

> "You fools, you've gone insane, and in your hearts
> no longer hide how much you eat and drink.
> You must be being incited by some god.
> So, now you've feasted well, return back home.
> When the spirit bids, you can get some rest.
> Still, I'm not chasing anyone away."

Telemachus spoke, and they all bit their lips,
astonished that he'd spoken out so boldly.
Then Amphinomus, splendid son of Nisus,
son of lord Aretias, spoke to them and said: 520

> "My friends, when a man says something just,
> no one should get enraged and answer him
> with hostile words. Don't abuse this stranger
> or any slaves in lord Odysseus' home.
> But come, let the wine server pour some drops
> into our cups so we can make libations,
> and then go home and rest. This stranger here,
> we'll leave him in Odysseus' palace,
> and Telemachus can cater to him—
> after all, it's his home which he came to."   530

Amphinomus finished. They were all delighted
with what he'd said. A herald from Dulichium,
lord Mulius, attending on Amphinomus,
mixed wine in a bowl for them and served it round,
coming to each man in his turn. They poured libations
to the sacred gods and drank wine sweet as honey.
Once they'd poured libations and had drinks of wine
to their heart's content, they all went on their way,
each man going to his own house to get some rest.

Book Nineteen
Eurycleia Recognizes Odysseus

[Odysseus and Telemachus hide the weapons; Telemachus leaves to go to bed; Penelope comes down; Melantho insults Odysseus a second time; Penelope upbraids her, then has a conversation with Odysseus; Penelope tells him of her deception of the suitors; Odysseus gives her a long false story of his Cretan ancestry and talks of meeting Odysseus; Penelope questions him about Odysseus' clothes and comrades; Penelope orders Eurycleia to wash Odysseus' feet; the story of the scar on Odysseus' knee, how Odysseus got his name; the hunting expedition with Autolycus; Eurycleia recognizes the scar; Odysseus threatens her; Penelope and Odysseus resume their conversation; Penelope tells about her dream; Odysseus comments on the interpretation of the dream; Penelope talks about the two gates of dreams, then proposes the contest of firing an arrow through twelve axe heads; Odysseus urges her to have the contest; Penelope goes upstairs to sleep.]

So lord Odysseus remained in the hall behind,
thinking of ways he might kill off the suitors,
with Athena's help. He spoke out immediately
to Telemachus—his words had wings:

> "Telemachus,
> all these war weapons we must stash inside,
> and when the suitors notice they're not there
> and question you, then reassure them,
> using gentle language:
>
>> 'I've put them away
>> in a place far from the smoke. Those weapons
>> are no longer like the ones Odysseus left   10
>> when he set off for Troy so long ago.
>> They're tarnished. That's how much the fire's breath
>> has reached them. Moreover, a god has set
>> a greater fear inside my heart—you may drink
>> too much wine and then fight amongst yourselves
>> and wound each other. That would shame the feast,

disgrace your courtship. For iron by itself
can draw a man to use it.'"

Odysseus finished.
His dear father's words convinced Telemachus.
He called his nurse, Eurycleia, and said to her:

"Nurse, come and help me. Keep the women
in their rooms, so I can put away in storage
these fine weapons belonging to my father.
Since the time he left, when I was still a child,
no one's looked after them, and smoky fires
have tarnished them. Now I want to keep them
beyond the reach of breathing fire."

His dear nurse, Eurycleia, then said to him:

"Yes, my child, may you always think about
caring for this house, guarding all its wealth.
But come, who will go off and fetch a light
and carry it for you, if you won't let
the servant women, who could hold torches,
walk out in front of you?"

Shrewd Telemachus
then answered her and said:

"This stranger will.
I won't let anyone who's touched my food
rest idle, not even if he's come here
from somewhere far away."

Telemachus spoke.
She did not reply—her words could find no wings.
So she locked shut the doors in that stately room.
Then both Odysseus and his splendid son jumped up
and carried away the helmets, embossed shields,
and pointed spears. In front of them Pallas Athena
held up a golden lamp and cast a lovely light.

Then suddenly Telemachus spoke to his father:

> "Father, what my eyes are witnessing
> is an enormous wonder. In this room
> the walls and beautiful pedestals,
> the fir beams and high supporting pillars
> are glowing in my eyes, as if lit up   50
> by blazing fire. Some god must be inside,
> one of those who hold wide heaven."

                        Resourceful Odysseus
then answered him and said:

>   "Keep quiet.
> Check those ideas and ask no questions.
> This is how gods who hold Olympus work.
> You should go and get some rest. I'll stay here,
> so I can agitate the servants even more—
> and your mother. As she laments, she'll ask
> for each and every detail."

                       Odysseus finished.
Telemachus moved off, going through the hall,   60
below the flaming torches, out into the room
where he used to rest when sweet sleep came to him.
Then he lay down there and waited for the dawn.
Lord Odysseus remained behind, in the hall,
thinking how to kill the suitors with Athena's help.

Then wise Penelope emerged out of her room,
looking like Artemis or golden Aphrodite.
Beside the fire where she used to sit, they placed
a chair for her, inlaid with ivory and silver.
Imalcius, a craftsman, had made it years ago.   70
He'd fixed a footstool underneath, part of the chair,
on which they usually threw a large sheep fleece.
Here wise Penelope sat, while white-armed servants
came from the women's hall and started to remove
the lavish amounts of food, the tables, and the cups

high-spirited suitors had been drinking from.
The embers in the braziers they threw on the floor,
then filled them up with plenty of fresh wood
for warmth and light. But then Melantho once again
went at Odysseus, chiding him a second time:

> "Stranger, are you still going to pester us
> even now, all through the night in here,
> roaming around the house, spying on women?
> Get outside, you wretch, and be satisfied
> with what you've had to eat, or soon enough
> you'll be beaten with a torch and leave that way."

Resourceful Odysseus scowled and said to her:

> "You're a passionate woman—why is it
> you go at me like this, with such anger
> in your heart? Is it because I'm filthy,   90
> wear shabby clothing on my body,
> and beg throughout the district? I have to—
> sheer need forces that on me. That's what
> beggars and vagabonds are like. But once
> I was wealthy and lived in my own home,
> in a rich house, too, among my people.
> I often gave gifts to a wanderer like me,
> no matter who he was or what his needs
> when he arrived. I had countless servants
> and many other things that people have   100
> when they live well and are considered rich.
> But then Zeus, son of Cronos, ruined me.
> That's what he wanted, I suppose. And so,
> woman, take care that you, too, someday
> don't lose all that grace which now makes you
> stand out among the woman servants here.
> Your mistress may lose her temper with you
> and make things difficult, or Odysseus
> may come home, for there's still a shred of hope.
> Even if he's dead and won't come home again,   110
> thanks to Apollo he's got Telemachus,

376

a son just like himself. And no woman
in these halls who acts with recklessness
escapes his notice. He's a child no longer."

Odysseus spoke. Wise Penelope heard his words
and rebuked Melantho, saying to her:

> "You can be sure,
> you bold and reckless bitch, I've noticed
> your gross acts. And you'll wipe away the stain
> with your own head. You clearly know full well,
> because you heard me say it—I'm intending   120
> to ask this stranger in my halls some questions
> about my husband, since I'm in so much pain."

Penelope paused, then spoke to Eurynome,
her housekeeper, and said:

> "Eurynome,
> bring a chair over here with a fleece on it,
> so the stranger can sit down and talk to me
> and hear me out. I want to question him."

Once Penelope had spoken, Eurynome
quickly brought a polished chair and placed it there.
She threw a sheep fleece over it. Lord Odysseus,   130
who'd been through so much, sat down on it. And then
wise Penelope began their conversation:

> "Stranger, first of all I'll ask this question—
> Who are you among men? Where are you from?
> From what city? And where are your parents?"

Resourceful Odysseus then answered her and said:

> "Lady, no human living on boundless earth
> could find fault with you. And your fame extends
> right up to spacious heaven, as it does
> for an excellent king who fears the gods   140

377

and governs many courageous people,
upholding justice. His black earth is rich
in barley and in wheat, and his orchards
are laden down with fruit. His flocks bear young
and never fail, while the sea yields up its fish.
All this from his fine leadership. With him
his people thrive. So here inside your home
ask me questions about anything except
my family or my native land, in case
you fill my heart with still more sorrow,   150
as I remember them. For I'm a man
who's suffered a great deal, and there's no need
for me to sit here weeping my laments
in someone else's house—for it's not good
to be sad all the time and never stop,
in case the slaves or you yourself resent it
and say I swim in tears because my mind
is now besotted, loaded down with wine."

Wise Penelope then answered him and said:

    "Stranger, the immortal gods destroyed   160
my excellence in form and body
when Argives got on board their ships for Troy.
Odysseus went with them, my husband.
If he would come and organize my life,
my reputation then would be more famous,
more beautiful, as well. But now I grieve.
Some god has laid so many troubles on me.
For all the finest men who rule the islands—
Dulichium, Same, wooded Zacynthus—
and those who live in sunny Ithaca,   170
these men are courting me against my will.
And they are ruining the house. That's why
I have no time for suppliants and strangers,
or for heralds who do the people's work.[1]

---

[1] . . . *people's work*: Public heralds work on public business, as opposed to heralds
retained by rich aristocrats to carry their private messages.

Instead I waste away my heart, longing
for Odysseus. They're all keen on marriage,
but I trick them with my weaving. Some god
first breathed into my heart the thought
that I should place a huge loom in the halls
and weave a robe, wide and delicate fabric.   180
So I spoke to them at once:

                              'You young men,
    my suitors, since lord Odysseus is dead,
    you're keen for me to marry, but you must wait
    until I'm finished with this robe, so I
    don't waste this woven yarn in useless work.
    It's a burial shroud for lord Laertes,
    for when the lethal fate of his sad death
    will seize him, so no Achaean woman
    in the district will get angry with me
    that a man who'd won much property   190
    should have to lie without a death shroud.'

"That's what I said, and their proud hearts agreed.
So every day I'd weave at the big loom.
But at night, once the torches were set up,
I'd unravel it. And so for three years
I tricked Achaeans into believing me.
But as the seasons came and months rolled on,
and many days passed by, the fourth year came.
That's when they came and caught me undoing yarn—
thanks to my slaves, those ungrateful bitches.   200
They all shouted speeches at me. And so,
against my will, I was forced to finish off
that piece of weaving. Now I can't escape
the marriage or invent some other scheme.
My parents are really urging me to marry,
and my son is worrying about those men
eating away his livelihood. He notices,
because he's now a man, quite capable
of caring for a household to which Zeus
has granted fame. But tell me of your race,   210

where you come from. For you did not spring up
out of an oak tree in some ancient story
or from a stone."

Odysseus, a man of many schemes,
then answered her and said:

"Noble lady,
wife of Odysseus, Laertes' son,
will you never stop asking your questions
about my family? All right, I'll tell you.
But you'll be giving me more sorrows
than those which grip me here—as is the rule
when a man's been absent from his native land   220
as long as I have now, wandering around,
through many towns of mortal men, suffering
great distress. Still, I'll answer what you ask,
the questions you have posed. There's a place
in the middle of the wine-dark sea called Crete,
a lovely, fruitful land surrounded by the sea.
Many men live there, more than one can count,
in ninety cities. The dialects they speak
are all mixed up. There are Achaeans
and stout-hearted native Cretans, too,   230
Cydonians and three groups of Dorians,
and noble Pelasgians. Their cities
include great Cnossos, where king Minos reigned,
after he'd talked with Zeus for nine full years,
the father of my father, brave Deucalion.
Deucalion had me and king Idomeneus.
But Idomeneus went away to Troy
in his beaked ships with Atreus' sons.
My name's well known—Aethon—the younger son,
but Idomeneus was older by birth   240
and was the finer man. I saw Odysseus there
and gave him welcoming gifts. The wind's force
brought him to Crete, as he was sailing on,
bound for Troy—it drove him off his course
past Malea. He'd moored at Amnisus,

where one finds the cave of Eilithyia,
in a difficult harbour, fleeing the storm,
but only just. He went immediately
up to the city, seeking Idomeneus,
saying he was his loved and honoured friend.   250
But by now nine or ten days had gone by
since Idomeneus had set off for Troy
in his beaked ships. So I invited him
into my house and entertained him well,
with a kind welcome, using the rich store
of goods inside my house. For the others,
comrades who followed him, I gathered up
and gave out barley from the public stores,
gleaming wine, and cattle for sacrifice,
enough to satisfy their hearts. And there   260
those Achaean lords remained twelve days.
The great North Wind held them there, penned them in—
he would not let them stand up on the earth.
Some angry deity had stirred him up.
But on the thirteenth day, the wind eased off,
and they put out to sea."

                    As Odysseus spoke,
he made the many falsehood seem like truth.
Penelope listened with tears flowing down.
Her flesh melted—just as on high mountains
snow melts away under West Wind's thaw,   270
once East Wind blows it down, and, as it melts,
the flowing rivers fill—that's how her fair cheeks
melted then, as she shed tears for her husband,
who was sitting there beside her. Odysseus
felt pity in his heart for his grieving wife,
but his eyes stayed firm between his eyelids,
like horn or iron, and he kept up his deceit
to conceal his tears. But then, when Penelope
had had enough of crying and mourning,
she spoke to him once more and said:

                            "Now, stranger,   280

I think I'd really like to test you out,
to see if you did, in fact, entertain
my husband and his fine companions there,
in your halls, as you just claimed. So tell me
what sort of clothes he had on his body
and the kind of man he was. And tell me
about his comrades who went there with him."

Resourceful Odysseus then answered her and said:

"Lady, it's difficult to tell you this
for any man who's been away so long—   290
it's now the twentieth year since he went off
and left my country. But I'll describe for you
how my heart pictures him. Lord Odysseus
wore a woolen purple cloak, a double one.
The brooch on it was made of gold—it had
a pair of clasps and a fine engraving
on the front, a dog held in its forepaws
a dappled fawn, gripping it as it writhed.
Everyone who saw it was astonished
at those gold animals—the dog held down   300
the fawn, as he throttled it, and the fawn
was struggling with its feet, trying to flee.
I noticed the tunic on his body—
glistening like the skin of a dry onion—
it was so soft and shone out like the sun.
In fact, many women kept watching him
in wonder. And I'll tell you something else.
Keep in mind I don't know if Odysseus
dressed his body in these clothes at home,
or if some comrade gave them to him   310
on his swift ship after he went aboard,
or perhaps a stranger did—Odysseus
was liked by many men. Few Achaeans
could equal him. I gave him gifts myself,
a bronze sword, a lovely purple cloak,
with a double fold, and a fringed tunic,
and I sent him off on his well-benched ship

382

with every honour. And in his company
he had a herald, older than himself,
but not by much. I'll tell you about him.   320
He looked like this—he had rounded shoulders,
a dark skin, and curly hair. And his name
was Eurybates. Odysseus valued him
more than any other of his comrades—
he had a mind that matched his own."

As Odysseus spoke, in Penelope he roused
desire to weep still more, because she recognized
in what Odysseus said signs that he spoke the truth.
But then, when she'd had enough of tearful sorrow,
she answered him and said these words:

                                        "Stranger,   330
        though I pitied you before, in my home
        you'll now find genuine welcome and respect.
        I was the one who gave him that clothing
        you talk about. I brought it from the room,
        folded it, and pinned on the shining brooch
        to be an ornament for him. But now,
        I'll not be welcoming him here again,
        when he returns to his dear native land.
        Odysseus set off with an evil fate
        to catch a glimpse of wicked Ilion,   340
        a place that never should be spoken of."

Resourceful Odysseus then answered her and said:

        "Noble wife of Odysseus, Laertes' son,
        don't mar your lovely skin or waste your heart
        by weeping for your husband any more.
        I don't blame you in the least, for anyone
        would mourn the husband she had married
        and then lost, one she'd had loving sex with
        and to whom she borne a child, even if
        he were not Odysseus, who, people say   350
        is like the gods. But end your crying,

383

and listen to my words. I'll tell you the truth,
hiding nothing—for I've already heard
about Odysseus' return. He's close by,
in the wealthy land of Thesprotians,
still alive and bringing much fine treasure
with him. He's urging men to give him gifts
throughout that land. He lost his loyal friends
on the wine-dark sea and his hollow ship,
as he was moving from the island Thrinacia.   360
Zeus and Helios were angry with him—
his crew had slaughtered Helios' cattle.
So they all perished in the surging sea.
But Odysseus, holding onto the ship's keel,
was tossed by waves on shore, in the land
of the Phaeacians, who by their descent
are close relations of the gods. These men
honoured him with all their hearts, just as if
he were a god. They gave him many gifts
and were keen to bring him home unharmed.   370
Odysseus would have been here long ago,
but to his heart it seemed a better thing
to visit many lands collecting wealth.
For above all mortal men, Odysseus
knows ways to win many advantages.
No other man can rival him in this.
That's what Pheidon, the Thesprotian king,
told me, and he swore to me in person,
as he poured libations in his home,
the ship was launched and comrades were prepared   380
to take him back to his dear native land.
But before they left he sent me away.
It happened that a Thesprotian ship
was sailing for wheat-rich Dulichium.
He showed me all the rich possessions
Odysseus had collected. There was enough
to feed his family for ten generations—
that's how much was lying in storage there
in that king's house. Odysseus, he said,
had gone to Dodona to find out there,   390

384

from the towering oak, what plans Zeus had
for the voyage back to his dear native land,
after being away so long. Should he come
openly or in secret? He's near by and safe
and will be here soon. He won't stay away
from his friends and native land much longer.
I'll make an oath on that for you. May Zeus
be my first witness, highest and best of gods,
and the hearth of excellent Odysseus,
which I've reached, all these things will happen   400
just as I describe. In this very month
Odysseus will come, as the old moon wanes
and the new moon starts to rise."

        Wise Penelope
then answered him and said:

                    "Oh stranger,
I wish what you have said might come about.
You'd soon come to recognize my friendship,
so many gifts from me that any man
who met you would call you truly blessed.
But my heart has a sense of what will be—
Odysseus won't be coming home again,   410
and you'll not find a convoy out of here,
because there are no leaders in this house,
not the quality of man Odysseus was,
if there was ever such a man, to welcome
honoured strangers and send them on their way.
But, you servant women, wash this stranger,
and prepare a place to sleep—a bed, cloaks,
bright coverlets—so in warmth and comfort
he may reach Dawn with her golden throne.
Tomorrow morning early give him a bath   420
and rub him down with oil, so he'll be ready
to take his seat inside the hall and eat his meal
beside Telemachus. Things will go badly
for any one of them who injures him
and pains his heart—that man will accomplish

nothing further here, even though his rage
is truly fierce. How will you learn from me,
stranger, that I in any way excel
among all women for my prudent plans
and my intelligence, if you dine here,   430
in my halls, dressed in filthy ragged clothes?
Men don't live long. And if a man is harsh
and thinks unfeelingly, then everyone
lays painful curses on his future life,
and when he's dead they all make fun of him.
But if a man is innocent and thinks
with no sense of injury, then strangers
bear his fame far and wide among all men,
and many say of him 'He's a true man.'"

Resourceful Odysseus then answered her and said: 440

"Honoured wife of Odysseus, Laertes' son,
I've hated cloaks and shining coverlets
since I first left the mountain snows of Crete,
when I departed on my long-oared ship.
So I'll lie down, as I've been doing before
through sleepless nights. I've lain many nights
on foul bedding, awaiting bright-throned Dawn.
And having my feet washed brings no delight
into my heart. No woman in your household
will touch my feet, none of the serving women   450
in your home, unless there is an old one,
who knows true devotion and has suffered
in her heart as many pains as I have.
I'd not resent it if she touched my feet."

Wise Penelope then answered him and said:

"Dear stranger, no guest from distant lands
who's come into my house has ever been
as wise as you or more welcome—your words
are all so sensible and thoughtful. I do have
an old woman with an understanding heart.   460

She gave my helpless husband her fine care
the day his mother first gave birth to him.
Although she's weak and old, she'll wash your feet.
So come now, stand up, wise Eurycleia,
and bathe a man the same age as your master.
Perhaps Odysseus has feet and hands like his,
for mortal men soon age when times are bad."

Penelope spoke, and the old woman held her hands
over her face and shed warm tears. She spoke out
uttering words of sorrow:

                        "Alas for you, my child.   470
There's nothing I can do. Zeus must despise you
above all people, though you have a heart
that fears the gods. No mortal up to now
has given Zeus, who hurls the thunderbolt,
so many rich burned pieces of the thigh,
or offered such well-chosen sacrifice
as you've made to him, praying you might reach
a sleek old age and raise your splendid son.
But now from you alone he's taken away
the day that you'll return. And it may be   480
that women in some strange and far-off land
make fun of him, as well, when he arrives
at some famous home, the way these bitches,
mock you here, all of them. To stop their slurs,
their insults, you won't let them wash your feet.
But Icarius' daughter, wise Penelope,
has asked me to do it, and I'm willing.
So for Penelope's sake I'll bathe your feet,
and for yours, since the heart in me is stirred
with sorrow. But come now, listen to me.   490
Hear what I say. Many worn-out strangers
have come here, but none of them, I tell you,
was so like him to look at—your stature,
voice, and feet are all just like Odysseus."

Then resourceful Odysseus answered her and said:

"Old woman, those who've seen the two of us
with their own eyes all say the same—we both
look very like each other, as you've seen
and mentioned."

After these words from Odysseus,
the old woman took the shining bowl to wash his feet.   500
She poured in plenty of cold water and added
warmer water to it. Odysseus then sat down
some distance from the hearth and quickly turned around
towards the darkness. For suddenly in his heart
he was afraid that, when she touched him, she might see
a scar he had, and then the truth would be revealed.
She came up and began to wash her master.
She recognized the scar immediately, a wound
a boar's white tusk had given him many years ago,
when he'd gone to Parnassus, making a visit   510
to Autolycus, his mother's splendid father,
and his sons. That man could surpass all others
in thievery and swearing. A god himself, Hermes,
had given him those skills. For him he used to burn
pleasing offerings, thighs of younger goats and lambs.
So Hermes traveled with him, bringing willing favours.
When he came to the wealthy land of Ithaca,
Autolycus had met his daughter's new born son,
and once he'd finished dinner, Eurycleia
set the child upon his knees and spoke to him: 520

"Autolycus, you must personally find
your daughter's child a name. We've been praying
for a long time now to have this child."

So Autolycus then answered her and said:

"My son-in-law and daughter, give the boy
whatever name I say. Since I've come here
as one who's been enraged at many people,
men and women, on this all-nourishing earth,

388

let him be called Odysseus, a man of rage.[1]
As for me, when he's become a full-grown man   530
and comes to see his mother's family home
at Parnassus, where I keep my property,
I'll give him some of it and send him off.
He'll be delighted."

               It was for that reason,
to get those splendid presents from Autolycus,
that Odysseus had come. Autolycus and his sons
clasped his hand in welcome, greeted him with kindness,
and his mother's mother, Amphithea, hugged him,
kissed him on the head and both his lovely eyes.
Autolycus then called out to his noble sons   540
to prepare a meal, and they answered his call.
Quickly they brought in a male ox, five years old,
flayed it, and prepared the beast, slicing up the limbs.
They cut these skillfully, pierced the meat with spits,
roasted them with care, and passed around the portions.
Then they dined all day long until the sun went down.
They feasted equally—their hearts were quite content.
But when the sun went down and darkness came,
they then lay down to rest and took the gift of sleep.
But as soon as rose-fingered early Dawn appeared,   550
they went off to the hunt, with Autolycus' sons
and dogs, as well. And lord Odysseus left with them.
They climbed up steep, tree-covered Mount Parnassus
and quickly reached its windy gullies. By this time,
Helios had just begun to strike the fields,
rising from deep streams of gently flowing Ocean.
The beaters reached a clearing. The dogs went first,
ahead of them, following the tracks. Behind them,
came Autolycus' sons, with lord Odysseus
in their group, close to the dogs. He was holding up   560
his long-shadowed spear. Now, right there a huge wild boar
was lying in a tangled thicket—it was so dense

---

[1] ... *Odysseus, a man of rage.* This explanation for Odysseus' name derives it from the Greek verb *odussomai*, meaning *to be angry* at.

the power of watery winds could not get through,
none of Helios' rays could pierce it, and the rain
would never penetrate. There were fallen leaves
in piles around the place. The sound of rustling feet
from men and dogs, as they pushed on the hunt,
came round the beast, and he charged from the thicket
to confront them, his back was really bristling,
eyes flashing fire—as he stood at bay before them.   570
Odysseus rushed in first, his strong hands gripping
the long spear, keen to strike the boar. But the beast
got the jump on him and struck him above the knee,
charging at him from the side, a long gash in his flesh
sliced by its tusk, but it didn't reach Odysseus' bone.
But then Odysseus struck the boar, hitting it
on its right shoulder. The bright point of his spear
went clean through—the boar fell in the dust, squealing,
and its life force flew away. Autolycus' dear sons
attended to the carcass. They skillfully bound up   580
the wound on noble, godlike Odysseus, staunching
with a spell the flow of his dark blood. And then
they quickly went back to their dear father's home.
When Autolycus and Autolycus' sons
had fully cured him and presented splendid gifts,
they soon sent him back in a joyful frame of mind
to his native land in Ithaca. When he got back,
his father and his honoured mother were delighted,
asked him every detail of how he'd got the wound,
and he told them the truth—how, while he was hunting   590
with Autolycus' sons when he'd gone to Parnassus,
a boar's white tusk had gored him. That was the scar
the old woman was then holding in her hands.
She traced it out and recognized it. She dropped his foot.
His leg fell in the basin, and the bronze rang out.
It tipped onto its side. Water spilled out on the ground.
All at once, joy and sorrow gripped her heart. Her eyes
filled up with tears, and her full voice was speechless.
She reached up to Odysseus' chin and said:

                    "It's true, dear child.

You are Odysseus, and I didn't know you,   600
not till I'd touched all my master's body."

She spoke, and her eyes glanced over at Penelope,
anxious to tell her that her husband had come home.
But Penelope could not see her face or understand,
for Athena had diverted her attention.
Then Odysseus' arms reached out for Eurycleia—
with his right hand he grabbed her by the throat,
and with the other pulled her closer to him.
Then he said:

                    "My good mother, why this wish
        to have me slaughtered? You yourself nursed me   610
        at this breast of yours. Now in the twentieth year,
        after suffering through numerous ordeals,
        I've come back to my native land. And now,
        you've recognized me—a god has put that
        in your heart. Stay silent, so in these halls
        no one else finds out. I'll tell you something—
        and it will happen. If a god overpowers
        these arrogant suitors, sets them under me,
        I'll not spare you, though you are my nurse,
        when I kill other women in my home."   620

Prudent Eurycleia then answered him:

                                    "My child,
        what words escaped the barrier of your teeth!
        You know how strong and firm my spirit is.
        I'll be as tough as a hard stone or iron.
        I'll tell you something else. Keep it in mind.
        If a god does overpower these lordly suitors
        and sets them under you, then I'll tell you
        about the women in your home, the ones
        dishonouring you and those who bear no shame."

Resourceful Odysseus then answered her and said: 630

"Good mother, why speak to me about them?
There's no need. I myself will look at them
and get to know each one. But keep this news
to yourself. Leave the matter with the gods."

Once Odysseus spoke, the old woman left the room
to fetch water for his feet, since what she'd had before
had all been spilled. When she'd finished bathing him,
she rubbed him with rich oil. Then Odysseus once more
pulled his chair closer to the fire to warm himself.
He hid the scar under his rags. Wise Penelope   640
began to speak. She said:

                              "Stranger, there's one small thing
I'll ask you for myself. Soon it will be time
to take a pleasant rest. And sleep is sweet
to anyone it seizes, even if he's troubled.
But some god has given me unmeasured grief,
for every day I get my joy from mourning,
from laments, as I look after my own work
and supervise the servants in the house.
But when night comes and Sleep grips everyone,
I lie in bed, and piercing worries crowd   650
my throbbing heart and give me great distress,
while I mourn. Just as Pandareus' daughter,
the nightingale of the green woods, sings out
her lovely song when early spring arrives,
perched up in thick foliage of the forest,
and pours forth her richly modulating voice
in wailing for her child, beloved Itylus,[1]
lord Zethus' son, whom with a sword one day
she'd killed unwittingly—that's how my heart
moves back and forth in its uncertainty.   660
Should I stay with my son and keep careful watch
on all possessions and my female slaves
and my large and lofty home, honouring

[1]Itylus, son of king Zethus, was killed by his mother Aedon accidentally. The mother
was then transformed into a nightingale, whose song is a constant lament for her dead
child. In some versions of the story, Itylus is a daughter.

my husband's bed and what the people say,
or go off with the best of those Achaeans
who court me in my halls—the one who offers
countless bridal gifts. My son, while young
and with a feeble mind, would not permit
that I got married and left my husband's home.
But now he's grown—his youth has reached its limit—   670
he's begging me to go back home again,
to leave this house, for he's very worried
about the property which these Achaeans
are using up. But come, listen to my dream
and interpret it for me. In this house
I have twenty geese come from the water
to eat my wheat. And when I look at them
I am delighted. Then from the mountains
a huge hook-beaked eagle came and killed them—
snapping all their necks. They lay there in piles,   680
inside my hall, while he was carried up
into a shining sky. Now in that dream
I wept and wailed. Meanwhile, all around me
fair-haired women of Achaea gathered,
as, in my sorrow, I was there lamenting
that the eagle had slaughtered all my geese.
But he came back and, sitting on a beam
projecting from the roof, checked my sorrow,
and in a human voice spoke out to me:

  'Daughter of famous Icarius,   690
  you must be brave. That was no dream,
  but a true glimpse of what will really happen.
  The suitors are those geese, and I am here—
  before I was an eagle, but now I've come
  as your own husband, who will execute
  a cruel fate on each and every suitor.'

"That's what he said. Then sweet sleep released me.
When I looked around the hall, I saw the geese—
they were pecking at the wheat beside the trough,
as they used to do before."

then answered her and said:

"Lady, it's quite impossible
to twist another meaning from this dream,
since the real Odysseus has revealed to you
how he will end all this. The suitors' deaths
are all plain to see, and not one of them
will escape destruction and his fate."

Wise Penelope then gave him her reply:

"Stranger, stories told in dreams are difficult—
their meanings are not clear, and for people
they are not realized in every detail.   710
There are two gates for insubstantial dreams,
one made of horn and one of ivory.
Those which pass through the fresh-cut ivory
deceive—the words they bring are unfulfilled.
Those which come through the gate of polished horn,
once some mortal sees them, bring on the truth.
But, in my case, I don't think that strange dream
came through that gate. It really would have been
a welcome thing to me and to my son.
But I'll tell you something else. Keep it in mind.   720
That morning is already drawing near
which will separate me from Odysseus' house,
a day of evil omen. I'll now organize
a competition featuring those axes
he used to set inside his hall, in a line,
like a ship's ribs, twelve of them in all.
He'd stand far off and shoot an arrow through them.
I'll now set up this contest for the suitors.
The one whose hand most deftly strings his bow
and shoots an arrow through all twelve axes   730
is the one I'll go with.[1] I'll leave my house,

---

[1] . . . *go with*: The details of this famous trial of shooting an arrow through a row of axes
have been much discussed. Some interpreters have suggested that it makes sense if we
imagine that there is a hole in the head of each axe and that they can be lined up so that

where I've been married, a very lovely home,
full of what one needs to live—even in dreams
it will stay in my memory forever."

Resourceful Odysseus then answered her and said:

"Honoured wife of Odysseus, Laertes' son,
don't delay this contest in your halls
a moment longer. I can assure you,
Odysseus will be here with all his schemes,
before these men pick up the polished bow,   740
string it, and shoot an arrow through the iron."

Wise Penelope then answered him:

                                        "Stranger,
if you wished to sit beside me in these halls
to bring me pleasure, sleep would never sit
on these eyelids of mine. But there's no way
men can go on forever without sleep.
Immortal gods have set a proper time
for every man on this grain-bearing earth.
So now I'll go up to my upper room
and lie down on the bed, which is for me   750
a place for grieving, always wet with tears,
since Odysseus went to wicked Ilion,
a name which never should be mentioned.
I'll lie down there. But you can stretch out here,
in the house, putting bedding on the floor.
Or let the servants make a bed for you."

Once she'd said this, she went to her bright upper room,
not alone, for two attendant women went with her.
When she and her servants reached the upper room,
she cried out for Odysseus, her dear husband,   760
till bright-eyed Athena cast sweet sleep on her eyelids.

an arrow might pass through them all (obviously a very difficult shot). Some ancient axes
apparently had this feature. Others have suggested that the holes are rings at the bottom
end of the shaft or that the holes are those which normally hold the axe shaft (so that the
line of axes is actually a line of axe heads with the shaft removed.

Book Twenty
Odysseus Prepares for his Revenge

[Odysseus has trouble sleeping; Athena visits him and gives him reassurance; Penelope prays to Artemis, longing for her life to end; Odysseus asks Zeus for two omens; Zeus peals his thunder and a woman grinding grain prays aloud to Zeus; Telemachus asks Eurycleia about the treatment of his guest; Eurycleia organizes the clean up of the house; Eumaeus arrives with some animals and talks to Odysseus; Melanthius insults Odysseus again; Philoetius arrives and talks to Eumaeus, then wishes Odysseus well; the suitors plan to kill Telemachus but are dissuaded by an omen; Telemachus tells Odysseus he'll protect him at the feast and speaks forcefully to the suitors; Ctesippus throws a piece of meat at Odysseus, but misses; Telemachus threatens him; Agelaus proposes that Penelope make up her mind; Pallas Athena makes the suitors laugh uncontrollably and sends images of disaster; Theoclymenus interprets them and warns the suitors; they all laugh at Telemachus; Penelope sits and listens to the conversations.]

So lord Odysseus went to the portico to sleep.
Underneath he spread an untanned hide and on top
fleeces from many sheep slaughtered for sacrifice
by the Achaeans. Eurynome spread a cloak on him,
once he lay down to rest. But he couldn't sleep.
His heart was hatching trouble for the suitors.
Then the women went out from the hall, the ones
who in earlier days had had sex with the suitors.
They were laughing, having fun with one another.
Odysseus' spirit in his chest was stirred—mind and heart   10
engaged in fierce debate whether he should charge out
and put each one to death or let them and the suitors
have sex one last and final time. Inside him
his heart was growling. Just as a bitch stands snarling
above her tender pups when she sees anyone
she does not recognize and is prepared to fight,
that how in his anger the heart within him growled
at their disgraceful acts. But he struck his chest and said,
as a rebuke to his own heart:

                       "Hang on, my heart.
You went through things worse than this that day   20
the Cyclops, in his frantic rage, devoured
your strong companions. You held out then,
until your cunning led you from that cave,
where you thought you would die."

                     He said these words,
to hold down the heart within his chest, and his spirit
submitted, enduring everything with resolution.
But he still tossed back and forth. Just as a man
turns quickly to and fro on a blazing fire a stomach
stuffed with fat and blood when he's keen to roast it fast,
that how Odysseus tossed around, wondering   30
how he might get the shameless suitors in his grip,
one man against so many. Then Athena came,
moving down from heaven, looking like a woman.
She stood above his head and spoke to him, saying:

     "Why now, you most ill-fated of all men,
     are you awake? This is your home, and here,
     inside this house, your wife and child, a man
     whom anyone would pray for as a son."

Resourceful Odysseus then answered her and said:

     "Yes, goddess, everything you say is true.   40
     But the heart inside my chest is worried—
     How can I handle those shameful suitors,
     just a single man against so many.
     And in the house they're always in a group.
     There's something else my heart is thinking of—
     it's more important, too—if I do kill them,
     with Zeus' help and yours, how do I find
     a way of making my escape? That's something
     I'd ask you to consider."

                   Then the goddess,
bright-eyed Athena, gave him her reply:

　　　　　　　　　　　　　　　　"You stubborn man,
men put their trust in weaker friends than me—
in a mortal man who lacks my wisdom.
I'm a god, and I'm there to protect you
to the end in all your troubles. I tell you—
to make things clear—if there were fifty groups
of mortal men taking a stand around us,
eager to slaughter us in war, even so,
you'd still drive off their cattle and fine sheep.
Let Sleep take hold of you. To stay awake,
on guard all night, will make you weary.
You'll soon come out from under these bad times."

After Athena spoke, she poured sleep on his eyelids.
Then the lovely goddess went back to Olympus.

While Sleep, who relaxes troubled human hearts,
relaxed his mind, his faithful wife woke up and cried,
sitting there on her soft bed. But when her heart
had had its fill of crying, the lovely lady
began by saying a prayer to Artemis:

　　　　　　　　　　　　　　　　　　　"Artemis,
royal goddess, Zeus' daughter, how I wish
you'd shoot an arrow in my chest right now
and take my life or a storm wind would come,
lift me up, carry me away from here,
across the murky roads, and cast me out
in Ocean's backward-flowing stream, just as
storms snatched up Pandareus' daughters,
whose parents the gods killed, thus leaving them
orphans in their home. Fair Aphrodite
looked after them with cheese, sweet honey,
and fine wine, while Hera offered them
beauty and wisdom beyond all women.
Chaste Artemis made them tall, and Athena
gave them their skills in famous handicrafts.
But when fair Aphrodite went away
to high Olympus, petitioning Zeus,

who hurls the thunderbolt, that the girls
could find fulfillment in a happy marriage,
for Zeus has perfect knowledge of all things,
what each man's destiny will be or not,
that's when storm spirits snatched away the girls
and placed them in the care of hateful Furies.[1]   90
How I wish those gods who hold Olympus
would do away with me like that, or else
that fair-haired Artemis would strike at me,
so with Odysseus' image in my mind
I could descend beneath this hateful earth
and never bring delight of any kind
into the heart of some inferior man.
But when a man laments all day, his heart
thick with distress, and sleep holds him at night,
that evil can be borne—sleep makes one forget   100
all things good and bad, once it settles down
across one's eyelids. But some god sends me
bad dreams as well. This very night again
a man who looked like him lay down beside me,
just as he was when he went with the troops.
My heart rejoiced—I thought it was no dream,
but finally the truth."

                            Penelope finished.
Then Dawn came on her golden throne. As she wept,
lord Odysseus heard her voice and lost himself in thought.
To his heart it seemed she knew him and was standing there,   110
beside his head. He gathered up the cloak and blankets
he was lying on and placed them on a chair
inside the hall. He took an ox-hide from the house,
set it on the ground, and, lifting up his hands,
made this prayer to Zeus:

                         "Oh Father Zeus,

---

[1] ... *hateful Furies.* This legend of the daughters of Pandareus is very different from the story of Pandareus' daughter Aedon, told in Book 19, who killed her son Itylus by accident and was turned into a nightingale. The Furies are the goddess of blood revenge who live underground and are generally hated by the other gods.

if you wished to bring me over land and sea
to my own land, when you had given me
so much distress, let someone in the house
wake up and say something in there for me,
a word of omen, and here outside the house
let there appear another sign from Zeus."

That's what he prayed. And Counselor Zeus heard him.
At once he thundered down from glittering Olympus,
from high beyond the clouds. Lord Odysseus rejoiced.
And then some woman grinding on the stones close by
sent out a word of omen from inside the place
where the shepherd of his people placed his millstones.[1]
At these grinding stones twelve women used to work,
making barley meal and flour, which feed men's marrow.
The other women had already ground their wheat
and were asleep, but this one, weaker than the rest,
had not yet finished. She stopped her grinding stone
and said these words, an omen for her master:

"Father Zeus, who rules both gods and men,
you've thundered loud up in the starry sky,
and yet there's not a single cloud up there.
You must be offering a sign to someone.
I'm a poor wretch, but what I have to say,
oh, make that happen. May these suitors here
for the last and final time this very day
have a pleasant dinner in Odysseus' home.
Those men have hurt my knees with this hard work
grinding flour—may they now sup their last."

She spoke. That word of omen and Zeus' thunder
made lord Odysseus happy—he thought he'd be revenged
on those malicious men.

Inside Odysseus' lovely home,

---

[1] *. . . had placed his millstones*: The millstones are flat stones set on the ground and used to grind wheat and barley. The servant women kneel on the ground to use them. Here they are, it seems, in a building adjacent to the main house.

other women slaves were up and making tireless fire
inside the hearth, and then godlike Telemachus
got out of bed, put on his clothes, and from his shoulders
slung a keen-edged sword. Under his shining feet he tied   150
his lovely sandals. He picked up a sturdy spear,
with a sharp bronze point, then went out to the threshold,
stood there, and said to Eurycleia:

                              "My dear nurse,
        have you shown our guest respect inside our home
        with bed and food, or is he still lying there
        unattended to? That's how my mother is,
        although she's wise. She seems to deal with men
        at random—some inferior mortal man
        she'll honour, while some finer person
        she'll send away with no respect at all."   160

Wise Eurycleia then answered him:

                              "My child,
        don't blame her now about such things. That man
        sat here drinking wine as long as he could wish.
        He said he had no appetite for food.
        She asked him. When he thought of going to bed
        to get some sleep, she told the women slaves
        to spread out bedding, but like a wretched man
        familiar with hard times, he had no wish
        to lie down under blankets on a bed.
        So he stretched out on the portico to sleep   170
        on sheep fleeces and an untanned ox-hide,
        and then we threw a cloak on top of him."

Once she'd finished, Telemachus went through the hall,
spear in hand, with two swift dogs accompanying him.
He went to join the group of finely dressed Achaeans.
Then that good woman Eurycleia, daughter of Ops,
Peisenor's son, called out to the female slaves:

"Come on, some of you get busy here—
sweep the hall and sprinkle it. Then spread out
purple covers on these well-fashioned chairs.   180
You others, wipe down all those tables
with sponges, clean up the mixing bowls,
those finely crafted double-handled cups.
And you others, get water from the spring.
Carry it back here. And do it quickly—
the suitors won't be absent from this hall
for very long. They'll be back really soon.
Today's a banquet day for everyone."

As Eurycleia spoke, they all listened carefully,
then acted on her words. Twenty of the women   190
went to the dark-water spring. The others stayed there,
busy working expertly throughout the house.
Then the men who served Achaean lords arrived.
While they were chopping wood skillfully and well,
the women slaves who'd gone off to the spring returned.
Behind them came the swineherd, leading in three hogs,
the best of all he had. He turned them loose to feed
inside the lovely yard, while he talked to Odysseus,
with words of reassurance:

                          "Stranger, these Achaeans—
         do they have any more regard for you?   200
         Or in these halls are they dishonouring you,
         they way they did before?"

                          Shrewd Odysseus
then answered him and said:

                          "Well, Eumaeus,
         I hope the gods pay back the injuries
         arrogant men so recklessly have planned
         in someone else's home, with no sense of shame."

As these two were saying these words to one another,
Melanthius, the goatherd, came up close to them,

leading the very finest she-goats in his flocks,
part of the suitors' feast. Two herdsmen came with him.
He tied the goats up by the echoing portico,
then started hurling his insults at Odysseus:

> "Stranger, are you still bothering us here,
> inside the house, begging from the people?
> Why don't you get out? I think it's clear
> the two of us won't say goodbye, until
> we've had a taste of one another's fists.
> The way you beg is not appropriate.
> Achaeans do have feasts in other places."

Melanthius spoke, but shrewd Odysseus said nothing. 220
He shook his head in silence. Deep in his heart
he was planning trouble. Then a third one joined them,
Philoetius, an outstanding man, bringing in
a sterile heifer and plump she-goats for the suitors.
Ferrymen, who transport other men across,
whoever comes to them, had brought them over
from the mainland. He tied these animals with care
below the echoing portico, walked up to the swineherd,
and questioned him in person:

> "Swineherd,
> who's the man who's just come to this house? 230
> What people does he claim to come from?
> Where are his family and his native lands?
> He's had bad luck, but in his appearance
> he seems to be a royal king. But still,
> the gods bring miseries to wandering men,
> whenever they spin their threads of trouble,
> even though those men are royalty."

Once he'd said this, he walked up to Odysseus,
held his right hand out in greeting, and spoke to him—
his words had wings:

> "Greetings, honoured stranger. 240

403

Though you're facing many troubles now,
may you find happiness in future days.
O Father Zeus, none of the other gods
is more destructive than you are. For men,
once you yourself have given birth to them,
you have no pity. You get them involved
with misery and painful wretchedness.
When I recall Odysseus and think of him,
I start to sweat. My eyes fill up with tears.
For he, too, I think, is dressed in rags like these,   250
wandering among men somewhere, if indeed
he's still alive, looking at the sunlight.
If he's already dead in Hades' home,
then I grieve for excellent Odysseus,
who, when I was still a boy, put me in charge
of cattle in the Cephallenians' land.[1]
Their numbers now are more than one can count—
this breed of broad-faced cattle has increased
more than it could in any other way
for a different man. Now strangers tell me   260
to drive the cattle in for their own meals.
They don't care about the son inside the house
or tremble at the vengeance of the gods.
Now they're keen to share amongst themselves
my master's goods—he's been away so long.
As for me, the heart here in my chest
keeps turning over many things—it's bad,
really bad, while his son is still alive,
for me to leave here with the cattle herds
and head off to some other district,   270
to a group of strangers. But it's even worse
to stay here, putting up with so much trouble,
to herd these cattle going to other men.
In fact, I would have run off long ago
to one of the other haughty kings—
for things are now unbearable—but still,

---

[1] ... *Cephallenians' land*: The word Cephallenian describes Odysseus' subjects generally, but Cephallenia is the name of a large island immediately to the west of Ithaca. In the *Iliad*, Odysseus' soldiers are called Cephallenians.

that unlucky man is always on my mind.
Perhaps he might come home from somewhere
and send the suitors packing from his home."

Resourceful Odysseus then answered him and said:

"Herdsman, you don't appear to be a man
who's bad or one who lacks intelligence.
I see for myself your understanding heart.
And so I'll swear a powerful oath to you.
I'll speak the truth—let Zeus be my witness,
first among the gods, and this guest table,
and the hearth of excellent Odysseus,
to which I've come—While you are present here
Odysseus will come home. With your own eyes,
you'll see the suitors killed, if that's your wish,   290
those men who act as if they own the place."

The cattle herder answered him:

                                    "Ah stranger,
how I wish Cronos' son might bring about
what you've just said. Then you'd find out
how strong I am and what my hands can do."

Eumaeus also prayed like that to all the gods
for wise Odysseus' return to his own home.

As they were talking in this way to one another,
the suitors were making plans against Telemachus,
scheming to bring him to a fatal destiny.   300
But then a bird went soaring past them, on their left,
an eagle flying up high, gripping a trembling dove.
So Amphinomus addressed them all and said:

"My friends, this plan to kill Telemachus
will not proceed the way we want it to.
We should instead prepare to have our feast."

405

Amphinomus spoke, and they agreed with him.
So they went inside godlike Odysseus' home,
threw their cloaks on stools and chairs, and sacrificed
big sheep and fattened goats. They killed plump swine, as well,   310
and the heifer from the herd. They roasted entrails,
passed them round, and blended wine in mixing bowls.
The swineherd handed out the cups. Philoetius,
an outstanding man, served bread in a fine basket.
Melanthius poured their wine. And then their hands
reached out to take the fine food set before them.
Thinking it would work to his advantage, Telemachus
sat Odysseus down inside the well-constructed hall,
beside the entrance made of stone, then set for him
a modest stool and tiny table. He placed before him   320
a share of inner organs and poured out some wine
into a golden cup. Then he said:

                                      "Sit here for now,
              among these men and drink your wine. I myself
              will protect you from all suitors' insults
              and their fists, for this is not a public house
              but a home belonging to Odysseus,
              and he acquired this place for me. You suitors,
              make sure your hearts do not encourage you
              to gibes and blows, so that no arguments
              or fights will happen here."

                                    Once he'd finished speaking,   330
all the suitors bit their lips. They were astonished
Telemachus had talked to them so forcefully.
Then Antinous, Eupeithes' son, spoke out to them:

              "Achaeans, what Telemachus has said
              is challenging, but let's accept his words,
              although his speech is a bold threat to us.
              For Zeus, son of Cronos, has not given
              his permission, or here within these halls
              by this time we'd have put a stop to him,
              for all his clear-voiced talk."

But Telemachus ignored what he'd just said.

Meanwhile, as heralds led offerings sacred to the gods
down through the city, long-haired Achaeans gathered
underneath archer god Apollo's shadowy grove.
They cooked the outer flesh and pulled away the spits,
then shared the meat and had a splendid banquet.[1]
The servers placed beside Odysseus a portion
matching what they received themselves—Telemachus,
godlike Odysseus' son, had given them those orders.
But there was no way Athena would permit   350
those proud suitors to hold back their bitter insults,
so that Odysseus, Laertes' son, would suffer
still more heartfelt pain. Now, among the suitors
there was man who had a lawless heart. His name
was Ctesippus, and he made his home in Same.
Relying on his prodigious wealth, he courted
the wife of Odysseus, who'd been away so long.
He now addressed the overbearing suitors:

> "You noble suitors, listen to me now—
> I've got something to say. This stranger here   360
> has for some time had an equal portion,
> as is right, since it's by no means proper,
> nor is it just, for Telemachus' guests
> to go without—no matter who it is
> who shows up at the house. So now I, too,
> will provide a gift to welcome him.
> Then he, for his part, can pass it along
> to some bath attendant or another slave
> here in the home of godlike Odysseus."

As he said this, his strong hand picked up an ox hoof   370
from the basket where it lay, and then he hurled it.
But by quickly pulling his head back, Odysseus

[1] . . . *splendid banquet*: This reference to a feast in the grove of Apollo is rather abrupt and confusing, since up to this point the feast has been taking place inside Odysseus' home and further details suggest the same location.

dodged the throw. In his heart he smiled with bitter scorn.
The gristle hit the solid wall. Telemachus
then went at Ctesippus and said:

"Ctesippus,
in your heart you understand what's good for you—
that's must be why you didn't hit the stranger.
He escaped your throw all on his own.
Otherwise, I'd have taken my sharp spear
and rammed you in the chest. Then your father   380
would be here planning for your funeral
and not a wedding feast. So none of you
make any show of trouble in my house.
For now I am observing every detail—
both good and bad—I know what's going on.
Before this point, I was still a foolish child.
But we still must see and bear these things—
the slaughtered sheep, the wine and bread consumed.
It's hard for one man to restrain so many.
So come, no longer show me such ill will   390
or give me so much trouble. If you're keen
to kill me with your swords, that's what I'd choose—
it would be far better to meet my death
than constantly to watch these shameful deeds,
strangers being abused and female servants
dragged through this lovely home. It's a disgrace."

Telemachus finished. They all sat there in silence,
saying nothing. At last Agelaus, Damastor's son,
addressed them:

"My friends, no man could answer
what's been so justly said and in his rage   400
respond with words provoking enmity.
So don't insult the stranger any more
or any of the servants in this home
belonging to godlike Odysseus. Still,
to Telemachus and to his mother
I have some reassuring things to say,

which both their hearts should find agreeable.
As long as you had in your hearts some hope
that wise Odysseus would return back home,
no blame attached itself to you by waiting,   410
holding off the suitors in your house.
This was the better choice, if Odysseus
had returned and come back to his palace.
But surely it's already clear by now
he won't be coming back, not any more.
So come, sit down beside your mother. Tell her
to marry whoever is the finest man
and offers the best bridal gifts. And then,
you can enjoy all your paternal goods
as yours to keep, all the food and wine,   420
while she looks after someone else's home."

Shrewd Telemachus then answered him and said:

"I swear to you, Agelaus, by Zeus
and by the sufferings of my father,
who's perished or is wandering around
somewhere far from Ithaca, there's no way
I'm trying to delay my mother's marriage.
I tell her to marry any man she wants,
and I'll give her innumerable gifts.
But I'm ashamed to drive her from the home   430
against her wishes, to give an order
which forces her to leave. I hope the god
will never bring about something like that."

Once Telemachus had spoken, Pallas Athena
roused them all to laugh with no sense of control.
She unhinged their minds, so laughter from their mouths
came from an alien source, and the meat they ate
became blood-spattered.[1] Their eyes filled up with tears.
Their hearts were crammed with thoughts of lamentation.
Then godlike Theoclymenus addressed them all: 440

[1] . . . *blood spattered*: The Greek says (literally) "they laughed with the jaws of other
men," an expression which seems to mean they had no idea of why they were laughing.

"Oh you miserable men, what troubles
are you suffering now? Your heads, your faces,
your lower limbs are shrouded in the night.
You're on fire with grief, faces wet with tears,
fine pedestals and walls have gobs of blood,
the porch is full of ghosts, so is the yard—
ghosts rushing in the dark to Erebus.
Up in the sky the sun has disappeared—
an evil mist is covering everything."

Theoclymenus finished. But they all laughed,   450
enjoying themselves at his expense. The first to speak
was Eurymachus, son of Polybus:

                              "He's mad,
        this stranger who's just recently arrived
        from some foreign land. Come on, young men,
        hurry and carry him outside the house,
        so he can make his way to the assembly,
        since he thinks it's like the night in here."

Godlike Theoclymenus then said in reply:

        "Eurymachus, I'm not requesting you
        to furnish me with guides. I've got my eyes   460
        and my two feet. And in my chest
        I've got a mind that's not made for a fool.
        I'll go outside with these, for I can see
        you're headed for disaster—no suitors
        who, in the home of godlike Odysseus,
        mistreat others and plan their reckless schemes
        will be able to avoid it or escape."

After he'd said this, he left the stately palace
and went to Peiraeus, who gladly welcomed him.
But all the suitors looked around at one another   470
and tried to hurt Telemachus with mockery,
laughing at his guests. Some arrogant young man
would make a comment using words like these:

410

"Telemachus,
no one is more unlucky with his guests
than you are. You have a man like this one,
a dirty tramp in need of food and wine,
with no work skills or strength, just a burden
on the land. Then some other man stood here
and made a prophecy. You'd be better off
to follow what I say. Let's throw these guests   480
onboard a well-decked ship and send them off
to the Sicilians. You'd get good prices there."

That's what the suitors said. But Telemachus
paid no attention to their words. He kept quiet,
looking at his father, always watching him
to see when his hands would fight the shameless suitors.

But wise Penelope, Icarius' daughter,
had set in place a lovely chair across from them.
She heard what each man in the hall was saying.
While they kept laughing, the men prepared a meal,   490
something sweet to satisfy their hearts, slaughtering
many beasts. But there would never be another meal
more sorrowful than the one the mighty warrior
and the goddess would set before them very soon.
With their shameful plans, the suitors brought this on.

Book Twenty-One
The Contest with Odysseus' Bow

[Penelope decides to set up the archery contest with the axes; she goes to a storeroom to fetch the bow, arrows, and axes; the story of how Odysseus got the bow from Iphitus; Penelope addresses the suitors, saying she will marry whoever succeeds in the competition; Eumaeus and Philoetius weep; Antinous upbraids them; Telemachus addresses the suitors, sets up the bows in line, and tries unsuccessfully to string the bow; Leiodes attempts to string the bow and fails; Antinous criticizes Leiodes, then suggests they rub fat on the bow by the fire to make it more supple; Odysseus reveals his identity outside to Eumaeus and Philoetius and gives them instructions; Eurymachus tries to string the bow and fails; Antinous proposes they postpone the contest for today; Odysseus suggests he be given a chance to succeed with the bow; Antinous objects; Penelope intervenes; Telemachus tells his mother to go upstairs; Eumaeus hands the bow to Odysseus and orders Eurycleia to lock the doors; Philoetius closes the courtyard gates; Odysseus inspects the bow, then fires an arrow through the holes in the axe heads; Telemachus arms himself and moves to stand with his father.]

Bright-eyed Athena then placed inside the heart
of wise Penelope, Icarius' daughter,
the thought that she should set up in Odysseus' halls
the bow and the gray iron axes for the suitors,
as a competition and the prelude to their deaths.
She climbed the lofty staircase to her chamber,
picked up in her firm grip a curved key made of bronze—
beautifully fashioned with an ivory handle.
With her attendants she went off to a storeroom
in a distant corner of the house, where they kept   10
her king's possessions—bronze and gold and iron,
all finely crafted work. His well-sprung bow was there,
and quivers, too, with lots of painful arrows,
gifts he had received from Iphitus, his friend,
son of Eurytus, a man like the immortals,
when they'd met in Lacedaemon, in Messene,
at the home of wise Ortilochus. Odysseus
had gone there to collect a debt the people owed—

Messenian men had run off with three hundred sheep
and seized the shepherds, too, leaving Ithaca   20
in their ships with many oars. Because of this,
Odysseus, who was just a boy, had been sent
a long way by his father and other senior men,
part of an embassy. Iphitus was searching
for twelve mares he'd lost and sturdy mules, as well,
still on the teat. Later on these animals
led him to a fatal destiny, the day he met
the mortal Hercules, Zeus' great-hearted son,
who knew all there was to know about great exploits.
Hercules slaughtered him, although he was a guest   30
in his own home—a cruel man who didn't care
about the anger of the gods or the dining table
he'd set before him. After their meal, he killed him
and kept the strong-hoofed mares with him at home
for his own use.[1] While Iphitus was enquiring
about these horses, he got to meet Odysseus
and gave him the bow. In earlier days, this weapon
had been used by mighty Eurytus, and when he died,
he'd left it for his son in his high-roofed home.
Odysseus had given him a keen-edged sword   40
and a powerful spear, as well. This was the start
of their close friendship. But they never bonded
as mutual dinner guests—before that happened
Zeus' son had murdered Iphitus, son of Eurytus,
a man like the immortals, who gave Odysseus
that bow of his. Lord Odysseus never took it
whenever he went off to war in his black ships.
It lay there in his home as a memorial
to a dear friend. He carried it in his own land.
When fair Penelope came to the storage room,   50

---

[1] ... *for his own use*: Iphitus went to see Hercules, who was his friend, about some stolen
cattle. But Hercules went insane (a fit brought on by Hera) and killed Iphitus by throwing
him off the walls of Tiryns. Hercules had to be purified and suffer some punishment for
this murder. It's not entirely clear how the horses mentioned in Homer's text brought
about Hercules' violence, unless the idea is that Hercules killed him to obtain the horses.
Hercules is called "mortal" because Iphitus met him when he was still a man, that is, before
he became deified after his death. The reference to the "dining table" is a reminder of the
special bond between a host and his guest once they had shared a meal together.

she crossed the wooden threshold—a long time ago
a skillful craftsman planed it, set it straight and true,
then fitted doorposts and set shining doors in place.
She quickly took the looped thong from its hook,
put in the key, and with a push shoved back the bolt.[1]
Just as a bull grunts when it grazes in a meadow,
that how the key's force made the fine door creak,
and it quickly swung ajar. She stepped high up,
onto the planking where the storage trunks were placed
in which they kept their fragrant clothing. There she stretched   60
to take the bow in its bright case down from its peg.
She then sat down, placed the bow case on her knees,
and wept aloud, as she took out her husband's bow.
When she'd had enough of her laments and tears,
she went off to the hall, to join the noble suitors,
holding in her hands the well-sprung bow and quiver,
with many pain-inflicting arrows. And with her
came some servants carrying a chest which held
lots of iron and bronze, her husband's battle weapons.
Once the lovely lady reached the suitors, she stood there,   70
by the door post of the well-constructed hall,
with a bright veil on her face. On either side
stood loyal attendant women. Then Penelope
addressed the suitors with these words:

                           "Listen to me,
bold suitors, who've been ravaging this home
with your incessant need for food and drink,
since my husband's now been so long absent.
The only story you could offer up
as an excuse is that you all desire
to marry me and take me as your wife.   80

---

[1] *... the bolt.* Merry, Riddell, and Monro, in their *Commentary on the Odyssey* (1886) explain
that the inside bolt was moved by a thong passing through a slit in the door. Once the door
was bolted shut by pulling the thong (when a person was leaving and was outside the door),
the thong was attached to a hook on the outside wall. To get into the room from the outside
required a key which fit a hole of the appropriate shape. Once the thong was taken off its
hook, the key was inserted in the hole, and it pushed the bolt back. The purpose of the
thong, it seems, was to prevent someone from opening the door from the inside (where it
would be impossible to remove the thong from its hook and thus to move the bolt).

So come now, suitors, since I seem to be
the prize you seek, I'll place this great bow here
belonging to godlike Odysseus. And then,
whichever one of you can grip this bow
and string it with the greatest ease, then shoot
an arrow through twelve axes, all of them,
I'll go with him, leaving my married home,
this truly lovely house and all these goods
one needs to live—things I'll remember,
even in my dreams."

When she'd said this,   90
she then told Eumaeus, the loyal swineherd,
to set the bow and gray iron axes for the suitors.
With tears in his eyes, Eumaeus picked them up
and laid them out. Philoetius, the goatherd,
was weeping, too, in another spot, once he saw
his master's bow. Then Antinous addressed them both
with this reproach:

"You foolish bumpkins,
who only think of what's going on today!
What a wretched pair! Why start weeping now?
Why agitate the heart inside the lady's breast?   100
Her spirit lies in pain, now that she's lost
the man she loves. So sit and eat in silence,
or go outside and weep. Leave the bow here.
The contest will decide among the suitors.
I don't think it's going to be an easy feat
to string that polished bow. Of all men here,
no one is like Odysseus used to be.
I saw him for myself, and I remember,
though at the time I was a little child."

Antinous spoke. In his chest his heart was hoping   110
he would string the bow and then shoot an arrow
through the iron.[1] But, in fact, he'd be the first

---

[1] . . . *through the iron:* As mentioned in the note at 19.731, the challenge required the

to taste an arrow from brave Odysseus' hands—
the very man he was disgracing shamefully,
as he sat in the hall, inciting all his comrades.
Then among them all Telemachus spoke out
with royal authority:

                    "Well now, Zeus,
son of Cronos, must have made me foolish—
my dear mother, although quite sensible,
says she'll be leaving with another man,   120
abandoning this home, and I just laugh.
My witless heart finds that enjoyable.
So come, suitors, since your prize seems to be
a woman who throughout Achaean land
has no equal, not in sacred Pylos,
Argos, or Mycenae, not on the mainland,
or in Ithaca itself. But you yourselves
know this. Why should I praise my mother?
So come on. Don't delay this competition
with excuses or use up too much time   130
diverting your attention from this bow string.
Then we'll see. I might try the bow myself.
If I can string it and shoot an arrow
through the iron, I won't get so upset
when my royal mother has to leave here
with another man. I'd be left behind,
as someone capable of picking up
fine prizes from my father in a contest."

After he'd said this, Telemachus threw off
the purple cloak covering his back, jumped up,   140
and removed the sharp sword from his shoulders.
First, he set up the axes. He dug a trench,
one long ditch for all of them, in a straight line.
Then he stamped the earth down flat around them.

contestant to string the bow (i.e., bend it back so that the string could be attached at both
tips) and then shoot an arrow through a series of holes in twelve ax heads set up in a
straight line. This appears to take place inside the great hall, which, as Merry, Riddell,
and Monro note, had a floor consisting of hard earth. However, the precise location of
the contest (inside or outside) has long been a matter of dispute.

Amazement gripped all those observing him
to watch him organize those axes properly,
although before that time he'd never seen them.
Then, going and standing in the threshold, he tried
to test the bow. Three times he made it tremble,
as he strove to bend it, and three times he relaxed,   150
hoping in his heart he'd string that bow and shoot
an arrow through the iron. On his fourth attempt,
as his power bent the bow, he might have strung it,
but Odysseus shook his head, motioning him to stop,
for all his eagerness. So Telemachus spoke out,
addressing them once more with royal authority:

> "Well, I suppose I'll remain a coward,
> a weak man, too, in future days, or else
> I'm still too young and cannot yet rely
> on my own strength to guard me from a man   160
> who gets angry with me first. But come now,
> you men who are more powerful than me,
> test this bow. Let's end this competition."

Once he'd said this, Telemachus placed the bow
down on the ground away from him, leaning it
against the polished panels of the door, and set
a swift arrow there beside the bow's fine tip,
then sat down again in the chair from which he'd stood.
Then Antinous, Eupeithes' son, addressed them:

> "All you comrades, get up in order now,   170
> from left to right, beginning from the place
> where the steward pours the wine."

Antinous spoke,
and what he'd just proposed they found agreeable.
The first to stand up was Leiodes, son of Oenops,
their soothsayer. He always sat furthest away,
beside the lovely mixing bowl—the only man
hostile to their reckless acts—he was angry
with the suitors, all of them. That was the man

who first picked up the bow and the swift arrow.
After moving to the threshold and standing there,
he tried the bow, but couldn't string it. His hands,
which were delicate and weak, grew weary,
before he could succeed in stringing up the bow.
He then spoke out among the suitors:

> "My friends,
> I'm not the man to string this bow. So now,
> let someone else take hold of it. This bow
> will take away from many excellent men
> their lives and spirits, since it's far better
> to die than live and fail in the attempt
> to have what we are gathered here to get,   190
> always waiting here in hope day after day.
> Now every man has feelings in his heart—
> he desires and hopes to wed Penelope,
> Odysseus' wife. But when he's tried this bow
> and observed what happens, then let him woo
> another of Achaea's well-dressed women,
> seeking to win her with his bridal gifts,
> and then Penelope can wed the man
> who offers her the most, whose fate it is
> to be her husband."

> When Leiodes had finished,   200
he set the bow away from him, leaning it
against the polished panels of the door
and placing a swift arrow by the fine bow-tip.
Then he sat again on the chair he'd risen from.
But Antinous took issue with what he'd just said,
talking directly to him:

> "Leiodes,
> that speech that passed the barrier of your teeth,
> what wretched, sorry words! As I listened,
> it made me angry—as if this bow would,
> in fact, take away the lives and spirits   210
> of the very finest men, just because

you couldn't string it. Your royal mother
did not produce in you the sort of man
who has sufficient strength to draw a bow
and shoot an arrow. But some other men
among these noble suitors will soon string it."

This said, Antinous called out to Melanthius,
the goatherd:

"Come now, Melanthius,
light a fire in the hall. Set beside it
a large chair with a fleece across it.   220
And bring a hefty piece of fat—there's some
inside the house—so the young men here
can warm the bow and rub grease into it,
then test the bow and end this contest."

When he'd said this, Melanthius quickly lit
a tireless fire. Then he brought a large chair up,
draped a fleece on it, and set it down beside the fire
and from inside the house fetched a large piece of fat.
Then the young men warmed the bow and tested it.
But they couldn't string it—whatever strength they had   230
was far too little. Antinous and godlike Eurymachus,
the suitors' leaders, still remained—the two of them
with their abilities, were the finest men by far.

Now, the cattle herder and the keeper of the swine
belonging to godlike Odysseus had gone out,
both together, so lord Odysseus himself
left the house to follow after them. And then,
when they'd gone beyond the gates and courtyard,
he spoke, addressing them with reassuring words:

"You there, cattleman and swineherd, shall I   240
tell you something or keep it to myself?
My spirit tells me I should speak to you.
If Odysseus were to come back suddenly,
brought from somewhere by a god, would you two

419

be the sort of men who would defend him?
Would you support the suitors or Odysseus?
Answer as your heart and spirit prompt you."

Then the cattle herder answered him:

                              "Oh Father Zeus,
would that you might fulfill this very wish—
may that man come, and led on by some god.   250
Then you would know the kind of strength I have
and how my hands can show my power."

And then Eumaeus, too, made the same sort of prayer
to all the gods that wise Odysseus would come back
to his own home. Once Odysseus had clearly seen
how firm their minds were, he spoke to them again,
saying these words:

                              "Well, here I am in person—
after suffering much misfortune, I've come home,
back in the twentieth year to my own land.
Of those who work for me, I recognize   260
that you're the only two who want me back.
Among the rest, I've heard no one praying
that my return would bring me home again.
I'll tell you both how this is going to end—
and I'll speak the truth—if, on my behalf
some god will overcome those noble suitors,
I'll bring you each a wife, and I'll provide
possessions and a house built near my own.
Then you'll be my companions—and kinsmen
of Telemachus. Come, I'll show you something,   270
a sure sign, so you will clearly know it's me
and trust me in your hearts—here's the old scar
I got from a boar's white tusk, when I'd gone
to Parnassus with Autolycus' sons."

As he said this, Odysseus pulled aside his rags,
exposing the great scar. Once those two had seen it

and noted every detail, they threw their arms
around the wise Odysseus, burst into tears,
and welcomed him, kissing his head and shoulders.
Odysseus did the same—he kissed their heads and hands.   280
They would have kept on crying until sunset,
if Odysseus himself hadn't called a halt and said:

> "Stop these laments. Let's have no more crying.
> Someone might come out from the hall, see us,
> and tell the people in the house. Let's go in,
> one by one, not all together. I'll go first.
> You come later. And let's make this our sign.
> All those other men, the noble suitors,
> will not allow the quiver and the bow
> to be given to me. But, good Eumaeus,   290
> as you're carrying that bow through the house,
> put it in my hands, and tell the women
> to lock their room—bolt the close-fitting doors.
> If any of them hears the noise of men
> groaning or being hit inside our walls,
> she's to stay quiet, working where she is,
> and not run off outside. Now, as for you,
> good Philoetius, I want you to lock
> the courtyard gates. Bolt and lash them shut.
> Do it quickly."

After he'd said this,   300

Odysseus went into the stately home and sat down
on the chair from which he'd risen. The two men,
godlike Odysseus' servants, then went in as well.

Eurymachus already had the bow in hand,
warming it here and there in the firelight.
But even doing that, he could not string it.
Then his noble heart gave out a mighty groan,
and he spoke to them directly—he was angry.

> "It's too bad. I'm frustrated for myself
> and for you all. I'm not that unhappy   310

421

about the marriage, though I am upset.
There are many more Achaean women—
some here in sea-girt Ithaca itself,
others in different cities. But if we are
so weak compared to godlike Odysseus
that we can't string his bow, it's a disgrace
which men will learn about in years to come."

Antinous, Eupeithes' son, then answered him:

"Eurymachus, that's not going to happen.
You yourself know it. At this moment,   320
in the country there's a feast day, sacred
to the god. So who would bend the bow? No,
set it to one side without saying anything.
As for the axes, what if we let them
just stand there. I don't think anyone
will come into the home of Odysseus,
Laertes' son, and carry them away.
So come, let the steward begin to pour
wine in the cups, so we can make libations.
Set the curved bow aside. In the morning,   330
tell Melanthius the goatherd to bring in
the finest goats by far from all the herds,
so we can set out pieces of the thigh
for Apollo, the famous archer god.
Then we'll test the bow and end the contest."

Antinous finished. They were pleased with what he'd said.
Heralds poured water on their hands, and young men
filled the mixing bowls up to the brim with drink
and served them all, pouring a few drops in the cups
to start the ritual. Once they'd poured libations   340
and drunk wine to their heart's content, Odysseus,
a crafty man who had a trick in mind, spoke out:

"Suitors of the splendid queen, listen to me,
so I can say what the heart inside my chest
is prompting me to state. It's a request,

a plea, especially to Eurymachus
and godlike Antinous, since what he said
was most appropriate—that for the moment
you should stop this business with the bow
and turn the matter over to the gods.   350
In the morning a god will give the strength
to whoever he desires. But come now,
give me the polished bow, so here among you
I can test my power and arms and see
if I still have strength in my supple limbs
the way I used to have, or if my travels
and my lack of food have quite destroyed it."

Odysseus finished. They were all extremely angry,
afraid that he might string the polished bow.
Then Antinous, speaking to him directly,   360
took Odysseus to task:

                       "You wretched stranger,
your mind lacks any sense—you've none at all.
Aren't you content to share a feast with us,
such illustrious men, without being disturbed
or lacking any food, and then to hear
what we say to one another as we speak?
No other beggar or stranger listens in
on what we say. The wine, so honey sweet,
has injured you, as it harms other men,
when they gulp it down and drink too much.   370
Wine befuddled even great Eurytion,
the centaur, in brave Perithous' house,
when he'd gone to the Lapiths. Afterwards,
when his heart went blind from drinking wine,
in a mad fit he committed evil acts
in Perithous' home. Grief seized the heroes.
They jumped up and hauled him out of doors,
through the gate, then cut off his ears and nose
with pitiless bronze. His wits were reckless,
and he went on his way, bearing madness   380
in his foolish heart. And that's the reason

423

the fight between centaurs and men began.
But he first discovered evil in himself,
when loaded down with wine.[1] And so I say
if you string the bow, you'll face great trouble.
You'll not get gentle treatment anywhere,
not in this land. We'll ship you off at once
in a black ship over to king Echetus,
who likes to kill and torture everyone.
You won't escape from him. So drink your wine   390
in peace, and don't compete with younger men."

Wise Penelope then answered him and said:

"Antinous, it's neither good nor proper
to deny guests of Telemachus a chance,
no matter who it is comes to this house.
And if, trusting in his strength and power,
the stranger strings Odysseus' great bow,
do you think he'll take me to his home
and make me his wife? I'm sure he himself
carries no such hope in that chest of his.   400
So none of you should be at dinner here
with sorrow in his heart because of him.
That would be undignified."

                    Then Eurymachus,
son of Polybus, answered her:

                    "Wise Penelope,
daughter of Icarius, we do not think
this man will take you home. That would be wrong.
But we would be ashamed by public gossip
from both men and women if later on
some low-born Achaean said something like:

---

[1] . . . *loaded down with wine*: Eurytion, a Centaur, was a guest at Perithous' wedding. A battle broke out between the centaurs and Perithous' people, the Lapiths. This version blames the fight on Eurytion's drinking.. Eurytion was later killed by Hercules. It's not clear here whether the Centaurs are pictured as normal human beings or, as they were later, as creatures with the head and torso of a human being and the body and legs of a horse.

'Those men wooing the wife of that fine man   410
are far worse than him—they can't even string
his polished bow, and yet another man,
a beggar who came here on his travels,
did so with ease and then shot through the iron.'

That's what men will say, and it would be
a slur on us."

                    Then wise Penelope replied:

"Eurymachus, there is no way at all
there will be in this district good reports
of those dishonouring and eating up
a noble's home. Why turn the matter now   420
into a slur? This stranger is very large
and strongly built. Furthermore, he claims
he comes by birth from a good father.
So come now, give him the polished bow,
and let us see. I will say this to you—
and it will happen—if he strings the bow
and Apollo grants him glory, I'll dress him
in some lovely clothes, a cloak and tunic,
and give him a sharp spear, as a defense
from dogs and men, and a two-edged sword.   430
I'll give him sandals for his feet and send him
wherever his heart and spirit tell him."

Shrewd Telemachus then answered her:

                              "Mother,
among Achaeans, no man has a right
stronger than my own to give the bow
to anyone I wish or to withhold it—
none of those who rule in rocky Ithaca
or in the islands neighbouring Elis,
where horses graze. Among these men, no one
will deny my will by force, if I wish   440
to give the bow, even to this stranger

as an outright gift to take away with him.
But you should go up to your own chamber
and keep busy with your proper work,
the loom and spindle, and tell your women
to go about their tasks. The bow will be
a matter for the men, especially me,
since the power in this house is mine."

Penelope, astonished, went back to her rooms,
taking to heart the prudent words her son had said.   450
With her servant women she walked up to her room
and then wept for Odysseus, her dear husband,
till bright-eyed Athena cast sweet sleep on her eyes.

The worthy swineherd had picked up the curving bow
and was carrying it. But all the suitors cried out
in the hall. One of those arrogant young men
then said something like:

                                        "What are you doing,
            you wretched swineherd, carrying that bow,
            you idiot? You'll soon be with the swine
            all alone, with no men around, being eaten   460
            by those swift dogs you yourself have raised,
            if Apollo and other immortal gods
            act with graciousness to us."

                                        That's what they said.
So, though he was carrying the bow, he put it down,
afraid because inside the hall so many men
were yelling at him. But then from across the room
Telemachus shouted out a threat:

                                        "Old man,
            keep on moving up here with that bow. You'll soon
            regret obeying them all. I'm younger than you,
            but I might force you out into the fields   470
            and throw rocks at you. I'm the stronger man.
            I wish my hands had that much strength and power

426

over all the suitors in the house. I'd send
some of them soon enough on their way home,
out of this house, and they'd be miserable.
For they keep coming up with wicked plans."

Telemachus finished speaking. But the suitors
all had a hearty laugh at his expense, relaxing
their bitter anger at Telemachus. Meanwhile,
the swineherd kept on going through the hall,   480
carrying the bow. He came to shrewd Odysseus
and placed it in his hands. Then he called the nurse,
Eurycleia, and said to her:

                         "Wise Eurycleia,
          Telemachus is telling you to lock up
          the closely fitted doorway to this hall.
          If anyone hears groans inside this room
          or any noise from men within these walls,
          she's not to run outside, but stay where she is,
          carrying out her work in silence."[1]

After he'd said this, her words could find no wings.   490
So she locked the doors of that well-furnished hall.
And Philoetius, without a word, slipped outside
and locked the courtyard gates inside the sturdy walls.
A cable from a curved ship was lying there,
under the portico, made of papyrus fibres.
With that he lashed the gates, then went inside,
sat down again on the seat where he'd got up,
and observed Odysseus, who already had the bow.
He was turning it this way and that, testing it
in different ways to see if, while its lord was gone,   500
worms had nibbled on the horns. One of the men,
with a glance beside him, would say something like:

          "This man knows bows—he must be an expert.

---

[1] _... in silence_. The doorway in question is the entrance to the women's quarters. They
are to be locked in so that they don't interrupt the revenge killings or run off to raise a
general alarm.

Either he has bows like this stored at home
or else he wants to make one. That's why
he's turning it around in all directions.
That beggar's really skilled in devious tricks."

And then another of those arrogant young men
would make some further comment:

"Well, I hope
the chance that this brings him some benefit   510
matches his ability to string this bow."

That's how the suitors talked. But shrewd Odysseus,
once he'd raised the bow and looked it over
on all sides, then—just as someone really skilled
at playing the lyre and singing has no trouble
when he loops a string around a brand-new peg,
tying the twisted sheep's gut down at either end—
that's how easily Odysseus strung that great bow.
Holding it in his right hand, he tried the string.
It sang out, resonating like a swallow's song,   520
beneath his touch. Grief overwhelmed the suitors.
The skin on all of them changed colour. And then Zeus
gave out a sign with a huge peal of thunder.
Lord Odysseus, who had endured so much, rejoiced
that crooked-minded Cronos' son had sent an omen.
Then he picked up a swift arrow lying by itself
on the table there beside him—the other ones,
which those Achaeans soon would be familiar with—
were stored inside the hollow quiver. He set it
against the bow, on the bridge, pulled the notched arrow   530
and the bow string back—still sitting in his seat—
and with a sure aim let the arrow fly. It did not miss,
not even a single top on all the axe heads.
The arrow, weighted with bronze, went straight through
and out the other end. And then Odysseus
called out to Telemachus:

"Telemachus, the stranger

sitting in your halls has not disgraced you.
I did not miss my aim or work too long
to string that bow. My strength is still intact,
in spite of all the suitors' scornful gibes.   540
Now it's time to get a dinner ready
for these Achaeans, while there's still some light,
then entertain ourselves in different ways,
with singing and the lyre. These are things
which should accompany a banquet."

As he spoke, he gave a signal with his eyebrows.
Telemachus, godlike Odysseus' dear son,
cinched up his sword, closed his fist around a spear,
moved close beside his father, right by his seat,
and stood there, fully armed with glittering bronze.   550

Book Twenty-Two
The Killing of the Suitors

[Odysseus stands in the doorway and shoots arrows at the suitors; he first kills Antinous; Eurymachus offers compensation for what the suitors have done; Odysseus kills him; Telemachus kills Amphinomus, then goes to fetch weapons from the storeroom; Melanthius reveals where the weapons are stored and gets some for the suitors; Eumaeus and Philoetius catch Melanthius and string him up to the rafters; Athena appears in the guise of Mentor to encourage Odysseus; Agelaus tries to rally the suitors; Odysseus, Telemachus, Eumaeus and Philoetius keep killing suitors until Athena makes the suitors panic; Leiodes seeks mercy from Odysseus but is killed; Odysseus spares Phemius and Medon; Odysseus questions Eurycleia about the women servants who have dishonoured him; he gets them to haul the bodies outside and clean up the hall; Telemachus hangs all the unfaithful female slaves; Melanthius is cut up and castrated; Odysseus purifies the house and yard; Odysseus is reunited with the faithful women servants.]

Then shrewd Odysseus stripped off his rags, grabbed up
the bow and quiver full of arrows, and sprang
over to the large doorway. He dumped swift arrows
right there at his feet and then addressed the suitors:

> "This competition to decide the issue
> is now over. But there's another target—
> one no man has ever struck—I'll find out
> if I can hit it. May Apollo grant
> I get the glory."

As Odysseus spoke,
he aimed a bitter arrow straight at Antinous,   10
who was just about to raise up to his lips
a fine double-handled goblet he was holding
in his hands, so he could drink some wine. In his heart
there was no thought of slaughter. Among those feasting,
who would ever think in such a crowd of people,
one man, even with truly outstanding strength,
would bring himself an evil death, his own black fate?

Odysseus took aim and hit him with an arrow
in the throat. Its point passed through his tender neck.
He slumped onto his side, and, as he was hit,   20
the cup fell from his hand. A thick spurt of human blood
came flowing quickly from his nose. Then, suddenly
he pushed the table from him with his foot, spilling
food onto the floor—the bread and roasted meat
were ruined. When the suitors saw Antinous fall,
they raised an uproar in the house, leaping from their seats,
scurrying in panic through the hall, looking round
everywhere along the well-constructed walls,
but there were no weapons anywhere, no strong spear
or shield for them to seize. They began to shout,   30
yelling words of anger at Odysseus:

                              "Stranger,
        you'll pay for shooting arrows at this man.
        For you there'll be no contests any more.
        It's certain you'll be killed once and for all.
        You've killed a man, by far the finest youth
        in all of Ithaca. And now the vultures
        are going to eat you up right here."

                              Each of them
shouted out some words like these. They did not think
he'd killed the man on purpose. In their foolishness,
they didn't realize they'd all become enmeshed   40
in destruction's snare. Shrewd Odysseus scowled at them
and gave his answer:

                              "You dogs, because you thought
        I'd not come back from Troy to my own home,
        you've been ravaging my house, raping women,
        and in your devious way wooing my wife,
        while I was still alive, with no fear of the gods,
        who hold wide heaven, or of any man
        who might take his revenge in days to come.
        And now a fatal net has caught you all."

As Odysseus said these words, pale fear seized everyone.
Each man looked around to see how he might flee
complete destruction. Only Eurymachus spoke—
he answered him and said:

                              "If, in fact, it's true
               that you're Odysseus of Ithaca,
               back home again, you're right in what you say
               about the actions of Achaeans here,
               their frequent reckless conduct in your home,
               their many foolish actions in the fields.
               But the man responsible for all these things
               now lies dead—I mean Antinous, the one   60
               who started all this business, not because
               he was all that eager to get married—
               that's not what he desired. No. For he had
               another plan in mind, which Cronos' son
               did not bring to fulfillment. He wanted
               to become the king of fertile Ithaca,
               by ambushing your son and killing him.
               Now he himself has died, as he deserved.
               So at this point you should spare your people.
               Later on we'll collect throughout the land   70
               repayment for all we've had to eat and drink
               inside your halls, and every man will bring
               compensation on his own, in an amount
               worth twenty oxen, paying you back in gold
               and bronze until your heart is mollified.
               Until that time, no one is blaming you
               for being so angry."

                      Shrewd Odysseus glared at him
and then replied:

                              "Eurymachus, if you gave me
               all the goods you got from your own fathers,
               everything which you now own, and added   80
               other assets you could obtain elsewhere,
               not even then would I hold back my hands

from slaughter, not until the suitors pay
for all their arrogance. Now you've a choice—
to fight here face to face or, if any man
wishes to evade his death and lethal fate,
to run away. But I don't think there's one
who will escape complete destruction."

Once Odysseus spoke, their knees and hearts went slack
right where they stood. Then Eurymachus spoke once more,   90
calling out to them:

          "Friends, this man won't hold in check
those all-conquering hands of his. Instead,
now he's got the polished bow and quiver,
from that smooth threshold he'll just shoot at us
until he's killed us all. So let's think now
about how we should fight. Pull out your swords,
and set tables up to block those arrows—
they bring on death so fast. And then let's charge,
go at him all together in a group,
so we can dislodge him from the threshold,   100
clear the door, get down into the city,
and raise the alarm as swiftly as we can.
Then this man should soon take his final shot."

With these words, Eurymachus pulled out his sword,
a sharp two-edged blade of bronze, and then charged out
straight at Odysseus, with a blood-curdling shout.
As he did so, lord Odysseus shot an arrow.
It struck him in the chest beside the nipple
and drove the swift shaft straight down into his liver.
Eurymachus' sword fell from his hand onto the ground.   110
He bent double and then fell, writhing on the table,
knocking food and two-handled cups onto the floor.
His forehead kept hammering the earth, his heart
in agony, as both his feet kicked at the chair
and made it shake. A mist fell over both his eyes.
Then Amphinomus went at glorious Odysseus,
charging straight for him. He'd drawn out his sharp sword,

to see if he would somehow yield the door to him.
But Telemachus moved in too quickly for him—
he threw a bronze-tipped spear and hit him from behind   120
between the shoulders. He drove it through his chest.
With a crash, Amphinomus fell, and his forehead
struck hard against the ground. Telemachus jumped back,
leaving his spear in Amphinomus, afraid that,
if he tried to pull out the long-shadowed spear,
some Achaean might attack and stab him with a sword
or strike him while he was stooping down. And so
he quickly ran away and then moved across
to his dear father. Standing close to him, he spoke—
his words had wings:

                    "Father, now I'll bring you   130
        a shield, two spears, and a bronze helmet,
        one that fits your temples. When I get back,
        I'll arm myself and hand out other armour
        to the swineherd and the keeper of the goats.
        It's better if we fully arm ourselves."

Quick-witted Odysseus answered him and said:

        "Get them here fast, while still I have arrows
        to protect myself, in case they push me
        from the doors, since I'm here by myself."

Odysseus spoke, and Telemachus obeyed   140
his dear father. He went off to the storeroom
where their splendid weapons lay. From the place
he took four shields, eight spears, and four bronze helmets
with thick horsehair plumes. He went out carrying these
and came back to his dear father very quickly.
First he armed himself with bronze around his body,
and the two servants did the same, putting on
the lovely armour. Then they took their places
on either side of skilled and sly Odysseus,
who, as long as he had arrows to protect him,   150
kept on aiming at the suitors in his house,

shooting at them one by one. As he hit them,
they fell down in heaps. But once he'd used his arrows,
the king could shoot no more. So he leaned the bow
against the doorpost of the well-constructed wall,
and let it stand beside the shining entrance way.
Then on his own he set across his shoulders
his four-layered shield, and on his powerful head
he placed a beautifully crafted helmet
with horsehair nodding ominously on top.   160
Then he grabbed two heavy bronze-tipped spears.
In that well-constructed wall there was a side door,
and close to the upper level of the threshold
into the sturdy hall the entrance to a passage,
shut off with close-fitting doors. So Odysseus
told the worthy swineherd to stand beside this door
and watch, for there was just one way of reaching it.[1]
Then Agelaus spoke, calling all the suitors:

> "Friends, can someone climb up to that side door
> and tell the men to raise a quick alarm?   170
> Then this man won't be shooting any more."

But Melanthius the goatherd answered him and said:

> "It can't be done, divinely raised Agelaus.
> The fine gate to the yard is awfully near,
> and the passage entrance hard to get through.
> One man could block the way for everyone,
> if he were brave. But come, let me bring you
> armour from the storeroom. You can put it on.
> It's in the house, I think—there's nowhere else
> Odysseus and his noble son could store   180

---

[1]For the architectural details see the ground plan of Odysseus' home at the back of this book. Odysseus has been shooting arrows from the entrance to the great hall (C) at the suitors inside the hall. The door at the back of the hall (z) has been locked. Odysseus wants to stop any suitor getting into the side passage (D) through the side door (s) and reaching the courtyard that way. So he's telling Eumaeus to stand at the door where that passage ends (t) to stop anyone leaving. The storage room for the weapons seems to be up the stairs by the door at point t. This would allow both Eumaeus and Melanthius to gain access to the room and would enable Eumaeus to see Melanthius when he returns for more weapons.

their weapons."

Once goatherd Melanthius said this,
he climbed a flight of stairs inside the palace,
up to Odysseus' storerooms. There he took twelve shields,
as many spears, as many helmets made of bronze
with bushy horsehair plumes. Once he'd made it back,
carrying the weapons, as quickly as he could
he gave them to the suitors. When Odysseus saw them
putting armour on and their hands brandishing
long spears, his knees and his fond heart went slack.
His task appeared enormous. He called out quickly   190
to Telemachus—his words had wings:

                              "Telemachus,
        it seems one of the women in the house
        is stirring up a nasty fight against us,
        or perhaps Melanthius might be the one."

Shrewd Telemachus then said in reply:

        "Father, I bear the blame for this myself.
        It's no one else's fault. I left it open—
        the close-fitting door of that storage room.
        One of them has keener eyes than I do.
        Come, good Eumaeus, shut the storeroom door.   200
        And try to learn if one of the women
        has done this, or if it's Melanthius,
        son of Dolius—I suspect it's him."

While they were saying these things to one another,
Melanthius the goatherd went back once more
to carry more fine armour from the storeroom.
But the loyal swineherd saw him and spoke out,
saying a quick word to Odysseus, who was close by:

        "Resourceful Odysseus, Laertes son,
        raised from Zeus, there's that man again,   210
        the wretch we think is visiting the storeroom.

436

Give me clear instructions—Should I kill him,
if I prove the stronger man, or should I
bring him to you here?—he can pay you back
for the many insolent acts he's done,
all those schemes he's thought up in your home."

Resourceful Odysseus then answered him and said:

"These proud suitors Telemachus and I
will keep penned up here inside the hall,
no matter how ferociously they fight.   220
You two twist Melanthius' feet and arms
behind him, throw him in the storeroom,
then lash boards against his back. Tie the man
to a twisted rope and then hoist him up
the lofty pillar till he's near the beams.
Let him stay alive a while and suffer
in agonizing pain."

             As Odysseus said this,
they listened eagerly and then obeyed his words.
They moved off to the storeroom, without being seen
by the man inside. He was, as it turned out, searching   230
for weapons in a corner of the room. So then,
when Melanthius the goatherd was coming out
across the threshold, holding a lovely helmet
in one hand and in the other an old broad shield
covered in mould—one belonging to Laertes,
which he used to carry as a youthful warrior,
but which now was lying in storage, its seams
unraveling on the straps—the two men jumped out
and grabbed him. They dragged him inside by the hair,
threw him on the ground—the man was terrified—   240
and tied his feet and hands with heart-wrenching bonds.
They lashed them tight behind his back, as Odysseus,
Laertes' royal son, who had endured so much,
had told them. They fixed a twisted rope to him,
yanked him up the lofty pillar, and raised him
near the roof beams. And then, swineherd Eumaeus,

you taunted him and said:

> "Now, Melanthius,
> you can really keep watch all night long,
> stretched out on a warm bed, as you deserve.
> You won't miss the golden throne of early Dawn,   250
> as she rises from the streams of Ocean—
> the very hour you've been bringing goats here,
> so the suitors can prepare their banquets
> in these halls."

They left Melanthius there,
tied up and hanging in bonds which would destroy him.
The two put on their armour, closed the shining door,
and made their way to wise and crafty Odysseus.
Filled with fighting spirit, they stood there, four of them
on the threshold, with many brave men in the hall.
Then Athena, Zeus' daughter, came up to them,   260
looking just like Mentor and with his voice, as well.
Odysseus saw her and rejoiced. He cried:

> "Mentor,
> help fight off disaster. Remember me,
> your dear comrade. I've done good things for you.
> You're my companion, someone my own age."

Odysseus said this, thinking Mentor was, in fact,
Athena, who incites armed men to action.
From across the hall the suitors yelled:

> "Mentor,
> don't let what Odysseus says convince you
> to fight the suitors and to stand by him.   270
> For this is how it will end up, I think,
> when our will prevails. Once we've killed these men,
> father and son, then you'll be slaughtered, too,
> for all the things you're keen to bring out
> here in the hall. You're going to pay for it
> with your own head. Once our swords have sliced

your strength from you, we'll mix your property,
all the things you have inside your home
and in the fields, with what Odysseus owns.
We won't allow your sons and daughters   280
to live within your house or your dear wife
to move in Ithaca, not in the city."

After they said this, Athena in her heart
grew very angry, and she rebuked Odysseus
with heated words:

            "Odysseus, you no longer have
that firm spirit and force you once possessed
when for nine years you fought against the Trojans
over white-armed Helen, who was nobly born.
You never stopped. You slaughtered many men
in fearful combat. Through your stratagems   290
Priam's city of broad streets was taken.
So how come now, when you've come home
among your own possessions, you're moaning
about acting bravely with these suitors?
Come on, my friend, stand here beside me,
see what I do, so you can understand
the quality of Mentor, Alcimus' son,
when, surrounded by his enemies,
he repays men who've acted well for him."

Athena spoke. But she did not give him the strength   300
to win that fight decisively. She was still testing
the power and resolution of Odysseus
and his splendid son. So she flew up to the roof
inside the smoky hall, and sat there, taking on
the appearance of a swallow.

            Meanwhile the suitors
were being driven into action by Agelaus,
Damastor's son, by Eurynomus, Amphimedon,
Demoptolemus, Peisander, Polyctor's son,
and clever Polybus. Among the suitors still alive

these were the finest men by far. Odysseus' bow
and his swift arrows had destroyed the others.
Agelaus spoke to them, addressing everyone:

> "Friends, this man's hands have been invincible,
> but now they'll stop. Mentor has moved away,
> once he'd made some empty boast. And now,
> they're left alone before the outer gates.
> So don't throw those long spears of yours at them,
> not all at once. Come, you six men throw first,
> to see if Zeus will let us strike Odysseus
> and win the glory. Those others over there 320
> will be no trouble after he's collapsed."

Agelaus spoke, and in their eagerness
to follow what he'd said, they all hurled their spears.
But Athena made sure their spear throws missed the mark.
One man hit a door post in the well-built hall.
Another struck the closely fitted door. One ash spear,
weighted down with bronze, fell against the wall.
When they'd escaped the suitor's spears, lord Odysseus,
who'd been through so much, was the first to speak:

> "Friends, now I'll give the word—let's hurl our spears 330
> into that crowd of suitors trying to kill us,
> adding to the harmful acts they did before."

Once Odysseus spoke, they all took steady aim,
then threw their pointed spears. Odysseus struck down
Demoptolemus, Telemachus hit Euryades,
the swineherd struck Elatus, and the cattle herder
killed Peisander. These men's teeth chewed up the earth,
all of them together. The suitors then pulled back
into the inner section of the hall. The others
then rushed up to pull their spears out of the dead. 340
The suitors kept throwing spears with frantic haste,
but, though there were many, Athena made them miss.
One man struck the door post of the well-built hall.
Another hit the closely fitted door. One ash spear,

weighted down with bronze, fell against the wall.
But Amphimedon did hit Telemachus' hand
a glancing blow across the wrist. The bronze point
cut the surface of his skin. And with his long spear
Ctessipus grazed Eumaeus' shoulder above his shield,
but the spear veered off and fell down on the ground.   350
Then the group surrounding sly and shrewd Odysseus
once more threw sharp spears into the crowd of suitors,
and once again Odysseus, sacker of cities,
hit a man—Eurydamas—while Telemachus
struck Amphimedon, and swineherd Eumaeus
hit Polybus. The cattle herder Philoetius
then struck Ctesippus in the chest and boasted
above the body, saying:

>   "Son of Polytherses,
>   you love to jeer—but don't yield any more
>   to your stupidity and talk so big.   360
>   Leave that sort of boasting to the gods,
>   for they are far more powerful than you.
>   This is your guest gift—something to pay back
>   the ox hoof you gave godlike Odysseus
>   back when he was begging in the house."

That's what the herder of the bent-horned cattle said.
At close range Odysseus wounded Damastor's son
with his long spear, and Telemachus injured
Leocritus, son of Evenor—he struck him
with his spear right in the groin and drove the bronze   370
straight through—so Leocritus fell on his face,
his whole forehead smashing down onto the ground.
Then Athena held up her man-destroying aegis
from high up in the roof. The suitors' minds panicked,
and they fled through the hall, like a herd of cattle
when a stinging gadfly goads them to stampede,
in spring season, when the long days come. Just as
the falcons with hooked talons and curved beaks
fly down from mountains, chasing birds and driving them
well below the clouds, as they swoop along the plain,   380

and then pounce and kill them, for there's no defense,
no flying away, while men get pleasure from the chase,
that's how Odysseus and his men pursued the suitors
and struck them down, one by one, throughout the hall.
As they smashed their heads in, dreadful groans arose,
and the whole floor was awash in blood.

                                        But then,
Leiodes ran out, grabbed Odysseus' knees,
and begged him—his words had wings:

                                        "Odysseus,
    I implore you at your knees—respect me
- and have pity. I tell you I've never   390
    harmed a single woman in these halls
    by saying or doing something reckless.
    Instead I tried to stop the other suitors
    when they did those things. They didn't listen
    or restrain their hands from acting badly.
    So their own wickedness now brings about
    their wretched fate. Among them I'm a prophet
    who has done no wrong, and yet I'll lie dead,
    since there's no future thanks for one's good deeds."

Shrewd Odysseus glared at him and answered:

                                        "If, in fact,   400
    you claim to be a prophet with these men,
    no doubt here in these halls you've often prayed
    that my goal of a sweet return would stay
    remote from me, so my dear wife could go
    away with you and bear your children.
    That's why you won't escape a bitter death."

As he said this, Odysseus picked up in his fist
a sword that lay near by—Agelaus, when he was killed,
had let it fall onto the ground. With this sword
Odysseus struck Leiodes right on the neck—   410
his head rolled in the dust as he was speaking.

And then the minstrel Phemius, son of Terpes,
who'd been compelled to sing before the suitors,
kept trying to get away from his own murky fate.
He stood holding his clear-toned lyre by the side door,
his mind divided—Should he slip out from the hall
and take a seat close to the altar of great Zeus,
god of the courtyard, where Laertes and Odysseus
had burned many thighs from sacrificial oxen,
or should he rush up to Odysseus' knee   420
and beg him for his life? As his mind thought it through,
the latter course of action seemed the better choice,
to clasp the knees of Laertes' son, Odysseus.
So he set the hollow lyre down on the ground,
between the mixing bowl and silver-studded chair,
rushed out in person to clasp Odysseus' knees,
and pleaded with him—his words had wings:

> "I implore you, Odysseus, show me respect
> and pity. There'll be sorrow for you later,
> if you kill me, a minstrel, for I sing   430
> to gods and men. I am self taught. The god
> has planted in my heart all kinds of songs,
> and I'm good enough to sing before you,
> as to a god. Don't be too eager then
> to cut my throat. Your dear son Telemachus
> could tell you that it wasn't my desire
> nor did I need to spend time at your house,
> singing for the suitors at their banquets.
> But their greater power and numbers
> brought me here by force."

                            As Phemius said this,   440
royal Telemachus heard him and spoke up,
calling to his father, who was close by:

> "Hold on. Don't let your sword injure this man.
> He's innocent. We should save Medon, too,
> the herald, who always looked out for me
> inside the house when I was still a child,

443

unless Philoetius has killed him,
or the swineherd, or he ran into you
as you were on the rampage in the hall."

Telemachus spoke. Medon, whose mind was clever,   450
heard him, for he was cowering underneath a chair,
his skin covered by a new-flayed ox-hide, trying
to escape his own black fate. He quickly jumped out
from beneath the chair, threw off the ox-hide,
rushed up to clasp Telemachus' knees, and begged—
his words had wings:

                            "Here I am, my friend.
Stop! And tell your father to restrain himself,
in case, as he exults in his great power,
he slaughters me with that sharp bronze of his,
in his fury with the suitors, those men   460
who consumed his goods here in his own hall,
those fools who did not honour you at all."

Resourceful Odysseus then smiled at him and said:

"Cheer up! This man here has saved your life.
He's rescued you, so you know in your heart
and can tell someone else how doing good
is preferable by far to acting badly.
But move out of the hall and sit outside,
in the yard, some distance from the killing,
you and the minstrel with so many songs,   470
until I finish all I need to do in here."

After Odysseus spoke, the two men went away,
outside the hall, and sat down there, by the altar
of great Zeus, peering round in all directions,
always thinking they'd be killed.

                            Odysseus, too,
looked round the house to check if anyone
was hiding there, still alive, trying to escape

444

his own dark fate. But every man he looked at—
and there were plenty—had fallen in blood and dust,
like fish which, in the meshes of a net, fishermen   480
have pulled from the gray sea up on the curving beach,
lying piled up on the sand, longing for sea waves,
while the bright sun takes away their life—that's how
the suitors then were lying in heaps on one another.

Resourceful Odysseus then said to Telemachus:

> "Telemachus, go and call the nurse in here,
> Eurycleia, so I can speak to her.
> Something's on my mind—I want to tell her."

Once Odysseus spoke, Telemachus obeyed
what his dear father said. He shook the door and called   490
to Eurycleia, saying:[1]

> "Get up, old woman,
> born so long ago—the one in charge
> of female servants in the palace.
> Come out. My father's calling for you.
> He's got something he wants to say."

He spoke. But Eurycleia's words could find no wings.
She opened up the door of the well-furnished hall
and came out. Telemachus went first and led the way.
There she found Odysseus with the bodies of the dead,
spattered with blood and gore, like a lion moving off   500
from feeding on a farmyard ox, his whole chest
and both sides of his muzzle caked with blood,
a terrifying sight, that's how Odysseus looked,
with bloodstained feet and upper arms. Eurycleia,
once she saw the bodies and huge amounts of blood,
was ready to cry out for joy now that she'd seen
such a mighty act. But Odysseus held her back

---

[1] *. . . to Eurycleia, saying.* The doorway here is the entrance to the women's quarters (in
the diagram at the back point v). At the start of the slaughter Eurycleia had locked it to
prevent any of the women coming into the great hall or escaping to raise the alarm.

445

and checked her eagerness. He spoke to her—
his words had wings:

"Old woman, you can rejoice
in your own heart—but don't cry out aloud.   510
Restrain yourself. For it's a sacrilege
to boast above the bodies of the slain.
Divine Fate and their own reckless acts
have killed these men, who failed to honour
any man on earth who came among them,
bad or good. And so through their depravity
they've met an evil fate. But come now,
tell me about the women in these halls,
the ones who disrespect me and the ones
who bear no blame."

His dear nurse Eurycleia   520
then answered him and said:

"All right my child,
I'll tell you the truth. In these halls of yours,
there are fifty female servants, women
we have taught to carry out their work,
to comb out wool and bear their slavery.
Of these, twelve in all have gone along
without a sense of shame and no respect
for me or even for Penelope herself.
Telemachus has only just grown up,
and his mother hasn't let him yet control   530
our female servants. But come, let's go now
to that bright upstairs room and tell your wife.
Some god has made her sleep."

Resourceful Odysseus
then answered her and said:

"Don't wake her up.
Not yet. Those women who before all this
behaved so badly, tell them to come here."

Once he'd said this, the old woman went through the house
to tell the women the news and urge them to appear.
Odysseus then called Telemachus to him,
together with Eumaeus and Philoetius.   540
He spoke to them—his words had wings:

> "Start carrying those corpses outside now,
> and then take charge of the servant women.
> Have these splendid chairs and tables cleaned,
> wiped with porous sponges soaked in water.
> Once you've put the entire house in order,
> then take those servants from the well-built hall
> to a spot outside between the round house
> and the sturdy courtyard wall and kill them.
> Slash them with long swords, until the life is gone   550
> from all of them, and they've forgotten
> Aphrodite and how they loved the suitors
> when they had sex with them in secret."

Odysseus spoke. Then the crowd of women came,
wailing plaintively and shedding many tears.
First they gathered up the corpses of the dead
and laid them out underneath the portico,
leaning them against each other in the well-fenced yard.
Odysseus himself gave them their instructions
and hurried on the work. The women were compelled   560
to carry out the dead. After that, they cleaned
the splendid chairs and tables, wiping them down
with water and porous sponges. Telemachus,
along with Philoetius and Eumaeus,
with shovels scraped the floor inside the well-built hall,
and women took the dirt and threw it in the yard.
When they'd put the entire hall in order,
they led the women out of the sturdy house
to a place between the round house and fine wall
around the courtyard, herding them into a narrow space   570
where there was no way to escape. Shrewd Telemachus
began by speaking to the other two:

                                                     "I don't want
        to take these women's lives with a clean death.
        They've poured insults on my head, on my mother,
        and were always sleeping with the suitors."

He spoke, then tied the cable of a dark-prowed ship
to a large pillar, threw one end above the round house,
then pulled it taut and high, so no woman's foot
could reach the ground.[1] Just as doves or long-winged thrushes
charge into a snare set in a thicket, as they seek out   580
their roosting place, and find out they've been welcomed
by a dreadful bed, that's how those women held their heads
all in a row, with nooses fixed around their necks,
so they'd have a pitiful death. For a little while
they twitched their feet, but that did not last long.

Then they brought Melanthius out through the doorway
into the yard. With pitiless bronze they sliced away
his nose and ears, then ripped off his cock and balls
as raw meat for dogs to eat, and in their rage
hacked off his hands and feet. After they'd done that,   590
they washed their hands and feet and went inside the house,
back to Odysseus. Their work was done. But he
called out to Eurycleia, his dear nurse:

                            "Old woman,
        bring sulphur here to purify the house.
        And bring me fire so I can purge the hall.
        Ask Penelope to come here with her slaves,
        and get all the women in the house to come."

His dear nurse Eurycleia answered him:

                            "My child,
        what you say is all well and good, but come,
        I'll fetch you clothing, a cloak and tunic,   600

[1] . . . *could reach the ground*: The round house is in one corner of the courtyard (point
g on the diagram in the back of this book). Telemachus hangs the servant women from
a cable attached to the top of the round house and to a nearby pillar.

so you don't stand like this in your own hall
with nothing but rags on your wide shoulders.
That would be the cause of some disgrace."

Resourceful Odysseus then answered her and said:

"But first make me a fire in the hall."

Dear nurse Eurycleia then followed what he'd said.
She brought fire and sulphur, so Odysseus
purged the house and yard completely. Eurycleia
went back through Odysseus' splendid home to tell
the women what had happened and to order them   610
to reappear. They came out holding torches,
then gathered round Odysseus, embracing him.
They clasped and kissed his head, his hands, and shoulders,
in loving welcome. A sweet longing seized him
to sigh and weep, for in his heart he knew them all.

Book Twenty-Three
Odysseus and Penelope

[Eurycleia wakes up Penelope to tell her Odysseus has returned and killed the Suitors; Penelope refuses to believe the news; Penelope comes down and sits in the same room as Odysseus but doesn't recognize him; Telemachus criticizes his mother; Odysseus invites her to test him and discusses with Telemachus what their next step will be to deal with the aftermath of the killings; they organize a fake wedding dance to deceive anyone passing the house; Odysseus is given a bath, and Athena transforms his appearance; Penelope tells Eurycleia to set his old bed up for him outside the bedroom; Odysseus tells the story of the bed; Penelope acknowledges Odysseus and embraces him; Odysseus tells her of the ordeals yet to come, according to the prophecy of Teiresias; Penelope and Odysseus go to bed, make love, and then she hears the story of his adventures; in the morning Odysseus gets up, tells Penelope to stay in her upper rooms, puts on his armour, instructs Eumaeus and Philoetius to arm themselves; Athena leads them out of the city.]

Old Eurycleia went up to an upstairs room,
laughing to herself, to inform her mistress
her beloved husband was inside the house.
Her knees moved quickly as her feet hurried on.
She stood beside her lady's head and spoke to her:

> "Wake up, Penelope, my dear child,
> so you can see for yourself with your own eyes
> what you've been wanting each and every day.
> Odysseus has arrived. He may be late,
> but he's back in the house. And he's killed   10
> those arrogant suitors who upset this home,
> used up his goods, and victimized his son."

Wise Penelope then answered her:

>   "Dear nurse,
> the gods have made you mad. They can do that—
> turn even someone really sensible

into a fool and bring the feeble minded
to a path of fuller understanding.
They've injured you—your mind was sound before.
Why mock me, when my heart is full of grief,
telling this mad tale, rousing me from sleep,   20
a sweet sleep binding me, shrouding my eyes?
I've not had a sleep like that since Odysseus
went off to look at wicked Ilion,
a place whose name no one should ever speak.
Come now, go back down to the women's hall.
Among my servants, if some other one
had come to tell me this, woken me up
when I was sleeping, I'd have sent her back
at once to the woman's quarters in disgrace.
But I'll be good to you because you're old."   30

The dear nurse Eurycleia then said to her:

"But I'm not making fun of you, dear child.
It's true. Odysseus has returned. He's back,
here in the house, exactly as I said.
He's that stranger all the men dishonoured
in the hall. For some time Telemachus
knew he was at home, but he was careful
to conceal his father's plans, until the time
he could pay back those overbearing men
for their forceful oppression."

                                Eurycleia spoke.   40
Penelope rejoiced. She jumped up out of bed,
hugged the old woman, tears falling from her eyelids,
then she spoke to her—her words had wings:

                                "Come now,
dear nurse, tell me the truth. If he's really here,
back home as you claim, then how could he
turn his hands against those shameless suitors?
He was alone, and in this house those men
were always in a group."

Her dear nurse Eurycleia
then answered her:

                                    "I didn't see or hear about it.
I only heard the groans of men being killed.   50
We sat in our well-built women's quarters,
in a corner, terrified. Close-fitting doors
kept us in there, until Telemachus,
your son, called me from the room. His father
had sent him there to summon me. And then,
I found Odysseus standing with the bodies—
dead men on the hard earth all around him,
lying on each other, a heart-warming sight—
and he was there, covered with blood and gore,
just like a lion. Now all those bodies   60
have been piled up at the courtyard gates,
and he's purging his fair home with sulphur.
He's kindled a great fire. He sent me out
to summon you. Now, come along with me,
so you two can be happy in your hearts.
You've been through so much misfortune, and now
what you've been looking forward to so long
has come about at last. He's come himself,
to his own hearth while still alive—he's found
you and your son inside these halls and taken   70
his revenge on all suitors in his home,
men who acted harmfully against him."

Wise Penelope then answered Eurycleia:

                                    "Dear nurse, don't laugh at them and boast too much.
You know how his appearance in the hall
would delight all men, especially me
and the son born from the two of us.
But this story can't be true, not the way
you've told it. One of the immortal gods
has killed the noble suitors out of rage   80
at their heart-rending pride and wicked acts.
There was no man on this earth they honoured,

452

bad or good, when he came into their group.
They've met disaster through their foolishness.
But in some place far away Odysseus
has forfeited his journey to Achaea,
and he himself is lost."

Dear nurse Eurycleia
then answered her:

"My child, what kind of speech has slipped
the barrier of your teeth, when you declared
your husband won't get home—he's in the house,   90
at his own hearth. Your heart just has no trust.
But come on, I'll tell you something else—
it's a clear proof—that scar a boar gave him
some time ago with its white tusk. I saw it.
I washed it clean. I was going to tell you,
but his hand gripped me by the throat—his heart
in its great subtlety wouldn't let me speak.
But come with me. I'll stake my life on it.
If I've deceived you, then you can kill me
and choose a painful death."

Wise Penelope   100
then answered her:

"Dear nurse, you find it hard
to grasp the plans of the eternal gods,
even though you're really shrewd. But let's go
to my son, so I can see the suitors
now they're dead—and the man who killed them."

Penelope spoke, then went down from the upper room,
her heart turning over many things—Should she
keep her distance and question her dear husband,
or should she come up to him, hold his head and hands,
and kiss them? Crossing the stone threshold, she went in   110
and sat down in the firelight opposite Odysseus,
beside the further wall. He was sitting there

453

by a tall pillar, looking at the ground, waiting
to learn if his noble wife would speak to him
when her own eyes caught sight of him. She sat there
a long time in silence. Amazement came in her heart—
sometimes her eyes gazed at him full in the face,
but other times she failed to recognize him,
he had such shabby clothing covering his body.
Telemachus spoke up, addressing a rebuke   120
directly to her:

                              "Mother, you're a cruel woman,
            with an unfeeling heart. Why turn aside
            from my father in this way? Why not sit
            over there, close to him, ask him questions?
            No other woman's heart would be so hard
            to make her keep her distance from a husband
            who's come home to her in his native land
            in the twentieth year, after going through
            so many harsh ordeals. That heart of yours
            is always harder than a stone."

                                    Wise Penelope   130
then answered him:

                              "My child, inside my chest
            my heart is quite amazed. I cannot speak
            or ask questions, or look directly at him.
            If indeed it's true he is Odysseus
            and is home again, surely the two of us
            have more certain ways to know each other.
            We have signs only we two understand.
            Other people will not recognize them."

As she spoke, lord Odysseus, who'd been through so much,
smiled and immediately spoke to Telemachus—   140
his words had wings:

                              "Telemachus, let your mother
            test me in these halls. She will soon possess

more certain knowledge. Right now I'm filthy,
with disgusting clothing on my body.
That's why she rejects me and will not say
I am Odysseus. But we need to think
how this matter can best resolve itself.
Anyone who murders just one person
in the district, even when the dead man
does not leave many to avenge him later,   150
goes into exile, leaving his relatives
and his native land. But we have slaughtered
the city's main defense, the best by far
of the young men in Ithaca. I think
you should consider what that means."

Shrewd Telemachus then answered him and said:

"Surely you must look into this yourself,
dear father. For among all men, they say,
your planning is the best—of mortal men
no one can rival you. And as for us,   160
we're keen to follow you, and I don't think
we'll lack the bravery to match our strength."

Resourceful Odysseus said this in reply:

"All right, I'll say what seems to me the best.
First of all, take a bath. Put tunics on.
Next, tell the female servants in the hall
to change their clothing. After that, we'll let
the holy minstrel, with his clear-toned lyre,
lead us in playful dancing, so anyone
who hears us from outside—someone walking   170
down the road or those who live close by—
will say it is a wedding. In that way,
the wide rumour of the suitors' murder
will not spread too soon down in the city,
before we go out to our forest lands.
There later on we'll think of our next move,
whatever the Olympian god suggests."

They listened eagerly to what Odysseus said
and were persuaded. So first of all they bathed
and put on tunics. The women got dressed up.   180
Then the godlike singer took his hollow lyre
and encouraged their desire for lovely songs
and noble dancing. The whole great house resounded
to the steps of men celebrating a good time
with women wearing lovely gowns. So any man
who listened in as he walked past outside the house
might offer a remark like this:

                "It seems that someone
    has married the queen with all those suitors.
    A heartless woman. She lacked the courage
    to maintain her wedded husband's home   190
    and persevere till he arrived back home."

That's what someone would've said—he'd never know
what was going on. Meanwhile, Eurynome,
the housekeeper, gave brave Odysseus a bath,
rubbed him with oil, and put a tunic on him,
a fine cloak, as well. Athena poured beauty on him
in large amounts to make him taller, more robust
to look at, and on his head she made his hair
flow in curls resembling a hyacinth in bloom.
Just as a man sets a layer of gold on silver,   200
a skillful artisan whom Pallas Athena
and Hephaestus have taught all sorts of crafts,
so he produces marvelous work, that's how Athena
poured grace onto his head and shoulders, as he came
out of his bath, looking like the immortal gods.
He sat back down in the chair from which he'd risen,
opposite his wife, and said to her:

                "Strange lady,
    to you those who live on Mount Olympus
    have given, more so than to other women,
    an unfeeling heart. No other woman   210
    would harden herself and keep her distance

from her husband, who, in the twentieth year,
came back to her in his own native land,
after going through so much misfortune.
So come, nurse, spread out a bed for me,
so I can lie down by myself. The heart
inside her breast is made of iron."

Wise Penelope then answered him:

                    "Strange man,
I am not making too much of myself,
or ignoring you. Nor is it the case   220
that I'm particularly offended.
I know well the sort of man you were
when you left Ithaca in your long-oared ship.
So come, Eurycleia, set up for him
outside the well-built bedroom that strong bed
he made himself. Put that sturdy bedstead
out there for him and throw some bedding on,
fleeces, cloaks, and shining coverlets."

Penelope said this to test her husband.
But Odysseus, angry at his true-hearted wife,   230
spoke out:

             "Woman, those words you've just uttered
are very painful. Who's shifted my bed
to some other place? That would be difficult,
even for someone really skilled, unless
a god came down in person—for he could,
if he wished, set it elsewhere easily.
But among men there is no one living,
no matter how much energy he has,
who would find it easy to shift that bed.
For built into the well-constructed bedstead   240
is a great symbol which I made myself
with no one else. A long-leaved olive bush
was growing in the yard. It was in bloom
and flourishing—it looked like a pillar.

I built my bedroom round this olive bush,
till I had finished it with well-set stones.
I put a good roof over it, then added
closely fitted jointed doors. After that,
I cut back the foliage, by removing
branches from the long-leaved olive bush.   250
I trimmed the trunk off, upward from the root,
cutting it skillfully and well with bronze,
so it followed a straight line. Once I'd made
the bedpost, I used an augur to bore out
the entire piece. That was how I started.
Then I carved out my bed, till I was done.
In it I set an inlay made of gold,
silver, and ivory, and then across it
I stretched a bright purple thong of ox-hide.
And that's the symbol I describe for you.   260
But, lady, I don't know if that bed of mine
is still in place or if some other man
has cut that olive tree down at its base
and set the bed up in a different spot."

Odysseus spoke, and sitting there, Penelope
went weak at the knees, and her heart grew soft.
For she recognized that it was true—that symbol
Odysseus had described to her. Eyes full of tears,
she ran to him, threw her arms around his neck,
kissed his head, and said:

                "Don't be angry, Odysseus,   270
not with me. In all other matters
you've been the cleverest of men. The gods
have brought us sorrows—they were not willing
the two of us should stay beside each other
to enjoy our youth and reach together
the threshold of old age. Now's not the time
to rage at me, resenting what I've done
because I didn't welcome you this way
when I first saw you. But in my dear breast
my heart was always fearful, just in case   280

some other man would come and trick me
with his stories. For there are many men
who dream up wicked schemes. Argive Helen,
a child of Zeus, would never have had sex
with a man who came from somewhere else,
if she'd known Achaea's warrior sons
would bring her back to her dear native land.
And some god drove her to that shameful act.
Not till that time did she start harbouring
within her heart the disastrous folly   290
which made sorrow come to us as well.
But now you've mentioned that clear symbol,
our bed, which no one else has ever seen,
other than the two of us, you and me,
and a single servant woman, Actoris,
whom my father gave me when I came here.
For both of us she kept watch at the doors
of our strong bedroom. You've now won my heart,
though it's been truly stubborn."

                              Penelope spoke
and stirred in him an even more intense desire   300
to weep. As he held his loyal and loving wife,
he cried. Just as it's a welcome sight for swimmers
when land appears, men whose well-constructed ship
Poseidon has demolished on the sea, as winds
and surging waves were driving it, and a few men
have swum to shore, escaping the grey sea,
their bodies thickly caked with brine, and they climb
gladly up on land, evading that disaster,
that how Penelope rejoiced to see her husband.
She simply couldn't stop her white arms holding him   310
around the neck. And rose-fingered early Dawn
would've appeared with them still weeping there,
if goddess Athena with the gleaming eyes,
had not thought of something else—she prolonged
the lengthy night as it came to an end, keeping
Dawn and her golden throne waiting by Ocean's stream—
she would not let her harness her swift horses,

who carry light to men, Lampros and Phaeton,
the colts who bring on Dawn.

                         Resourceful Odysseus
then said to his wife:

                         "Lady, we've not yet come   320
to the end of all our trials. Countless tasks
must still be carried out in days to come,
plenty of hard work I have to finish.
That's what the spirit of Teiresias
prophesied to me when I descended
inside Hades' house to ask some questions
concerning our return, my companions
and myself. But come, wife, let's go to bed,
so we can lie down and enjoy sweet sleep."

Wise Penelope then answered him:

                         "You'll have a bed   330
when your heart so desires, for the gods
have seen to it that you've returned back here
to your well-built home and native land.
But since you've thought of it and some god
has set it in your heart, come and tell me
of this trial. For I think I'll hear of it
in future, so to learn of it right now
won't make things any worse."

                         Resourceful Odysseus
then answered her and said:

                         "Strange lady,
why urge me so eagerly to tell you?   340
All right, I'll say it, and I'll hide nothing.
But your heart will not find it delightful.
I myself get no enjoyment from it.
Teiresias ordered me to journey out
to many human cities, carrying

in my hands a well-made oar, till I reached
a people who know nothing of the sea,
who don't put salt on any food they eat,
and have no knowledge of ships painted red
or well-made oars that serve those ships as wings.   350
He told me a sure sign I won't conceal—
when someone else runs into me and says
I've got a shovel used for winnowing
on my broad shoulders, he told me to set it
in the ground there, make rich sacrifice
to lord Poseidon with a ram, a bull,
and a boar that breeds with sows, then leave,
go home, and there make sacred offerings
to immortal gods who hold wide heaven,
all of them in order. My death will come   360
far from the sea, such a gentle passing,
when I'm bowed down with a ripe old age,
with my people prospering around me.
He said all this would happen to me."

Wise Penelope then said to him:

                              "If it's true the gods
          are going to bring you a happier old age,
          there's hope you'll have relief from trouble."

While they went on talking to each other in this way,
Eurynome and the nurse prepared the bed
with soft coverlets, by light from flaming torches.   370
Once they'd quickly covered up the sturdy bed,
the old nurse went back to her room to rest,
and the bedroom servant, Eurynome, led them
on their way to bed, a torch gripped in her hands.
When she'd brought them to the room, then she returned.
Odysseus and Penelope approached with joy
the place where their bed stood from earlier days.
Telemachus, Philoetius, and Eumaeus
stopped their dancing feet, made the women stop as well.
Then they, too, lay down in the shadowy hall to sleep.   380

Odysseus and Penelope, once they'd had the joy
of making love, then entertained each other
telling stories, in mutual conversation.
The lovely lady talked of all she'd been through
in the house, looking at that destructive group,
the suitors, who, because of her, had butchered
so many cattle and fat sheep and drained from jars
so much wine. Odysseus, born from Zeus, then told
all the troubles he'd brought down on men, all the grief
he'd had to work through on his own. Penelope   390
was happy listening, and sleep did not come down
across her eyelids until he'd told it all.

He began by telling how he first destroyed
the Cicones, and then came to the fertile land
of Lotus-eating men, and all the Cyclops did—
and how he forced him to pay the penalty
for his brave comrades eaten by the Cyclops—
then how he came to Aeolus, who'd taken him in
quite willingly and sent him on his way.
But it was not yet his destiny to reach   400
his dear native land. Instead, storm winds once more
caught him, drove him across the fish-filled seas,
for all his weary groans. He told how he next came
to Telepylos where the Laestrygonians live,
men who destroyed his ships and well-armed comrades,
all of them, and how Odysseus was the only one
to escape in his black ship.[1] He went on to talk
of Circe's devious resourcefulness and how
in his ship with many oars he'd then gone down
to Hades' murky home in order to consult   410
the spirit of Teiresias of Thebes and seen
all his companions and his mother, who bore him
and raised him as a child, and how he'd listened to
the Sirens' voices, in their never-ending song,

---

[1] . . . *his black ship.* In this incident with the Laestrygonians, narrated in Book 10,
Odysseus loses all his men and ships except his own ship and crew, because he had the
foresight not to moor his boat with the others inside the harbour. These lines
obviously do not mean that from this point on he was totally alone.

then come to the Wandering Rocks, dread Charybdis,
and to Scylla, whom men have never yet escaped
without being harmed, how his comrades slaughtered
the oxen of the sun god Helios, how his ship
was shattered by a flaming lightning bolt thrown down
from high-thundering Zeus, how his fine comrades perished,   420
all at once, while he alone escaped from fate,
how he reached the nymph Calypso on her island,
Ogygia, how she kept him in her hollow caves,
longing for him to be her husband, nurturing him
and telling him she'd make him an immortal
who through all his days would not get any older,
but she could not convince the heart within his chest,
how, after suffering a great deal, he then had come
to the Phaeacians, who greatly honoured him,
as if he were a god, and sent him in a ship   430
to his dear native land, after offering gifts
of bronze and gold and rich supplies of clothing.
He stopped his story at that point, when sweet sleep,
which makes men's limbs relax, came over him,
and eased disturbing worries he had in his heart.

Then Athena, goddess with the gleaming eyes,
came up with something else. When she thought Odysseus
had had his heart's fill of pleasure with his wife and slept,
from Ocean she quickly stirred up early Dawn
on her golden throne to bring her light to men.   440
Odysseus rose from his soft bed and told his wife:

> "Lady, the two of us by now have had
> sufficient trouble—you here lamenting
> my hazardous return, while, in my case,
> Zeus and the other gods kept me tied up
> far from my native land, in great distress,
> for all my eagerness to get back home.
> Now that we've come back to the bed we love,
> you should tend to our wealth inside the house.
> As for the flocks those arrogant suitors stole,   450
> I'll seize many beasts as plunder on my own,

463

and Achaeans will give others, till they fill up
each and every pen. Now I'm going to go
out to my forest lands, and there I'll see
my noble father, who on my behalf
has suffered such anxiety. Lady,
since I know how intelligent you are,
I'm asking you to follow these instructions—
once sunrise comes, the story will be out
about the suitors slaughtered in our home.   460
So you should go up to your upper room
with your female attendants. Then sit there.
Don't look in on anyone or ask questions."

Once he'd said this, he put his lovely armour on,
around his shoulders, and roused Telemachus,
Philoetius, and Eumaeus, and told them all
to get weapons in their hands to fight a war.
They did not disobey, but dressed themselves in bronze,
opened the doors, and went outside, with Odysseus
in the lead. By now light was shining on the ground,   470
but Athena kept them hidden by the night,
as she led them quickly from the city.

Book Twenty-Four
Zeus and Athena End the Fighting

[Hermes conducts the shades of the dead suitors down to Hades, where they meet Achilles, Patroclus, Antilochus, and Agamemnon; Agamemnon and Achilles talk; Agamemnon gives details of Achilles' burial; Amphimedon complains to Agamemnon about his death at Odysseus' hands; Agamemnon pays tribute to Odysseus and Penelope; Odysseus goes out to find his father; Laertes and Odysseus talk in the vineyard, and Odysseus tests his father with a false story and then reveals his identity; the two men return to Laertes house, where Eumaeus, Philoetius, and Telemachus have prepared dinner; Laertes' appearance is transformed; Dolius and his sons arrive; the men in Ithaca hear about the slaughter and collect their dead; Eupeithes urges action against Odysseus; Medon and Halitherses advises against such action; the majority decide to follow Eupeithes; Athena questions Zeus about his intentions regarding Odysseus; Zeus tells her to deal with the situation; Odysseus and his followers arm themselves and go out to meet the Ithacan army; Athena urges Laertes to throw a spear; Laertes kills Eupeithes; Athena stops the Ithacan army and sends it back to the city; a thunderbolt from Zeus stops Odysseus; Athena establishes a lasting oath between both sides.]

Meanwhile Hermes of Cyllene summoned up
the spirits of the suitors. In his hand he held
the beautiful gold wand he uses to enchant
the eyes of anyone he wishes or to wake
some other man from sleep. With it he roused and led
these spirits, who kept squeaking as they followed him.
Just as inside the corners of a monstrous cave
bats flit around and squeak when one of them falls down
out of the cluster on the rock where they cling
to one another, that how these spirits squawked   10
as they moved on together. Hermes the Deliverer
conducted them along the murky passageway.[1]
They went past the streams of Ocean, past Leucas,

---

[1] *Hermes the Deliverer.* Hermes, in addition to his other roles as messenger of the gods, traditionally escorted the souls of the dead down into Hades, hence the epithet "Deliverer."

past the gates of the Sun and the land of Dreams,
and very soon came to the field of asphodel,[1]
where spirits live, the shades of those whose work is done.

Here they found Achilles' shade, son of Peleus,
and of Patroclus, too, noble Antilochus,
and Ajax, who had the finest form and shape
of all Danaans, after the son of Peleus,   20
who had no peer. These shades were gathered there,
in a group around Achilles. Then to them came
the spirit of Agamemnon, son of Atreus,
full of sorrow. Around him were assembled shades
of all those who'd been killed with him and met their fate
in Aegisthus' house. The son of Peleus' shade
was the first to speak to him:

                                  "Son of Atreus,
we thought of you as one well loved by Zeus,
who hurls the thunderbolt, for all your days,
more so than every other human warrior,   30
because on Trojan soil you were the king
of many powerful men, where we Achaeans
went through so much distress. And now it seems
destructive Fate was destined to reach you,
as well, and far too soon, the mortal doom
that no man born escapes. Oh, how I wish
you'd met your fatal end in Trojan lands,
still in full possession of those honours
you were master of. Then all Achaeans
would have made a tomb for you—for your son   40
you'd have won great fame in future days.
But as it is, your fate was to be caught
in a death more pitiful than any."

The shade of Atreus' son then answered him:

      "Godlike Achilles, fortunate son of Peleus,
killed in the land of Troy, far from Argos.

[1] . . . *field of asphodel*: Leucas is the "White Rock" at the entrance to Hades.

Other men fell round you, the finest sons
of Trojans and Achaeans, in the fight
above your corpse. You lay in the swirling dust,
a great man in your full magnificence,   50
with your skill in horsemanship forgotten.
As for us, we fought there all day long.
We never would have pulled back from the fight,
if Zeus had not brought on a storm to end it.
We took you from the battle to the ships,
laid you on a bier, and with warm water
and oil we cleaned your lovely skin. And then,
standing around you, the Danaans wept,
shedding plenty of hot tears, and cut their hair.
When your mother heard the news, she came   60
with immortal sea nymphs from the sea.[1]
An amazing cry arose above the water—
all Achaeans were then seized with trembling.
They would've all jumped up and run away
to the hollow ships, if one man, well versed
in ancient wisdom, had not held them back.
I mean Nestor, whose advice in earlier days
had seemed the best. Using his wise judgment,
he addressed them all and said:

                'Hold on, Argives.
You young Achaean men, don't rush away.   70
This is his mother coming from the sea
with her immortal sea nymphs to look on
the face of her dead son.'

                   "That's what Nestor said,
and the brave Achaeans stopped their running.
Then the daughters of the Old Man of the Sea
stood round you in a piteous lament,[2]
as they put immortal clothing on you.

---

[1] ... *up from the sea*: Achilles' mother is Thetis, a minor deity of the sea.

[2] ... *in piteous lament*: The phrase Old Man of the Sea to refers to different minor sea gods. The father of the sea nymphs is Nereus, not Proteus, the Old Man of the Sea whom Menelaus talks about in his adventures in Egypt in Book 4.

And Muses, nine in all, sang out a dirge,
their lovely voices answering each other.
You'd not have seen a single Argive there
without tears, their hearts so deeply moved
by the Muses' clear-toned song. We mourned you
for seventeen days and nights together,
both mortal humans and immortal gods.
On the eighteenth we gave you to the fire.
Around you we killed many well-fed sheep
and bent-horned cattle. You were cremated
in clothing of the gods, with sweet honey
and much oil. Many Achaean warriors
moved around the funeral pyre in armour,
as you were burning, both foot soldiers
and charioteers, making an enormous noise.
And then, Achilles, once Hephaestus' flame
was finished with you, we set your white bones
in unmixed wine and oil. Your mother gave
a two-handled jar of gold. She said it was
a gift from Dionysus, something made
by illustrious Hephaestus. In this jar,
glorious Achilles, lie your white bones,
mixed in with those of dead Patroclus,
son of Menoetius.[1] Separate from these
are Antilochus' bones, whom you honoured
above all the rest of your companions
after Patroclus.[2] Then, over these bones
we raised a huge impressive burial mound,
we—the sacred army of Argive spearmen—
on a promontory projecting out
into the wide Hellespont, so that men,
those now alive and those in future days,
can view it from a long way out at sea.
Your mother asked the gods for lovely prizes

---

[1] ... *son of Menoetius*: Patroclus is Achilles' closest companion in the *Iliad*. In that
poem, his dying request to Achilles is to have their bones placed together in a funeral
urn when Achilles is killed.
[2] ... *after Patroclus*: Antilochus is a son of Nestor. He was killed in the fighting around
Troy. His name is mentioned in Book 3 when Telemachus visits Nestor in Pylos.

and set them out among the best Achaeans
for a competition. In earlier days
you've been present at the funeral games
of many warriors, when, once a king dies,
the young men, after tying up their clothes,
prepare to win the contests. But if you'd seen
that spectacle you'd have truly marveled—
the goddess, silver-footed Thetis, set
such beautiful prizes in your honour.   120
The gods had that much special love for you.
So even in death, your name did not die.
No. Your glorious fame, Achilles, will endure
among all men forever. As for me,
I finished off the war, but what pleasure
does that give me now? When I got back home,
Zeus organized a dreadful fate for me,
at Aegisthus' hands and my accursed wife's."[1]

As they talked this way to one another, Hermes,
killer of Argus, came up close to them, leading down   130
the shades of suitors whom Odysseus had killed.
When they observed this, the two, in their amazement,
went straight up to them. The shade of Agamemnon,
son of Atreus, recognized the well-loved son
of Melaneus, splendid Amphimedon,
a guest friend of his from Ithaca, his home.
The shade of Atreus' son spoke to him first, saying:

> "Amphimedon, what have you suffered,
> all of you picked men of the same age,
> to come down here beneath the gloomy earth?   140
> If one were to choose the city's finest men,
> one would not select any men but these.
> Did Poseidon overwhelm you in your ships

---

[1] . . . *accursed wife*: This is the second fairly direct accusation in the *Odyssey* that
Clytaemnestra was complicit in the actual murder of Agamemnon. Most other references
place the blame squarely on Aegisthus or else are ambiguous about Clytaemnestra's role
in the killing. The shade of Agamemnon in 11.509 says she butchered Cassandra and
insulted him as he lay dying. Further on, he states she slaughtered him (11.573). There's
another fairly explicit accusation from Agamemnon later in this book, at line 263

by rousing violent winds and giant waves?
Or did hostile forces on the mainland
kill you off, while you were taking cattle
or rich flocks of sheep, or were they fighting
to protect their city and their women?
Answer what I'm asking. For I can claim
I am your guest friend. Don't you remember   150
the time I made a visit to your home
with godlike Menelaus—to urge Odysseus
to come with us in our well-benched ships
to Ilion? It took us an entire month
to cross all that wide sea, and it was hard
to win Odysseus, sacker of cities,
over to our side."

               Amphimedon's shade
then answered him and said:

                 "Noble son of Atreus,
Agamemnon, Zeus-fostered king of men,
I do remember all these things you say,   160
and I'll describe for you every detail,
the truth of how we died, a wicked fate,
and how it came about. For many years,
Odysseus was away from home, so we
began to court his wife. She did not refuse
a marriage she detested, nor did she
go through with it. Instead, she organized
a gloomy destiny for us, our death.
In her heart she thought up another trick.
She had a huge loom set up in her rooms   170
and on it wove a delicate wide fabric.
And right away she said this to us:

                    'Young men,
my suitors, since lord Odysseus is dead,
you're keen for me to marry—you must wait
until I'm finished with this robe, so I
don't waste this woven yarn in useless work.

It's a burial shroud for lord Laertes,
for when the lethal fate of his sad death
will seize him, so no Achaean woman
in the district will get angry with me   180
that a man who'd won much property
should have to lie without a death shroud.'

"That's what she said, and our proud hearts agreed.
So day by day she'd weave at that great loom.
At night she'd have torches placed beside her
and keep unraveling it. She tricked Achaeans
for three years with this scheme—they believed her.
But as the seasons changed and months rolled on,
and many days passed by, the fourth year came.
Then one of her women, who knew the plan,   190
spoke out, and we came in and caught her
undoing the lovely yarn. So after that
we made her finish it against her will.
Once she'd woven it and washed the fabric,
she displayed the robe—it shone like the sun
or like the moon. But then some malignant god
brought Odysseus back from some foreign place
to the borders of the field where the swineherd
has his house. And there, too, came the dear son
of godlike Odysseus, once he'd returned   200
in his black ship, back from sandy Pylos.[1]
The two hatched a plan against the suitors,
to bring them to a nasty death, then left
for the well-known city. Telemachus
made the journey first, whereas Odysseus
got there later. The swineherd led his master,
who wore shabby clothing on his body—
he looked like an ancient worn-out beggar
leaning on a stick, rags covering his skin.
So none of us could recognize the man   210
when he suddenly showed up, not even

---

[1] . . . *from sandy Pylos.* It's not clear just how Amphimedon, who was one of the suitors in Odysseus' home, could know all these details about what went on between Odysseus, Eumaeus, and Telemachus. Death in Homer's world does not convey such knowledge.

older men. We pelted him with insults,
hurled things at him, but for a little while
his firm heart kept enduring what we threw
and how we taunted him in his own home.
But when aegis-bearing Zeus aroused him,
with Telemachus' help he took away
the lovely weapons, put them in a storeroom,
and locked the bolt. Then, with his great cunning,
he told his wife to place before the suitors   220
his bow and gray iron axes, a contest
for those of us who bore an evil fate,
the prelude to our death. None of us
could stretch the string on that powerful bow.
We weren't nearly strong enough. But then,
when the great bow was in Odysseus' hands,
we all called out to say we should not give
that bow to him, no matter what he said.
Telemachus alone kept urging him—
he told him to do it. Once lord Odysseus,   230
who had endured so much, picked up the bow,
he strung it with ease and shot an arrow
through the iron axes. Then he went and stood
inside the doorway with a fearful glare
and kept shooting volleys of swift arrows.
He hit lord Antinous and went on shooting,
aiming at other men across the room,
letting lethal arrows fly. Men collapsed,
falling thick and fast. Then we realized
some god was helping them, when all at once   240
they charged out in a frenzy through the house,
butchering men everywhere. The screams
were hideous, as heads were smashed apart.
The whole floor swam with blood. That's how we died,
Agamemnon, and even now our bodies
are lying uncared for in Odysseus' house.
Each man's friends at home don't know what's happened,
the ones who'd wash the black blood from our wounds,
then lay our bodies out and weep for us,
the necessary rites for those who've died."   250

The shade of Atreus' son then answered Amphimedon:

> "Oh, son of Laertes, happy Odysseus,
> a resourceful man, who won himself
> a wife whose excellence was truly great.
> How fine the heart in faultless Penelope,
> daughter of Icarius! She remembered well
> the husband she was married to, Odysseus.
> The story of her excellence will not die—
> immortal gods will make a pleasing song
> for men on earth about faithful Penelope.   260
> Tyndareus' daughter acted differently,[1]
> when she planned to carry out her evil acts
> and killed her wedded husband—among men
> there'll be a hateful song for her. She gives
> all women an evil reputation,
> even one whose actions are done well."

So these two talked to one another, as they stood
in the house of Hades, deep beneath the earth.

Once Odysseus and his men had left the city,
they soon reached Laertes' fine, well-managed farm,   270
which Laertes had once won by his own efforts,
working really hard. His house was there, with sheds
surrounding it on every side, where his servants,
bonded slaves who worked to carry out his wishes,
ate and sat and slept. An old Sicilian woman
lived inside his house, looking after the old man,
caring for him at the farm, far from the city.
Odysseus then spoke to his servants and his son:

> "You should go inside the well-built home.
> Hurry up and kill the finest pig there is,   280
> so we can eat. I'll sound out my father,
> to find out if he can recognize me,
> see who I am, once he's laid eyes on me,
> or if he doesn't know me any more,

---

[1] *... Tyndareus' daughter.* This is a reference to Agamemnon's wife, Clytaemnestra.

since I've been away so long."

                              Odysseus spoke,
then gave his battle weapons to his servants.
They quickly went inside the house. Then Odysseus,
walking out to test his father, came up beside
the fruitful vineyard and from there continued down
to the extensive orchard, where he failed to find   290
Dolius or any sons of his father's slaves.
They'd gone off to gather large rocks for the wall
around the vineyard, with the old man in the lead.
In the well-established vineyard he found his father.
He was digging round a plant, all by himself,
dressed in a filthy, shabby, patched-up tunic.
Around his legs he'd tied shin pads stitched from ox-hide
to protect himself from scratches, and on his hands
he had on gloves, since there were thistles in that spot.
On his head he wore a goatskin hat. In these clothes   300
he was dealing with his grief. When lord Odysseus,
who had endured so much, saw him worn down with age
and carrying so much heavy sorrow in his heart,
he stood under a tall pear tree and shed a tear,
debating in his mind and heart whether he should
embrace and kiss his father, or describe for him
in detail how he got back to his native land,
or start by questioning him, to test him out
on every point. As he thought about his options,
the best decision seemed to be to test him first,   310
using words which might provoke him. With this in mind,
lord Odysseus went straight up to his father,
who was digging round a plant with his head down.
His splendid son stood there beside him and spoke out:

        "Old man, from the way you tend this orchard
        you've no lack of skill. No. Your care is good.
        There's nothing here—no plant, fig tree, vine,
        olive, pear, or garden plot in all the field—
        that needs some care. I'll tell you something else—
        don't let this make you angry in your heart—   320

474

you yourself are not being well looked after.
Along with your old age, you're filthy dirty,
and badly dressed in those disgusting clothes.
Surely it can't be because you're lazy
your lord refuses to look after you.
In appearance you don't seem to be a slave,
not when one sees your stature and your shape.
You're like a king, the kind of man who bathes
and eats and goes to sleep in a soft bed,
as old men should. So come now, tell me this,   330
and speak out candidly—Whose slave are you?
Whose orchard are you tending? And tell me
the truth about this, too, so I understand—
Is this place we've reached really Ithaca,
as some man I just met on my way here
told me. His mind was not too clever—
he didn't try to tell me any details
or listen to my words when I asked him
about a friend of mine, if he's still alive
or is in Hades' home, already dead.   340
I'll explain it to you. Listen to me,
and pay attention. In my dear native land,
I once entertained a man, someone who'd come
to my own home. No other human being
from far away has visited my house
as a more welcome guest. He said he came
from Ithaca. He told me his father
was Laertes, son of Arcesius.
I took him to the house, entertained him
with generous hospitality, and gave him   350
a kind reception with the many things
I had inside my home, providing him
appropriate friendship gifts. I gave him
seven talents of finely crafted gold,
a silver mixing bowl etched with flowers,
twelve cloaks with single folds, twelve coverlets,
as many splendid cloaks, and, besides these,
as many tunics and, what's more, four women
skilled in fine handicrafts and beautiful,

the very ones he wished to choose himself."

Then his father shed a tear and answered him:

> "Stranger, yes indeed, you've reached the country
> which you asked about. But it's been taken over
> by arrogant and reckless men. Those presents,
> the countless gifts you freely gave, are useless.
> If you'd come across him still living here,
> in Ithaca, he'd have sent you on your way
> after paying you back with splendid presents
> and fine hospitality—that's the right
> of him who offers kindness first. But come, 370
> tell me this, and make sure you speak the truth.
> How many years ago did you welcome him,
> that unlucky guest, my son, if, indeed,
> such an ill-fated man ever was alive?
> Somewhere far from his native land and friends
> the fish have eaten him down in the sea,
> or on land he's been the prey of savage beasts
> and birds. Neither his father nor his mother,
> we who gave him birth, could lay him out
> for burial or lament for him. Nor did 380
> the wife he courted with so many gifts,
> faithful Penelope, bewail her husband
> on his bier, closing up his eyes in death,
> as is appropriate, though that's a rite
> we owe the dead. And tell me this, as well—
> speaking the truth so I can understand—
> Among men who are you? Where are you from?
> What is your city? Who are your parents?
> Where did you and your god-like companions
> anchor the swift ship that brought you here? 390
> Or did you come on other people's ship
> as passenger, men who let you disembark
> and then set off again?"

Resourceful Odysseus
then answered him:

                "All right, I'll tell you everything
quite truthfully. I come from Alybas,
where I have a lovely home. I'm the son
of Apheidas, lord Polypemon's son.
My name's Eperitus. But then some god
made me go off course from Sicania,
so I've come here against my will. My ship   400
is anchored over there, close to the fields
far from the city. As for Odysseus,
this is the fifth year since he went away
and left my country. That unlucky man!
There were auspicious omens from some birds
flying on the right, when he departed.
So when I sent him off, I was happy,
and so was he. The hearts in both of us
hoped we'd meet again as host and guest,
and give each other splendid presents."   410

As Odysseus said these words, a black cloud of grief
swallowed up Laertes. With both hands he scooped up
some grimy dust and dumped it over his gray hair,
moaning all the time. He stirred Odysseus' heart.
Already, as he looked at his dear father, sharp pains
were shooting up his nostrils. He jumped over,
embraced Laertes, kissed him, and then said:

                                              "Father,
I'm here—the very man you asked about.
I've returned here in the twentieth year,
back to my native land. Stop your grieving,   420
these tearful moans. I'll tell you everything,
though it's essential we move really fast.
I've killed the suitors in our home, avenged
their heart-rending insolence, their evil acts."

Laertes then answered him and said:

                                          "If that's true,
if you are indeed my son Odysseus

and have come back, show me some evidence,
something clear so I can be quite certain."

Resourceful Odysseus replied to him and said:

"First, let your eyes inspect this scar—a boar   430
inflicted that on me with its white tusk,
when I went to Parnassus, sent there
by you and by my honourable mother,
to her cherished father, Autolycus,
so I could get the gifts he'd promised me,
what he'd agreed to give when he was here.
Come, I'll tell you the trees you gave me once
in the well-established vineyard—back then
I was a child following you in the yard,
and I asked about each one. It was here—   440
we walked by these very trees. You named them,
and described them to me. You offered me
thirteen pear trees and ten apple trees
along with forty fig trees. In the same way,
you said you'd give me fifty rows of vines,
bearing all sorts of different types of grapes,
when Zeus' seasons load their tops with fruit."

As Odysseus spoke, his father's fond heart and knees
gave way—he clearly recognized the evidence
Odysseus had presented. He threw both his arms   450
around the son he loved and struggled hard to breathe.
Lord Odysseus, who had endured so much, held him.
After he'd revived and his spirit came once more
into his chest, Laertes spoke again and said:

"Father Zeus, it seems you gods are still
on high Olympus, if it's true those suitors
have paid the price of their proud arrogance.
But now my heart contains a dreadful fear—
all the men of Ithaca will soon come here
against us, and they'll send out messengers   460
all through Cephallenia, to every city."

Resourceful Odysseus then answered him and said:

> "Take courage, and don't allow these things
> to weigh down your heart. Let's go to the house,
> the one close to the orchard, where I sent
> Telemachus, together with the swineherd
> and the keeper of the goats, so they could
> prepare a meal as soon as possible."

After they'd talked like this, they went to the fine house.
Once they reached Laertes' well-furnished home, they found   470
Telemachus with the swineherd and goat keeper
carving lots of meat and mixing gleaming wine.

Inside the home the Sicilian servant woman
gave great-hearted Laertes a bath, then rubbed him
with oil and threw a lovely cloak around him.
Athena then approached and fleshed out the limbs
on that shepherd of his people. She made him
taller than before and sturdier to the eye.
When he left the bath, his dear son was astonished—
as he looked at him he seemed like the immortals.   480
Odysseus spoke to him—his words had wings:

> "Father, surely one of the eternal gods
> has made you handsomer to look at—
> both your form and stature."

                         Wise Laertes
then answered him and said:

>   "By Father Zeus,
> Athena, and Apollo, I wish I were
> just like I was when I took Nericus
> on the mainland coast, that well-built citadel,
> when I was king of Cephallenians.
> With strength like that, I could've stood with you   490
> yesterday, my armour on my shoulders,
> and driven off the suitors in our home.

479

I'd have made many of their knees go slack
inside the hall—I'd have pleased your heart."

In this way, the two men conversed with one another.

Meanwhile, the other men had finished working
Dinner was prepared. So they sat down one by one
on stools and chairs. As they were reaching for the food,
old Dolius appeared. The old man's sons were with him,
tired out from work. The ancient Sicilian woman,   500
their mother, had gone outside and summoned them.
She fed them and took good care of the old man,
now that his age had laid its grip on him. These men,
once they saw Odysseus and their hearts took note of him,
stood in the house astonished. Then Odysseus
talked to them with reassuring words and said:

> "Old man, sit down and have some dinner.
> Forget being so amazed. For some time now
> we've been keen to turn our hands to dinner,
> but we kept expecting you'd be coming,   510
> so we've been waiting in the house."

                              Odysseus spoke.
Dolius went straight up to him, both arms outstretched,
grabbed Odysseus' hand and kissed it on the wrist.
Then he spoke to him—his words had wings:

>   "My friend,
> you're back with us, who longed for your return
> but never thought to see it! The gods themselves
> must have been leading you. Joyful greetings!
> May gods grant you success! Be frank with me
> and tell me so I fully understand—
> Does wise Penelope now know for certain   520
> you've come back here, or should we send her
> a messenger?"

                    Resourceful Odysseus answered him

and said:

> "Old man, she already knows.
> Why should you be so concerned about it?"

Odysseus spoke, and Dolius sat down again
on his polished stool. Then Dolius' sons
also came up around glorious Odysseus,
clasping his hands with words of welcome. Then they sat,
in a row alongside Dolius, their father.
So these men occupied themselves with dinner   530
inside the house.

> Meanwhile, Rumour the Messenger
sped swiftly through the entire city, speaking
of the suitors' dreadful death, their destiny.
People heard about it all at once and came in
from all directions, gathering with mournful groans
before Odysseus' home. Each one brought his dead
outside the house and buried them. All the men
from other cities they sent home, placing them
aboard swift ships to be escorted back by sailors.
Then, with sorrowful hearts, they went in person   540
to meet in an assembly. Once they'd got there
together in a group, Eupeithes rose to speak.
Constant grief lay on his heart for his own son,
Antinous, the first man killed by lord Odysseus.
Weeping for him, he spoke to the assembly:

> "My friends, this man has planned and carried out
> dreadful acts against Achaeans. He led
> many fine courageous men off in his fleet,
> then lost his hollow ships, with all men dead.
> Now he's come and killed our finest men by far   550
> among the Cephallenians. So come on,
> before he can quickly get to Pylos
> or to holy Elis, where Epeians rule,
> let's get started. If not, in future days
> we'll be eternally disgraced, since men

481

yet to be born will learn about our shame,
if we don't act to take out our revenge
on those murderers of our sons and brothers.
As far as I'm concerned, the life we'd live
would not be sweet. I rather die right now   560
and live among the dead. So let us go,
in case those men have a head start on us
and get across the sea."

                              As Eupeithes said this,
he wept, and all Achaeans were seized by pity.
Then Medon and the godlike singer, released
from sleep, approached them from Odysseus' house,
and stood up in their midst. They were astonished.
Then Medon, a shrewd man, spoke out.

                              "Men of Ithaca,
now hear me. Odysseus didn't plan these acts
without the gods' consent. I myself observed   570
an immortal god who stood beside him,
looking in every detail just like Mentor.
The deathless god appeared before Odysseus
at that time to spur him on to action,
and, at another time, charged through the hall,
terrifying the suitors. They collapsed in droves."

As Medon spoke, pale fear gripped them all. And then,
old warrior Halitherses, son of Mastor, addressed them.
He was the only man who could see past and future.
Bearing in the mind their common good, he spoke out,   580
saying these words:

                              "Men of Ithaca,
listen to me now, hear what I have to say.
What's happened now, my friends, has come about
because of your own stupidity.
You just would not follow my instructions
or Mentor's, that shepherd of his people,
and make your sons stop their reckless conduct,

their monstrous acts of wanton foolishness,
squandering a fine man's property and then
dishonouring his wife, claiming the man   590
never would come back. So now, let that be,
and agree with what I'm going to tell you—
we should not move out, in case some men here
run into trouble they've brought on themselves."

He ended. Some men stayed together in their seats,
but others, more than half, jumped up with noisy shouts.
Their hearts had not responded to what he'd just said.
They'd been won over by Eupeithes. And so,
they quickly rushed away to get their weapons.
Once they'd put gleaming bronze around their bodies,   600
they gathered in a group on the spacious grounds
before the city. Eupeithes was the leader
in this foolishness. He thought he could avenge
the killing of his son, but he would not return—
that's where he was going to meet his fate.

Then Athena spoke to Zeus, Cronos' son, saying:

> "Father of us all and son of Cronos,
> highest of all those who rule, answer me
> when I ask this—What are you concealing
> in that mind of yours? Will you be creating   610
> further brutal war and dreadful battle,
> or bring both sides together here as friends?"

Cloud-gatherer Zeus then answered her and said:

> "My child, why are you asking this of me?
> Why these questions? Were you not the one
> who devised this plan all on your own,
> so Odysseus could take out his revenge
> against these men, after he got back?
> Do as you wish. But I'll lay out for you
> what I think is right. Since lord Odysseus   620
> has paid back the suitors, let them swear

a binding oath that he'll remain their king
all his life, and let's make them forget
the killing of their sons and brothers.
Let them love each other as they used to do,
and let there be wealth and peace in plenty."

His words stirred up Athena, who was already keen.
She swooped down from the heights of Mount Olympus.

Meanwhile, once his group had eaten their hearts' fill
of food as sweet as honey, lord Odysseus,   630
who had endured so much, was the first to speak:

    "Someone should go outside to look around,
    see whether they are getting close to us."

Once he said this, a son of Dolius went out,
as he had ordered. He stood in the doorway
and saw all those men approaching. At once
he called out to Odysseus—his words had wings:

    "They're here, close by. Let's get our weapons—
    we'd better hurry!"

             At these words, they leapt up
and put on their armour. Odysseus and his men   640
were four, the sons of Dolius six, and with them
Dolius and Laertes, though they had gray hair,
were dressed in armour, too, forced to be warriors.
When they'd put glittering bronze around their bodies,
they opened up the doors and went outside. Odysseus
led them out. But then Athena, Zeus' daughter,
with the shape and voice of Mentor, came up to them.
When lord Odysseus, who'd endured so much, saw her,
he was glad and quickly spoke up to Telemachus,
his dear son:

    "Telemachus, now you've reached   650
    the field of battle, where the finest men

are put to the test. Soon enough you'll learn
not to disgrace your ancestral family—
for in earlier times we've been pre-eminent
for strength and courage everywhere on earth."

Shrewd Telemachus then answered him and said:

"Dear father, if that's what you want, you'll see
that I, with my heart as it is at present,
won't shame your family. I'll do what you say."

When he said this, Laertes felt great joy and said: 660

"You dear gods, what a day this is for me!
I'm really happy when my son and grandson
compete for excellence with one another."

Then Athena with the glittering eyes came up,
stood by Laertes, and said to him:

"Child of Arcesius,
by far the dearest of all those I cherish,
pray to the young girl with the flashing eyes
and to Father Zeus, then without delay
raise that long spear of yours and throw it."

Pallas Athena spoke and then breathed into him   670
enormous power. Laertes said a prayer
to great Zeus' daughter, and quickly lifting up
his long-shadowed spear, he threw it. It hit home,
through the bronze cheek piece on Eupeithes' helmet,
which didn't stop the spear—the bronze point went on through.
Eupeithes fell down with a thud, his armour
crashing round him. Odysseus and his splendid son
charged at the fighters in the front, striking them
with swords and two-edged spears. They'd have killed them all,
cut them down so none of them returned, had not   680
Athena, daughter of aegis-bearing Zeus, cried out—
her voice held back every man in that whole army.

485

"Men of Ithaca, stop this disastrous war,
so you can quickly go your separate ways
without spilling any blood."

                                   Athena spoke,
and pale fear gripped the men. They were so terrified
they dropped their weapons and all fell on the ground,
at that goddess' resounding voice. They turned round,
back towards the city, eager to save their lives.
Then much-enduring lord Odysseus gave out   690
a fearful shout, gathered himself, and swooped down
like an eagle from on high. But at that moment,
Zeus, son of Cronos, shot a fiery thunderbolt.
It struck at the feet of the bright-eyed daughter
of that mighty father. And then Athena,
goddess with the glittering eyes, said to Odysseus:

        "Resourceful Odysseus, Laertes' son,
        and child of Zeus, hold back. Stop this fight,
        this impartial war, in case thundering Zeus,
        who sees far and wide, grows angry with you."   700

Once Athena spoke, Odysseus obeyed,
joy in his heart. And then Pallas Athena,
daughter of aegis-bearing Zeus, in shape and form
looking just like Mentor, had both parties swear
a solemn treaty designed to last forever.

Appendices

Ground Plan of Odysseus' Palace

Glossary of Names

Map of the Eastern Mediterranean

Map Showing Locations of Odysseus' Adventures

Odysseus' Palace, According to Voss (1820)

(used with permission of Carlos Parada of the Greek Mythology Link)

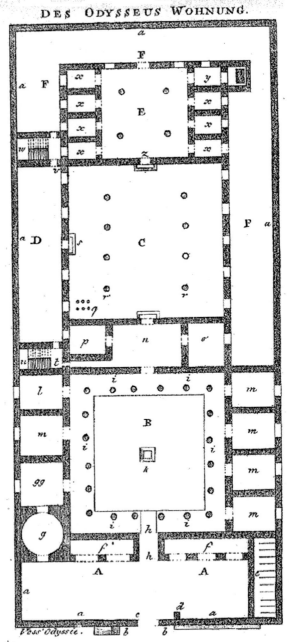

DES ODYSSEUS WOHNUNG.

Labels for the Diagram on the Facing Page

a. the outer wall

b. the entrance

c. the gates

d. location of the dog Argus

e. standing place for mules

f. two halls

g. the dome

h. the entrance to the court

i. the hall

k. Zeus' altar in the court

l. Telemachus' room

m. various rooms

n. vestibule

o. room for bathing

p. activity room

q. wine preparation room

r. pillars

s. simple doors

t. door from vestibule

u. stair to Odysseus' rooms

v. door to women's rooms

w. stairs to Penelope's room

x. ground floor rooms

y. Penelope's bedroom

z. door

A. courtyard and fence

B. level middle court

C. the hall

D. passage by-passing the hall

E. Penelope's work room

F. rear courtyard

When Odysseus kills the Suitors he is standing with his bow at the lower entrance to the main hall, C. The doors to the women's quarters (at v and z) have been locked. The only way out for the Suitors is a small door at s, which leads to the passageway D. Odysseus places Eumaeus at the end of the passage (at point t) to prevent any Suitor getting out into the courtyard B.

Glossary of Names

The following glossary includes the names of the main characters and places in the *Odyssey* and a few others.

Achaeans: a collective name of the Greeks (used interchangeably with **Danaans** and **Argives**)

Achilles: son of Peleus, greatest of the Achaean warriors at Troy, where he died and was buried.

Aegisthus: son of Thyestes, lover of Clytaemnestra and murderer of Agamemnon.

Aeolus: son of Hippotas, god of the winds, living on the island **Aeolia**.

Agamemnon: son of Atreus, king of Argos, leader of the Achaean forces which attacked and destroyed Troy.

Agelaus: son of Damastor, one of the Suitors.

Ajax: (1) son of Telamon, greatest Achaean warrior after Achilles at Troy, where he died and was buried; (2) son of Oïleus, Achaean warrior at Troy.

Alcinous: son of Nausithous, husband of Arete, king of the Phaeacians.

Amphimedon: son of Melaneus, one of the Suitors.

Amphinomus: son of Nisus, one of the Suitors from Dulichium.

Amphitrite: divine wife of Poseidon, a sea goddess.

Anticleia: daughter of Autolycus, mother of Odysseus.

Antinous: son of Eupeithes, one of the leaders of the Suitors.

Antiphates: king of the Laestrygonians.

Aphrodite: divine daughter of Zeus and Hera, goddess of erotic love.

Apollo: divine son of Zeus and Leto, often called Phoebus or Phoebus Apollo.

Arcesius: father of Laertes and thus Odysseus' grandfather.

Ares: divine son of Zeus and Hera, god of war.

Arete: wife of Alcinous, queen of the Phaeacians.

Argives: see **Achaeans**.

Artemis: divine daughter of Zeus and Leto, goddess of the hunt.

Athena: divine daughter of Zeus, goddess of wisdom.

Atreus: father of Agamemnon and Menelaus, who are often called "sons of Atreus."

Autolycus: father of Penelope and thus grandfather of Odysseus.

Calypso: daughter of Atlas, goddess living on the island of Ogygia.

Cephallenia: an island close to Ithaca, part of Odysseus' kingdom, often applied to that kingdom and its people generally (Cephallenians).

Charybdis: a divine sea monster which acts as a whirlpool.

Cicones: inhabitants of Ismarus, a city close to Troy.

Circe: a goddess living on the island of Aeaea.

Clytaemnestra: daughter of Tyndareus, wife of Agememnon.

Cyclopes (singular **Cyclops**): monstrous creatures with one eye.

Cronos: father of Zeus, overthrown by his son and imprisoned deep in the earth.

Ctesippus: son of Polytherses, one of the Suitors from Same.

Danaans: see **Achaeans**.

Demodocus: the blind minstrel in the court of Alcinous in Phaeacia.

Dolius: an old servant of Laertes and Penelope.

Dulichium: an island close to Ithaca, part of Odysseus' kingdom.

Elpenor: the youngest of Odysseus' crew.

Eumaeus: a servant of Odysseus, keeper of pigs.

Eupeithes: father of Antinous (one of the Suitors).

Euryalus: a young Phaeacian nobleman.

Eurycleia: daugher of Ops, elderly family servant to Odysseus, Penelope, and Telemachus.

Eurylochus: one of Odysseus' companions, related to him by marriage.

Eurymachus: son of Polybus, one of the leading Suitors.

Eurynome: housekeeper in Odysseus' and Penelope's home.

Furies: goddesses of blood revenge.

Giants: the race of divinities before Zeus, many now imprisoned by Zeus deep in the earth.

Hades: god of the underworld, also the underworld itself.

Halitherses: son of Mastor, an older prophet in Ithaca, a colleague of Odysseus.

Helen: daughter of Leda and Zeus, wife of Menelaus.

Hephaestus: divine son of Zeus and Hera, god of the forge, divine artisan.

Hercules: mortal son of Zeus, made into a god after his death.

Hermes: divine son of Zeus and the nymph Maia, messenger god, often called "killer of Argus."

Hyperion: god of the sun (also called **Helios**)

Icarius: father of Penelope.

Ilion: another name for Troy.

Irus: a beggar at Odysseus' palace.

Ithaca: island off the west coast of mainland Greece, kingdom ruled by Odysseus.

Lacedaemonia (or **Lacedaemon**): a region in the central Peloponnese surrounding **Sparta**. The names are often used interchangeably.

Laertes: son of Arcesius, father of Odysseus.

Laestrygonians: race of giants living in Telpylus.

Laodamas: son of Alcinous, a prince in Phaeacia.

Leiodes: son of Oenops, one of the Suitors, a soothsayer.

Leocritus: son of Euenor, one of the Suitors.

Megapenthes: bastard son of Menelaus.

Medon: a herald in Odysseus' palace.

Melampus: a prophet from Pylos many years ago.

Melanthius: son of Dolius, a goatherd friendly to the Suitors.

Melantho: daughter of Dolius, a servant woman in Penelope's household.

Menelaus: son of Atreus, brother of Agamemnon, husband of Helen, king of Sparta.

Mentor: son of Alcimus, steward of Odysseus' place, an old companion of Odysseus.

Nausicaa: daughter of Arete, princess of the Phaeacians.

Neriton: a mountain in Ithaca.

Nestor: son of Neleus, king of Pylos, sometimes called the "Geranian horseman."

Noemon: son of Phronius, a friend of Telemachus in Ithaca.

Oceanus: the river running around the outer rim of the world.

Odysseus: king of Ithaca, son of Laertes, husband of Penelope, father of Telemachus.

Old Man of the Sea: a name applied to different sea divinities (Proteus, Phorcys and Nereus)

Olympus: mountain in northern Greece where the major deities live (the Olympians).

Ogygia: island where Calypso lives and where she detains Odysseus.

Orestes: son of Agamemnon and Clytaemnestra, killer of Aegisthus.

Peiraeus: son of Clytius, a close comrade of Telemachus.

Peisenor: a herald in Odysseus' palace.

Peisistratus: son of Nestor, friend of Telemachus.

Penelope: daughter of Icarius, wife of Odysseus, mother of Telemachus.

Persephone: wife of Hades, goddess of the underworld.

Phaeacians: inhabitants of Scheria, master sailors.

Phemius: son of Terpes, the professional minstrel in Odysseus' palace.

Philoetius: a goat and cattle herder on Ithaca friendly to Odysseus.

Polyphemus: a cyclops, son of Poseidon.

Pontonous: a herald in the court of Alcinous in Phaeacia.

Poseidon: god of the sea, brother of Zeus, often called "shaker of the earth" or "Earthshaker."

Priam: king of Troy, killed when the city was captured by Achaeans.

Pylos: city state in the south Peloponnese ruled by Nestor.

Pytho: the location of the shrine of Apollo.

Same: an island close to Ithaca, part of Odysseus' kingdom.

Scheria: distant land where the Phaeacians live.

Scylla: a monster with many heads.

Sirens: two singers who lure sailors to their destruction.

Sparta: city in the central Peloponnese ruled by Menelaus.

Styx: river in Hades by which the gods swear their most solemn oaths.

Suitors: aristocratic young men courting Penelope in hopes of marrying her.

Taphians: inhabitants of some islands close to Ithaca.

Teiresias: a blind prophet from Thebes.

Telemachus: son of Odysseus and Penelope.

Theoclymenus: a prophet who meets Telemachus in Pylos and returns to Ithaca with him.

Thesprotians: a group of people living on mainland Greece close to Ithaca.

Thrasymedes: son of Nestor.

Troy: city in Asia Minor, near the Hellespont, besieged by the Achaean (Greek) forces for ten years.

Zacynthus: an island close to Ithaca, part of Odysseus' kingdom.

Zeus: major divine presence on Olympus, often called "son of Cronos."

Ancient Greece and
Western Asia Minor

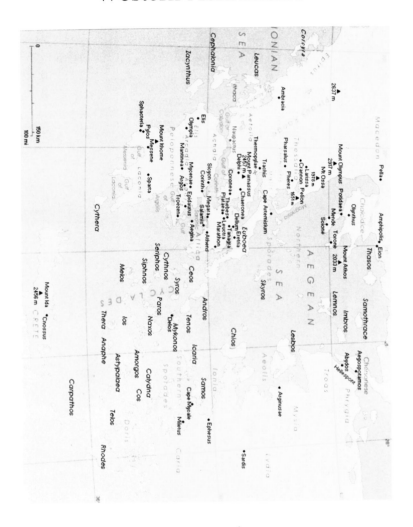

Map of Odysseus' Wanderings

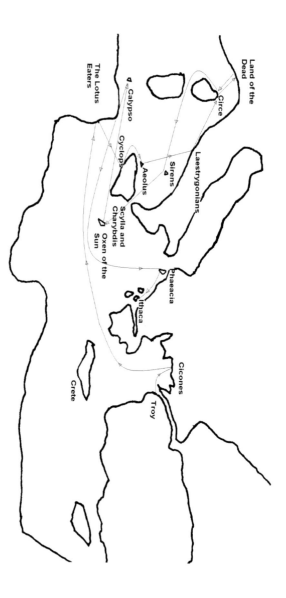

This map represents a possible route for Odysseus' wanderings. The most confusing geographical point is the location of Calypso's island, which some commentators place far in the west at the Straits of Gibraltar, others just off the coast of North Africa, and others further to the east.

Suggestions for Further Reading

For those wishing to read critical and historical commentary on the *Odyssey*, there are a great many works available. The following is a very short list of suggestions.

Austin, Norman. *Archery at the Dark of the Moon: Poetic Problems in Homer's Odyssey.* University of California, 1975.

Bloom, Harold. *Homer: Modern Critical Views.* NY: Chelsea House. 1986.

Finley, M.I., *The World of Odysseus.* New York: The Viking Press, 1954.

Griffin, Jasper. *Homer: The Odyssey* Cambridge: Cambridge University Press, 1987

Heubeck, Alfred, J.B. Hainsworth, *et al. A Commentary on Homer's Odyssey.* 3 Vols. Oxford: Oxford University Press, 1988.

Segal, Charles. *Singers, Heroes and Gods in the Odyssey.* Ithaca: Cornell University Press, 1994.

Thalmann, William G., *The Odyssey: An Epic of Return.* NY: Twayne Publishers, 1992.

Twentieth Century Interpretations of the Odyssey: A Collection of Critical Essays. Ed. Howard W. Clarke. Prentice-Hall, 1983.

There are a great many resources on the Internet as well, including an essay by the translator of this volume available at the following address:

http://www.mala.bc.ca/~johnstoi/introser/homer.htm